W9-BFY-398

# Addiction, Progression & Recovery

Understanding the
Stages of Change on the
Addiction Recovery Learning Curve

"Man is not so lost that Eternal Love
may not return—so long as Hope
retaineth ought of green."

—Dante

# Addiction, Progression & Recovery

## Understanding the Stages of Change on the Addiction Recovery Learning Curve

Dale Kesten, LCSW, LADC

 HEALTHCARE

Eau Claire, Wisconsin
2004

Copyright © 2004 Dale Kesten.
All Rights Reserved.

Published by
PESI HEALTHCARE, LLC
PO Box 1000
200 Spring Street
Eau Claire, Wisconsin 54702

Printed in the United States of America
FIRST EDITION
First Printing—May, 2004
Second Printing, Revised—December, 2004

ISBN: 0-9749711-2-X

PESI HealthCare strives to obtain knowledgeable authors and faculty for its publications and seminars. The clinical recommendations contained herein are the result
of extensive author research and review. Obviously, any recommendations for
patient care must be held up against individual circumstances at hand. To the best
of our knowledge any recommendations included by the author reflect currently
accepted practice. However, these recommendations cannot be considered universal and complete. The author and publisher repudiate any responsibility for unfa-
vorable effects that result from information, recommendations, undetected omis-
sions or errors. Professionals using this publication should research other original
sources of authority as well.

**For more information on this and other PESI HealthCare products
please call 800-843-7763**

**www.pesihealthcare.com**

**This book is dedicated to Art and Dotty Kesten:**

My parents, role models, and inspiration.

Honored, admired, and treasured friends to countless people.

Life partners, business partners, and creative partners.

They have shown me how to be a decent and honest person;

how to love people and bring them together;

how to find my own passion, purpose, and vision in life;

and slowly turn a dream into reality, one day at a time.

# TABLE OF CONTENTS

# About the Author

**Dale Kesten** brings solid professional credentials and a depth of practical wisdom and authority to his writing, speaking, public seminars, and clinical training workshops which are drawn not only from his extensive professional experience but also from his unique experience with the process of achieving and sustaining long-term personal change.

He is a licensed clinical social worker and a licensed alcohol and drug abuse counselor who has helped thousands of clients learn how to change some of their most addictive, compulsive, or self-defeating attitudes and behaviors through his work in the mental health and addictions treatment field since 1987.

Equally important for the development of his unique perspective on changing addictive behavior, Dale is also a recovering compulsive overeater who has achieved 23 years of sustained success through his active participation in a self-help recovery program since 1981. At that time, he was morbidly obese and weighed more than 300 pounds—and he has now been maintaining a normal weight (and a remarkable weight loss of about 140 pounds) since 1983.

He earned his Bachelors degree in Government from Cornell University and then worked as a Congressional staff assistant in Washington, DC. Dale has also worked as the editor of a professional journal focused on U.S. Army Aviation, and he later completed the intensive Training Program for Alcoholism and Chemical Dependency Counseling sponsored by the National Council on Alcoholism and Other Drug Addictions/Westchester prior to earning his Masters degree in clinical social work from the Columbia University School of Social Work.

Dale has worked as a front-line clinician or clinical supervisor at outpatient psychiatric and substance abuse clinics, intensive outpatient chemical dependency treatment programs, partial hospital dual-diagnosis programs, residential alcohol and drug-abuse treatment centers, and on inpatient psychiatric and medical detoxification units as well.

Dale now works primarily as an author, speaker, trainer, personal growth seminar leader, and consultant, and he is currently working on two closely related books for general readers:

*Rational Spirituality:*
*Tapping the Life-Transforming Power of Unconditional Love,*

and a companion volume to be called:

*The Addiction Recovery Learning Curve:*
*What It Really Takes to Really Change Harmful Addictive Behavior.*

Dale is the founder and sole proprietor of **The HIGHLIGHT ZONE Personal Growth Programs,** a publishing and educational services company located in Westport, Connecticut, where he also remains active as a psychotherapist in private practice. He is married to Elizabeth Lamberton Kesten, a certified alcohol and drug abuse counselor working at Silver Hill Hospital in New Canaan, Connecticut.

# ACKNOWLEDGEMENTS

**"No man is an island . . ."**

—John Donne

♦ ♦ ♦

I sometimes like to make a joke and say: "There are two kinds of people in the world—those who practice patience, kindness, tolerance, and unconditional love, and those who give others the opportunity to practice." Generally speaking, I like to count myself among the first group, but I know that during the prolonged process of writing this book I have probably given my wife Liz far more opportunities to practice these virtues than she ever bargained for when we first committed our lives and our love to each other. Choosing to "follow my bliss" has meant walking a path that hasn't always been very secure or blissful, so I'd like to thank Liz from the deepest part of my soul for all of her love and support through many good times and some fairly tough times and for her wonderful and perceptive feedback as an addictions treatment professional.

I'd also like to thank Lois Longwell, LCSW, BCD, for her ongoing personal encouragement, wise advice, professional validation, and many insightful and constructive comments during this creative process. Erika Steffen, EdD, has shared her expertise on career development issues for many years, along with her unwavering friendship and confidence in my potential. Alex Skutt, my old college-friend and owner of McBooks Press in Ithaca, NY, has been incredibly generous with his time and advice at several critical points and Attorney Cliff Ennico has also been a remarkable source of wisdom about the world of publishing and the nuances of the author-publisher relationship.

I will be forever grateful to Mike Conner, President of PESI HealthCare, LLC, for first giving me the opportunity to work with his outstanding company, and I'm especially indebted to Mike Olson, Mental Health Education Project Manager at PESI Healthcare, for the reassuring confidence he has continually shown in the value of my work and for the almost superhuman patience, kindness, and professionalism he has shown working with a first time author during a writing process that has taken much longer than any of us had imagined. Drew Clausen, Product Manager at PESI HealthCare, has also been great to work with on the design and production of this book.

My sister, Lynn Kesten Coakley, has been very generous with her time and support helping me deal with various computer hardware and software problems and questions over many years, and I'd also like to thank the following people who have been particularly helpful in sharing their experience, wisdom, support, or encouragement with me at various times in my personal or professional development:

Anthony Abeson, David Avila, Cynthia Barnett, Jill Ross Beres, Ed Bialek, Douglas Budde, Susan Chouinard, Tony Contorelli, Jim Cooney, Priscilla Egan, Valerie Enders, Jan Fable, George & Connie Fitzelle, Jim Francek, Chris Greene, Florence Johnson, Pat Kearns, June Lee, Maria Lilliedahl, Stuart Losen, Brian McHugh, Matt McHugh, Bill Metzger, Carmine Moffa, Carl Palmieri, Robert Perry, Bill Pietsch, Jane Pollak, Mark Rego, Ben Rosenthal, Pearl Schwartz, Bob Skane, Dick Sperry, Stella Tamsky, Nancy Wheeler, Jodi Whiting, and Irwin Zucker.

# NOTICE

This book is primarily intended to meet the continuing education needs of licensed or certified professionals currently working with patients or clients in healthcare, mental health, addictions treatment, counseling, education, or prevention.

It is not intended to serve as a substitute for appropriate professional education, training, licensure or certification, clinical supervision, or the "practice wisdom" that can only come from years of direct clinical experience.

In particular, it is not intended serve as a substitute for the specialized training and clinical experience required for professional licensure or certification in alcohol and drug abuse counseling or addictions treatment.

This book is also not intended to offer specific clinical or therapeutic advice in particular individual cases. Readers must assume the responsibility to assimilate and apply the information presented in this book into their practice in an individualized, clinically appropriate, and professional way.

Neither the author nor publisher assumes any liability for any misuse or inappropriate application of the information contained in this book in a manner that would constitute professional malpractice or practicing without appropriate professional licensure, certification, or supervision.

Certification or licensure as an addictions treatment or counseling professional, and information about the specialized training required to achieve this, is available from a number of organizations. These include:

The American Academy of Health Care Providers in the Addictive Disorders
314 West Superior Street, Suite 702, Duluth, MN 55802
(218) 727-3940 — www.americanacademy.org

The American Society of Addiction Medicine—ASAM
4601 North Park Avenue, Arcade Suite 101, Chevy Chase, MD 20815
(315) 656-3920 — www.asam.org

NAADAC—The Association for Addiction Professionals
901 North Washington Street, Suite 600, Alexandria, VA 22314
(800) 548-0497 — www.naadac.org

"Defer not till tomorrow to be wise. Tomorrow's sun for thee may never rise."

—William Congreve

"When you are good to others, you are best to yourself."

—Benjamin Franklin

"All who joy would win must share it—happiness was born a twin."

—Lord Byron

"Those who bring sunshine to the lives of others cannot keep it from themselves."

—Sir James Matthew Barrie

"There's nothing worth the wear of winning but laughter and the love of friends."

—Hillaire Belloc

"The life-transforming power of unconditional love is like a chisel in the hands of a sculptor—it only works when we tap it."

—Dale Kesten

# PREFACE

"I finally figured out the meaning of life—and then they changed it!"

—George Carlin.

"What if the hokey pokey really is what it's all about?"

♦ ♦ ♦

## BEGINNING WITH THE END IN MIND

I'm a licensed clinical social worker and a licensed alcohol and drug abuse counselor and I've worked as a front-line clinician or clinical supervisor at outpatient psychiatric and substance abuse clinics, intensive outpatient chemical dependency treatment programs, partial hospital dual-diagnosis programs, residential alcohol and drug-abuse treatment centers, and on inpatient psychiatric and medical detoxification units as well.

In May, 1987, I began my first job working in the mental health and addictions treatment field as a nurses-aide level Mental Health Worker on the day shift of an inpatient chemical dependency treatment program at Hall-Brooke Hospital—a psychiatric and substance abuse treatment facility located in my hometown of Westport, Connecticut.

My interest in this field had developed slowly over the previous six years because of my active participation in voluntary service in a self-help recovery program for compulsive overeating. I worked at Hall-Brooke for just over two years, and I completed 12 credits toward a masters degree in clinical social work while I was there—and a one year intensive training program in alcoholism and chemical dependency counseling as well—before moving on to start my first year social work internship as a full-time graduate student.

I have many warm, funny, and striking memories of my time in that first job at Hall-Brooke, and I especially remember something that "Flo" used to say to the assembled patient group now and then. "Flo" was the lone substance abuse counselor assigned to our treatment unit, working amid an array of psychiatrists, psychologists, clinical social workers, nurses, mental health workers, and psychology and social work interns. Her full name was Florence Johnson, and she was a short, feisty African-American woman with a great sense of humor and a warm heart not too well hidden under her sometimes gruff, challenging manner.

I was privileged to co-lead a late morning psychoeducational discussion group on our unit with Flo five days per week which focused exclusively on addiction and recovery issues. Attendance at this group was required for all of our patients—many of whom had been legally mandated into treatment by the courts as a condition of probation, or otherwise coerced into treatment by the pressure of employers, family members, or others.

About once every other month or so—after most patients in the standard 21 to 28 day rehab program had completed treatment and the normal rate of turnover had produced a mostly new patient group—or whenever a particularly negative or opinionated patient would start grumbling too loudly about what some community volunteer in recovery or some staff member had the nerve to say to them—Flo would interrupt the typical indignant and impassioned tirade with the following comments:

> "Excuse me, but let me just remind you that you didn't exactly fly in here on the wings of victory, and neither did anyone else. As a matter of fact, it was your own best thinking that got you here.
>
> So, let me tell you something:
>
> If you come in here and you're not ready to change, then nothing that I or anyone else can say will ever help you.
>
> But, if you come in here and you really are ready to change, then nothing that I can say—or that anyone else can say—will ever hurt you.
>
> So why don't you just take the cotton out of your ears and put it in your mouth?"

I don't entirely agree with Flo's first point—that nothing you can say will ever help someone who "isn't ready to change"—because over many years in many different practice settings I've personally observed countless times how the seeds of knowledge and insight that can get planted during one apparently unsuccessful treatment episode will often lie dormant—while a person continues to drink or use drugs and keeps on getting worse—only to sprout, grow, and bear fruit in a successful recovery much later on.

Nevertheless, since alcoholism, drug addiction, and other forms of harmful addiction are so often characterized by high rates of relapse and recidivism, her comments do raise a vital question:

What does it really mean—or what does it really take—for a person to really become "ready, willing, or able" to permanently change a habitual pattern of harmful addiction?

The philosophical approach to addiction treatment and recovery issues presented in this book is based on the following fundamental premises:

**First,** that the *most practical path* to permanent recovery for people who struggle with serious harmful addiction will be to develop a deep, passionate devotion to a healthy alternative—a positive addiction that will ultimately prove to be far more reliable, rewarding, meaningful, satisfying, and fun.

**Second,** that the painful personal experience of repeated failure—when they try to "just say no"—strongly suggests that for many people the only *possible* path to permanent success may be to develop a truly enjoyable, healthy, positive addiction to which they can passionately and wholeheartedly "just say yes!"

**Third,** that any superficial "solution"—or purely hedonistic alternative—will eventually be doomed to failure for many of the people who develop the most severe, intractable, and life-threatening forms of harmful addiction. For them, a viable healthy alternative will usually have to address their deepest sense of the ultimate meaning and purpose of a good life—in a positive and practical manner—and somehow provide them with a *rational* and *reliable* way to access, experience, and practice

### the life-transforming power of unconditional love.

In his book, *The 7 Habits of Highly Effective People: Restoring the Character Ethic*—just after noting that highly effective people will habitually tend to "Be Proactive"—Stephen Covey also recommends that readers seeking to develop greater "self-efficacy"—to use a closely related clinical concept—should also learn to:

### "Begin with the End in Mind."

(Covey, 1989)

So, what's the bottom line going to be when we turn that final page?

Another basic premise of this book is that when people *begin* to *understand, accept,* and *practice* sound spiritual principles at a relatively early age—perhaps even during an initial treatment episode for alcohol or drug abuse—and thus *begin* to develop a coherent and positive sense of meaning and purpose in their lives—they may eventually be empowered to find a new way of life so *"reliable, rewarding, meaningful, satisfying, and fun"* that they could be effectively "inoculated" against developing or sustaining any serious harmful addiction—even when they might otherwise be mentally, emotionally, physically, or spiritually "predisposed" for such an unhealthy and unfortunate development.

As clinicians, I believe we should always be devoted to empowering our clients—at any age or stage of life—to continue learning and growing toward greater maturity and wisdom as human beings, and to help them develop a conscious commitment to practice dealing with the problems and opportunities presented by their daily lives in a positive, healthy way.

The therapeutic approach that will be presented in this book represents an eclectic blend of some key elements drawn from a number of different sources. These approaches include: Reality Therapy, Transactional Analysis, Cognitive-Behavioral and Rational-Emotive Therapy, the Voice Dialogue Method, Motivational Enhancement Therapy, Relapse Prevention, Twelve-Step Facilitation, Logotherapy, Transpersonal Psychology, and other sources. The book will identify some central principles and practices in each approach that can be especially relevant to the addiction treatment and recovery process, but I will not try to present a full introduction, or even a complete outline, of each of these approaches within the limited context of this work.

In technical, clinical terms—for those professional readers who may prefer or occasionally need to use them—I have chosen to call the overall eclectic therapeutic approach presented in this book:

### "Transpersonal Cognitive Therapy."

It is based on three simple principles of *"rational spirituality"* which suggest that:

- Many people are apparently unable to use sound rational and emotional coping skills without first calming their minds and centering themselves spiritually.
- True spirituality is natural, healthy, and enhances our rational thinking, and
- Unconditional love is the most peaceful, powerful, and practical spiritual energy in the universe.

However, as we will see very clearly when we consider the critical issues of personal responsibility and motivation for change in harmful addiction, there is a vital corollary to these core principles which gently but firmly reminds us—and hopefully our clients as well—that

**the life-transforming power of unconditional love is like a chisel in the hands of a sculptor**—*it only works when we tap it.*

I have chosen to use the word "we" very carefully and deliberately here—rather than saying "you" or "they"—because I have a personal bias which presumes that a good clinician can only communicate and transmit those values, principles, and practices that they have personally embraced and embodied and can therefore role model in a healthy therapeutic relationship with authenticity and integrity.

Thus—if we actually know it for ourselves as an experiential fact—we can suggest to our clients that when we do tap into this awesome power we will begin to gradually remove from our lives all those things that don't belong in a beautiful work of art.

We can let our clients know that when we thoughtfully reflect upon the core principles and practices of *"rational spirituality,"* we will understand that this mighty power is "alive and well" inside all of us—flowing freely through the deepest spiritual core of our being.

Therefore, when we make a decision to devote our lives to the daily practice of patience, kindness, tolerance, and unconditional love for ourselves and for all others, we will tap into a deep source of inner peace, inner power, personal freedom, and enduring joy that is always dependable and can never be seriously disturbed, diminished, depleted, or destroyed.

For people struggling with serious harmful addictions this is often the best path—and sometimes it may prove to be the only effective path—toward achieving a real and lasting recovery.

"Human perfection," of course, is an absurd oxymoron, but truly practicing the power of unconditional love and forgiveness will allow each of us to find the humility and self-acceptance to remember that our lives will always be an unfinished "work-in-progress"—hopefully right up to the day we die—on the path of true happiness as we keep tap, tap, tapping away.

Above all else, when we finally see the futility of approaching life like a vacuum cleaner—vainly trying to fill our spiritual emptiness with anything or anyone we can find outside ourselves—and when we make a conscious and deliberate decision to allow the life-transforming power of unconditional love to flow freely through our daily lives from a hidden wellspring deep inside ourselves—like water through a garden hose—to refresh, nourish, and brighten our days and the days of all those whose lives we are privileged to touch—then we will come to understand why the principles of *rational spirituality* would suggest that the one primary purpose of a good and meaningful life could be:

> **"Always to add whatever we can to the stream of goodness and light in our sometimes dark and troubled world, and to help others do likewise."**

Dale Kesten
*Westport, Connecticut*
*April 4, 2004*

# INTRODUCTION

"I gave up drinking, smoking, drugs, and sex. It was the hardest 15 minutes in my life!"

"Anyone who imagines that all fruits ripen at the same time as the strawberries knows nothing about grapes."

—Paracelsus.

"Habit is habit, and not to be flung out of the window by any man, but to be coaxed down the stairs one step at a time."

—Mark Twain.

◆ ◆ ◆

## MAKING THE TRANSITION INTO RECOVERY

This book is primarily intended to meet the continuing education needs of licensed or certified professionals currently working with patients or clients in the disciplines of medicine, nursing, healthcare, psychiatry, psychology, clinical social work, marriage and family therapy, counseling, other mental health or behavioral health services, and in any form of addictions treatment, alcohol and drug abuse counseling, or substance abuse education and prevention.

The title of the book may strike some readers as a bit misleading since it is not intended serve as a comprehensive training manual or to offer everything you would ever want or need to know about addiction, progression, and recovery. In particular, we will *not* be taking a detailed look at the traditional stages of change and growth that commonly occur in the long-term addiction recovery process—nor reviewing the critical developmental tasks that are normally linked to achieving and maintaining permanent recovery at each stage.

Rather, *Addiction, Progression, & Recovery* is designed to help readers achieve a better understanding of the *signs, symptoms, and stages of progression* in harmful addiction, and of the long-term learning process that is usually involved for those people who successfully *make the transition* from active progression into active and sustained recovery.

Alcoholism, drug addiction, and other harmful addictions frequently tend to develop in a recognizable pattern of signs and symptoms that often emerge gradually over a period of many years in a series of identifiable and progressively worsening stages.

Moreover, it is only through the direct personal experience of numerous signs, symptoms, and negative consequences—and especially through the direct and humbling experience of repeated failure in all serious attempts at control or abstinence—that most people will ever become truly convinced that they are actually in the grips of a serious harmful addiction. Furthermore, even after they have achieved the crucial insight that a serious problem truly exists, most people will only begin to understand through a long process of trial and error what methods will work or apparently won't work for them individually as they attempt to control it or stop it.

As a licensed clinical social worker and a licensed alcohol and drug abuse counselor, I've worked with thousands of clients in the mental health and addictions treatment field since 1987.

As a recovering compulsive overeater, I've also made innumerable direct observations and have had personal interactions with thousands of people dealing with the same problem through my active participation in a self-help recovery program since 1981.

I've also learned much about the extended course of inner change and growth that's usually required in a long-term addiction recovery process through my personal experience maintaining a normal weight and a weight loss of about 140 pounds since 1983.

The core concept of learning through repeated trial and error is the theoretical foundation for a *unified addiction recovery model* that I have developed and will present in this book that is designed to help clients:

- understand the compulsive nature of harmful addiction more thoroughly,
- recognize the signs, symptoms, negative consequences and progression of a harmful addiction in their personal history more clearly,
- make sense of their own past, present, and *future* experiences more easily,
- self-diagnose and identify any problem they may have—or may be developing—with a harmful addiction more promptly, and thus
- facilitate the overall process of making permanent change more effectively.

I call this new perspective:

**"The Face to Face Unified Addiction Recovery Model."**

"Face to Face" is an acronym that stands for:

*"Formal Addiction Control Experiments"*

and

*"Failed Addiction Control Experiments."*

This model identifies an **Addiction Recovery Learning Curve** that describes five stages of change that many people with the most serious harmful addictions will usually have to go through on their long road to achieving a real and lasting recovery.

These five *naturally-occurring* and *easily observable* stages are identified in the *Face to Face Model* as follows:

1. **Uncontrolled Use with Consequences**
2. **Attempted Common Sense Control**
3. **Attempted Analytical Abstinence**
4. **Attempted Spiritual Sobriety** and
5. **Rational Spiritual Sobriety**

These five stages of change are purely descriptive and *not* theoretical.

In other words, they are *not* based on quantitative, experimental research studies testing abstract academic theories or plausible scientific hypotheses about how people *might* be able to change some of their most harmful, self-defeating, or self-destructive behaviors.

Rather, these five plateaus of learning and growth commonly found on the rugged path of painful personal experience actually represent a retrospective "synthesis and description" of a reality that is readily observable and widely repeated in the experience of many users.

For example?

- Most people will usually have to experience the negative consequences of unrestricted use *repeatedly* before they would ever be seriously motivated to consistently attempt controlled use.
- Most people will usually have to fail at controlled use *repeatedly* before they would ever be seriously motivated to attempt complete abstinence through the conscious use of rational coping skills.

- Most people will usually have to fail in their efforts to achieve some kind of "rational-secular" sobriety *repeatedly* before they would ever be seriously motivated to attempt any kind of a "spiritual solution."
- And, finally, many people will often have to "fail" *repeatedly* at an attempted spiritual solution—that will often be quite vaguely defined and poorly understood by them in practical terms—before they would ever be seriously motivated to *personally identify* and *persistently practice* a set of universal spiritual principles that they can easily understand, accept, and coherently express in clear, simple, modern, rational terms.

This developmental "learning curve" model is solidly based on the empirical foundation of countless direct personal observations that I have made over two decades during interactions with thousands of people dealing with very serious harmful addictions.

The sum total of all the data that I have gathered during the past 23 years of "naturalistic, qualitative field research" has made it very clear to me that:

> this is how *most* people who develop the most serious harmful addictions actually *do* change or ultimately *fail* to change over the long term.

In essence, the *Face to Face Unified Addiction Recovery Model* and the *Addiction Recovery Learning Curve* merely *describe observable reality* in a systematic way with some original clinical concepts and some newly coined technical terms.

**Why do I call the approach presented in this book the Face to Face *Unified* Addiction Recovery Model?**

Because it's designed to help people reconcile many of the *apparent philosophical "differences"* which often seem to be so glaring in the addiction treatment and recovery field when the overall process of addiction, progression, recognition, and recovery is only seen short-sightedly in a superficial, partial, and fragmented manner.

Historically, the addiction treatment and recovery field has been marked by a number of "serious" and often heated *philosophical disagreements*, and this sad tendency shows little or no sign of abating.

In this book, we will examine the three most significant areas of toxic misunderstanding, misinformation, disagreement, and debate in the addiction field—for which an open mind and a decent sense of humor are often a good antidote.

These three "core conflicts" involve:

- Social learning models of addiction "versus" the disease model,
- Controlled-use or moderation based models of recovery "versus' the total abstinence approach, and
- Cognitive-behavioral, "rational," or "secular" recovery models "versus" the twelve step "spiritual" model.

In his 1985 article "Craftsman versus Professional: Analysis of the Controlled Drinking Controversy," D. R. Cook described a serious polarization that had existed in the addiction treatment field historically for several decades—which still lingers to this day. He referred to the tension between proponents of a "craft-paraprofessional" approach aimed at achieving total abstinence from the use of all mood altering substances—with treatment being provided by trained counselors utilizing the AA recovery model who are also sober alcoholics themselves—and partisans for a "scientist-professional" approach aimed at a range of options including total abstinence or "controlled drinking"—with treatment provided by "empirically oriented researcher-clinicians" who may or may not have ever had any personal experience with harmful addiction.

Cook examined the philosophical conflicts involved and concluded, quite reasonably, that:

> "It is . . . possible for a craftsman alcoholism counselor to take an open-ended position on abstinence for any given patient. It is also possible for a scientist-professional alcoholism counselor to take an absolute position on the necessity of permanent abstinence for any given patient. It is possible for the scientist-professional to utilize the AA steps in treatment and for the craftsman to learn and implement effective relapse prevention techniques."

> (Cook, 1985: 441).

The experiential reality of the long-term process of change described in the *Addiction Recovery Learning Curve* has been widely recognized and openly discussed for decades by many people who are active in the addiction treatment field and in various self-help recovery programs.

Indeed, it has been widely recognized that this *basic learning process* is often—and perhaps even universally—repeated among those people who eventually develop and then struggle to overcome the most serious harmful addictions.

What's been sadly missing—thus far—has been any widespread recognition of the powerful underlying unity and coherence that binds all of these superficially "competing" addiction treatment and recovery philosophies together into a seamless whole that this new model merely seeks to explain and formalize.

This essential unity can be recognized quite clearly when we take the time to look at *all* of the different philosophical approaches holistically. In fact, we can easily see how well all of these approaches actually fit together and complement each other when we start to look at them in a logical sequence on a simple continuum of change.

My ultimate aim as an author, speaker, trainer, and seminar leader dealing with addiction and recovery issues is to help more clinicians and clients achieve a clear understanding of this deeper unity.

All of the different philosophical approaches to addiction treatment and recovery can fit easily and comfortably into the *Face to Face Unified Addiction Recovery Model* and all of them are accepted and understood as being *legitimate* and *clinically appropriate* for *certain* people when they are dealing with *certain* issues at *particular* stages in the overall process of change on the *Addiction Recovery Learning Curve.*

It is crucial to understand, however, that this is not because the particular approach, methods, or goals that are employed at a particular stage would always be expected or predicted to "work" for every client who seriously tries it.

Rather, each of these different approaches to change will probably have to be given a serious effort in a logical sequence by most clients who develop serious harmful addictions simply because:

> most people will have to *find out for themselves*—through their own *direct personal experience*—whether or not a given approach will work for them before they will *ever* be ready—usually after repeated, painful failures—to move on to the next stage.

Indeed, very often it is only the direct personal experience of a five-level "Addiction Control Failure Sequence" at each stage on the *Addiction Recovery Learning Curve* that ultimately convinces most people of the severity of their condition and of their need to try something different to effectively deal with it.

Naturally, those people who genuinely have *milder problems* will be able to successfully and permanently drop out of the "learning curve" model at an earlier stage—sometimes "right off the bat" at the simple stage of "Attempted Common Sense Control." This is not, however, because some abstract, academic, scientific, or partisan theory or philosophy says that they should or shouldn't be able to so, but simply because in real-life they can, they will, and they do.

Sadly, many of the people who genuinely have *more serious problems* won't become *ready, willing, or able* to move on to the next stage on the *Addiction Recovery Learning Curve* until long after they've passed a point of painful desperation and futility in their failed attempts at control or abstinence at a given stage—and "strike out" over and over again.

At some point, however, many of the people who repeatedly fail to abstain or control their use may have to reluctantly admit defeat at a particular stage on the learning curve and move on to try a different set of addiction recovery methods or goals in the next stage.

Happily, many people who repeatedly fail to abstain or control their use with one set of methods or goals will be able to use the enhanced insight and improved coping skills gained in this learning process quite constructively at some point in the future—if they have given the recommended approach at each stage a *serious and open-minded effort.*

Indeed, for many people, fully mastering the fundamentals of each approach in a logical sequence—including the knowledge base, core principles, and practical skills involved—will often prove to be indispensable. This is because the practical insights and skills that clients can learn at each stage will often represent crucial developmental tasks and essential building blocks for change that they will eventually need as they move forward through the overall process of change.

For example, a person who *really learns and practices* sound rational and emotional coping skills—using cognitive-behavioral or rational-emotive therapy in the "Attempted Analytical Abstinence" stage—will eventually have a more solid foundation for long-term recovery that someone who leapfrogs or is prematurely pushed ahead into the "Attempted Spiritual Sobriety" stage without ever learning these skills. This will be true even if they find that using these purely "rational-secular" principles alone leads to a pattern of repeated failure and they eventually decide that they will also need to seek a deeper "spiritual solution."

◆ ◆ ◆

While virtually anyone could potentially develop a harmful addiction—and there is no universal *"addictive personality"* per se—it's also fair to say that irrational beliefs, distorted thinking patterns, selfish desires, shallow motives, emotional over-reactivity, and poor impulse control are all strongly linked to the problem of harmful addiction in many cases—and to many other mental, emotional, and behavioral problems as well.

Therefore, in addition to presenting the *Face to Face Unified Addiction Recovery Model* and the *Addiction Recovery Learning Curve*, this book will also introduce a closely related system—already mentioned indirectly in the preface—that could be crucial to helping addiction clients achieve a deep and lasting recovery and could also be of great value for many other people who are dealing with altogether different issues.

Over the past 23 years, during professional and personal interactions with thousands of people struggling with serious harmful addictions, distressing mental, emotional, or physical problems, and difficult relationship issues, interpersonal conflicts, or communication problems, I have repeatedly observed a troubling phenomena that seems to occur quite frequently among people in all of these "diverse" groups:

> Many people seem to be driven so compulsively by their most *shallow desires, selfish motives, irrational beliefs,* and *unreasonable fears*—and their emotional reactivity and lack of healthy impulse control seems to be so intense or persistent—even when they are consciously *trying* to stop and think rationally—that they are apparently *unable* to use sound rational and emotional coping skills without first calming their minds and centering themselves spiritually.

I have seen so many sad or even tragic consequences unfold because of this problem that I am now completely convinced there is an urgent need for clinicians to offer people a simple and effective way to integrate and practice sound rational *and* spiritual principles in a fully unified and consistent manner.

In an effort to provide clinicians and clients alike with a clear example, an ideal model, and a simple vocabulary illustrating how this sort of *"rational-spiritual" integration* might be accomplished, I have developed a self-help system that will be introduced in the final chapter of this book.

This system is called:

### RS—Rational Spirituality ®

The *"RS"* model was initially crafted as a self-help system for people who are working through the fifth and final stage on the *Addiction Recovery Learning Curve—Rational Spiritual Sobriety.* However, as it has gradually evolved, the *RS model* is now intended to benefit anyone who may be interested in learning how to

- *center* themselves spiritually,
- *control* their own emotional reactivity, thoughts, feelings, words, and deeds more consistently,
- become *healthier* and *happier*, and
- learn how to live in a more *rational, effective, rewarding, and meaningful* way.

*Emotional over-reactivity* seems to be the hallmark of almost all unhappiness and it provides the impetus for many crimes against our better nature—whether one routinely plays the stereotyped role of perpetrator, victim, rescuer, bystander, avenger, fugitive, prisoner, judge, jury, or executioner in the typical dramas of everyday life.

About 150 years ago—in his classic book *Walden*—Henry David Thoreau made a timeless observation about the human condition when he wrote:

> The mass of men lead lives of quiet desperation.
>
> (Thoreau, 1960: 10)

For this reason, I would include among the ranks of the "emotionally over-reactive" even those "strong, silent," and superficially stoic types who just seem to "grin and bear it" while slowly dying inside—literally and figuratively—from rampant, often unacknowledged emotional stress.

The typical "bulldozer," "bully," "dictator," or "rageaholic" is a loud, painfully obvious, and unpleasant example of emotional over-reactivity at its worst. However, I would also include all of the "martyrs," "people-pleasers," "doormats," and "clowns" among the emotionally over-reactive—right along with the "strong, silent stoics"—because all of them are either consciously suppressing or "stuffing" their negative emotional reactions to difficult people, circumstances, or life events, or else they are unconsciously repressing, denying, or otherwise disowning these vital signals indicating that something is seriously wrong—inside or out.

I would also include among the *emotionally over-reactive* those men and women who *seem* to be more "emotionally expressive"—because they seem to cry, suffer, whine, complain, or just talk a lot—and really "get their feelings out." Most of the time, however, this kind of person merely blurts out, talks out, pours out, or acts out their negative emotions in an ineffectual, dysfunctional manner without ever genuinely expressing them or taking action to resolve them in a healthy way.

In the final chapter of this book, we will see how *Rational Spirituality* addresses the central problems of ego-level emotional reactivity and poor impulse control by seamlessly blending the proven tools for rational change that are currently found in cognitive-behavioral and rational-emotive therapy with a practical translation of twelve-step program principles—and other universal spiritual principles—into

> *clear, simple, modern terms and a set of effective self-management techniques that most people can easily understand, accept, and begin to practice.*

We will review the stages of faith development and consider why it is that so many people—especially chronic relapsers—often tend to react with sincere confusion or reflexive antagonism to the generic spirituality of twelve-step recovery programs. In this developmental context, we will also examine the apparent *pre-existing biases* that may be held by many advocates for purely "rational-secular" approaches to addiction recovery. We will consider how so many of them often seem to be reacting negatively to their own *misunderstanding* of the simple universal spiritual principles that are actually involved in the spiritual recovery process.

In the simplest possible terms, as we have already noted in the preface, we will see how the *Rational Spirituality* model proposes a thoughtful and reasonable way for people to tap into a deep source of inner peace, inner power, personal freedom, and enduring joy through daily devotion to the intelligent practice of

patience, kindness, tolerance, and unconditional love.

The ultimate purpose of this book is to provide concerned and caring clinicians with some useful information and a fresh perspective that might assist you in your worthy efforts to help people who are struggling with harmful addictions learn what they have to learn and do what they have to do in order to achieve a real and lasting recovery. Hopefully, this information will help some of them do so much sooner than might otherwise have been the case, and will also help some of them learn how to live healthier, happier, more meaningful, and more rewarding lives in the process.

Ideally, the *Face to Face Unified Addiction Recovery Model,* and the *Addiction Recovery Learning Curve* presented in this book—along with the clear, simple, modern terms that I've tried to use in the *Rational Spirituality* self-help model—will all work together to help clinicians and clients achieve a better understanding of the key dynamics that are usually involved in the frequently extended, overlapping, and complex processes of "Addiction, Progression, and Recovery."

# LEARNING OBJECTIVES

---

"I keep six honest serving men, they taught me all I knew. Their names are what and why and when and where and how and who."

—Rudyard Kipling.

♦ ♦ ♦

Healthcare and mental health treatment providers encounter a wide range of problems linked to alcohol and drug abuse and other harmful compulsive or addictive behaviors in virtually every practice setting.

As noted above, this book is primarily intended to meet the continuing education needs of licensed or certified professionals currently working with patients or clients in the fields of medicine, nursing, healthcare, psychiatry, psychology, clinical social work, mental health counseling, marriage and family therapy, or addictions treatment.

The *most important* Learning Objective for the book as a whole is to provide treatment professionals with the ability to:

> *Assess, educate, motivate*, and *empower* clients with this information and *help* them overcome any rationalization, minimization, or denial that might block their ability to recognize the signs and symptoms of a past, present, or future problem with harmful addiction, and take effective action to control or stop any harmful addictive behavior.

## PLAN OF THE BOOK

**Part One** of this book will focus on the basic phenomena of **ADDICTION**, and will also look at some basic assessment and diagnosis issues.

**Part Two** of the book will take a detailed look at the traditional signs, symptoms, and stages of **PROGRESSION** in harmful addiction.

**Part Three** will focus on helping people understand and self-diagnose harmful addiction and successfully make the transition into **RECOVERY**.

# PART ONE

---

# ADDICTION

# CHAPTER 1

# Understanding Addiction

> "There is in all men a demand for the superlative, so much so that the poor devil who has no other way of reaching it attains it by getting drunk."
>
> —Oliver Wendell Holmes, Jr.

◆ ◆ ◆

Many honest and well-intentioned people who drink or use some other kind of drug will eventually find themselves asking a very serious question:

**"How do I really know if I have an alcohol or drug abuse problem?"**

Some of these people will find that they can't answer this question objectively for themselves, because their capacity to perceive the truth of the matter—which may seem very clear to outside observers—has become lost or obscured in an unconscious fog of **minimization, rationalization, self-deception,** or **denial.**

One well-known answer to this classic question therefore suggests, only half-jokingly:

**"If you have to ask, then you've got a problem."**

In the addiction treatment field it is a very common practice to provide clients with a great deal of basic information regarding addiction and recovery issues. Indeed, it's fair to say that this is a universal practice in the "best" treatment programs. This is primarily an educational task and it is often accomplished through the use of lectures, videotapes, readings, handouts, worksheets, and homework assignments. This basic information will then be processed in topic-centered psychoeducational discussion groups where a skilled clinician will keep the client group focused on one critical question:

**"How does all of this apply to me?"**

This educational experience is deemed to be an essential element in addiction treatment because it helps clients achieve two critical goals in the early stage of the recovery process:

> First, they gain **factual information** that helps them understand the true nature of alcoholism or drug addiction in objective terms.

> Secondly, this learning process also helps them begin to see through some of their own denial, dishonesty, or self-deception and start to make an **accurate self-diagnosis** of their own condition.

In their clinical text *A Concise Guide to Treatment of Alcoholism and Addictions,* Avram Mack, John Franklin, and Richard Frances make the following observations:

> In the United States, *substance use disorders (SUDs)* present a tremendous medical and social challenge . . . Treatment of SUDs can be extremely difficult. Helping the patient to *recognize a problem* and to *accept help* are the *two most important steps* in treatment, recognized both by self-help groups and by research concerning motivational interviewing and stages of awareness. These two steps are frequently difficult because of the nature of addictive disorders, which leads to denial, lying, and organicity (central nervous system pathology). Both patient and therapist may struggle with the stigma of substance disorders and with accepting that the patient has an illness. *Most patients will wish to achieve controlled use* and will have difficulty accepting the therapist's standard of *abstinence* as the goal for treatment.

> (Mack, Franklin & Frances, 2001: xv, 1–2. Emphasis added).

One primary purpose of this book is to give you as a clinician the essential information you would need to conduct a thorough psychoeducational assessment and feedback interview with your individual clients—or to facilitate an effective psychoeducational discussion group—that could help some of your clients begin to honestly answer that vital question—"How does all of this apply to me?" In this regard, however, we will *not* get into the area of generic clinical interviewing skills or group facilitation skills, but will keep our focus on improving your knowledge and understanding of the basic signs, symptoms, and stages of progression into harmful addiction and the long-term learning process that is often involved in helping clients make the vital transition into recovery.

## ADDICTION DEFINED

"A problem well-stated is a problem half solved."

—Charles Kettering.

◆ ◆ ◆

The word "addiction" is highly charged with emotion for many people. It often evokes strong negative stereotypes and images of "junkies," "crack heads," "dope fiends," or "drug addicts." The word "alcoholism" carries much of the same negative baggage in our society, evoking negative stereotypes of the "alcoholic" as a "hopeless drunk," a "lush," a "wino," or a "skid row bum."

Prestigious academic, scientific, medical, and government organizations —such as the American Medical Association, the American Psychiatric Association, the American Society of Addiction Medicine, the United States Department of Health and Human Services, and the World Health Organization, among many others—have long recognized that serious problems with alcohol or drug abuse are manifestations of a chronic "disease" or "disorder."

Despite this, many negative stereotypes persist and harsh terms such as those mentioned above are still used by some people as insulting and judgmental labels that stigmatize people with alcohol or drug abuse problems as being weak, shameful, sinful, or morally bankrupt. Even when the terms "alcoholism" or "addiction" are vaguely understood to represent some kind of illness, we find that the words "sick" or "pathological" may often be used in an angry and abusive way to demean and insult the person involved rather than objectively describe a condition from which they suffer.

Virtually all professionals working in the addiction treatment field today have rejected the old-fashioned "moral model" of addiction as fundamentally flawed—even those who also dispute the newer "disease model." Advocates of the "social learning model" of addiction, for example, propose that addiction is essentially "a learned behavior that can be unlearned." For them, alcohol or drug abuse problems do not reflect the absence of "strong values, good character, or moral fiber" in the addicted person *nor* do they reflect the presence of any "disease." For social learning theorists, serious addiction problems stem mostly from a lack of adequate coping skills in the addicted person.

American public attitudes toward addiction have also shifted radically away from the "moral model" over the past few decades, and the overall concept of addiction has also expanded to suggest something much larger and all-inclusive than ever imagined before. The basic meaning of the word "addiction" in our popular culture today now extends far beyond the limits of alcohol or drug abuse to embrace a much wider range of problem substances or activities. These would include things such as nicotine addiction; compulsive gambling; compulsive overeating; food addiction; sugar addiction; caffeine addiction; compulsive spending and debting; workaholism; rage, anger, and abusiveness; dysfunctional and dependent relationships; sexual addiction; pornography; hoarding and clutter; internet surfing; computer and video games; excessive television viewing; spectator sports; excessive exercise; and so forth.

While this broader concept of addiction has become the butt of jokes at times—as reflected by the humorous or sarcastic use of hybrid terms such as "chocoholic," "foodaholic," or "shopaholic"—it has also been applied more seriously with the use of terms such as "workaholic" or "rageaholic." This relatively new notion has also been recognized clinically in many significant ways and this trend is reflected by the growing acceptance and use of more objective, technical terms such as:

### "compulsive-addictive behavior."

In their book *Craving for Ecstasy: The Consciousness & Chemistry of Escape,* Harvey Milkman and Stanley Sunderwirth talk about "the compelling urge to feel wonderful," and they also use various terms such as "compulsive pleasure seeking," "mood-altering behaviors," and "pathological habits." They stress the validity of this broader understanding of addiction as a central tenet of their book, and note that:

> The term *addiction* was once reserved for dependence on drugs. Today it is applied to a range of compulsive behaviors as disparate as working too hard and eating too much chocolate. In fact, there are essential biological, psychological, and social common denominators between drug use and other habitual behaviors. Whether your pleasure is meditation or mescaline, cocaine or cults, you are addicted when you cannot control when you start or stop an activity.

> Gradually, addiction came to imply psychological need over and above the traditional constructs of physical demand and distress upon withdrawal.

> Compulsion, loss of control, and continuation despite harmful consequences became new criteria for the determination of addiction.

Specifically, Milkman and Sundwerwirth identify three preferred styles of coping that will usually lead people of different personality types to prefer one of three basic types of addiction:

**satiation, arousal,** or **fantasy.**

In this regard, they also point out that:

> People do not become addicted to drugs or mood-altering behaviors as such, but rather to *the sensations of pleasure* that can be achieved through them. We repeatedly rely on three distinct types of experience to achieve feelings of well-being: *relaxation, excitement,* and *fantasy.* As they say in show business:
>
> *'You've gotta feed 'em, shock 'em, or amuse 'em.'*
>
> (Milkman & Sunderwirth, 1987: ix, xi–xii,<br>1–2, 6, 18, 174. Emphasis added)

Jalie Tucker, senior editor of the book *Changing Addictive Behavior*, clearly acknowledges this trend—as reflected in the title chosen for the book itself. In her introductory chapter reviewing historical and contemporary perspectives on addiction she points out that:

> medical notions about the disease of alcoholism have . . . been disseminated and generalized on such a scale that they have become *a cultural metaphor for all impulse control problems* (e.g. alcohol and drug abuse, gambling, overeating, sex and computer addiction) at least in the United States.
>
> (Tucker, 1999:6. Emphasis added)

*So what does the word "addiction" really mean?* In layman's terms, most people would say that an "addiction"—by way of definition—has to involve some kind of habitual behavior that sooner or later gets "out of control." In order to qualify as a *genuine* addiction, this "bad habit" must also be something that the "addict" is "unable to stop"—often because they experience some kind of "painful withdrawal symptoms" whenever they try to "go cold turkey," and "kick the habit." Beyond this, in order to qualify as a *real addiction*, most people would say that the negative habit involved *must* cause a significant number of "serious problems" and produce major "negative consequences" for the addicted person, and for his or her family, friends, or co-workers.

My favorite dictionary tells me that the word "addiction" actually means:

- To habitually devote oneself—or give oneself up—to a particular behavior or activity.

The word "addiction," is drawn from the Latin word "*addictus*," and the related verb: "*addicere*," which is derived from the words "*ad*," meaning "to," and "*dicere*," meaning "say," and what the word really means is:

- "To give assent."

Addiction, in the original sense of the word, essentially involves making an affirmative choice. Expressed in the simplest terms, to become "addicted" literally means:

- To say "yes."

To "devote," also involves making an affirmative choice. Its roots are found in the Latin verb "*devovere*," (to dedicate by vow), and it means:

- To dedicate, consecrate, give up, or apply oneself to some purpose, activity, or person.

To "give up," while also defined as making an affirmative choice, involves making a choice that might be considered as positive, negative, or value neutral. To "give up" means:

- To despair and lose hope.
- To admit failure and stop trying.
- To hand over, turn over, relinquish, or surrender.
- To sacrifice and wholly devote.

## THE BIG QUESTION

"Out, out, brief candle! Life's but a walking shadow, a poor player that struts and frets his hour upon the stage and then is heard no more: it is a tale told by an idiot, full of sound and fury, signifying nothing."

—William Shakespeare.

♦ ♦ ♦

There's a classic question that most good actors are always asking themselves as they prepare a to enter a role, develop a character, and play a particular scene:

**"What's my motivation?"**

One day a background extra working on a movie was given the direction to stand up, glance at his watch, look around, and then walk out a side door on the set when he heard a certain cue in the script.

He asked the Assistant Director who had quickly told him to do all this:

"What's my motivation?"

And the Assistant Director—who probably had about two minutes available to give individual directions to a crowd of background extras working in that particular shot—said to the budding actor:

> "You're motivation is to stand up when you hear that line, glance
> at your watch, look around, and then walk out that door or you're
> fired."

When talking about actors or extras working in comedy or drama on stage or screen it's easy to joke about inner direction or motivation, but in real life this isn't a joking matter.

In fact, nothing could be more serious.

Life constantly poses *one very big question* that we all have to answer in one way or another many times every day. Philosophically, some people feel strongly that this is the only question we all must face on a daily basis that *really counts:*

> "What I am going to think, feel, say, or do—right now—in this
> very moment?"

This one vital question, put another way, asks simply:

> "What do I really care about deeply enough, right here and now,
> to say:

> *'Yes, that's what I'll do?'"*

During every waking moment of our lives, with every choice we make, whether consciously or unconsciously, we are always answering this fundamental question by saying: "yes" to something. Moreover, we all tend to become deeply "devoted" or "dedicated" to our most habitual choices—even if we don't think about our choices or behavior in those terms. In fact, most of us will become so attached to our most habitual choices that these behaviors eventually start to look much more like *automatic, unthinking* "responses" rather than *conscious or deliberate* "choices." And when that happens, as it routinely does for most of us, it's probably fair to say that we're "hooked."

This is why "addiction" in one form or another is now so widely recognized as being *an almost universal phenomena*, and why so many people today can relate very easily to the idea that:

"We're *all* addicted to something."

More accurately, it's probably fair to say:

"We're all addicted to *many* things."

When we ponder the persistent problem that so many people face in controlling their own blatant or subtle emotional over-reactivity it might be valuable for us to ask our clients to think about any irrational beliefs or distorted thinking patterns they may be able to identify in themselves in the following terms:

- Am I *addicted* to feeling frustrated, angry, intolerant, or impatient when people don't do what I want or things don't go my way?
- Am I *addicted* to feeling sad, hurt, disappointed, or angry when people don't seem to like me, love me, accept me, respect me, recognize me, reward me, or treat me the way I'd like them to?
- Am I *addicted* to leaping to conclusions or to personalizing things in my imagination that actually may have nothing to do with me?
- Am I *addicted* to feeling tense or pressured by a never-ending list of shoulds and musts and resentful, guilty, or ashamed because of my own sense of imperfection, inadequacy, laziness, or rebellion?
- Am I *addicted* to comparing myself with other people and feeling ashamed, unworthy, inferior, judgmental, arrogant, proud, angry, self-righteous, or superior?
- Am I *addicted* to seeing people or situations in simplistic terms that reflect a critical all-or-nothing, black-or-white, good-or-bad, always-or-never attitude with no real understanding or tolerance for gray areas of imperfection, ambiguity, or uncertainty?
- Am I *addicted* to seeing only the worst or most negative aspects of a person or a situation and to consistent blindness regarding their positive features or possibilities?
- Am I *addicted* to pessimism, fear, worrying about the future, and feeling anxious, depressed, or doomed, because I always irrationally predict or expect the worst?
- Am I *addicted* to regretting or resenting the past and harshly judging myself or others for past failures, mistakes, misdeeds, or missed opportunities?

- Am I *addicted* to projecting blame and responsibility for my own problems, feelings, reactions, mistakes, or failures onto other people or outside circumstances?
- Am I *addicted* to compulsively pursuing a futile quest to satisfy my inner emptiness and fill my spiritual void with anyone or anything outside of myself?

## HARMFUL VERSUS POSITIVE ADDICTIONS

"O God, that men should put an enemy in their mouths to steal away their brains!"

—William Shakespeare.

"This is the true joy in life, the being used for a purpose recognized by yourself as a mighty one; the being thoroughly worn out before being thrown on the scrap heap; the being a force of nature instead of a feverish selfish clod of ailments and grievances, complaining that the world will not devote itself to making you happy."

—George Bernard Shaw.

♦ ♦ ♦

Every day in America alone, thousands of people are being killed, injured, or sickened by the impact of various harmful compulsive-addictive behaviors, and millions of other lives are being slowly destroyed, damaged, diminished, or otherwise affected.

So many powerful negative stereotypes still linger around the concept of addiction that we can easily forget how the generic phenomena of addiction is a universal human experience that is neither good nor bad in itself.

When we remember the root definition of the word "addiction"—which is "to habitually devote oneself—or give oneself up—to a particular behavior or activity"—it becomes obvious that there *must* be such a thing as *positive addiction.*

Indeed, our human ability to feel idealism, altruism, compassion, and unconditional love—and our ultimate capacity for devotion, dedication, and passionate commitment to a beloved person, a noble cause, a healthy activity, or even a good habit or a regular routine—can all be seen as examples of positive addiction.

Many of us can become so deeply committed to some of our positive addictions that we will literally get "hooked." We will start to feel uncomfortable withdrawal symptoms whenever our healthy habit or routine is interrupted—and this is one of the classic signs of true addiction.

Ultimately, whether any given addiction turns out to be a positive or negative experience for the person involved will depend upon several important factors:

- What purpose, activity, or person has become the object of devotion?
- Are there any negative consequences associated with the addictive behavior?
- How harmful or destructive have these negative consequences become?
- Does the addictive behavior flow from a position of personal autonomy and true freedom of choice?

This last point suggests an apparent contradiction and raises a very important question: if someone is truly "hooked" on a positive addiction, and feels uncomfortable withdrawal symptoms when the addictive behavior is skipped, how could this behavior *possibly* "flow from a position of personal autonomy and true freedom of choice?"

William Glasser, a psychiatrist who is widely known for his book *Reality Therapy,* addresses this crucial issue in another book called *Positive Addiction,* and he makes the following points:

> Negative addicts are totally involved with their addiction, having long since given up on finding love and worth. The positive addict enjoys his addiction, but it does not dominate his life. From it he gains *mental strength* which he uses to help him accomplish whatever he tries to do more successfully. Unlike a negative addict, who is satisfied completely to live for his addiction, to the exclusion of everything else, a positive addict uses his extra strength to gain more love and more worth, more pleasure, more meaning, more zest from life in general.

> (Glasser, 1976: 39-40)

Let me briefly reiterate here that a fundamental premise of this book is to suggest that the *most practical path* to permanent recovery for many people dealing with serious harmful addictions will be for them to develop a passionate devotion to an alternative positive addiction that will prove to be more *reliable, rewarding, meaningful, satisfying,* and *fun.*

Now, let's consider a critical question:

What is the *key factor* that determines whether or not a particular addiction is healthy or harmful?

Many experts agree on one central idea:

The experience of "COMPULSION" is the *most crucial element* involved in the whole process of developing, sustaining, and defining a HARMFUL ADDICTION.

My dictionary defines "compulsion" as "the fact or state of being forced, coerced, or constrained," and, within the realm of psychopathology, it is described as:

"An irresistible impulse to perform an irrational act."

There are two essential elements in this definition that are crucial to understanding and defining the phenomena of harmful addiction. First, let's consider what constitutes an "irrational act?" Most "normal" people—who are reasonably sane and healthy—would probably agree that it would be "irrational" for them to engage in any behavior that produces negative consequences that are clearly harmful or destructive for them or for others. Negative consequences, then, must be involved for any habitual behavior to qualify as a harmful addiction. But this alone is not enough, because the crucial test—to establish the presence of compulsion—is that the impulse to perform the irrational act that produces the negative consequences has become *irresistible*.

Mark Twain made a profound observation about the difficulty many people encounter when they try to change harmful compulsive or addictive behaviors when he joked:

"It's easy to give up smoking. I've done it a thousand times."

And Oscar Wilde made another telling remark that describes the sad plight of so many people in this predicament when he said:

"I can resist everything . . . except temptation."

How can people start to change compulsive behaviors that have reached the level of harmful addiction or that may be heading in that direction?

The first essential step on the path toward changing any behavior—or fixing any problem—is simply to recognize that a problem actually exists and, even more importantly, to clearly identify what the problem actually is.

When we begin to identify many of the specific signs and symptoms of harmful addiction in Part Two of this book, let's remember that our most crucial task as clinicians will be not merely to help our clients recognize and admit which signs and symptoms they've already experienced, but, much more importantly, to help them understand the true nature of compulsion and to honestly face the question, regarding both the past and present, and especially in the future:

"Am I really in control of my own behavior?"

## "ALCOHOLISM" AND "ADDICTION" AS SYMBOLIC TERMS

"Once a cucumber has turned into a pickle, it can never be a cucumber again."

"The serious problems we face today cannot be solved at the same level of thinking we were at when we created them."

—Albert Einstein.

♦ ♦ ♦

The legendary CBS television correspondent Edward R. Murrow reportedly once said about Vietnam:

"If you're not confused, you don't really understand the situation."

In order to communicate effectively about any subject it's important to define the key terms and core concepts involved. So let's quickly review the key terms we've already established:

**Addiction**—To habitually devote oneself—or give oneself up— to a particular behavior or activity.

**Positive Addiction**—A healthy form of self-enhancing addictive behavior that is based upon personal commitment and freedom of choice, maximizes the strength and wellness of the addicted person, and ultimately contributes to greater success and satisfaction in life.

**Harmful Addiction**—An unhealthy form of self-defeating addictive behavior that is based on compulsion, produces unwanted negative consequences for the addicted person, diminishes or destroys their strength and wellness, and ultimately sabotages their success and satisfaction in life.

**Compulsion**—An irresistible impulse to perform an irrational act—the core element in all harmful addictions.

Let me emphasize that these are my own definitions—based on my trusty dictionary, my clinical education, training, and study, 23 years of personal recovery experience, and 17 years of clinical practice in the mental health and addictions treatment field.

In this field, unfortunately, there is no universal agreement regarding the actual meaning of many key terms that are widely used and frequently misunderstood. Of course, it's not really accurate in many cases to say that these terms are just *"misunderstood."* The same terms are very loosely defined, casually and informally used, and understood by different people to mean very different things.

In fact, there are so many conflicting assumptions regarding the meaning and value of most key terms in the addiction treatment and recovery field, and so many competing definitions—all hotly debated by well meaning, well-educated, and highly credentialed advocates of different theoretical approaches—that no one is really in a position to define *any* of these key terms with any real authority.

The words "alcoholic," and "alcoholism," for example, are strongly denounced by some people as being nothing more than stigmatizing labels, as we have already seen, and the same holds true for the emotionally charged terms "addict," and "addiction."

Technically speaking—in terms of formal clinical diagnoses—none of these words are officially accepted or used as a part of our current diagnostic terminology. A particular person may meet the diagnostic criteria for Alcohol Abuse or Alcohol Dependence that can be found in the *Diagnostic and Statistical Manual of Mental Disorders (Fourth Edition—Text Revision)*—which is published by the American Psychiatric Association—and is commonly referred to as the "DSM-IV-TR." Or they might satisfy the diagnostic criteria for some other form of substance abuse or substance dependence disorder found in the DSM-IV-TR. But, to be rather blunt about it, there is no such thing as "alcoholism" or "addiction" in our current official clinical terminology, and hence, *technically speaking,* there are no "alcoholics" or "addicts." For the sake of simplicity and clarity, therefore, we actually have no need to use any of these archaic terms, or try to understand, define, debate, or even discuss them as meaningful technical terms. In fact, we could easily dismiss them all as being essentially *meaningless and irrelevant.*

Let's look at an excellent example of the semantic fog of confusion and conflict that currently prevails regarding the proper use and real meaning of the word ""alcoholism." In his preface to a book called *Alternatives to Abstinence: A New Look at Alcoholism and the Choices in Treatment,* Frederick Rotgers points out that:

> Problem drinkers in the United States are faced with a daunting dilemma when they seek help. They can either accept the prevailing myth that abstinence is the *only* effective means to resolve a drinking problem, or they can be accused of being 'in denial' and dismissed from (or coerced into) an abstinence-only treatment that may be neither desirable nor appropriate for them.

> (Rotgers, 2001: xiii)

The point that Rotgers makes here is completely valid and the term he uses to describe the people involved is also entirely accurate—he calls them "problem drinkers."

The difficulty here is with the subtitle of the book itself—which asks us to take "a new look at *'alcoholism'* and the choices in treatment."

If the book were subtitled "a new look at *problem drinking"* there would be no problem, no confusion, and no real grounds for much conflict or debate.

For many people in our culture, however, and for most people working professionally in the addiction treatment field:

> an "alcoholic"—*by definition*—is someone who has demonstrated—repeatedly and beyond any shadow of reasonable doubt—that they cannot consistently control their drinking.

By *this* definition of alcoholism, of course, there is *no* sane "alternative to abstinence" for a *real* alcoholic, and the subtitle of this book would be considered absurdly and perhaps even dangerously misleading to imply that there could be.

Historically, however, the treatment coercion problem that Rotgers points out for "problem drinkers" has often been quite real. Some addiction treatment providers have operated with a therapeutic style that could be rather narrow-minded or semi-authoritarian. Their "confrontational approach"—which was actually in vogue for quite some time—is now widely seen as inappropriate and ineffective. This is because it violates all of the basic principles of motivational interviewing and fails to recognize the generic stages of change that most people have to go through in order to really recognize and change a problem behavior.

Some other problems with this outmoded approach have involved:

- a "cookie-cutter" or "one size fits all" mentality;
- leaping to conclusions;
- arbitrary labeling;
- partial, biased, or imaginary "assessments," and
- inaccurate or premature diagnosis.

Sadly, this discredited "confrontational approach" has given the addiction treatment field a "bad name" with some people over the past few decades and it has also created an exaggerated negative stereotype that still lingers on in many quarters. This has also been responsible for much of the bitterness and hostility that so often hinders reasonable discussion or debate of some "controversial" issues that do exist in the realm of addiction and recovery.

Remember, one of our first goals in addiction treatment will be to help our clients make an *accurate* and *timely* self-diagnosis.

You may remember the distinguished actor John Houseman, who did a classic television commercial for a stock brokerage firm many years ago in which he declared, with a rather arrogant sneer:

"We make our money the old fashioned way—we *earn* it!"

The model for the character and tone of voice used in this commercial was the gruff and intimidating Professor Kingsfield, whom Houseman had portrayed in his earlier film and television role in "The Paper Chase." One memorable moment from the film gave us another classic line so powerful that it was included as part of the opening sequence for the weekly television series that followed. Professor Kingsfield looks out at a large classroom full of first-year law students—sitting in front of him nervously on their first day of classes at Harvard Law School—and he declares—in exactly the same challenging and arrogant tone:

"You come in here with your head full of *mush*—and you *leave* thinking like a lawyer!"

With all due respect, we must always bear in mind as clinicians that most of our client's will come to us with a metaphorical "head full of mush" regarding the two confusing and controversial terms "alcoholism" and "addiction," and a head equally full of negative images, simplistic clichés, and exaggerated stereotypes regarding the potentially stigmatizing labels "alcoholic" and "addict."

How could it be otherwise when so many treatment professionals apparently suffer from so much of the same confusion?

For myself, I would find it difficult, awkward, and ultimately counter-productive to try to strike these traditional words from my clinical vocabulary and dispense with them entirely.

Why? Because no matter how confusing or controversial they may be, these common everyday words are simply not going away. Therefore, one way or another, we will have to help our clients begin to understand and "come to terms" with these terms.

I firmly believe that these traditional terms can eventually come to have an accurate and powerful symbolic meaning for ourselves and for our clients that can greatly enhance their understanding and acceptance of their own reality. If some of our clients are actually progressing toward the development of a full-blown harmful addiction then a clear understanding of these terms can significantly improve their ability to honestly answer the crucial question:

"What does all of this have to do with me?"

I draw my own definition of the terms "alcoholic" and "alcoholism," from the book *Alcoholics Anonymous,* which is widely known by the nickname "the Big Book." This text was first published in 1939, and it was initially drafted by AA co-founder Bill Wilson, and then reviewed and revised by the early sober members of the AA fellowship. The AA twelve-step program for recovery first appeared in this book near the beginning of Chapter Five, entitled "How It Works," which describes, retrospectively, the steps these early members had taken in order to achieve and maintain their sobriety. At the time, their staying sober represented an almost miraculous achievement because they were a group of people whose alcoholism had often progressed well past the point of being considered "hopeless" by themselves, their families, and their doctors.

Let me quote and highlight some of their insights about the true nature of their problem, from the beginning of Chapter Two of the Big Book, entitled "More About Alcoholism:"

> Most of us have been unwilling to admit we were *real alcoholics.* . . . Therefore, it is not surprising that our drinking careers have been characterized by countless vain attempts to prove we could drink like other people. *The idea that somehow, someday he will control and enjoy his drinking is the great obsession of every abnormal drinker. The persistence of this illusion is astonishing. Many pursue it to the gates of insanity or death.* . . .

> We learned that we had to fully concede to our *innermost selves* that we were alcoholics. This is the first step in recovery. . . .

> *We alcoholics are men and women who have lost the ability to control our drinking.* We know that no real alcoholic *ever* recovers control. . . . We are convinced . . . that alcoholics of our type are in the grip of a progressive illness. Over any considerable period we get worse, never better.

> *We are like men who have lost their legs: they never grow new ones.*

> (Alcoholics Anonymous, 1976: 30. Emphasis added.)

## THE "DISEASE MODEL" OF ADDICTION

> "Enjoy'd no sooner but despised straight;
> Past reason hunted, and no sooner had,
> Past reason hated, as a swallow'd bait
> On purpose laid to make the taker mad . . ."

> —William Shakespeare.

◆ ◆ ◆

Our primary goal in the early stage of addiction treatment is to help our clients conduct an accurate self-diagnosis and recognize any current problem that they might have with alcohol, drug abuse, or any other form of harmful compulsive or addictive behavior. Of course, many of them will probably be getting plenty of competing ideas from some of their friends who are actively using—and even from family members in many cases.

When I was working on an inpatient substance abuse treatment unit many years ago, I wasn't terribly surprised to see one of our former patients readmitted just a few weeks after he had "successfully" completed a 21-day substance abuse rehab program. He had been very fond of saying, with apparent conviction, "I know what I have to do this time," but he never seemed to really "get it."

When asked what had caused his most recent relapse he said:

> As soon as I got home I went over to hang out with some of my old friends and one of them offered me a drink. Of course, I told him 'I can't drink anymore because I'm a recovering alcoholic.' But then all my friends started saying: 'Don't be ridiculous! You're not an alcoholic. You don't drink any more than we do!' Well, for some crazy reason that actually made sense to me—even though I really know better by now. So I took the first drink and 'Bam!'—before I even knew what hit me—I was completely out of control again.

Despite our best efforts, many clients will leave treatment unconvinced that they really have a problem or quite confused about what they really have to do about it. Therefore, we also need to give them the information they will need in order to make sense of their own *future* experience more quickly than might otherwise be the case. We will want to help them identify any problem that they might be in the process of developing—sooner rather than later—and recognize the emerging signs and symptoms as they become more apparent over time.

We have seen how the emotionally charged words "alcoholism" and "addiction" are not "official" clinical terms with clear-cut meanings that are universally accepted. At the same time—even though they can only be used informally—we have also seen how important it is for clients to develop their own personal understanding of these powerful, symbolic terms—and to evaluate how accurately they may apply to themselves personally. It is equally important for us as clinicians to clarify our own understanding of these terms if we really want to help our clients conduct an accurate self-diagnosis.

The educational challenge we face as clinicians involves much more than simply providing "good information" and dispelling the normal ignorance or confusion that all students bring to the study of a new subject. We also have to confront deeply-rooted negative stereotypes—images derived exclusively from the most extreme cases—and challenge the all-or-nothing thinking that insists:

> "I can't possibly be an alcoholic, or an addict, because I'm not like that."

We must help our clients appreciate the significance of the word "yet." We must help them to look at the facts of their own experience and to fearlessly ask themselves:

- What path am I on?
- How far have I gone?
- Where am I heading?
- Is that where I really want to go?

When some of our clients actually begin to take an objective look at the nature of harmful addiction—and closely examine the raw facts of their own experience—they may start to realize that perhaps "the shoe fits" after all.

At that point, we will often have to help them accomplish five additional tasks:

> **First,** to recognize and admit how their harmful compulsive-addictive behavior has failed so miserably to produce any real happiness, health, harmony, success, or genuine satisfaction in their life—and to identify specifically the many negative consequences it has produced instead.

> **Second,** to recognize how insidiously their own deeply ingrained patterns of rationalization, minimization, self-deception, or denial empower their addiction and allow it to continue—and become willing to let go of them all.

> **Third,** to accept complete personal responsibility for their own life, health, harmony, happiness, success, and satisfaction—and become willing to take a fearlessly objective and compassionate look at their own dysfunctional ego-level personality and character traits.

> **Fourth,** to identify and take effective action to change any negative attitudes, shallow motives, selfish desires, irrational beliefs, or distorted thinking patterns that are usually the root cause for any emotional distress they may experience, and

**Fifth,** to identify and take effective action to resolve any residual feelings of guilt, remorse, stigma, or shame that they may still be holding on to.

Building on this foundation, our primary role as clinicians will then be to help our clients:

- **identify** and **understand** any problem that they may have or may be developing with harmful compulsive or addictive behavior;
- **accept** and **embrace** complete personal responsibility for changing the harmful behavior;
- **generate** and **sustain** the internalized motivation they will need in order to do so permanently,
- **devote** and **dedicate** themselves to new lifestyle centered on an active process of self-help and personal growth, and finally
- **learn** and begin to **practice** the healthy attitudes and effective coping skills they will need to develop in order to live a truly rewarding and meaningful life.

We will not be able to do any of this very effectively as clinicians if we are using informal language to describe the addiction problem our clients may be facing in a loose or vague manner. Nor can we remain completely neutral when faced with apparently irreconcilable differences between the definitions and concepts proposed by advocates for various "competing" philosophical approaches to addiction treatment and recovery.

The "disease model" of alcoholism and addiction that has taken root in America over the past 70 years represents a radical departure from the old moral model and other traditional views that came before. While it was not a completely new idea when it began to emerge from relative obscurity and enter the mainstream in the mid-1930's with the founding of Alcoholics Anonymous, it was certainly considered very unconventional at the time and it has remained controversial ever since.

Over the years, however, the conventional wisdom of the disease model has become the predominant point of view in the addiction field—although it has been strongly challenged by some social learning theorists on fairly accurate and reasonable grounds—which suggest that harmful addiction is in many ways a learned behavior that needs to be "unlearned"—and on far more dubious grounds by some of the more dogmatic advocates for controlled-use who insist that absolutely *anyone* can learn how to control their drinking or drug use and use in moderation if they really wanted to.

In fact, there are many good reasons for the persisting popularity and pre-dominance of the disease model in the addiction treatment and recovery field, and the model has developed an extensive vocabulary that includes sound definitions for concepts such as "alcoholism," "addiction," "substance abuse," and "chemical dependency."

Personally, I strongly agree with the central tenet of the disease model that total abstinence will ultimately prove to be the only viable approach for virtually all people who have developed the most serious alcohol or drug abuse problems—if real recovery and the achievement of a healthy, balanced, normal life are the ultimate goals being pursued.

Providing simple health protection measures like clean needles to prevent the transmission of HIV and other blood-borne pathogens, and basic human services such as food, clothing, and shelter for people who are still drinking or using drugs deeply offends many people—both inside and out of the addiction treatment and recovery field. This is because it seems to be "enabling" the harmful addictive behavior to continue by protecting the drinker or drug user from experiencing the full negative consequences of their behavior as an essential motivation for change.

However, the harm reduction approach—which does provide this kind of help to active drinkers and drug users without judgment, question, criticism, or coercion—also makes complete sense for those hardcore early, middle, or late stage alcoholics or addicts who are not yet *ready, willing, or able* to stop or even *try* to stop their drinking and drug use. This makes sense, of course, if the immediate goal is to offer people enough psychosocial stability and security to keep them alive and treat them with enough human dignity, simple respect, personal acceptance, and unconditional love that they may begin to feel the kind of hope and self-worth that is usually an essential prerequisite for any genuine, internalized motivation for change. (Ringwald, 2002: 159–185)

Generally speaking, I use the basic terminology of the disease model comfortably, and I tend to endorse many of the core concepts of the model. At this point in my professional development, however, after thoughtfully considering everything I've seen, heard, experienced, and learned about addiction over the past 23 years—and carefully constructing the basic structure and terminology of *Face to Face Unified Addiction Recovery Model* and the *Addiction Recovery Learning Curve* to reflect what I've learned—I will no longer refer to harmful addiction automatically or uncritically as "the disease"

Using this term, of course, is common parlance in traditional recovery circles, but I now prefer to use the simple, more precise, less ambiguous, and less debatable term "harmful addiction" to describe this kind of problem. I do so out of sincere respect for advocates of social learning approaches, and out of consideration for many others who reject, resist, resent, or simply misunderstand the use of the term "disease" for a wide variety of reasons.

In Part Three of this book, we will examine and discuss some of the most common criticisms and misunderstandings of the disease model in more detail and hopefully resolve some of the unfortunate semantic confusion and conflict that exists in the field and help people better grasp the underlying practical and philosophical unity of the *Face to Face model.*

One of my fondest hopes would be to help end some of the confusion and resistance that blocks some very intelligent and well-intentioned people from being able to understand and use the term "disease" now and then in a flexible and open-minded way that can often be very appropriate and helpful for our clients.

For example, cognitive-behavioral and rational-emotive therapy, transactional analysis, and the voice dialogue method, among other therapeutic approaches all seem to propose some variation of the basic notions that all human beings have automatic, primary process thoughts, internalized parent or child ego-states, and quite a few semi-autonomous sub-personalities functioning within our psyche—such as the "addictive self." These very real and psychodynamically powerful aspects of the archetypal human personality are generally experienced subjectively by most people in the form of automatic thoughts or "self-talk" that do not reflect or respect but actually supplant or simply overpower the rational, deliberative, and healthy functioning of the "mature, adult, sober self."

One self-help program that harshly condemns the disease model and the twelve-step spiritual approach to addiction recovery was based solidly on rational-emotive and cognitive-behavioral principles when it was first developed. In my view, this program very properly and usefully identifies the powerful, irrational, and compulsive part of the personality that drives people to drink or use drugs or engage in other harmful addictive behavior against their better judgment—sometimes despite their sincere, desperate desire to stop—as the *"Addictive Voice."* It then goes on, quite appropriately in my view, to suggest that people use their healthy, creative imagination and their healthy, rational mind to personalize, dramatize, and essentially demonize that addictive voice metaphorically by calling it: *"The Beast."* (Trimpey, 1989)

Two of the most insightful, practical, and powerful recovery slogans that I've ever heard come out of the ethos of the disease model and in my view they are virtually 100 percent consistent in spirit and practical content with this "beastly" approach—despite the superficial, semantic difference reflected in the choice of words and metaphors.

These two slogans are:

**"That's the disease talking,"** and

**"I have a disease that talks to me in my own voice."**

Personally, I think it would be wonderful if these two slogans could be more widely understood, accepted, and applied by rational people who are completely comfortable with calling the addictive voice *"the Beast,"*—and creatively imagine how it would metaphorically tear them to shreds if they should ever fail to rationally recognize and reject it—but apparently can't bring themselves to call this very same inner voice *"the Disease"* because of an irrational and completely unfounded fear that doing so somehow amounts to an irrevocable "prescription for learned helplessness" that would somehow give people a permanent "license for relapse."

So, I hope it's clear that from my point of view many aspects of the disease model of harmful addiction are very accurate and that some of the core concepts of this model can be very useful for many people in many ways.

Indeed, Part Two of this book—which focuses on "Progression"—is devoted to exploring one of those core ideas—which is that harmful addictions will often develop in a recognizable pattern with identifiable signs and symptoms that often emerge gradually in discernible and progressively worsening stages.

In their *Clinical Textbook of Addictive Disorders,* Richard Frances and Sheldon Miller stress the importance of this clinical perspective:

> The training of physicians, nurses, social workers, and psychologists has often not led to the development of clinical skills, attitudes, and knowledge that are adequate and essential for evaluating and treating patients with substance abuse. The stigma associated with substance-related disorders affects the public's willingness to make treatment resources available. It can also cause treating staff to develop attitudinal problems. These attitudes can be altered by updating their skills and knowledge. The battle continues between a moral model—viewing addicts as having defects in character which require punishment—versus a medical model, in which addiction is viewed as a treatable illness with a biopsychosocial etiology, morbidity, mortality, and a clinical course.

> The myths, misinformation, and misunderstandings regarding addicted patients lead to avoidance of important issues and to stigmatization, which further contributes to denial, neglect, fear, and suffering.

(Frances & Miller, 1998: 6, 7)

# A DRUG IS A DRUG

"Switching addictions is like changing deck chairs on the Titanic."

♦ ♦ ♦

Most people are probably familiar with the supposedly humorous and good-natured but often far too accurate invitation frequently made by a bartender to a customer asking them to:

**"Name your poison."**

Throughout this book, in our discussion of the disease model specifically—and of harmful addiction generally—we will often be looking at specific information or using illustrative quotations coming from sources that are focused exclusively on problems related to alcohol.

However, many of the specific points being made regarding alcohol abuse or alcoholism will often prove to be highly relevant and instructive when considered in broader terms. Although they may not apply perfectly across the board, many of the core concepts related to alcohol problems can and should be generalized and applied metaphorically as we consider the whole range of different compulsive-addictive behaviors.

Most proponents of the "disease model," as noted above, would strongly insist that complete and permanent abstinence is the only realistic treatment or recovery goal for people with serious harmful addictions. Many would condemn any suggestion that an "alcoholic" could someday learn how to drink safely as absurdly, obscenely, and even dangerously irresponsible. By the same token, they would also reject the idea that an "addict" could someday safely use their drug of choice or their preferred addictive behavior.

Taking this basic notion a few steps further, there's an addiction recovery slogan that unequivocally reminds people:

**"A drug, is a drug, is a drug."**

Most proponents of the disease model would also strongly maintain—in addition to insisting on the need for complete and permanent abstinence from all identified "drugs of choice"—that any "real" alcoholic or addict who wants to prevent relapse and stay clean and sober will ultimately have to abstain permanently from *all* mood-altering substances.

Now, with this introductory discussion under our belts, let's take a look at some basic concepts from the disease model of addiction:

According to this model, harmful addiction is a *"Bio-Psycho-Social-Spiritual" disorder.*

This means that harmful compulsive-addictive behavior has a mixture of causes that are biological, psychological, social, and spiritual in nature and that the behavior also produces negative consequences in all of these vital areas—the mental, emotional, physical, social, and spiritual.

In their book *Don't Help—A Guide to Working with the Alcoholic,* Ronald Rogers and Chandler Scott McMillin inform us that a "disease" may be defined generically as:

> A morbid process with characteristic identifying symptoms . . .

They review a number of theoretical models of alcoholism and explain their reasons for believing that becoming an alcoholic is not a secondary symptom of underlying emotional or psychological problems, nor a reflection of any moral weakness or a lack of character, strength, or willpower.

Rather, while acknowledging the dangers of overgeneralization, they identify a number of reasons why they find it most helpful "for the greatest number of our patients" to describe alcoholism as a disease that it is:

- biological,
- psychological,
- social,
- spiritual,
- primary,
- chronic,
- progressive,
- incurable, and
- often fatal.

Bearing all of this in mind, Rogers and McMillin stress their conclusion that:

*Alcoholism is NOT caused by:*

- Irresponsible Use of Alcohol
- Emotional Stress, or
- An Unhappy Childhood

*Alcoholism IS caused by:*

- Being Biologically Susceptible, and
- Taxing that Susceptibility with alcohol.

They expand on this idea by emphasizing that:

> The focus, then, isn't on the drug alone . . . or on the personality of the drug user . . . but on the relationship between the agent (alcohol) and the biological system (the alcoholic).

> (Rogers & McMillin, 1988).

According to the American Medical Association (AMA):

> Alcoholism is an illness characterized by significant impairment that is directly associated with persistent and excessive use of alcohol. Impairment may involve physiological, psychological, or social dysfunction.

> (Kinney & Leaton, 1982: 39).

The American Association of Addiction Medicine (ASAM) offers a slightly different definition:

> Alcoholism is a primary, chronic disease with genetic, psychosocial, and environmental factors influencing its development and manifestations. The disease is often progressive and fatal. It is characterized by impaired control over drinking, preoccupation with the drug alcohol, use of alcohol despite adverse consequences, and distortions in thinking, most notably denial. Each of these symptoms may be continuous or periodic.

> (Graham, Schultz & Wilford, 1998).

Jean Kinney and Gwen Leaton offer the following simple definition of alcoholism in their book *Understanding Alcohol:*

> Alcoholism is a disease in which the person's use of alcohol continues despite problems it causes in any area of life.

Kinney and Leaton also emphasize the importance of understanding the difference between *"acute"* versus *"chronic" illnesses.* They point out that acute illnesses—such as appendicitis or the flu—tend to flare up quickly. The patient gets sick, gets treated, gets better, and "that's the end of it." By contrast, they stress that *chronic diseases*—such as diabetes, heart disease, cancer, and alcoholism—tend to develop slowly. They note that there will often be *warning signs and symptoms* prior to the point at which a chronic disease is clearly present, but "once you have it, you have it." Kinney and Leaton note that chronic diseases "may be amenable to treatment" and their progression "may be arrested" in many cases. However, they also note that chronic conditions are usually incurable, and they stress the fact that *"there is always a possibility of relapse."*

*"Management"*—rather than seeking a complete "cure"—is the medical approach to most chronic diseases, according to Kinney and Leaton, and they report that this usually involves specific medical or psychological treatment of "acute flare-ups;" emotional support and counseling; education, so the patient can understand the illness and learn how to provide self-care; and "rehabilitative measures, to make the life changes necessary to live within the limitations imposed by the illness."

(Kinney & Leaton, 1982: 41, 44).

Bill Burnett, a former President of the National Association of Alcoholism and Drug Abuse Counselors (NAADAC), takes all of these basic notions a few steps further and responds to some critics of the disease model when he argues that:

> addiction is comparable to numerous other diseases in many ways . . . if alcoholism is compared based on the degree to which it has a biological basis, the degree to which the condition shows a predictable course and outcome, and the degree to which the condition or its manifestations are caused by volitional acts, then the disease of alcoholism is very comparable to coronary heart disease, hypertension, diabetes mellitus, gout, cancer, and syphilis.

(Burnett, 2000).

In his book *Heavy Drinking: The Myth of Alcoholism as a Disease,* Herbert Fingarette vigorously attacks a very narrowly defined "classic" disease concept of alcoholism as a purely physiological malady, and he confidently asserts "no leading research authorities accept the classic disease concept." He thoroughly debunks the exaggerated and discredited all-or-nothing notion that *every single time* an "alcoholic" consumes any alcohol whatsoever this will immediately and invariably trigger an intense *physical* craving for more alcohol leading to an irresistible compulsion to drink and a complete loss of control over the amount consumed.

Yet the fact is that virtually no one in the addiction treatment or recovery field seriously endorses this rigidly narrow definition of the slogan "One Drink, One Drunk," which Fingarette describes and then proceeds to knock down quite effectively and legitimately.

When ambiguity abounds, and potential multiple meanings go unexamined and unrecognized, and exaggerated stereotypes and hair-splitting semantic differences are taken too seriously by too many intelligent and well-intentioned people, genuine confusion and needless philosophical conflict often seem to be the inevitable result.

For example, Fingarette himself favorably quotes alcoholism researcher Mark Keller who describes his repeated experience with many "alcoholics" who were apparently able to drink in moderation on numerous occasions "and then stopped without further drinking." However, Fingarette and Keller himself both seem to miss the real significance of the rest of Keller's own observation. He reported that these alcoholics ". . . stopped without further drinking, until on some other occasion, days or weeks later, they did not stop. Some could take a drink or two daily for days or weeks without going off on a bout."

The truly significant pattern being reported here—but not really noticed or understood—clearly indicates that taking "one drink" apparently put all of these alcoholics onto a slippery slope that inevitably led each of them—*sooner or later*—to be an active "drunk" once again.

Playing "Russian Roulette" is an almost perfect analogy for this alcoholic behavior. A player may not blow their brains out the first time they spin the cylinder and pull the trigger but if they keep playing long enough they'll certainly find out—sooner or later—why sane people don't play that particular game.

This is what the slogan "One Drink, One Drunk" really means in simple terms:

> *an alcoholic who takes one drink will <u>sooner or later</u> wind up drunk (or be a drunk).*

This apparently inevitable *eventual* loss of control, almost by definition, is what will clearly identify him or her as an alcoholic.

Oddly enough, despite his contention that it's a "myth" to call alcoholism a disease, Fingarette favorable cites George Valliant of Harvard University with respectful approval as an "extremely influential voice in the field of alcoholism studies" and he notes that:

> Valliant still advocates characterizing alcoholism as a disease but, like many other contemporary researchers, his views differ markedly from the classic disease concept.

He also notes that:

> Another influential group of research and clinical authorities who also support a *highly-modified disease concept of alcoholism* reject the classic stereotype in these words: "the person suffering from [the alcohol dependence syndrome] is not an automaton in the grip of an all-controlling and pathological process which totally denies his self-responsibility.

When the author of a book subtitled *The Myth of Alcoholism as a Disease* favorably cites highly respected researchers who describe alcoholism as a "disease," this only highlights the semantic confusion that so often dominates the addiction field regarding the definition of key terms. A much more appropriate and accurate subtitle for this book, therefore, would probably be: *The Myths About Alcoholism as a Disease.* (Fingarette, 1988: 2–3, 43–44; Valliant, 1983; Edwards et al., 1979)

Clinicians and theorists who endorse the disease model of "alcoholism," cite scientific evidence establishing the existence of many biological and hereditary factors involved in the problem. They point to biochemical differences in the way "alcoholics" metabolize alcohol, which may often produce a physical experience of craving that *eventually* causes or contributes to their pattern of compulsive and excessive use. We should bear in mind, however, that the actual onset of the disease process in the earliest stage of alcoholism is virtually impossible to detect—as noted by James Milam and Katherine Ketchum, in their book *Under the Influence:*

> Because the early alcoholic shows no sign of disease, the *logical but wholly mistaken idea* persists that alcoholism begins only when the drinker does suffer from drinking and does show some deterioration in physiological functioning, such as severe withdrawal symptoms, personality disintegration, or inability to control his intake. Before these visible signs appear, most people assume that alcoholics and nonalcoholics experience precisely the same physical reaction to alcohol.
>
> In fact, they do not. *The alcoholic reacts physically in an abnormal way to alcohol, and his disease begins long before he behaves or thinks like an alcoholic. The reactions or adaptations of the body's cells to alcohol remain hidden in the early stages of the disease, but they are nevertheless happening.* In months or years, the cells will have become so altered by alcohol that the alcoholic's behavior and thought processes will be affected. Then the disease will no longer be hidden, and the alcoholic will clearly be in trouble with alcohol.

(Milam & Ketcham, 1981: 47–49. Emphasis added.)

In their book *Craving for Ecstasy,*—which is significantly subtitled *The Consciousness & Chemistry of Escape*—Milkman and Sunderwirth look beyond specific phenomena—such as different physical adaptations occurring on a cellular level in early stage alcoholics or addicts to the use of alcohol or other psychoactive substances—and point to a general biochemical process which occurs on a physical level in *all* forms of pleasurable, compulsive, or addictive behaviors.

They state that:

> Advances in scientific understanding of the *mechanisms of neuro-transmission* have led to a significant departure from the increasingly archaic spiritual and moralistic definitions of addiction. It has become obvious that *individuals can change their brain chemistry* through immersion in salient mood-altering activities as well as through ingesting intoxicating substances . . . we are inescapably led to *redefine addiction* . . . (as) *self-induced changes in neurotransmission that result in behavior problems.*
>
> This new definition encompasses a *multidisciplinary understanding of compulsive problem behaviors* that involves the concepts of *personal responsibility* (the behaviors are self-induced); *biochemical effects* (the body's neurotransmission changes); and *social reactions* (society absorbs the costs and consequences of problem behaviors).
>
> (Milkman & Sunderwirth, 1987: 6. Emphasis added)

I've already mentioned that the "disease model" of harmful addiction was considered very unconventional when it first began to emerge into prominence with the founding of Alcoholics Anonymous in the 1930's, and that it has remained controversial ever since.

In fact, various features of this model are involved, in one way or another, with all three of the "core philosophical conflicts" that have dominated the addiction treatment and recovery field historically:

- **social learning** models of harmful addiction "versus" the **disease** model;
- **controlled-use** models of recovery "versus' the **total abstinence** approach; and
- **"rational,"** or **"secular"** recovery models "versus" the twelve-step **"spiritual"** model.

We will examine various critiques of the disease model later on in Chapters Seven and Eight of this book, when we begin to explore the philosophical premises underlying the *Addiction Recovery Learning Curve* and the *Face to Face Unified Addiction Recovery Model.*

Let's preview that discussion briefly here by addressing one common criticism that reflects a deep misunderstanding of the basic tenets of the disease concept of harmful addiction and the basic principles of the AA twelve-step spiritual recovery program. This is the mistaken view that calling a harmful addiction a disease is a powerful prescription promoting *learned helplessness, perpetual relapse, and the complete abandonment of all rational thought and all personal responsibility for your own sobriety,* especially when it is coupled with the language of the First Step which says:

> "We admitted we were powerless over our addiction—that our lives had become unmanageable,"

In his book *The Soul of Recovery: Uncovering the Spiritual Dimension in the Treatment of Addictions,* however, Christopher Ringwald observes that "the AA approach contradicts the extreme versions of the disease concept," and he notes that the AA "Big Book" uses the word "disease" to describe alcoholism only once, whereas is uses the words "illness," "malady," or "condition" repeatedly to describe the actual plight of the alcoholic.

In a similar vein, Ringwald also notes that the word "recovered" is used 28 times in the Big Book to describe the sober alcoholic, while the open-ended word "recovering"—which is often used by proponents of the disease model to lay special emphasis on the chronic and incurable nature of harmful addiction and the lifetime risk of relapse—is employed only twice.

Ringwald also addresses some basic misunderstandings regarding both AA and the disease concept when he observes that

> One of AA's central contributions was in disentangling morality from the debate. It basically determined, for its members, that while alcoholics were not necessarily to blame for their conditions, they were responsible for doing something about them. Powerful in the 1930's, when the condemnations of nineteenth-century reformers were still echoing over the land, this insight continues to liberate prospective members and patients in treatment from self-castigation.

Finally, he also quotes Steven Hyman, who was Director of the National Institute of Mental Health, in 1998 when he made a similar point in a public television interview with Bill Moyers:

> Take heart patients. We don't blame them for having heart disease, but we ask them to follow a certain diet, to exercise, to comply with medication regimes. So it is with the addicted person—we shouldn't blame them for the disease, but we should treat them as having responsibility for their recovery.

> (Ringwald, 2002: 14–23).

## REDEFINING SUCCESS

> "For freedom's battle, once begun, bequeathed by bleeding sire to son, though baffled oft, is ever won."

—Lord Byron

"Progress not perfection."

"If at first you don't succeed, just *redefine success*!"

"The only place where "success" comes before "sweat" is in the dictionary."

◆ ◆ ◆

As clinicians, you will surely find that many of your clients will not be ready, willing, or able to face the issue of harmful addiction honestly—or to self-disclose openly—or to make significant changes in their lives.

Nevertheless, when you can communicate the core concepts and basic information presented in this book to your clients effectively you may be able to gently plant some seeds of knowledge, self-awareness, and motivation that could make it much more difficult for them to continue avoiding the issue indefinitely.

In *The Soul of Recovery,* Christopher Ringwald points out the widely recognized and increasingly accepted fact that:

> Relapse is the most common treatment outcome. Rare is the alcoholic or addict who goes through treatment once and stays clean and sober forever.

He then goes on to observe:

> Thankfully, abstinence is no longer the single measure of success. The Physician's Leadership Council, quite reasonably, demanded that alcoholism and addiction be judged in the same light as other chronic illnesses with behavioral aspects, such as diabetes or hypertension. With all these illnesses, repeated efforts at change may fail but *eventually* lead to recovery. To judge one relapse as proof of failure is harsh, unreasonable, and medically useless.
>
> Progress, not perfection, should count.

(Ringwald, 2002: 121–122)

Thus, it is important to remember that the seeds which you plant during one treatment episode with a client may not bear fruit until many years later during a later treatment episode with another clinician. Therefore, when you consider the vastly over-simplified concept of "treatment outcomes," I hope you will recognize the crucial role that your own episode of "treatment failure" may have played on the client's long journey through the addiction recovery learning curve toward their eventual destination of "treatment success" and lifetime sobriety.

# CHAPTER 2

# Assessment and Diagnosis

"First the man takes the drink,
then the drink takes the drink,
then the drink takes the man."

♦ ♦ ♦

## PATTERNS OF USE

There's a wonderful greeting card which shows the cartoon character "Cathy" smiling on the front cover panel as she confidently declares:

"The body is the temple of the spirit."

And then, on the inside of the card, she frowns as she sadly laments:

"Unfortunately, mine has been invaded by some strange, fat worshipping cult!"

This stunning and brilliant observation offers a memorable and amusing insight into the perplexing subjective experience of compulsive overeating, and I believe that this deeply perceptive insight is equally relevant to many other forms of compulsive-addictive behavior as well—especially when we take time to recall the hoard of semi-autonomous subpersonalities—which we talked about briefly in the last chapter—that so often dominate both the normal and abnormal human psyche.

Let's take a moment to remember where we started out in Chapter One. Some of our clients or patients may be honestly asking themselves:

"How do I really *know* if I have an alcohol or drug abuse problem?"

Of course, many other clients or patients may be desperately trying to avoid facing this question or anything remotely like it. However, our job as clinicians addressing the complex and contradictory interplay of motivational and behavioral variables involved in harmful addiction will be to help our clients begin to answer this question objectively for themselves—whether they really want to or not—and enhance their capacity to perceive the truth of the matter—whether they like it or not.

In order to help our clients clear away any unconscious fog of minimization, rationalization, self-deception, or denial that might be obscuring their perception of reality—so that they can then make an accurate self-diagnosis of their own condition—we will need to start by educating them about the typical signs, symptoms, and stages of progression in harmful addiction.

In order to help our clients understand the distinctive features of abnormal, unhealthy, or pathological behavior, of course, it will also be crucial to provide them with some accurate information about the general nature and range of normal, healthy, or functional behavior.

In their book *Understanding Alcohol,* Jean Kinney and Gwen Leaton describe how prevailing social, family, and personal attitudes toward alcohol consumption can vary widely between different national, ethnic, racial, cultural, or religious groups.

They identify the four primary patterns of alcohol use that might prevail as follows:

### DRINKING PATTERNS

**Total Abstinence**

- Drinking is "forbidden."

**Ritual Use**

- Drinking is "connected to religious practice, ceremonies, and special occasions.

**Convivial Use**

- Drinking is tied to social occasions, with the emphasis on social solidarity and camaraderie.

**Utilitarian Use**

- People are allowed "to drink for their own personal reasons, to meet their own needs . . ."

(Kinney & Leaton, 1982: 66)

Please recall that many of the points that will be made throughout this book which happen to be focused specifically on problems related to alcohol will often be highly relevant and instructive when they are generalized conceptually and applied broadly to our consideration of a whole range of different **harmful compulsive-addictive behaviors.**

In the addiction treatment and recovery field we often speak in terms of people "using" a particular substance or addictive behavior in order to help themselves "feel better"—or just "feel good"—in some way. When this occurs, it's an example of what Kinney and Leaton are calling "utilitarian use."

People "use" the substance or the behavior for their own reasons, in order to meet their own needs. Initially, they might feel the need for a "social lubricant" just to help them relax or unwind, overcome their normal shyness or social inhibition, and have some fun with other people. Sometimes, however, they might be using a substance or activity as an actual "coping mechanism"—however functional or dysfunctional it might actually be—to help them try to deal with everyday stress, personal problems, painful emotions, or difficult life events.

Regardless of the specific addictive substance or potentially harmful compulsive behavior involved—or the person's subjective reasons for using it—there can also be a wide range of potential Levels of Use among various "users."

It can be helpful for us to think of these levels as occurring on a progressively serious scale as follows:

**LEVELS OF USE**

1. Abstinence.

2. Experimental Use.

3. Rare, Minimal, or Occasional Use.

4. Normal, Social, Recreational, or Moderate Use.

5. Heavy or Frequent Use.

6. Excessive or Problem Use.

7. Abuse.

8. Dependence.

It's important to understand that many people (perhaps even most people) who are engaged in potentially harmful compulsive-addictive behaviors—such as eating, social drinking or drug use, gambling, sex, relationships, work, and so on—will never experience *any* negative consequences from their use. Therefore, they'll never even reach the level of "problem use" on this scale, even though some of them may be heavily involved with a particular substance or behavior. Indeed, many *positive addictions* are marked by frequent and heavy involvement with a healthy behavior or beneficial activity.

The National Institute on Alcohol Abuse and Alcoholism (NIAAA) makes a distinction between "moderate" and "social" drinking by noting that:

> Moderate drinking is difficult to define because it means different things to different people. The term is often confused with "social drinking," which refers to drinking patterns that are accepted by the society in which they occur. However, social drinking is not necessarily free of problems. Moderate drinking may be defined as drinking that does not generally cause problems, either for the drinker or for society . . .

> (NIAAA, 1992)

While drawing this distinction may make some sense in technical terms, it's not especially helpful in practical terms because it goes so strongly against the grain of common usage and the widespread public understanding of these terms. Generally speaking, when most people use the term "social drinking" they are clearly thinking of a normal, moderate, or recreational level of alcohol use that does not lead to any problems or negative consequences. Public opinion is not always ignorant and conventional wisdom is not always wrong, and I personally think that this general characterization is completely valid.

Therefore, I make no meaningful distinction between so-called "normal," "social," "recreational," and "moderate" levels of use, but have chosen to distinguish this entire pattern or level of use from the next two levels that follow— "heavy or frequent use" and "excessive or problem use."

## IN THE EYE OF THE BEHOLDER

Now, let's take a moment to consider the distinctions that can to be made between "heavy use," and "excessive" or "problem use" of a particular substance or behavior. Where do we draw that line? To answer this question, we would first need to determine how to measure or define the term "heavy use?" Of course, since this level of use has to be defined in comparison to "normal, social, recreational, or moderate use," we would have to start by asking how to measure or define those terms?

**This is often very subjective.**

Exercise, for example, can be a very healthy form of "positive addiction." Consider the hypothetical case of someone who works out in a gym for an hour or so several days per week. Does this constitute the "heavy use" of exercise? Ask any "couch potato" and they would probably say "yes"—or, at least, "that's a bit too heavy for me." Ask the person doing the exercise, however, and they would probably describe this quite reasonably as a moderate, normal, healthy amount of exercise. For them, and for most people generally, a fair definition for the "heavy use" of exercise would be more likely to involve compulsively working out several hours per day, seven days per week.

What about drinking? Does consuming two or three drinks *per day of use* constitute "heavy use?" What about having three or four drinks? For many non-drinkers or social drinkers, anyone consuming more than four drinks on a given day would probably meet their threshold to qualify as a "heavy" drinker—at least for that day. What about drinking frequency? What about having four or five drinks, but only once per week? Or maybe only once per month? What about drinking that amount several days per week? Or daily? What about the person who has an admitted drinking binge one or two times per year?

Some people—who might be demonstrating just a bit of rationalization, minimization, or denial—can say in all sincerity that drinking a six pack of beer is clearly "moderate drinking" for them, and that "heavy" drinking would have to involve consuming two six packs or more on a given day.

So, where do we draw the line between "normal, social, moderate use" and "heavy use?"

### It is all very subjective.

Reasonable people, however, can usually reach some general agreement on broad objective standards to define the "heavy use" of alcohol in quantitative terms—within the context of a given drinking culture or subculture—without getting deeply mired in conflicting value-judgments that might support or condemn the amount used as "appropriate" or "inappropriate." By any objective standard, for example, weekend binge drinking on American college campuses—behavior that might be considered stupid, dangerous, and "excessive" within our wider American culture—clearly involves the "heavy use" of alcohol. This is an objective "fact" that's almost impossible to dispute from any perspective. Even people who are deeply devoted members of the *weekend binge drinking subculture* within the larger *college drinking subculture* in America today—who consider the behavior to be nothing more than harmless fun, totally cool, and perfectly "appropriate"—will usually concede as much.

Moderation Management is a self-help program for non-alcoholics who have had some alcohol problems and would like to get some support to help them moderate and control their drinking. In their basic text, "MM" cites a study that offers the following "objective" definitions, along with the percentage of people whom that particular study found to be in each drinking category:

**ABSTAINER**—46.4%

• No Drinks in the Past Month.

**LIGHT DRINKER**—27.4%

• 1 to 10 drinks in the Past Month.

**MODERATE DRINKER**—21.5%

• 11 to 59 Drinks in the past Month.

**HEAVY DRINKER**—4.7%

• 60 or More Drinks in the Month.

(Silva, Calkins & Rafferty, 1993)

*Moderation Management* also proposes some specific "drinking limits" to help people understand objectively just what *they* mean by the potentially ambiguous term "moderate" drinking." They stress that these *suggested limits* should never be considered as drinking *targets*.

The MM Limits are:

• Never drive while under the influence of alcohol.
• Do not drink in situations that would endanger yourself or others.
• Do not drink every day. MM suggests that you abstain from drinking alcohol at least 3 or 4 days per week.
• For women: Do not drink more than 3 drinks on any day, and no more than 9 drinks per week.
• For men: Do not drink more than 4 drinks on any day, and no more than 14 drinks per week.
• If you weigh very little, use the BAC limit of .055% instead of the "number of drinks" limits noted above.

(Kishline, 1994: 113–115)

According to an "Alcohol Alert" published by NIAAA:

A standard drink is generally considered to be 12 ounces of beer, 5 ounces of wine, or 1.5 ounces of 80-proof distilled spirits. Each of these drinks contains roughly the same amount of absolute alcohol— approximately 0.5 ounce or 12 grams.

I find it very interesting that the suggested guidelines for defining "moderation" published by Moderation Management still seem to reflect the widespread popular notion in our culture that "more is better" when compared to moderate drinking guidelines published by the U.S. Government.

In the same publication previously cited that defined moderate drinking as "drinking that does not generally cause problems," NIAAA also states that:

> It would be useful if the above definition of moderate drinking were bolstered by numerical estimates of "safe" drinking limits. However, the usefulness of quantitative definitions of moderate drinking is compromised by the likelihood that a given dose of alcohol may affect different people differently . . .

> Despite the complexity, numerical definitions of moderate drinking do exist. For example, guidelines put forth jointly by the U.S. Department of Agriculture and the U.S. Department of Health and Human Services define moderate drinking as no more than one drink a day for most women, and no more than two drinks a day for most men . . .

NIAAA also states that some people should simply not be drinking at all and notes that:

> These guidelines exclude the following persons, who should not consume alcoholic beverages: women who are pregnant or trying to conceive; people who plan to drive or engage in other activities that require attention or skill; people taking medication, including over-the-counter medications; recovering alcoholics; and persons under the age of 21. Although not specifically addressed by the guidelines, alcohol use also is contraindicated for people with certain medical conditions such as peptic ulcer.

(NIAAA, 1992)

Subjectively speaking, it may be difficult for some people to draw a clear line between "moderate" use and "heavy" use.

Objectively speaking, however, it isn't quite so difficult for us to draw a clear line between "non-problem use" and "excessive" or "problem" use—especially when the matter is seen through the eyes of an outside observer.

When we talk about "heavy" or "light" use of a particular substance or behavior we will usually be thinking of this in *quantitative terms* that involve the "frequency" or "amount" used.

It's important to remember here that *even "heavy use" of a particular substance or behavior will not necessarily lead to any "problems" for the user.*

On the other hand, when we speak of "excessive" or "problem" use, we will have to begin thinking in strictly *qualitative terms* that often have nothing whatsoever to do with the "frequency" or "amount" of use.

For some people, any level of involvement with certain addictive substances or behaviors can consistently lead to serious problems almost every time they use—even when they only use a small amount on rare occasions.

By contrast, many regular social users of certain addictive substances or behaviors who generally experience no problems whatsoever from their use—most of the time—will nevertheless manage to get themselves into some really big trouble on some rare, isolated occasions when they use.

For myself, a good working definition of "excessive use" or "problem use" is very simple, direct, and uncompromising.

> **"Excessive use" or "Problem Use" involves:**
>
> **ANY use,**
>
> **in ANY amount,**
>
> **with ANY frequency,**
>
> **that causes ANY NEGATIVE CONSEQUENCES**
>
> **of ANY kind,**
>
> **at ANY time,**
>
> **for the user**
>
> **or for ANYONE else.**

## CROSSING THE LINE

Everything that's been said thus far about the most effective clinical approach to helping our clients identify their own "excessive" or "problem" use remains true as we try to help them determine whether or not they have officially reached either of the two final levels of use—**"abuse"** or **"dependence."** Here, however—besides just helping them understand the full range of signs, symptoms, and progressive stages of harmful addiction in general terms and identify specifically those signs, symptoms, and consequences that they have experienced personally—we will finally have some fairly clear-cut, objective guidelines to follow in the process of determining whether or not a formal diagnosis is actually warranted. To do this, we will need to understand and employ the specific set of **diagnostic criteria** officially presented in the DSM-IV-TR—the Diagnostic and Statistical Manual of Mental Disorders (Fourth Edition—Text Revision).

In a nutshell, the presence of any negative consequences is the essential feature defining "excessive use" or "problem use," but many clients presenting with some history of "excessive" or "problem" use will not actually meet the more stringent criteria needed to establish a formal diagnosis "abuse."

To qualify officially as "abuse," these negative consequences would all have to add up to a pattern of "clinically significant impairment or distress," and within that context one of the *most essential identifying features* defining "abuse" is: **continued use despite recurring major negative consequences.**

Recurrent use in situations where it is physically hazardous to use is another *crucial identifying feature* for "abuse," and many people in our culture clearly tend to trivialize and minimize the actual life or death risks involved with any level of intoxication. I personally tend to set the bar very low on this matter because it's so clear to me how dangerous and potentially life-threatening using any psychoactive substance to the point of intoxication can actually be.

For example, I vividly recall hearing news stories about a major movie star who *slipped and fell down* while he was *walking across his living room*—because he was *drunk.* Generally speaking, of course, this would not be news—even though this gentleman was an Oscar winning international celebrity. Unfortunately, on this particular occasion, he *cracked his head* on the sharp edge of a coffee table and *bled to death.*

We've all heard of the legal charge driving while intoxicated—which is illegal and negligent because it is so blatantly and obviously dangerous. Well, when we bear this tragic accident in mind, we might benefit from considering the *equally dangerous and potentially deadly practice* of walking while intoxicated.

For myself and for many others who prefer not to trivialize or minimize this kind of problem—when we consider the genuine physical danger of accidental injury or death that's always present for the user and others:

> merely using a substance to the point of *intoxication* would qualify as "abuse."

There is one important caveat that should be noted right here:

> some people, of course, may not even survive their *first* experience with this kind of behavior.

I've heard it said that for many people

> the *first* recognizable symptom of heart disease may be sudden death

In a similar fashion, for some people:

> the *first* negative consequence that they experience from their substance use may also be their *last*—because they will be dead.

This tragic outcome is far more common than most people would care to acknowledge, and in many cases the victims are adolescents or young adults. This particular negative consequence, of course, makes the hypothetical question of whether the deceased would have ever developed a pattern of problem use, abuse, or dependence a rather moot point.

Along with the phenomena of progressively serious *Levels of Use* in potentially harmful addictive behaviors, there is also a progressively worsening range of problem severity that can be formulated as follows:

**RANGE OF PROBLEM SEVERITY**

**1.** None

**2.** Mild

**3.** Moderate

**4.** Serious

**5.** Severe

**6.** Grave

For some activities such as smoking—regardless of the substance involved—it may be that any use whatsoever is inherently "unhealthy." However, in particular cases, the actual level of use may be so rare, minimal, or occasional that it would be quite a stretch to call it "problem use." With a substance like nicotine, however, even a "normal, social, or recreational" level of use could prove to be very unhealthy in the long run, and most people would be quite hard-pressed trying to claim that this is *not* a "problem."

In an introductory chapter to the book *Changing Addictive Behavior: Bridging Clinical and Public Health Strategies,* the senior editor Jalie Tucker reviews historical and contemporary perspectives on harmful addiction and makes the following observations that are pertinent when we consider either the level of use or degree of problem severity:

> In contrast to the stereotype of the alcoholic or addict as an end-stage, out-of-control drug fiend who is impervious to the negative consequences of drug use, research has consistently shown that 1) drug use is sensitive to environmental contingencies, even among physically dependent users; and 2) substance use patterns and problems are *heterogeneous and lie along a continuum of severity.* Most persons have *less severe problems* that do not prevent them from working (albeit with diminished capacity in some cases) and from fulfilling at least some of their family and social responsibilities. This strongly suggests that *intensive treatment,* which removes individuals from their usual environment for extended periods, is *excessively costly, disruptive,* and *sweeping* in scope for those with *mild to moderate problems,* although it may be necessary for those with severe problems.
>
> (Tucker, 1999: 6–7. Emphasis added.)

Of course, both the level of use and the degree of problem severity for a particular user can be perceived and described in two distinct ways—subjectively by the people involved in the behaviors, and objectively by outside observers. Generally speaking, it is only when problem use progresses to the level of abuse, and then progresses even further to reach the level of dependence—and when the associated negative consequences have become "serious"—that the whole syndrome might truly be described as

a full-blown harmful addiction.

Even then, however, we must always be careful to distinguish between the existence of solid objective evidence pointing toward the presence of a problem or potential problem—as perceived by an outside observer be they clinical or otherwise—and the subjective experience or interpretation of any negative consequences by the actual user.

The observations and perceptions that flow from the subjective and objective perspectives, and especially the conclusions drawn regarding problem severity, are often radically different—and the user will often feel that the benefits of continued use far outweigh the cost of any consequences involved.

Thus, two other key variables that will always be crucial to the process of behavior change and problem resolution in harmful addictions are the degree of a client's insight into the reality of their problem and the relative intensity or laxity of their internalized motivation for change.

## ASSESSMENT INSTRUMENTS

"If a man will devote his time to securing facts in an objective, impartial manner, his worries will usually evaporate in the light of knowledge."

– Herbert E. Hawkes.

♦ ♦ ♦

Rudyard Kipling is best known for his poetry and his fictional stories that take place in the time of Colonialism and British Imperial Rule in India during the reign of Queen Victoria in the 19th Century. The story of "Gunga Din" may be his best known work because it was made into a classic Hollywood movie starring Errol Flynn back in the 1930s. For myself, however, the first thing that comes to mind whenever I think of Kipling is a powerful quotation in which he offers a wise, witty, and memorable perspective that could help almost anyone who would like to answer questions, evaluate situations, resolve problems, or approach life more successfully:

> "I keep six honest serving men,
> they taught me all I knew.
> Their names are what and why
> and when and where and how and who."

Many screening questionnaires and diagnostic assessment instruments have been developed over the years to help clinicians ask the right questions in order to identify the existence and determine the severity of potential alcohol or drug abuse problems in their clients. Additionally, many informal self-evaluation quizzes or questionnaires have been developed to help people determine for themselves whether or not they may have a problem with alcohol or drugs.

Four widely used examples that indicate the type of questions we need to be asking our clients in the overall process of assessment and diagnosis are

1. a twelve-item self-evaluation questionnaire published in pamphlet form by Alcoholics Anonymous,
2. the CAGE Alcoholism Screening Questionnaire,
3. the MAST – Michigan Alcoholism Screening Test, and
4. The Diagnostic Criteria for Substance Use Disorders in the DSM-IV-TR.

(Alcoholics Anonymous, 1973)<br>
(Volpicelli and Szalavitz, 2000: 14)<br>
(Mack, Franklin, & Frances, 2001: 102–103)<br>
(American Psychiatric Association, 2001)

More importantly, of course, we must also encourage our clients to take a good hard look in the mirror and to start honestly asking themselves exactly the same kind of uncompromising questions.

It's not appropriate for copyright reasons for me to reproduce these four items here *in full*—but they are widely available and can be located through the references noted above for readers who are especially interested. Later on, however– when we take a look at "the big picture" and focus on identifying many of the signs and symptoms that are most commonly linked to the **Early, Middle,** and **Late Stages** of progression in harmful addiction in Part Two of this book— we *will* be able to see how *all* of the specific indicators included in each of these instruments fit into this larger context *individually*.

The first three assessment instruments mentioned above—and many more like them – can be very valuable when used *informally* to help us understand more about any problem that our clients may have with harmful addiction. However, it's important to remember that none of them can be used to make a clinically acceptable formal diagnosis that would officially establish the presence of a recognized Substance Use Disorder. This task can *only* be accomplished when using the formal diagnostic criteria found in the DSM-IV-TR.

# DIAGNOSTIC CRITERIA

"He who conceals his disease cannot expect to be cured."

—Ethiopian Proverb.

♦ ♦ ♦

William Shakespeare raises an important point when he asks us to consider the following question:

"What's in a name? A rose by any other name would smell as sweet."

The words "alcoholism," "addiction," "chemical dependency," and "substance abuse" all point us toward the reality of a powerful and devastating disorder. Even those people who detest using the words "disease" or "disorder" in this context—and prefer to think of these problems a nasty set of "learned behaviors," or "bad habits"—still agree with one undeniable truth: if a "harmful addiction" sounds like a problem, looks like a problem, feels like a problem, and tastes like a problem—whatever the addictive substance or behavior may be—then it's a problem—and it's perfectly valid for us to ask:

"What's in a name? A harmful addiction by any other name will smell as bad."

If we *really* want to understand alcohol and drug abuse problems and discuss them in an informed way—then we all need to *know* the official diagnostic criteria and terminology. If, technically speaking, there is no such thing as "alcoholism" or "addiction" in our current clinical terminology, and, hence, there are no "alcoholics" or "addicts," then it's also perfectly valid for us to ask:

what are the appropriate clinical terms that we should be using?

As we have already seen, the Diagnostic and Statistical Manual of Mental Disorders (Fourth Edition—Text Revision)—which is published by the American Psychiatric Association and commonly referred to as the "DSM-IV-TR"—is the official "Bible" that provides us with a clinical glossary to formally define the terms that "really count" in the mental health and addiction treatment fields.

When we consider the full range of "compulsive-addictive behaviors," however, even this "Bible" has some huge and often controversial gaps. For example, when we look beyond the formal category of Substance Use Disorders, we will see that while the DSM-IV-TR does include a formal diagnosis for "Pathological Gambling," many other widely recognized compulsive-addictive behaviors are not yet included—such as compulsive overeating, over-spending, debting, workaholism, sexual addiction, and dysfunctional, dependent, or pathological relationships— to name just a few. They have not yet achieved an official "status" as identifiable disorders in their own right.

While there has been a "Binge Eating Disorder" under *consideration* for inclusion as a formal diagnosis for quite some time, it has not yet "made the grade" officially. Therefore, a classic pattern of compulsive overeating—without the purging behavior that would characterize Bulimia Nervosa—would probably have to coded as an "Eating Disorder, NOS," (Not Otherwise Specified). For diagnostic or insurance billing purposes, many classic harmful addictions might have to be coded—rather vaguely and inappropriately—as an "Impulse Control Disorder, NOS" or perhaps as one of the "V-Codes," which identify "other conditions or problems that may be a focus of clinical attention."

Let's consider the phenomena of "sexual addiction" for a moment to illustrate an area where the DSM-IV-TR is not very clear or helpful. There is absolutely no question that this problem is real—just ask any of the thousands of people who have joined self-help programs such as "Sex and Love Addicts Anonymous," or "Sex Addicts Anonymous." Many addiction treatment professionals also find that "sexual addiction" is an accurate and useful term that describes excessive sexual acting out quite well as a harmful compulsive-addictive behavior.

So, where do we find this syndrome when we look into the DSM-IV-TR? Try to find it—or anything like it—and you might begin to feel like you've started playing an old-fashioned game of "hide-and-seek." A quick glance at the table of contents might prompt us to look for this kind of pathology under the heading "Sexual and Gender Identity Disorders." And, when we get to that section, we might feel that we're getting even "warmer" when we find the sub-heading "Sexual Desire Disorders." But what to we find there? Only "Hypoactive Sexual Desire Disorder" and "Sexual Aversion Disorder." So close, so close, and yet, so far.

What's the problem? Simply that there is no "*Hyperactive* Sexual Desire Disorder" anywhere to be found. Why not? I don't know. That term could be used quite accurately to describe what we generally call sexual addiction—but it's just not in there. For diagnostic purposes, I suppose we could fall back on "Sexual Desire Disorder, NOS?" Sorry. There's nothing like that to be found anywhere either. The only thing that even seems come close is "Sexual Dysfunction NOS." But that diagnostic label doesn't seem to fit the typical "hyper-functioning" that gets so out of control in classic sexual addiction. When I look into this section of the manual a bit more closely, however, I notice that the generic heading "Sexual Dysfunctions" is used to cover the whole gamut of sexual disorders and this hardly seems to fit the bill.

When we consider classic alcohol or drug abuse problems, however, the DSM-IV-TR has no such shortage of diagnostic categories. What we commonly refer as ""substance abuse," "alcoholism," or "drug addiction" are officially called "Substance Use Disorders" and they can all be referred to by using the generic acronym "SUDs." (When we think about helping our clients get "Clean and Sober," however, we have to remember that "SUDs" are part of the problem and not part of the solution). The DSM-IV-TR includes diagnostic categories for "Substance Intoxication," (which may be associated with the normal, social, or recreational use of some substances), "Substance Withdrawal," and "Substance Induced Disorders." For our purposes, however, there are two crucial sets of diagnostic criteria on which we need to focus—those used to establish the presence of "Substance Abuse" or the more serious problem of "Substance Dependence."

These diagnoses can be made and coded individually for each of the following substances:

- Alcohol
- Amphetamines, or similar substances.
- Cannabis
- Cocaine
- Hallucinogens
- Inhalants
- Nicotine—dependence only.
- Opioids
- Phencyclidine (PCP)—or similar substances.
- Sedatives, Hypnotics, or Anxiolytics.
- Polysubstances—dependence only.
- Other (or Unknown) Substances.

An *official diagnosis* of "abuse" or "dependence," therefore, can only be made formally for the specific substances noted immediately above. Informally, however, if we want to think creatively in broader terms about a "Level of Use" that would constitute *"abuse"* or *"dependence"* for a wider range of potentially harmful addictive substance or behaviors, then I believe it would still be important to follow the *general diagnostic principles* found in the DSM-IV-TR as closely as possible—even if certain features such as *"increased tolerance"* or *"withdrawal symptoms"* might not apply very well across the board.

Unfortunately, copyright considerations prevent me from simply reprinting all of the specific DSM-IV-TR diagnostic criteria for Substance Abuse and Substance Dependence for you verbatim right here. However, you *will* be able to find *all* of these criteria embedded *individually* within the comprehensive list of the signs, symptoms, and negative consequences included in a detailed examination of the stages of progression in harmful addiction that will follow shortly in Part Two of this book.

In the meantime, however, I believe I can give you a quick paraphrased overview of the subject as follows:

To qualify for an informal "diagnosis" that would place their Level of Use within the range of "abuse," a person would have to use an addictive substance or behavior in a dysfunctional, harmful, or self-defeating manner that repeatedly produces either painful negative consequences or significant personal distress for the user or for others.

Specifically, this *"maladaptive pattern of use"* would have to lead to one or more of the following problems occurring within a one-year period:

- Failure to meet important personal responsibilities on the job, or in school, with the family, or at home because of the repeated use of an addictive substance or behavior.
- Repeated use of an addictive substance or behavior under dangerous circumstances where using might lead to serious injury or death.
- Recurring legal problems related to the use of an addictive substance or behavior.
- Continuing to use an addictive substance or behavior despite ongoing problems in *social situations* or *personal relationships* that are caused or made worse by using.

To qualify for an informal "diagnosis" that would place their Level of Use within the range of "dependence," a person would also have to use an addictive substance or behavior in a dysfunctional, harmful, or self-defeating manner that repeatedly produces either painful negative consequences or significant personal distress for the user or for others.

In specific terms, this *"maladaptive pattern of use"* would have to be marked by three or more of the following features occurring within a one-year period:

- **Increased tolerance**—which would involve the person needing to use a significantly *increased amount* of the addictive substance or behavior in order to become intoxicated or achieve a desired effect—

or by their experiencing a significantly *decreased effect* when continuing to use the same amount.

- **Withdrawal**—which would involve the person experiencing uncomfortable *physical or emotional withdrawal symptoms* when use of the addictive substance or behavior is *reduced or stopped*—*or*—actually using the addictive substance or behavior—or a very similar substance or behavior—to either relieve the discomfort associated with the withdrawal symptoms or to avoid experiencing them altogether.

  ○ If *either one* of the conditions above are present—plus *one or more* from the list below for a total of *three altogether*—then that would amount to *physical dependence*. If neither of these conditions are present, then the presence of *three or more* of the following conditions would amount to what may be informally referred to as *"psychological dependence."*

- **Loss of Control**—which would involve the person *unintentionally* using a significantly greater amount of an addictive substance or behavior than was initially planned or expected—or using the substance or behavior for a significantly longer time than was initially anticipated.

- **Failed Attempts at Control**—which could simply involve the person developing a *persistent desire* to cut down or control the addictive substance use or behavior or could actually involve their making one or more *unsuccessful efforts* to do so.

- **Significant Time Impact**—which would typically involve the person spending *a large amount of time:*

  ○ **acquiring** the addictive substance or **arranging** to engage in the addictive behavior

  ○ actually **using** the addictive substance or **engaging** in the addictive behavior

  ○ or later **recovering** from the effects of using the addictive substance or behavior.

- **Reduced Sober Activities**—which would typically involve the person cutting back or completely eliminating significant social, family, job, school, or recreational interests because of their addictive substance use or behavior.

- **Continued Use Despite Personal Consequences**—which would typically go beyond the essentially external *social and interpersonal problems* that might qualify the person for a "diagnosis" of "abuse" to

51

include significant recurring *medical or emotional problems* that are either caused or made worse by using an addictive substance or behavior and now *directly affect* the person's physical health or psychological well-being.

The DSM-IV-TR also provides a list of "course specifiers" for *substance dependence* which clearly indicate that once a person has qualified for this diagnosis it would be *clinically appropriate and prudent* for them to carry it with them for the rest of their life. Clinically, if nothing else, this would represent a *critical fact* about their past history of harmful addiction—even when the condition itself is in full remission.

In formal diagnostic terms, the course specifiers for substance dependence are:

- Sustained Full Remission
- Early Full Remission
- Sustained Partial Remission
- Early Partial Remission
- On Agonist Therapy
- In a Controlled Environment

(American Psychiatric Association, 2001)

When we think of *the whole range of potentially harmful addictive substances and behaviors* in broader terms—many of which do not officially qualify for a formal diagnosis of "abuse" or "dependence"—one thing about this list of "course specifiers" seems to be especially significant:

The absence of any category called "cured" seems to acknowledge a basic tenet of the traditional "disease model" of harmful addiction—which suggests that "alcoholism," "addiction"—or any form of "serious harmful addiction"—are chronic conditions that can never be "cured" but in the final analysis can only be **"active"** or **"arrested."**

Negative stereotypes, ignorance, and confusion about the nature of harmful addiction can dramatically interfere with our client's ability to perform an objective and accurate self-diagnosis. When we educate clients about the objective diagnostic criteria for substance abuse and substance dependence—and help clients recognize these signs and symptoms from their own personal experience should they be present—we can constructively avoid using any highly charged terms that may needlessly impede their progress because they are interpreted as negative "labels."

This clinical focus can often help neutralize some of the harsh and inaccurate stereotypes that may be associated with the words "alcoholism" or "addiction" in our client's minds and thus reduce any inappropriate sense of shame or stigma they might otherwise feel.

Remember, one of our main tasks as clinicians will be to educate our clients and help them understand how harmful addictions can develop:

- in a recognizable pattern;
- with identifiable signs and symptoms;
- that emerge gradually over time;
- in identifiable and progressively worsening stages.

To accomplish this task, we will be looking at the various assessment and diagnostic criteria we have considered thus far—as they often occur within a larger context—as we move on to examine the progressive stages of harmful addiction in Part Two of this book. Increased knowledge and objectivity can make a real difference for our clients in the early stage of addiction treatment because it starts to eliminate that metaphorical "head full of mush" that so many people carry around on this controversial subject that is so frequently misunderstood.

# PART TWO

# PROGRESSION

# CHAPTER 3

# Stages of Progression

"Experience isn't interesting until it begins to repeat itself—in fact, till it does that, it hardly *is* experience."

—Elizabeth Bowen.

"He who neglects to drink from the spring of experience is likely to die in the desert of ignorance."

—Ling Po.

◆ ◆ ◆

## THE ADDICTION CYCLE

Mark Twain once observed, rather wisely I suspect, that:

"Someone who has a cat by the tail knows a lot more about cats than someone who has merely read about them."

Some behavioral clinicians and academic theorists who advocate the "social learning model" of addiction vigorously contend that "alcoholism" is a learned behavior, and that most so-called "alcoholics" can actually "unlearn" it—and then learn instead how to successfully control their drinking. The most extreme version of this theory insists that there is, in fact, no such thing as "alcoholism," and that the term "alcoholic" is merely a rude, insulting, and self-fulfilling negative label. Furthermore, there are a number of "true believers" who insist that virtually anyone can learn how to "control" their drinking—if they really want to and make a firm, committed choice to do so. They would dismiss any suggestion that this might be "impossible" for some people as ignorant and foolish nonsense.

To the best of my knowledge, however, most of the theorists espousing these radical, "all-or-nothing" views on "controlled drinking" from an academic, clinical, or scientific perspective have never had to deal with any serious alcohol or drug abuse problems personally. Thus, their views often seem to be based on abstract theorizing, personal bias, mere opinion, or a concrete, stubborn devotion to the ideals of "logic, reason, and plain common sense" that displays virtually no insight into the powerful, irrational, and "irresistible" nature of compulsion as it is commonly experienced by people struggling with harmful addiction.

At best, the "facts" or "data" used to support the argument that "anyone, including alcoholics, can learn how to control their drinking" often seem to flow from scholarly or scientific "research" resting on naïve or simplistic premises that seem to make little sense out in the real world. In one case, for example, a client was apparently counted as "successfully" abstaining from alcohol during a period of time when he actually couldn't drink anyway because he was spending time in jail on an alcohol-related conviction for an offense that took place after he had "successfully" completed a controlled-drinking program designed to teach him how to drink in moderation.

Of course, many so-called "alcoholics" would strongly endorse the idea that "anyone 'should' be able to control their drinking." Indeed, many of them have gone to great lengths trying to be a successful "guinea pig" in their own "addiction control experiments" and thus prove to themselves and to others that they can drink moderately and safely. Some have been badly mangled in the process and—based on my own understanding of the term "alcoholic"—none have ever been truly successful over the long-run.

I remember seeing a tee-shirt on sale in a souvenir shop in Key West, Florida, amid a vast array of bars that I never visited—most of which apparently have signs in their men's room proudly proclaiming that

"Hemingway pissed here."

Anyway, this tee-shirt offers an interesting perspective on the kind of problem some people seem to have when they try to maintain "controlled use" or "total abstinence" when it boldly declares:

"I always say no to drugs—they just don't listen!"

The treatment philosophy based on the "disease model" of addiction is deeply rooted in the "total abstinence" approach followed by Alcoholics Anonymous. Clinicians and theorists who subscribe to the disease model will often scorn any treatment approaches that involve "controlled drinking," "moderation," or "harm reduction" as foolish, doomed, dangerous, and irresponsible for clients dealing with alcoholism.

However, even the original text of the AA program—the AA "Bible" first published in 1939 and referred to affectionately as the "Big Book"—indicates that trial and error through direct personal experience will often prove to be the best, or only, effective teacher for many alcoholics:

> We do not like to pronounce any individual as alcoholic, but you can quickly diagnose yourself. Step over to the nearest barroom and try some controlled drinking. Try to drink and stop abruptly. Try it more than once. It will not take long for you to decide, if you are honest with yourself about it. It may be worth a bad case of the jitters if you get a full knowledge of your condition.

> (Alcoholics Anonymous, 1976: 31–32).

Remember, our primary goal as clinicians in the early stage of addiction treatment is to help our clients conduct an accurate self-diagnosis. We will try to help them recognize and understand any problem that they might currently have with harmful compulsive or addictive behavior—or any problem that they might be in the process of developing. Although it would certainly be ideal in theory, merely providing our clients with a clear and "convincing" diagnostic snapshot, at one static moment in time, is rarely enough to help them learn how to recognize the existence or emergence of a harmful addiction. More often— while we will always try to promote insight and motivation for change sooner rather than later—the best that we can realistically hope for in many cases will be to facilitate a gradual process of recognition, understanding, and acceptance that may have to take place over many years.

Harmful addictions tend to develop rather slowly in most cases—sometimes over a period of decades. Therefore, while a recognizable pattern of telltale signs and symptoms will often emerge—in identifiable and progressively worsening stages—this progression will often occur quite gradually over a long period of time. Hence, in many cases, the actual facts of our client's experience may not yet support a clear-cut diagnosis of dependence—or even abuse—especially when we are seeing them in early, involuntary treatment episodes that have been mandated because their use has gotten them into some kind of trouble. This is why another key goal in early stage addiction treatment is to give our clients the solid factual information they will need in the future in order to recognize, understand, and admit any problem that they might be developing more quickly as it gradually unfolds and becomes more apparent over time.

At this point, it's important to remember that the phrase "accurate generalization" is virtually an oxymoron whenever we're trying to describe the nature of harmful addiction.

So, let's just take a moment right here to note the well-established fact that the experience of a "gradual progression" is by no means a universal phenomenon in harmful addiction.

Some users—even some who meet the diagnostic criteria for substance dependence—may experience serious, recurrent negative consequences in a repetitive but relatively stable way that doesn't significantly change or worsen over time.

Other users may experience a virtually "catastrophic progression" that seemingly explodes almost overnight into a pattern that looks much like a full-blown "late stage" harmful addiction.

During the "crack epidemic" of the 1980s, for example, the word "compression" was often used to describe the rapid onset of apparently irresistible cravings in many users who started to smoke cocaine that had been processed into a solid form. In many cases, a devastating loss of control and relentlessly compulsive use would follow almost immediately after the first use—sometimes literally overnight. This reaction would often occur even among many users who had been sniffing powdered cocaine for quite some time in quite large amounts without ever experiencing this degree of intense inner compulsion. The term "compression"—or perhaps the even more graphic phrase "train wreck"—also describes the swift course of physical, emotional, social, economic, and family destruction that often followed the onset of crack use much more accurately than the more sedate word "progression."

In the domain of alcohol abuse and alcoholism, C. Robert Cloninger and his associates have identified a pattern that they have labeled "Type II" alcoholism. This pattern tends to occur more often among the adolescent or young adult sons of male alcoholics than it does among other types of users and it usually involves rapid onset, recurrent alcohol-related antisocial or criminal behavior, and swift progression into the experience of serious alcoholic symptoms and significant negative consequences. They contrast this unmistakable emergence of a major problem early in life with a far more common pattern that they have labeled "Type I" alcoholism.

"Type I" refers to the broad pattern that we've been discussing thus far and will now proceed to examine in more detail. This syndrome usually involves a more gradual onset and a slower progression with the initial appearance of inconclusive early warning signs generally occurring in late adolescence or young adulthood. In this more widely experienced model of gradual progression, the convincing emergence of major symptoms and serious negative consequences does not generally occur until somewhat later in adulthood.

(Cloninger, Sigvardsson, & Bohman, 1996)

Allen Zweben and Michael Fleming offer useful advice for clinicians about maintaining a long-term perspective in their chapter on "Brief Interventions for Alcohol and Drug Problems" in the book *Changing Addictive Behavior:*

> Providers need to maintain a sense of *optimism* about the prospects for *eventual problem resolution*. Alcohol and drug problems are chronic, relapsing, and remitting problems. Some individuals are amenable to treatment and some are not and, even among those who are, stable behavior change often does not occur immediately . . . *Changing addictive behavior is a long-term process,* and many persons with problems need to hear concerns from several people or experience further negative consequences before they see the need for and become committed to change. Expressions of concern may lead to problem resolution *many months or years later.*

(Zweben & Fleming, 1999: 263. Emphasis added.)

In his book, *I'll Quit Tomorrow: A Practical Guide to Alcoholism Treatment,* Vernon Johnson gives us an overview of how alcoholism develops that is relevant and quite instructive when we look at harmful compulsive-addictive behaviors in broader terms. Please recall once more that many of the variables associated with alcohol abuse or alcoholism can and should be generalized conceptually as we consider problems involving other compulsive-addictive substances or behaviors—even though some may not apply perfectly across the board.

Johnson identifies four progressive phases in the development of a harmful addiction:

> **Phase One**—Learn the Mood Swing
> **Phase Two**—Seek the Mood Swing
> **Phase Three**—Harmful Dependence
> **Phase Four**—Using to Feel Normal

In phase one, the user learns that the addictive behavior can provide a mood swing towards euphoria. He or she also learns how to control the degree of the mood swing by regulating the amount of use, and that his or her mood will return to normal after the euphoria of using.

In phase two, the user seeks this euphoric mood swing by applying what has been learned within his or her social, cultural, and life situation. Social users are able to easily develop and adhere to self-imposed rules about use.

Problem users, however, will start to regularly break their self-imposed rules governing use as they move into the third phase of harmful dependence. Eventually they will  start to behave in ways that violate their own personal value system because of their persistent loss of control over use, and they will end up using primarily to relieve the emotional pain caused by problem use.

By the time they cross the line into the fourth phase, a user will typically experience frequent and severe loss of control over the amount used and suffer increasingly serious negative consequences and almost constant emotional pain. Ultimately, they will be using just to survive emotionally and try to feel normal again because they can no longer feel any euphoria when using due to their increased tolerance.

(Johnson, 1980)

In their book, *Staying Sober: A Guide to Relapse Prevention,* Terence Gorski and Merlene Miller offer a useful sketch of the progressively worsening stages that are often involved in the gradual development of a full-blown harmful addiction—which they summarize in the following two ways:

## Addictive Disease Progression

1. Early Stage
   GROWING TOLERANCE AND DEPENDENCY

2. Middle Stage
   PROGRESSIVE LOSS OF CONTROL

3. Chronic Stage
   DETERIORATION OF BIO-PSYCHO-SOCIAL HEALTH

## The Addiction Cycle

1. Short-Term Gratification
2. Long-Term Pain and Dysfunction
3. Addictive Thinking
4. Increased Tolerance
5. Loss of Control
6. Bio-Psycho-Social Damage

(Gorski & Miller, 1986: 45–50)

**Question:** Why would anyone in their right mind subject themselves to all this?

**Answer:** They wouldn't.

Please recall that according to the disease model, harmful addiction is a:

**"Bio-Psycho-Social-Spiritual" Illness or Disorder**

This means that harmful compulsive-addictive behavior has biological, psychological, social, and spiritual causes as well as harmful biological, psychological, social, and spiritual consequences. Psychologically, as we have already seen, many experts agree that "compulsion" is the most crucial element involved in the phenomena of harmful addiction, and within the realm of psychopathology, compulsion is defined as:

"An irresistible impulse to perform an irrational act."

Consider the following observations from "The Big Book" of Alcoholics Anonymous on this point:

> *Why does he behave like this?* If hundreds of experiences have shown him that one drink means another debacle with all its attendant suffering and humiliation, *why is it he takes that one drink? . . .*

> These observations would be academic and pointless if our friend never took the first drink, thereby setting the terrible cycle in motion. Therefore, *the main problem of the alcoholic centers in his mind,* rather than in his body. . . .

> Whatever the precise definition of the word may be, *we call this plain insanity.* How can such a lack of proportion, of the ability to think straight, be called anything else?

> . . . there was always the *curious mental phenomenon* that parallel with our sound reasoning there inevitably ran some *insanely trivial excuse* for taking the first drink. Our sound reasoning failed to hold us in check.

> *The insane idea won out.*

> (Alcoholics Anonymous, 1976: 22–23, 37. Emphasis added.)

This vaguely reminds me of another one of those Key West tee-shirts:

"I'm out of my mind—I'll be back in five minutes."

On a more serious note, the twelve-step recovery program developed by Alcoholics Anonymous starts out with the following blunt declaration:

**Step One**—We admitted we were powerless over alcohol—that our lives had become unmanageable.

In the first step of other twelve-step programs modeled closely after AA, the word "alcohol" will be replaced by whatever addictive substance or behavior that its members are struggling with, such as: "drugs," "gambling," "food," "sex," "relationships," "debting," "spending," and so on.

For many people, of course, it's often very difficult to fully understand or accept the idea of being "powerless" as *a basic fact of life* for them when it comes to using certain substances or engaging in certain behaviors. In the final chapter of this book, which introduces the *Rational Spirituality* self-help system I've developed, I will offer a practical "translation" of the entire twelve-step program into clear, simple, modern terms that I believe most people can easily understand, accept, and begin to practice.

In order to help our clients—and ourselves—better understand the real meaning of the words used in the first step, for example, I believe we can make a valid, modern translation as follows:

> **Step One**—I admit that I have a problem dealing with compulsion—irresistible impulses to perform irrational acts that produce negative consequences in my life.

The concept of "powerlessness" as found in the first step of the twelve-step program is controversial in some circles because it is widely misunderstood as a virtual prescription for "learned helplessness." Essentially, however, "powerlessness" is a term that is best understood when used retrospectively—not prescriptively—to describe a key factor in a user's already established history with two basic problems:

1. Loss of Control, and
2. Inability to Abstain.

Of course, many people with milder problems will be able to control their use once they have finally decided to do so—and the term "powerless" will clearly not apply to those people who can do so successfully—which means *complete, permanent, lifetime control with <u>no</u> exceptions.*

Eventually, however—as we will see in greater detail in Part Three of this book when we look at the *"Addiction Recovery Learning Curve"*—those people who continue to experience further episodes of loss of control over the amount used—or over the amount of time spent using—will eventually have to concede to themselves that they have reached a point where *they cannot reliably or safely predict the outcome once they have started to use.*

Despite their best intentions and their serious attempts to exert their "willpower"—some people will find eventually, but inevitably, that they lose control again—even when they are sincerely and strongly motivated to control their use. In many cases, moreover, this continued loss of control will usually lead to further negative consequences for the user—sooner or later if not immediately—and for many people the frequency and severity of their loss of control will also become progressively worse over time.

Because of these mounting negative consequences—which also tend to become progressively worse over time in many cases—many people progressing through the *Addiction Recovery Learning Curve* eventually decide that they must abstain completely and permanently from their harmful addictive substance or behavior.

Of course, at this point, many people with milder problems will be able to abstain completely once they have finally decided to do so—and the terms "powerless" or "compulsive" will clearly not apply if to those people who can do so successfully—which means complete, permanent, lifetime abstinence with *no* exceptions.

Many people, however, although they will often be able to abstain for weeks, months, or even years at a time, will find that they are apparently unable to abstain permanently—even after they have truly developed *a sincere, deep, and sometimes desperate desire to do so.*

Despite their best intentions and their serious attempts to use their "willpower"—many people with more serious problems will eventually, but inevitably, begin to use again—even when they are sincerely and strongly motivated to stop. In most of these cases, moreover, this recurrent inability to abstain is inevitably followed by further loss of control and further negative consequences.

Many people who reach this point in the progression of harmful addiction feel that this second aspect of "powerlessness"—their apparent inability to abstain—is far more baffling, mysterious, and frightening than the loss of control that so often follows the onset of use. Many recovering people have found that it took a long time for them to finally recognize their own lack of control and fully accept their need to abstain. For many recovering people it takes even longer to fully understand and accept their own apparent inability to abstain and become willing to learn and do whatever it takes holistically—mentally, emotionally, physically, *and* spiritually—in order to deal with this problem successfully.

When we see a person who appears to have developed an abnormally high tolerance for painful consequences and still continues to use—even when the consequences seem to far outweigh any rational benefit they may derive—then we are probably looking at someone who is in the grips of a serious harmful addiction. Another identifying characteristic of this syndrome will be the problem of real ambivalence about cutting down or stopping harmful addictive behavior and a persistent pattern of *fluctuating, inconsistent, or insufficient motivation for change.*

In fact, most so-called "normal" people—whose "bad habits" never reach the level of diagnosable pathology—will not even begin to seriously contemplate cutting down or stopping an enjoyable addictive behavior until they sense—*based on their own, direct, personal experience*—that the pain of continuing will be far worse than the pain of stopping. Hence, it is only when they see that the actual costs of continued use—and the anticipated pain involved—finally add up to the point where they far outweigh the actual benefits of continued use—and the anticipated enjoyment involved—that most people will really become internally motivated for change.

It almost seems to be a basic fact of life—perhaps even a hallmark of human nature—that painful personal experience is often the most effective teacher many people will ever have. Indeed, for some people it seems to be the only teacher that can ever make a deep or lasting impression. In AA, for example, many people who are now successfully maintaining long-term sobriety initially experienced one or more serious relapses before they "finally" got sober. They will often jokingly refer to their last binge or relapse as "the convincer." Similarly, many people who have returned to AA after "going out" and failing one more time to control their drinking—or those who have made the same unsuccessful experiment without ever leaving the rooms of AA—will often joke:

> "I was out there in the 'research division.'"

According to Oscar Wilde:

> "Experience is the name everyone gives to their mistakes."

Countless times in my own clinical experience—wherever I've worked—at every level of care—I've heard clients who were coming back to treatment after a serious relapse say something like this:

> I didn't actually believe anything you guys said the last time I was here—and I guess I didn't really understand most of it either.
>
> And, to be completely honest, I didn't even want to be here, so I didn't really want to hear it anyway.
>
> So I just went right out and did my own thing all over again and before very long everything fell apart and got even worse than it ever was before.
>
> So, now I'm back—and I think what you've all been saying is finally starting to make some sense.

In many cases, the recovery information that client's begin to absorb in their early treatment episodes—or in their early exposure to self-help programs—is not really understood, believed, or accepted at any deep level. In fact, for most people, the information presented actually *can't* be genuinely understood or accepted until it's been "field-tested" out in the real world laboratory of painful personal experience.

Hopefully, all of this information will eventually "click," and the seeds planted in earlier treatment episodes—or self-help efforts—will all start to sprout sooner or later because, to paraphrase a great aphorism that I've heard attributed anecdotally to Oliver Wendell Holmes, Jr.:

> "Once a mind has been stretched by a new idea it can never shrink back to it's original size."

## THE STAGES OF PROGRESSION

During the war of 1812, U.S. Navy Commodore Oliver Hazard Perry won a decisive victory in battle against a fleet of British warships on the waters of Lake Erie between the United States and Canada. His brief statement reporting the news of this victory to his superior officer became one of the most memorable lines in American history:

> "We have met the enemy and they are ours!"

Today, this line is often remembered and widely misquoted to read: "We have met the enemy and *he is ours*." I believe our faulty memory on this point has been influenced greatly by another famous quotation that came to us from the cartoon character Pogo in the 1960s. Commenting on the American culture and politics of that tumultuous time, he boldly declared:

> "We have met the enemy—and he is us!"

We have examined the concept of harmful addiction as the behavioral manifestation of a powerful bio-psycho-social-spiritual disorder. As such, the ultimate causes of harmful addiction may be seen as deeply rooted in the heart, mind, body, and soul of the alcoholic, addict, or compulsive-addictive user. Sooner or later, the expression: "I am my own worst enemy" will start to make sense for those who develop this kind of problem. In the long run, however, for those who progress into the middle and late stages of harmful addiction, this truism will eventually become a powerful, devastating, and tragic reality that will no longer seem to make any sense at all.

In many ways, the self-destructive behavior of the alcoholic, addict, or user will never make much "sense" in rational terms because at the core of the most harmful addictive behavior there lies the reality of a *powerful, irresistible, often subtle, and consistently irrational compulsion.*

As previously noted, Terence Gorski and Merlene Miller identify three basic stages in addictive disease progression in their book, *Staying Sober,* and it may be useful for us to take a quick look at them again as we begin our examination of the signs, symptoms, and stages of progression in harmful addiction. They are:

1. Growing Tolerance and Dependency
2. Progressive Loss of Control
3. Deterioration of Bio-Psycho-Social Health

(Gorski & Miller, 1986: 45)

Our primary goal as clinicians, as we learn about the signs, symptoms, and stages of progression, will be to understand this process and be able to pass this knowledge on to our clients who have, or who may be developing, a problem. We will want to help them make an accurate self-diagnosis so that they can recognize an existing or emerging problem and perhaps begin to develop a healthier, more effective, and more satisfying way of life sooner rather than later.

The classic model for understanding the stages of progression in alcoholism was first developed by E.M. Jellinek, "a pioneer in modern alcohol studies" who started his work at Yale University in the 1940's and 1950's. Jellinek authored a pivotal book called *The Disease Concept of Alcoholism* in 1960, and he has since been called "the father of alcohol studies in the United States and the world."

Jellinek initially identified four stages in the development of alcoholism, which he called the **pre-alcoholic, prodromal, crucial,** and **chronic** stages. These four stages have subsequently been absorbed into a model that describes **early, middle,** and **late** stages of progression. In the next three chapters of this book, we will be examining the specific signs and symptoms of harmful addiction as they typically occur within the overall context of Jellinek's model which—with the Gorski and Miller concepts blended in—now looks like this:

**EARLY STAGE**
"Pre-Alcoholic Phase"
"Prodromal" or "Warning Phase"
GROWING TOLERANCE AND DEPENDENCY

**MIDDLE STAGE**
"Crucial Phase"
PROGRESSIVE LOSS OF CONTROL

**LATE STAGE**
"Chronic Phase"
DETERIORATION OF BIO-PSYCHO-SOCIAL HEALTH

(Gorski & Miller, 1986: 45; Jellinek, 1960; Kinney &
Leaton, 1982: 38,41; Milam & Ketchum, 1981: 78).

Before moving on to look at the signs, symptoms, and stages of progression in detail in the next three chapters of this book, I'd like to take a moment to reiterate a point I've already stressed before:

> It is only by *repeated* trial and error that most people will ever be convinced of their own need for total abstinence.

Only time and repeated experiences with unsuccessful attempts at control, can truly identify the minority of problem drinkers or drug users who are in the process of developing a serious problem. It is only when a person seriously tries and fails—over and over again—to control or stop their use and has established a factual record—their own track record of unsuccessful attempts at control—that we can convincingly demonstrate the presence of compulsive use and clearly identify the existence of a serious harmful addiction.

Therefore, it may be very helpful when working with a client to identify the specific signs, symptoms, and consequences they have experienced—and make a diagnostic assessment of where they currently stand within the classic stages of progression—to also help them examine their own history of failed attempts at control or abstinence in order to determine where they presently stand on the *Addiction Recovery Learning Curve*.

I've already outlined the five stages of change on the *Addiction Recovery Learning Curve* briefly in the Introduction to this book, and we will explore this new developmental learning model in greater detail in Chapters Seven and Eight, but I would like to take a moment to repeat these stages here to refresh your memory:

## The Addiction Recovery Learning Curve

1. Uncontrolled Use with Consequences.
2. Attempted Common Sense Control.
3. Attempted Analytical Abstinence.
4. Attempted Spiritual Sobriety.
5. Rational Spiritual Sobriety.

Most alcoholics, addicts, problem drinkers, or other users will have to suffer repeated negative consequences from unrestricted use before making any serious attempts to control their use. Then, most of them will also have to make repeated personal experiments with "controlled drinking" or "controlled use"—often over a period of many years—before becoming completely "convinced" of their need to stop. This persistent pattern often holds true despite strong clinical recommendations that they "must" abstain completely. In fact, this experimental process of trial and error is usually the only way that most people will ever be convinced that they "can't" control their drinking or drug use.

Sadly, even then, many people will not seem to care deeply enough about themselves or the negative consequences they suffer—and inflict on others—to muster the overpowering desire that is often required to take all the necessary steps—in terms of attitude, behavior, and lifestyle changes—to stop and stay stopped permanently.

These informal "addiction control experiments," are actually "endorsed" by the AA Big Book as being necessary in many cases for a person to learn for themselves whether or not total abstinence is truly required. As we have seen, the basic text of the AA twelve-step program makes it very clear that many people *must* try and fail at controlled drinking repeatedly before they will ever be convinced that they need to stop completely. It also insists—very accurately and wisely—that this understanding, and the decision to stop, must eventually come freely, from within their "innermost selves," and can never be successfully imposed from outside.

Among the entire population of those who have ever experienced any kind of problem with alcohol or drugs—or with any other addictive substances or behaviors—we must always remember that the vast majority are not really "alcoholics" or "addicts" and never will be. Therefore, we must recognize that those people with milder problems will actually be able to control or stop their drinking or drug use quite successfully once they are sufficiently motivated to do so. Most of them will also have no trouble doing so on their own, with no outside help being required.

## BECOMING TEACHABLE

One critical transitional moment in the addiction treatment process is said to occur anecdotally sometime after a person becomes at least partially "convinced" that they may have a serious problem, and this is the moment when they finally become open-minded and "teachable" on two vital questions:

1. What exactly *is* my problem? and
2. What do I have to do about it?

There's a recovery slogan that presents a little pearl of practical wisdom that may be very helpful when a person is still somewhat defensive and resistant and may be teetering right on the edge and just need a little nudge because he or she still hasn't made this crucial transition into "teachability." This slogan suggests simply—and gently one would hope—that some people may need to:

"Take the cotton out of your ears, and put it in your mouth."

Most good addiction treatment programs will present their clients with an overview and summary of the classic signs, symptoms, and stages of progression in harmful addiction on some kind of printed handout—which is occasionally referred to as "a Jellinek Chart." This written material is often distributed as part of an extensive client education program consisting of lectures, videotaped presentations, worksheets, or group exercises that focus on a variety of addiction and recovery issues. The factual information presented to the clients in this way is usually processed with them by the presenter—as part of the presentation itself or else immediately afterward—in psychoeducational discussion groups—which are usually a core element in most addiction treatment programs.

As a part of this process, each client will usually be asked to review his or her own alcohol or drug use history—often in writing on a blank worksheet designed for the purpose—or the history of their compulsive gambling, overeating, sexual addiction, or whatever it may be that brings them into treatment. And then, last but not least, clients are usually asked to complete one of the most important assignments in the addiction treatment process—a personal symptom checklist.

If someone needed one of the printed progression handouts we've just discussed—and for some reason they couldn't think of what it was called—almost anyone involved in the addiction treatment field would know what they meant if they just said:

"Could you get me one of those U-Shaped Charts?"

While a multi-page symptom checklist format may be used just as often—and some of the more artistic charts may actually present the progressive signs and symptoms in the form of a downward spiral—the most classic and memorable model for presenting the kind of information we will be looking at in the next three chapters—in terms of graphic design—involves a "progression chart" with the clinical data arranged in a rough chronological order moving from left to right on a *U-Shaped curve*.

On the upper left, we will see some of the typical signs presented by a normal, social drinker or user—who fits the profile of a "non-alcoholic" or "pre-alcoholic" as the case may be. Then, many of the typical, progressive signs and symptoms of early, middle, and late stage harmful addiction are arranged on a downward slope on the left-hand side of the graph—growing worse and worse over time until finally "hitting bottom"—at the bottom of the "U"—where we will see the most severe late stage symptoms.

In the next three chapters, we will take a look at the long slide that a hypothetical user could take all the way down the left-hand side of a hybrid "progression chart" that represents a combination of many signs and symptoms that I have drawn together from a number of different sources.

The classic U-Shaped charts we are talking about here might actually best be described as "progression and recovery charts" because the right-hand side of the chart—which represents the upward arm of the "U"—presents the signs of the slow but steady upward progress that can be made by the recovering alcoholic, addict, or user as they move through the progressive stages of recovery—including the most crucial developmental tasks that are most commonly linked to the achievement of permanent sobriety at each stage.

In Part Three of this book, however, after completing our review of the basic signs, symptoms, and stages of progression into harmful addiction, we will not be moving very far up the right-hand side of the "U." We will examine the long-term learning process that is often involved in helping clients make the vital transition into recovery, but any detailed examination of the long-term addiction recovery process itself will have to wait for another day and another book.

Before we step out onto "the slippery slope" let me acknowledge the unavoidable oversimplification and overgeneralization that will necessarily be a part of this presentation—and discuss how best to take them. When we consider the stereotypical, unchecked "course of illness" in harmful addiction, we can see that several clearly differentiated stages of progression have been identified and are well documented. Many specific signs and symptoms have also been identified and these are also well-documented. Many of these symptoms—like increased tolerance, for example—can be linked rather firmly to a particular stage of progression while other signs—like driving while intoxicated—cannot be pinned down quite so precisely. In particular cases, these "floating" signs or symptoms may emerge somewhat earlier or later than they typically appear on most progression charts, and in many individual cases they may not be present at all.

Although a general pattern can often be seen across a wide range of cases, none of what follows should be taken as a conceptual model intended to fit all clients uniformly. There is simply *no specific order* in which these signs and symptoms emerge in all cases. Hence, any written progression chart or symptom checklist can only represent a rough approximation that can try to present them—at best—in a "rough chronological order."

Each client is a unique individual and within any group of clients we will often see a wide array of different symptom clusters that may occur in sequences that can differ radically from individual to individual.

# THERE'S NOTHING NEW UNDER THE SUN

"He whose genius appears deepest and truest excels his fellows in nothing save the knack of expression; he throws out occasionally a lucky hint at truths of which every human soul is profoundly though unutterably conscious."

– Nathaniel Hawthorne.

♦ ♦ ♦

There's a little aphorism I've always loved which says:

"All genius is plagiarism—only stupidity is original."

Of course, someone had to be the person who first said or wrote this little gem, and I'd love to be able to cite a specific source for it. Unfortunately, I have absolutely no idea where I first heard it, and I can't find a source for it on-line or in any of my basic desk reference books of quotations.

In presenting the material that follows in the next three chapters I have essentially blended a mass of clinical, research, and anecdotal data that I've drawn together over many years from many different sources—including professional journal articles, clinical textbooks, and popular self-help books. Whenever possible—meaning whenever I actually know the sources involved—I've cited sources in the section on References and Resources. However, I've also drawn much of the material that follows from a large collection of anonymously prepared client education handouts, symptom checklists, and progression charts that I've gathered from various treatment programs over the years—most of which seem to bear a striking resemblance to each other.

Of course, I'd like to apologize in advance if I haven't properly credited anything that I should have—but that's not actually the main point I'd like to make here. Another important fact to bear in mind is that the diverse body of material on which this presentation is based also contains *many significant differences.*

I've arranged the long list of signs and symptoms that follow into a specific sequence that makes good sense to me—based on my own clinical education, training, experience, knowledge, and best judgment. It might be helpful for you to think of this generic presentation as a symptom checklist that could reflect how a specific hypothetical individual might experience all of these symptoms. Seen from that perspective, the next three chapters would represent a kind of "case study from hell"—reflecting the history of someone who would experience every single symptom on this list as they move inexorably downward through the stages of progression.

It may appear to some readers that I've arranged some of the "progressively worsening" signs and symptoms of harmful addiction into the sequence that follows in a rather subjective or arbitrary manner. However, since there is no definitive or universal "clinical model" to simply quote, regurgitate, paraphrase, or plagiarize for you, I've made what are essentially "editorial choices" based loosely on the following logic:

> "If you haven't already seen this particular sign or symptom before, you should start to see it by now."

Therefore, you may notice a virtual refrain written into the fabric of the next three chapters that goes something like this:

> "By now, in many cases, if it hasn't already happened long before . . ."

## A TALE OF TWO DRIVERS

> "A journey of a thousand miles begins with a single step."

◆ ◆ ◆

Before we "get on with the show" and look at the full range of progressive signs and symptoms, let's briefly consider some questions regarding the diagnostic validity and predictive value of *driving while intoxicated* as a symptom of harmful addiction or a sign that a serious problem is likely to develop.

What should we make of this when we see it in our client's history?

I've already cited DWI as an example of a sign or symptom that

- cannot be firmly linked to a particular stage of progression,
- may often occur much later in particular cases than where it would typically appear on most generic progression charts, and
- may or may not be present at all in many individual cases.

Driving while intoxicated—or merely "driving under the influence"—is often a very early sign of a possible long-term problem that is frequently seen in the "pre-alcoholic" or "early warning" stage of progression. However, a history that includes driving while intoxicated—when taken all by itself—does not establish that a particular person is actually an alcoholic or even a potential alcoholic. If there are no other signs or symptoms present to suggest that possibility, this simply means that the person may be a potential alcoholic—or they may merely be *an irresponsible and dangerous criminal.*

I'm sorry if this choice of words seems a little harsh or offensive to some readers, but I've attended too many Victim's Impact Panels run by Mothers Against Drunk Driving (MADD) to mince words or to trivialize or minimize the seriousness of this potentially deadly criminal offense.

Although I usually won't hesitate—in my personal or professional roles—to assertively challenge deplorable words or deeds whenever it's necessary or appropriate, I will usually do so with patient, understanding, and compassionate firmness. At this point in my life, it takes an incredible provocation for me to actually judge or criticize anyone personally for anything they may say or do. When this does happen, my negative emotional reaction is almost always silent and quite brief, because I quickly try to step into the other person's shoes and attempt to understand what's really happening inside them on a deeper level.

But I am human, and some things will definitely trigger an initial negative reaction.

For example, I once saw someone wearing a supposedly humorous tee-shirt that read:

> "Don't drink and drive. You might spill your drink!"

I must confess, my immediate gut reaction triggered the automatic thought:

> "That shirt really needs to have the word *IDIOT* printed on the neckline with a great big arrow pointing upward."

My wife Liz dislikes it when I occasionally blurt out the word "idiot" in response to things I see or hear on TV, so I *try* to avoid using this word completely in deference to her feelings. To use this "taboo" term so deliberately right here in print, therefore, may suggest how strongly I feel about the reckless folly of taking DWI so lightly.

In my own view—if a person drives under the influence more than once in their lifetime—they are clearly an alcohol abuser.

Why? Because they have started to develop a *pattern* of "recurrent use in situations where it is physically hazardous to use." Does this diagnostic assessment sound premature, or perhaps even harsh, or judgmental? Many people—including many clinicians, I'm sure—might suggest that we should "lighten up" a little and "give the guy a break?"

### Sure, why not give someone the "benefit of the doubt?"

Because there's no real room for doubt that a person with two episodes of driving while intoxicated—even if they are uneventful and undetected—would qualify for a diagnosis alcohol abuse. Well, okay, that's not quite true.

Technically speaking, a pattern of recurrent use in hazardous situations –meaning two or more episodes—would have to occur within a twelve month period to formally qualify for the diagnosis of alcohol abuse—but I hope you get my general drift.

To think of driving while intoxicated under any circumstances—no matter how infrequently it may occur—as being anything other than alcohol abuse would be sensible and acceptable only if I wanted to minimize, trivialize, rationalize, or excuse illegal and dangerous behavior and learn how to become *a good professional enabler.*

I don't necessarily want to belabor this point—but I do want to be sure to really make it:

> When evaluating the potentially life-or-death question of harmful addiction it is essential that we take all signs and symbols very seriously and probably best if we tend to err on the side of *caution* rather than complacency.

So, please ask yourself honestly—and after you have established a good therapeutic relationship with your clients or patients—based on a solid foundation of empathy, trust, and rapport—please be just as blunt when asking them:

**What does the word "recurrent" mean to you?**

**For me, it means "more than once."**

Another serious question for you to ask yourself and your clients:

**What does the word "pattern" mean to you?**

**For me, it's the second dot on a frequency chart.**

As a quick test to evaluate how seriously or lightly we should take these matters in potentially ambiguous cases, please consider the following hypothetical case scenario:

> Mr. Smith" has established a "pattern" of getting drunk and driving while intoxicated after his daughter's wedding receptions. Otherwise, he never drinks and he uses no other mood altering substances except for caffeine in moderation. His first incident of driving while intoxicated occurred five years ago after his oldest daughter was married. The second incident took place three years ago—when his middle daughter got married. These two episodes were uneventful. Luckily, there were no accidents, and no one was injured or killed. Unfortunately, however, Mr. Smith was neither caught nor arrested for DWI on either occasion and consequently he has learned nothing from his experience.

> His youngest daughter is getting married tomorrow.

> I had planned to address my concern over this issue with him in our therapy session today, but Mr. Smith brought in a long agenda related to his presenting problem of anxiety regarding his recent financial set-backs in the stock market. He was particularly distressed over the cost of the tomorrow's wedding, and we never got around to discussing his obvious risk for further DWI behavior.

How would you like to recall writing this kind of hypothetical progress note at Mr. Smith's funeral next week? Or perhaps have it read aloud in court at his trial for vehicular homicide? Or how would you like to have something like this be one of those things that you would never actually write down—but that you might have to carry around on your conscience for the rest of your life?

How seriously will you take it if you ever have a similar "Mr. or Ms. Smith" sitting in a therapy session with you? How will you respond if you find yourself dealing with a client who is focused intensely on other issues, but also presents a similar "pattern" of driving while intoxicated in their history—perhaps someone with even a few more dots on their frequency chart—but still with no arrests, no accidents, and no negative consequences—yet.

### Would you appropriately challenge or confront a client about this kind of dangerous behavior?

Technically, "Mr. Smith" doesn't formally meet the diagnostic criteria for "alcohol abuse"—because he has had no drinking episodes of any kind within the past twelve months—and he is clearly not "alcohol dependent" or an "alcoholic." *Never was, and probably never will be.*

Nevertheless, because of my preference to err on the side of caution, I'd informally consider "Mr. Smith" to be an alcohol abuser—despite his reported history of drinking only two times in the past five years.

"Mr. Smith," by the way, is a totally fictional creation. Now let's tweak this scenario a bit and talk about another hypothetical client who actually resembles many people I actually worked during a four-year period when I conducted hundreds of psychoeducational "DWI Classes."

> "Bobby" Smith reports no family history of alcohol or drug abuse "except for one uncle who went to a rehab once, like a really long time ago." Bobby got drunk and drove while intoxicated after his older brother's wedding reception three months ago—shortly after turning 17. He was caught and arrested for DWI and—because this is his first offense—he was then given the option of entering this "pre-trial alcohol education program" as an alternative to prosecution.

"Bobby" reports that he only began drinking within the past year, and that he has had "a few beers" with his friends "a couple of times." When probed he said this means that he has had "three or four beers" with a frequency of "about once every other month or so."

In fact, not counting the episode at his brother's wedding—which he called "a big exception because it was a special occasion"—he reports only four other drinking episodes altogether in his lifetime—so far. He denies any other drug use or experimentation, and there is no collateral evidence to suggest or confirm that he is lying about any of this.

He reports that he has driven a car on each occasion after these four drinking episodes—including one episode of drinking and driving which occurred after his DWI arrest while he was already enrolled in this DWI program. He voluntarily reported drinking two beers "at a party" on the "weekly drinking log" he has been asked to maintain as part of this program. He said this was the only drinking episode he has had since the arrest. He added that he thought it was okay for him to drink because this program does not require abstinence except on the day of our weekly meeting. He also said he thought it was okay, and "legal" for him to drive after drinking "because I wasn't even close to being drunk."

"Bobby" was oblivious to the fact that it is illegal for him to drink under any circumstances because he is underage and he seemed to be genuinely puzzled when this was raised as an issue. He said he sees nothing wrong with his pattern of drinking occasionally and would probably have "a few beers again" if a special occasion arose with his friends—"maybe once every other month or so." He said: "I'm not even a social drinker. I drink less than a social drinker." He admitted that if it were ever offered to him he "might like to try marijuana *once* just to see what it's like, but I don't hang out with the 'potheads' in school." He stressed: "I'm not like that at all. I'm a jock. I'm on the football team. I don't do drugs, and I'm going to college."

He said he is looking forward to joining a fraternity when he gets to college but denied any particular interest in "partying" once he gets there.

**Is "Bobby" Smith an alcoholic? Certainly not—yet.**

**Is he a potential alcoholic? Maybe. Maybe not. Time will tell.**

**Is he an alcohol abuser? You decide.**

Let me repeat the main point of all this. Generally speaking, driving while intoxicated can be a very early warning sign of a possible future problem—but it usually doesn't tell us very much by itself.

Only time and the emergence of more symptoms will tell the story. The extended scenario that unfolds in the next three chapters presents the full range of signs, symptoms, and stages of progression into harmful addiction. In the particular scenario that follows, you will notice that problems with drinking and driving emerge well after our user has amassed many other "check marks" on his or her hypothetical symptom checklist. In this hypothetical scenario, therefore, we will be looking at a user who has started out with good judgment and strong scruples against drinking and driving. In this particular case, therefore, we will see an atypical but not uncommon pattern unfold where it takes quite awhile before we see the erosion and eventual breakdown of our users initial values and good judgment on the issue of drinking and driving.

## BELIEVE IT OR NOT

Please remember, we are about to look at a long downward slide through the full array of signs and symptoms and the progressively worsening stages of a full-blown harmful addiction. Anyone who actually goes down this sad road will eventually see many things come to pass in their personal behavior and life experience that would have been shocking, surprising, and utterly unbelievable had someone with a good crystal ball ever dared to predict them in advance.

In the same way, if a treatment professional with strong diagnostic and clinical skills were ever to make a well-informed, objective, and reasonable prediction—relatively early in the process—that this could be where they were heading—most people who are actually embarked on this tragic, unintended path would simply never believe them.

As clinicians, if we ever find ourselves making this kind of an objective and well-intended warning, and getting this kind of a skeptical and disbelieving response, that would be a good time for us to stress the fact that, for many people, "seeing is believing."

Then, I believe we can also tell any one of our clients—no matter who they are, no matter how far down the scale they may or may not have gone, and no matter how good or bad they may look in their own eyes, or in the eyes of the world:

> I think this may be a good time for you to take a really good look in
> the mirror. I can help you, if you think you might be ready, and if you
> can be honest enough with yourself to really try.

Let's just take an honest look at the facts of your own experience. Take a real look at *exactly* how far you've already gone down this path and then *you tell me* why you don't think you're really on it?

And if you tell me that you *can* see that you're on this self-defeating and self-destructive path and then say that you "just don't care"—then I'm afraid that you just don't see what I can see in you.

Believe it or not, the good that I can see in you is really there, it's really awesome, and it's really wonderful.

I think it's time for you to wake up and open your eyes.

Please let me help.

# CHAPTER 4

# Early Stage Progression

"How do you spell relief?"

"Better living through chemicals."

"I betcha can't eat just one."

—Television Commercial Slogans.

"Candy is dandy, but liquor is quicker!"

—Ogden Nash.

♦ ♦ ♦

During a recent trip, I remember seeing some fascinating, funny, and rather troubling tee-shirts displayed for sale in the front windows of many souvenir and gift shops in Key West, Florida—scattered amid the countless bars and nightclubs in a tourist town that seems to be dedicated to a perpetual, year-round "Spring Break." Most normal, social drinkers, of course, and even most purely recreational users of other drugs, probably wouldn't be caught dead wearing a tee-shirt like one of these.

Here's a little sampler of the messages:

**"I have a serious drinking problem—two hands and only one mouth!"**

**"I read so much about the evils of drinking that I finally had to give up reading."**

**"I'm not drunk—I'm just chemically imbalanced."**

**"I believe in drug testing—which drugs should we test tonight?"**

**"Why go to High School when you can go to school high?"**

**"Rehab is for Quitters!"**

**"I'm not an alcoholic—I'm a drunk! Alcoholics go to meetings."**

**"Spring Break Triathlon—Drink. Party. Puke."**

**"One tequila. Two tequila. Three tequila. Floor."**

The messages on these tee-shirts humorously and unashamedly reflect the pro-drinking and pro-drug attitudes that are commonly found among heavy drinkers or users, problem drinkers or excessive users, alcohol or drug abusers, early stage alcoholics or addicts, and other people who may or may not be in the early stage of progression into harmful addiction.

### Why are these attitudes so proudly and publicly promoted?

Realistically, of course, it's probably fair to say that many bar and liquor store owners and other members of the liquor, wine, and beer industry, along with cigarette manufactuers and sellers, restaurant owners, fast food franchisers, and the many purveyors of junk food—as well as many other kinds of illegal drug dealers, pushers, and promoters—all have a serious, selfish monetary interest involved. Whenever there's money to be made, some people will have a strong motivation to cynically or naively minimize the seriousness of harmful addiction—while deviously or candidly using humor, sex, fantasy, or whatever else will sell the product—in an attempt to blatantly or subtly manipulate public attitudes in favor of further consumption.

But, when we look at the defensive and brash use of overtly pro-alcohol and drug humor on these souvenir tee-shirts, we still have to ask ourselves what else is really going on among the people who might actually buy or wear them—besides the typical, docile, mindless, and herd-like response to the manipulation and brainwashing that's such a standard feature of any mass marketing consumer culture?

Of course, a cynical conspiracy theorist might suggest that virtually no one actually buys or wears most of these shirts and that they're displayed so prominently in so many gift shop windows in order to subliminally legitimize excessive consumption and the resulting free flow of cash in a tourist town? Perhaps.

But, in thinking about the signs, symptoms, and stages of progression in harmful addiction specifically, we still might ask ourselves why these overtly pro-alcohol and drug messages are so funny to some drinkers and drug users—even if they'd never be caught dead in one of the shirts?

In simple terms, this may reflect the fact that many drinkers or drug users are still happily engaged in that early stage in the development of a harmful addiction when using is still generally "fun" for most people, and there is often very little or no significant motivation for change. It other cases, it may be because some users have moved on to a more serious stage of progression where sarcasm, self-righteousness, and humor are quite useful as potent psychological defenses that serve to keep them as far out of touch as possible with the painful reality that they actually have a problem.

Before we move on to examine the early stage signs, symptoms and stages of progression into harmful addiction, let's quickly review an abbreviated summary of the Diagnostic Criteria for Substance Use Disorders which we already reviewed during our discussion of assessment and diagnostic issues:

**SUBSTANCE ABUSE**—*One* or more of the following:
- Failure to meet important personal responsibilities.
- Repeated use under dangerous circumstances.
- Recurrent legal problems related to use.
- Continued use despite ongoing *social* or *interpersonal* problems likely to have been caused or made worse by use.

**SUBSTANCE DEPENDENCE**—*Three* or more of the following:
- Increased Tolerance—Needing to use more to achieve a desired effect or experiencing a decreased effect when using the same amount.
- Withdrawal—Physical or emotional withdrawal symptoms when use is stopped, or using the same or a similar substance or behavior to relieve or avoid withdrawal symptoms.
- Loss of Control—Unintentionally using more or using for a longer time than planned.
- Failed Attempts at Control—Persistent desire or unsuccessful efforts to control or stop use.
- Significant Time Impact—Much time is spent obtaining, using, or recovering from effects of use.
- Reduced Sober Activities—Important social, family, job, school, or recreational activities cut back or eliminated due to use.
- Continued Use Despite Personal Consequences—Involving significant medical or emotional problems.

(Paraphrased from American Psychiatric Association, 2001)

The actual DSM-IV-TR diagnostic criteria will be found embedded within the presentation of the progressive signs and symptoms that follows. I have also included all the elements found in Johnson's four phase model of progression discussed above, and all of the items found on the assessment instruments we have discussed—the AA Questionnaire, the CAGE Alcoholism Screening Questionnaire, and the MAST—Michigan Alcoholism Screening Test. The following letter codes—with the appropriate identifying criteria number attached—will be used below to identify signs and symptoms that match these items:

| | |
|---|---|
| A = Abuse | D = Dependence |
| L = Learn the Mood Swing | S = Seek the Mood Swing |
| H = Harmful Dependence | U = Using to Feel Normal |
| M = MAST | AA = AA Self-Assessment |
| CC = CAGE—Attempted Control | CA = CAGE—Annoyed |
| CG = CAGE—Guilty | CE = CAGE—Eye-Opener |

Now let's move on to take a detailed look at the classic signs, symptoms, and stages of progression into harmful addiction:

## EARLY STAGE

### The "Pre-Alcoholic Phase"

In this initial phase the "user" of a potentially addictive substance or activity learns:

- That the substance or activity can provide a mood swing towards euphoria when used. L1.
- That the substance or activity will provide this positive mood swing every time it is used. L2.
- To trust the substance or activity and its effects. L3.
- To control the degree of the mood swing by regulating the amount of use. L4.
- That his or her mood will return back to normal after the euphoria of using. L5.

Now that the user has "learned the mood swing," he or she:

- Seeks the mood swing and applies what has been learned within his or her social, cultural, and life situation. S1.
- Uses the substance or activity at appropriate times and places. L2.
- Enjoys using the substance or activity now and then. M0.
- Develops self-imposed rules about use and adheres to them easily. S3.

- May suffer some physical pain from occasional overuse but no emotional pain. S4.
- Is able to control the time spent using, the amount used, and the outcome when using. S5.
- Uses the substance or activity for ritual or social motives with the emphasis on social interaction—with no special focus on enjoying the potentially addictive substance or activity itself or on seeking to experience its psychoactive effects.

Normal, social, or recreational users will continue using at this level indefinitely—with absolutely *no* negative consequences of any kind—now or in the future. S6

Potential compulsive-addictive users will move on to the next phase:

## The "Prodromal or Warning Phase"

According to James Milam and Katherine Ketchum, in their book *Under the Influence,* it has been established to their satisfaction that no

> . . . psychological or social factors are unique to the alcoholic or non-alcoholic . . . The same variety of personality traits is found in both groups. Earlier advocates of an 'alcoholic personality' have abandoned the hypothesis, and the theory of an 'addictive personality' has also been discredited by lack of supportive evidence.
>
> (Milam & Ketchum, 1981: 33)

In their book *Cognitive Therapy of Substance Abuse,* however, Aaron Beck, Fred Wright, Cory Newman, and Bruce Liese contend that we can positively identify a number of commonly occurring traits among people who develop serious problems with alcoholism, drug addiction, or other forms of harmful compulsive-addictive behavior. They describe a generic phenomena of addiction and identify the following as predispositional characteristics:

- Over-sensitivity to unpleasant emotions and normal mood swings.
- Deficient motivation to control behavior and a desire for instant gratification.
- Inadequate techniques for controlling behavior and coping with problems.
- A pattern of *automatic* non-reflective yielding to impulses.
- Excitement seeking and low tolerance for boredom.
- Low frustration tolerance (LFT).

85

- Diminished capacity to focus on the future consequences of present choices.

(Beck, et al., 1993: 39)

While the actual amount of self-consciousness or shyness that the user of a potentially addictive substance or activity might feel in social situations could easily be "within normal limits," a person who is moving into the early warning phase often:

- Feels awkward or uncomfortable in some social situations.
- Begins to use the addictive substance or activity as a "social lubricant."
- Starts to develop a *psychological dependence* on using to reduce or eliminate their self-consciousness and enhance or establish their ability to relax around other people and socialize more easily.

When this happens, our user has now found a social "crutch"—whether they consciously think of it in that way or not. Now, as a result of using this crutch, he or she will often fail to improve or develop new interpersonal, communication, recreational, or social skills.

At this stage, our user may react to personal problems, troubling events, or difficult life situations with a normal or elevated level of stress and emotional discomfort. In either case, we will often see that a person progressing into the early warning phase now:

- Begins to use their addictive substance or activity for stress reduction, emotional relief, problem avoidance, escape, or "relaxation," and
- Starts to develop a psychological dependence on using the substance or activity for these purposes.

When this happens, our user has now found an emotional and physical "crutch"—whether they consciously think of it that way or not. Now, as a result of using this crutch, he or she will often compound their previous failure to develop good social skills with a further failure to improve or develop healthy stress reduction, problem solving, or emotional coping skills.

Herbert Fingarette would undoubtedly reject any simplistic concept of "progression" as a symptom of a disease because, as we've already seen, he soundly rejects what he narrowly defines as the mythical "classic" disease concept of alcoholism as a purely physiological disorder. At the same time, he also comments favorably on the work of respected figures in the alcoholism field who endorse a "highly modified disease concept," and he himself describes a progressive pattern of problem avoidance in the development of harmful addiction. Fingarette points out that:

> Some people catch themselves in the act of dodging their problems and difficulties and call a halt to their evasive tactics. But at times any of us may find it easier to avoid a problem than to face it squarely. We find ourselves repeating the avoidance activities to maintain the evasion, and slowly the avoidance activities take on a momentum of their own. Eventually, the avoidance pattern becomes easier and easier, more and more spontaneously favored in response to a variety of threatening or anxiety-producing situations. Over time, an avoidance response like overeating or gambling or drinking may in itself become a focal activity for a small number of people.
>
> (Fingarette, 1988: 109)

Thus far, the actual "negative effects" experienced by our user are very passive and subtle indeed—involving the development of *deficits in social and emotional coping skills* that are actually quite common in our culture. Hence, it would be very difficult at this stage for most users—or for those around them—to recognize the warning signs of these emerging deficits and see them as a potentially serious problem. Moreover, a pattern of slowly growing social and psychological dependence of this kind can take place quite comfortably within the commonly accepted boundaries of *"normal, social, or recreational use."*

When we look at harmful addiction as a bio-psycho-social-spiritual disorder, we can see how it often involves a number of significant psychological causes and a wide range of negative mental and emotional effects as well. In this book we will be focusing our attention on trying to understand the signs, symptoms, and stages of progression in harmful addiction as they occur when the addiction manifests itself as a free-standing "primary diagnosis." It would be appropriate at this point, however, to say a few words about the phenomena of "dual-diagnosis." This is what we see when a harmful addiction develops—as a primary disorder in its own right—before, during, or after the development of a "co-existing psychiatric illness" or "mental disorder" that must also be understood and treated as a primary disorder in its own right.

Within the context of the disease model of harmful addiction, this means that the addiction is not merely a symptom of an underlying emotional disorder—and that the users level of emotional distress is not merely a consequence of the harmful addiction. A genuine "dual-diagnosis" exists when both types of disorders are present concurrently and independently—even though the disorders will often interact over time and mutually impact on the severity of each other.

There are three critical clinical implications that we must always bear in mind when the possibility of an emerging "dual-diagnosis" situation exists:

**First,** our potential early stage user may be doing much more at this stage than merely developing a maladaptive social, emotional, or physical "crutch" that might be a sign or symptom of a possible addiction problem. They may also be "self-medicating" the early signs of a genuine psychiatric or mental disorder—in lieu of seeking professional help, accurate diagnosis, and appropriate psychotherapeutic or psychopharmacological treatment.

**Second,** even with appropriate diagnosis and treatment for a co-existing psychiatric or mental disorder, our potential early stage user may still be in the process of developing a harmful addiction. If a co-existing addiction problem is left undiagnosed or untreated, it will often radically interfere with or destroy the effectiveness of any mental health treatment efforts.

**Third,** if a co-existing psychiatric or mental disorder is left undiagnosed or untreated, the symptoms of emotional distress involved will often radically interfere with or destroy the effectiveness of any addiction treatment or self-help recovery efforts and thus contribute to a pattern of chronic relapse.

Returning now to our overview of the signs, symptoms, and stages of progression in harmful addiction—*we will work on the premise that no "dual-diagnosis" is involved as a complicating factor*. However, as clinicians we must always bear this possibility—even this likelihood—in mind when working with specific clients and develop the knowledge base and clinical skills needed to make an accurate differential diagnosis.

At this point, we will see that some users will begin to move past the generally accepted limits of "social use" and go on to the next level, which is "heavy use." They will:

- Begin to have episodes of "heavy use" beyond their tolerance—and end up getting drunk, high, or otherwise intoxicated. A2.
- Start to *plan* on having deliberate episodes of "heavy use" *in order* to get drunk, high, or otherwise intoxicated —because they enjoy the sensation.
- Begin *increasing the amount* of use on many occasions—without changing their overall frequency of use—thus deliberately get drunk, high, or otherwise intoxicated *more often* when they are using the substance or activity.
- Eventually find that *getting drunk, high, or otherwise intoxicated* has become their *primary purpose* in using the substance or activity and

that they are doing so on still *more or even most occasions* when they use.

In the case of alcohol, many of these "heavy drinkers," manage to "handle their liquor" very well, and very often they will experience little or no negative impact. Indeed, as Milam and Ketchum have observed:

> In the early hidden stage of alcoholism, the only visible difference between the alcoholic and the nonalcoholic is improved performance in the alcoholic when he drinks and a deterioration in performance when he stops drinking.

> (Milam & Ketchum, 1981: 57. Emphasis added.)

Why is that? It is simply because some users will now start to experience:

- A cellular adaptation in their body to the presence of their chosen addictive substance in the bloodstream—or to the biochemical effects of engaging in their chosen addictive activity.
- A gradual increase in their physical tolerance for the substance or activity as a result and the ability to use comfortably in greater amounts.
- Improved performance when using in moderation.
- A continuing increase in physical tolerance over time and—eventually—a need to use more greater amounts to achieve the desired effect. D1A.
- A diminished effect with continued use of the same amount due to this increasing tolerance for the substance or activity. D1b.

In response to this change in their tolerance, however, some users may:

- Find that they are not only using *more* of their chosen substance or activity in order to get drunk, high, or otherwise intoxicated, but that they are also using it *more often* than they had before. In assessment terminology, this means that the *"frequency"* and *"amount"* of their use are both increasing.
- Try to get "extra" drinks—or to use more of a substance or activity at a party or on other using occasions—because they feel they "do not get enough." AA 8.
- Begin "pre-drinking" or "post-drinking"—using *more* of the substance or activity *before* and/or *after* an occasion where it is used socially.
- Start to hear casual comments from others about the amount they use or jokes about the amount they can handle.

- Begin to make jokes about their own capacity to use in large amounts and perhaps even develop a positive social identity or a sense of pride about this.
- Start playing an unconscious *"game"* that allows this social *"role"* to serve as an acceptable *"excuse"* for their increased use.
- Begin to "show off" the amount they can handle and even "compete" with others who are so inclined.
- Start to realize that he or she is not a "normal" drinker or user and to recognize that they are using more than most other people—and certainly more than most normal, social, or recreational users. M1.
- Begin to feel self-conscious or embarrassed when people notice or make comments or jokes about the amount they use.
- Start sneaking drinks or using surreptitiously.

At this point, our user has moved beyond the realm of normal, social drinking—and they have also gone past the boundaries of merely "heavy use." Our user has now reached the level of "excessive" or "problem use."
Why?

> Because a person with *no* problem would have *no* reason to feel embarrassed.

Our normal, social user—or heavy user—has now become a problem user—and this would be true even if embarrassment is the only subjective problem that they have experienced up to this point. Let me re-emphasize the point that

> a person with *no* problem whatsoever will have *no* reason to feel embarrassed or to hide any aspect of their behavior.

Minimization, rationalization, self-deception, and denial are an insidious poison that are central to the whole process of developing a harmful addiction. Therefore, as an antidote to this subtle poison, we as clinicians need to remember and clearly communicate to our clients that even the mildly negative emotional reactions that a user starts to experience at this early stage are

> *not normal*—except, of course, for problem users.

At this crucial point, a person who is not a potential alcoholic, addict, or harmful compulsive-addictive user would start to change their behavior and they would certainly not feel any need to *defend it, excuse it, continue it,* or *cover it up.*

In many cases, however, feeling some mild embarrassment and self-consciousness is just the beginning of a long, sad, and painful experience with the negative consequences of harmful addiction. For those who continue on this path, it gets much, much worse. For example, on the morning after heavy drinking—or some other form of drug use—some users will now start to experience occasional:

- Hangovers,
- Headaches,
- Dry Mouth,
- Nausea, or
- Vomiting.

Some users who continue down this path—*if this hasn't already happened long before*—may now start to:

- Hear comments from their friends or relatives indicating that they think he or she is not a "normal" drinker or user—meaning that they use "more than most other people." M6.
- Do things that are foolish or belligerent while drunk or under the influence. H4.
- Behave in ways that violate his or her own value system while drunk or under the influence. H4.
- Embarrass, hurt, confuse, intimidate, or anger family, friends, co-workers, or strangers by their behavior while under the influence. H4.
- Create tension, conflict, and personal problems between themselves and their spouse or primary partner, or parents, or other family members. M11–AA 7.
- Hear complaints and expressions of concern, worry, or anger over their behavior from their spouse or primary partner, family, friends, co-workers, or others. M3.
- Feel genuine emotional pain such as embarrassment, guilt, shame, or remorse about their drinking or other drug use and their "bad behavior" while under the influence. M5–CG

Please recall that a person only has to meet one of the DSM-IV-TR criteria for substance abuse in order to qualify for that diagnosis. By my own personal standards, someone who has progressed to this point with their use of mood altering substances would qualify for a diagnosis as a substance abuser. This is because using any psychoactive substance to the point of intoxication, in my view, is potentially dangerous and would therefore qualify as substance abuse by the criteria of "recurrent use in situations where it is hazardous to use."

Many people in our culture, however, or perhaps even most people—including many or perhaps even most clinicians—might tend to trivialize and minimize this danger. They would probably evaluate the level of use here as "problem use" that does not yet meet the criteria for "abuse." This is because there seems to be a general consensus in our culture that "merely" getting intoxicated is not really dangerous or irresponsible—as long as you are "careful."

I would challenge this minimization, however, by recalling the potentially fatal danger involved in "walking while intoxicated" as demonstrated by the case of a famous actor, already discussed, where merely trying to walk across his own living room when drunk proved to be a "hazardous situation." (In fact, it turned out to be a deadly situation when he stumbled, cracked his head against the sharp edge of a coffee table, and bled to death).

In many cases, of course, a person who already "does things that are foolish or belligerent while drunk or under the influence" and "behaves in ways that violate his or her own value system" would probably be drinking and driving by this point anyway. That would make this whole discussion a moot point because driving under the influence is so clearly hazardous. But, let's say that our hypothetical user has very high standards and remarkably strong values on this issue and hasn't gone there—yet.

Please remember that:

> One of the hallmarks of "abuse" is *continued use* despite the existence of significant problems or negative consequences associated with using.

So, our "problem user" will not have to go much further down this path in order to qualify as a diagnosable substance abuser. Please recall that in most cases a person who is not a potential alcoholic, addict, or a compulsive-addictive user would have already started to change their behavior well before they ever reached this point. They would not have tried to defend it, excuse it, continue it, or cover it up. Moreover, they would also have found—long before now in most cases—that they were able change their problem behavior successfully, easily, and permanently.

So, our user now stands at another crucial moment of truth. If he or she now finds—for whatever "reason"—that they cannot or will not make needed changes, this may be because they are starting to experience:

> An internalized *compulsion*—or irresistible impulse—to continue irrational behavior that is creating negative consequences for themselves and others.

If so, our user may not be *able* to change their problem behavior, even if they really wanted to. Indeed, if their compulsion to continue using at this stage is deeply ingrained and powerful enough it will often be so subtle that they will not even want to resist it. At this point, in their mind, the perceived benefits of continued use will usually far outweigh the perceived costs. Indeed, it may not even occur to them to resist their impulses to use because they are still enjoying themselves and will often have *absolutely no desire to change.*

Therefore, our truly devoted "problem user" who continues to use at this stage will clearly "cross the line" and qualify as a bona fide "substance abuser" if they now:

- Continue using to a level of intoxication despite ongoing social or interpersonal problems that are likely to have been caused or made worse by use. A4.
- Continue their pattern of excessive use in ways that violate their own values; embarrass, hurt, or anger others; and provoke further expressions of concern, worry, or anger from others.
- Compromise their own value system when not using in order to accommodate, rationalize, and justify their behavior to themselves and others
- Angrily deny drinking or using too much when challenged.
- Try to avoid any conversational references to alcohol or drug problems.
- Feel annoyed should anyone criticize their drinking or drug taking, and wish that people would mind their own business and stop telling them what to do. CA–AA 2.
- Continue drinking or using to a level of intoxication despite the danger of serious physical injury or death due to overdose, accidents, fights, or assaults. A2.
- Start to drive while intoxicated or under the influence—risking serious injury or death for themselves or others and/or arrest and criminal charges. A2.
- Risk assault, robbery, injury, or death by going into dangerous situations or high-crime areas to obtain or use illegal substances. A2.
- Get into one or more physical fights when drinking or using—with a family member, friend, co-worker, or stranger. M10.
- Start to prefer the company of fellow drinkers or other users and to spend time bars, taverns, or other locations centered on using.

- Begin to lose interest in non-drinking or using activities and companions, and start to reduce or give up important personal, family, social, recreational, or work activities in order to use. D6.
- Make frequent conversational references to drinking, drunkenness, using, or getting high.
- Have accidents or injuries while under the influence. A2.
- Get arrested for drunk driving, driving while intoxicated, or driving under the influence. M24.
- Get arrested—or taken into custody without formally being charged—for public intoxication, disorderly conduct, domestic disturbance, fighting or assault, or because of other behavior while drunk or under the influence. M25.
- Get arrested—or taken into custody without formally being charged—for illegal possession or use, for dealing in illegal substances, or on other drug-related charges.
- Get arrested for a second or third time on some alcohol or drug-related charge—or for illegal behavior while under the influence—and continue using despite this recurrence of substance-related legal problems. A3.

At this point, our user definitely qualifies for a diagnosis of substance abuse and he or she has now started to meet some of the criteria for substance dependence as well. He or she has satisfied three of the four criteria for abuse and only one is needed for the diagnosis. Our user has also met two of the seven criteria for dependence, and only three are needed for the diagnosis.

The user who has reached this stage is now demonstrating some real resistance to change by angrily defending their "right" to keep on using exactly as they have before. Most of them would "love" to be able to continue using their preferred addictive substance or activity with complete impunity while making no changes whatsoever and experiencing no further negative consequences of any kind. However, most normal people—with even average reality testing abilities—would probably be wise enough to recognize the irrationality or stupidity of thinking that this could ever actually work.

Most users at this stage, will not have the motivational intensity or the irrational compulsivity required to try to prove an impossible proposition—that they can get somehow magically do whatever they want—whenever they want to—and never have to pay *any* price for it.

Rather, most users at this level will soon understand and accept their need to try to exercise some kind of self-restraint and control over their use. Thus, they will be able to leave the first stage on the Addiction Recovery Learning

Curve—which involves Uncontrolled Use with Consequences—and move on without too much fuss to enter the second stage—which is focused on Attempted Common Sense Control.

Thus far, in this particular hypothetical sequence of signs and symptoms, we have been talking about a pattern of substance abuse flowing from deliberate, conscious, and willful "choices" being made by the user regarding the frequency and amount of use. Any compulsion to continue using that may have been involved up to this point has been operating on an unconscious level. There have not as yet been any conscious desires manifested nor any attempts made to change any behavior—which, of course, would have occurred long before this point in many actual cases.

Thus far, moreover, we have seen "heavy users" who embark on using with a deliberate plan and intention to use excessively *in order* to get drunk, high, or otherwise intoxicated—because they enjoy the sensation. We have seen that for some users this has become their primary purpose in using the addictive substance or behavior on more and more occasions and that some will eventually find themselves using both in greater amounts and with greater frequency as time goes by. Up to this point, however, all of the behavioral choices we have seen regarding the frequency, amount, and duration of use have been essentially voluntary.

Now, *if it hasn't already happened long before*—as it will have in many cases because these signs and symptoms emerge in a different sequence for many people—some users may start to experience isolated episodes of "loss of control" that involve:

- Using more than originally intended and sometimes getting drunk, high, or otherwise intoxicated when they had not planned to do so. D3.
- Using for a longer period of time than originally intended. D3.

There is a widely held negative stereotype about harmful addiction which seems to be based on the false impression that the term "loss of control" means that a drinker, drug user, or other user will be completely unable to stop using once they begin to use. Another common misconception about the term "loss of control" is the mistaken idea that this inability to stop using will inevitably occur every single time they start using. Therefore, many users who begin to experience "loss of control" on some occasions may foolishly conclude that:

"I can't possibly be an alcoholic or an addict because that doesn't happen to me."

There is a little three-letter word that is often useful to remember in such cases—"yet."

While an almost total lack of control of this kind described above may often develop by the late middle stage of progression into harmful addiction, it normally takes quite a long time for it to emerge. The phenomena of "loss of control" usually starts to emerge in the early stage of progression with some isolated episodes of using more than intended. Thus, what really happens in most cases is a partial or gradual loss of control.

Initially, episodes of loss of control might take place very rarely when a person uses—in some cases perhaps as few as one time out of a hundred. In many cases, it might then take a long time before the frequency rate for episodic loss of control gets up to one time out of ten. Even a late stage, chronic, skid-row type of alcoholic might have some isolated episodes of drinking in moderation—perhaps even as often as one time out of ten— which, by the rather twisted "logic" of harmful addiction, might lead them to conclude

> "I can't possibly be an alcoholic, because I don't lose control every time I drink!"

I remember a great cartoon showing a group of angels sitting together on some clouds up in Heaven. They were all wearing white robes with halos and wings, of course, but one of them—who was standing up and speaking to the others—was also wearing an old-fashioned leather pilot's helmet and goggles. Pointing one finger up into the air, he proudly exclaims:

> "I flew for *ten* years and I only had *one* accident!"

If you were driving a car at a high speed would you settle for being "in control" of your vehicle 90 per cent of the time? How about 99 per cent control? That sounds pretty good, doesn't it? Sure it does—if you have a death wish.

The fact is that

- *any* loss of control,
- at *any* time,
- for *any* reason

can be fatal when driving a car at a high speed—and it can be just as deadly when it involves getting buzzed, drunk, high, stoned, wasted, or intoxicated in any way regardless of whether or not the user ever gets into a moving vehicle.

Although they are actually placing themselves at just as much risk when they get intoxicated on purpose, it's somehow more frightening for most users when this is something that seems to start happening *to* them "by mistake."

So, at this point—*if it hasn't already happened long before*—many users will start to:

- Feel a need to cut down or control their drinking or drug use. CC.
- Develop a persistent desire to control or stop their use. D4.
- Make self-imposed rules to control their drinking or use.
- Make sincere promises to family and friends to follow these rules.
- Set limits on the amount they will allow themselves to drink or use.
- Set limits on the frequency of their drinking or use.
- Switch from one kind of drink or drug to another in the hope that this will keep them from losing control and using too much. AA 3.
- Change their usual patterns and try to limit their drinking or using to certain times of the day, or certain days of the week. M7.
- Change their patterns to limit their drinking or using or to certain places or to avoid certain people or places.

At this point. our user has clearly reached the most serious "level of use" and he or she now qualifies for the diagnosis of substance dependence. He or she has met two more of the criteria for dependence, and this now makes four out of seven, with only three being needed to make the diagnosis.

By this point, our user has also started to recognize that the costs of continued uncontrolled use now outweigh the perceived benefits and they can no longer *consciously* defend it or excuse it—not even to themselves—much less to others. As already noted, a person who is not a potential alcoholic, addict, or compulsive-addictive user would have successfully changed their behavior long before reaching this point—and would not have even tried to defend it, excuse it, or cover it up.

At this stage, he or she recognizes very clearly that something is wrong and they sincerely want to change their behavior by cutting down and controlling their use in order to avoid any further negative consequences.

Now, our user comes to another critical moment of truth and a crucial question:

### Can I do it?

It bears repeating here that for most people—even for many of those who have progressed this far into the early warning stage of harmful addiction—this will be *no problem.*

So, there should be no further problem for our user—right? He or she has finally made a "firm decision." They have "made up their mind," and now they "really mean it."

Our user has finally "seen the light" and they have now very sincerely

- set some real limits,
- made some real rules, and
- made some real promises.

So common sense and sound logic suggests that they *should* be able to control or completely stop their use—successfully, easily, and permanently. Right? Of course they can! Unless they are slipping even further into the grip of:

An internalized *compulsion*—or irresistible impulse—to continue irrational behavior that is creating negative consequences for themselves and others.

If this particular phrase looks and sounds rather familiar that's because you have already seen it here before—several times. Please understand that I'm not actually trying to bore you by repetition. I just want to make sure that you really remember the single most essential factor that can help our clients understand and recognize their own *harmful compulsive-addictive behavior.*

So, what happens next on the slow downward spiral into harmful addiction? At this point, in many cases, our user will:

- Start to regularly break his or her own self-imposed rules governing use. H2.
- Not always be able to stop drinking or using when they want to. M8.
- Feel guilty about their drinking or using. CG
- Find that they often cannot stop drinking or using without a struggle after having starting out with one or two drinks or drug uses. M4.
- Sometimes decide to stop drinking or using for a week or so, only to find that they can only abstain completely for a couple of days at most. AA 1.

At this point, we may begin to see that our user:

- Has failed in their attempts to control or stop their use despite their persistent desire to do so. D4.
- Can no longer consistently or safely predict the outcome once use begins. H3.
- Is deeply ambivalent and has mixed feelings and mixed motives about actually cutting down or controlling their use one hundred percent of the time.
- Continues to drink or use to the point of intoxication—sometimes deliberately and sometimes unintentionally. D4.

- Often tells him or herself that they can stop drinking or using any time they want to—even though they keep getting drunk or high when they don't mean to. AA 9.
- May become increasingly uncomfortable in non-using situations.
- Drinks or uses for emotional relief or escape with increasing frequency.
- Starts to tell more and more lies about the frequency and amount of use.
- Begins to lead a "double-life" of secrecy and deception.
- Continues to experience increasing tolerance.
- Sees that their pattern of excessive use is gradually escalating in the frequency, duration, and amount of use.
- Finds that the frequency and intensity of the hangovers, headaches, and other types of physical pain or discomfort that they feel on the morning after heavy drinking or other drug use are gradually increasing.
- Begins to experience an urgent sense of "need" for their first drink or use.
- May begin to drink or use earlier in the day or in the morning.
- Sometimes awakens after drinking the night before and cannot remember part of the evening due to an alcohol-induced "blackout"— not because they "forgot," but because their brain wasn't storing any memory of the events as they occurred due to the harmful neurological impact of alcohol—even though they were awake, aware, and functioning at the time. M2–AA 11.
- Sometimes envies people who can drink or use without getting into trouble. AA 5.
- Sometimes feels that his or her life would be better if they stopped drinking or using completely. AA 12.

When discussing the typical stages of progression into harmful addiction, it is often stressed in addiction treatment and recovery circles that in many cases:

"Work is the last thing to go."

This thought reminds me of another one of those Key West tee-shirts:

"I've used up all of my sick days—I think I'll call in dead."

Thus far—no matter how bad it may already seem to be—we have still been describing the pattern of a so-called "functioning" alcoholic or addict. Obviously, some people who reach this stage in the progression into harmful addiction may already be unemployed or unemployable —or they may be otherwise dysfunctional or impaired for any number of reasons. In general terms, however, most of the people who have reached this stage are "still holding a job" successfully—or they are otherwise successfully fulfilling their major role obligations at home, or school, or in the community.

In many cases—even at this stage of clear dependence and harmful use—there may still be little or no negative impact spilling over into these various functional areas. However, this immunity doesn't last forever and—*if it hasn't already happened long before*—as it certainly will in many cases—we may see that our user now:

- Starts failing to fulfill major role obligations at home, work, or school, and experiences even more negative consequences with family and friends associated with ongoing episodes or periods of excessive use. A1–AA 6.

At work or school, for the user who has reached this stage, we may now start to see:

- Poor concentration, focus, motivation, energy, and effort at certain times.
- Occasional inattention and poor judgment.
- Inefficiency. Mistakes. Missed deadlines. Poor work quality.
- Occasional lateness for work or school.
- Returning to work or school late from breaks or meals.
- Leaving work or school early.
- Occasional absences due to drinking or using. AA 10.
- Getting medical excuses for absences for a variety of reasons.
- Fellow workers or other students starting to complain.
- Some tension with co-workers, subordinates, or supervisors, other students, or teachers.
- Some complaints or warnings from employers, supervisors, or teachers.
- Overreacting to real or imagined criticism.
- Feeling defensive, fearful, and resentful.
- Making excuses and alibis for lateness, absences, poor performance, and strained relationships at work or school.
- Getting into "trouble" at work or school. M14.
- Suspensions or expulsions from school.
- Quitting or getting fired from jobs.

I remember another great cartoon that was published at a time when thousands of people were turning out to attend self-help conventions for "Adult Children of Alcoholics." It showed a huge auditorium with a large banner hung across the stage that read *"Adult Children of Normal Families"* and a speaker at the podium on the stage addressing a group of about a half dozen people—scattered amid hundreds of empty seats.

While "normality" is often a subjective notion that can be quite hard to define in any family, it's an even more elusive quality within the primary family system of compulsive-addictive users who have reached this point in the progression of a harmful addiction.

In the early stage alcoholic or addicted family system, we may often begin to see an escalating array of problems that can include:

- Embarrassment, shame, and confusion.
- Complaints, warnings, and threats.
- Getting home late and spending more time away from home.
- Emotional walls and distancing.
- Decreased communication.
- Broken promises and repeated disappointments.
- Lies, disgust, compromises, and guilt.
- Jealousy, suspicion, and distrust.
- Irritability, confrontation, and arguments.

The bottom line here adds up to increasingly strained relationships that will often drive some of our user's addictive behavior "underground." Therefore, we may now start to see that

- Complaints and anger expressed by family and friends are escalating because of broken promises, continued excessive use, and the user's obnoxious, embarrassing, hurtful, or detestable behavior while under the influence. A4–AA 6.
- The user starts hiding or sneaking their use, using surreptitiously, and/or hiding and protecting their supply—no longer just to save face or avoid their embarrassment over using excessively—but to avoid active complaints and open conflict with concerned or angry family or friends.

Mentally and emotionally, users who reach this stage may often respond to their own baffling lack of control—and to the mounting array of problems in their lives –with painful feelings of:

101

- Embarrassment.
- Guilt, shame, and remorse.
- Confusion, fear, and anxiety.
- Sadness and depression.
- Anger and resentment.

*If it hasn't already started long before,* this is where we will often see that our user:

- Starts to minimize and rationalize their use—to themselves and other—in order to block their conscious awareness of all these painful negative feelings. H6.
- Makes up plausible excuses and alibis for their use. H6.
- Starts projecting their own negative feelings onto others and blaming others for their problems. H6.
- Experiences a loss of conscious insight that becomes a growing delusion. H7.
- Is unable to resolve their hidden negative feelings—often because they can't even identify them. H8.
- Therefore, starts to feel a growing sense of chronic emotional pain and distress. H9.
- Experiences flashes of aggressiveness and grandiose behavior.
- Starts to seriously harm their own health, emotional stability, roles, and relationships. H10.
- Continues to seek euphoria through drinking or using in order to relieve the mounting emotional pain that is actually being caused or greatly exacerbated by their problem use. H12.
- Begins to realize consciously—at times—that their own mental and emotional distress is often caused or made much worse by their drinking or using. D7.
- Makes repeated, increasingly desperate, and ultimately futile attempts to cut down or control their use in order to continuing enjoying the perceived benefits of use and eliminate all of the negative consequences involved.
- Experiences more frequent and severe loss of control and mounting negative consequences.
- Starts to develop a deeply ingrained and rigid set of irrational beliefs and distorted thinking patterns about drinking or using that are

marked by self-deception and denial in order to sustain the alibis and excuses that allow his or her use to continue unabated.

- Experiences "Euphoric Recall" and can only seem to remember the pleasurable aspects of drinking or using—not the pain and suffering it causes.

The person who has reached this point in the early stage of progression into harmful addiction has now gone far past the bounds of normal, social, recreational use. They have also pushed far beyond the usually understood limits that identify "heavy use" or "problem use." Our user, in fact, now meets the DSM-IV-TR diagnostic criteria for both abuse and the more serious problem of dependence. In popular terms, although they would almost certainly reject the label in most cases, they now satisfy the generally accepted informal standards that would clearly and indisputably identify them as an *early stage alcoholic, addict, or compulsive-addictive user.*

In their book *Cognitive Therapy of Substance Abuse,* Aaron Beck, Fred Wright, Cory Newman, and Bruce Liese go beyond the initial list of "predispositional characteristics" that we've already examined to identify a snowballing sequence of internal and external factors that contribute to what they call *the phenomena of addiction.*

I've put together a summary of these factors just below and I've arranged them —for greater clarity—in the order in which they would tend to occur within a particular individual. (The relevant page numbers from Beck et al., 1993, are cited in parentheses).

I believe that this summary offers a useful perspective on the inner dynamics of harmful compulsive-addictive behavior and a valuable model for helping us understand how many diverse variables often come together to determine the self-defeating and ultimately self-destructive behavior of our early stage user:

### THE PHENOMENA OF ADDICTION

#### Predispositional Characteristics. (39)

Over-sensitivity to unpleasant emotions and normal mood swings.

Deficient motivation to control behavior and a desire for instant gratification.

Inadequate techniques for controlling behavior and coping with problems.

A pattern of *automatic* non-reflective yielding to impulses.

Excitement seeking and low tolerance for boredom.

Low frustration tolerance (LFT).

Diminished capacity to focus on the future consequences of present choices.

**Activating Stimulus.** (14)

Apparently irrelevant prior decisions. (14)

External cues, triggers, stimulus situations. (14)

Internal emotional states. (14)

Attachment of special symbolic meaning to activating stimulus. (50)

**First Conditioned Reflex.** (48)

Dysfunctional core beliefs, regarding: (43–44)

Personal abilities, strengths, and self-efficacy. (13)

Personal value, self-worth, and acceptability. (43–44)

Distorted and irrational automatic thoughts or "conditioned reflexes" (48)

Emotional discomfort and distress. (39)

Low frustration tolerance. (39)

**Second Conditioned Reflex.** (48)

Addictive beliefs and related irrational automatic thoughts. (38)

Anticipatory beliefs. (45)

Euphoric recall. (52)

Positive outcome expectancy for use. (13, 33)

Psychological dependency. (44)

Cravings, urges, and desire to use. (31)

Facilitating or permissive beliefs. (45)

Attributions of internal or external causality for behavior. (13)

**Attempted Exercise of Willpower and Positive Choice.** (35)

Personal motivation for change. (14)

Current stage of change. (15)

Internal capacity for self-control. (35)

Internal degree of commitment to change. (35)

Conflicting beliefs and desires. (46)

Ambivalence about continued use. (14)

Internal power of compulsion, cravings, or urges to use. (35)

**Decision Making Processes.** (14)

"Cognitive blockade" or "tunnel vision" reducing awareness of the potential negative consequences of use, positive coping options, or attractive alternatives to using. (51)

**Coping Response.** (12)

Use of cognitive-behavioral, relapse prevention, and recovery skills. (12)

Increased self-efficacy and positive feelings. (13)
  **Refusal Decision.** (35)
    **Reduced Probability of Relapse.** (13)
**No Coping Response.** (12)
  **Permission Giving Decision.** (12)
    Instrumental strategy for use. (47)
    Make plan to obtain and use drugs. (47)
    Implement of plan to obtain and use drugs. (47)
  **Lapse into Initial Substance Use.** (13)
    Temporary relief. (9)
    Negative internal or external consequences. (9)
  **Abstinence Violation Effect (AVE).** (12)
    Increased emotional distress. (12)
    Feelings of guilt and shame. (12)
    Addictive belief that further use is inevitable due to "loss of control." (12)
  **Increased Probability of Full-Blown Relapse.** (12)

Beck et al. also make the following crucial point about how our early stage user may be able to change their self-destructive behavior:

> The delay between the experience of craving and the implementation of the urge does provide an interval for . . . the technical application of control, or what is called in common parlance 'willpower," which we define as *an active process of applying self-help techniques,* not simply a passive enduring of discomfort.

> (Beck, et al, 1993: 32. Emphasis added.)

For our early stage alcoholic, addict, or compulsive-addictive user, of course, the "passive enduring of discomfort" is not really a viable option. People with poor impulse control, a propensity for low frustration tolerance, and a penchant for instant gratification will generally have little choice but to continue in their pattern of harmful addictive behavior—unless they can begin to *learn and use* some new and more effective social and emotional coping skills.

In many cases, however, even this will not be enough. Many of them will also have to find and devote themselves to at least one new, truly gratifying, and healthy *positive addiction.*

As they mature and grow older—and sometimes simply *because* they mature and grow older—many people who reach this stage of harmful addiction will manage somehow—with or without any professional help—to pick up some effective coping skills and make some real and healthy changes in their lives. Many of these people will then proceed no further into the progression of harmful addiction.

Sadly, however, it often seems that many other early stage users will manage to develop a set of *"coping skills"* that consist of little more than the ability to briefly grit their teeth and clench their fists when dealing with anything unpleasant. The coping theory here seems to be that there is no problem—big or small—that it can't be handled by a well-developed set of "white knuckles" and a stoic capacity to just *"grin and bear it."*

Sadly, this "grin, grit, grip, and bear it" approach to problem-solving doesn't actually work very well for most people.

In his book, *Emotional Intelligence,* Daniel Goleman explores the topic of "multiple intelligences" and explains the vital roles that must be played in emotionally healthy, well-adjusted people by *both* the rational and emotional aspects of our human intelligence. He reports:

> In a very real sense, we have two minds, one that thinks, and one that feels . . .
>
> These two fundamentally different ways of knowing interact to construct our mental life. One, the rational mind, is the mode of comprehension we are typically conscious of: more prominent in awareness, thoughtful, able to ponder and reflect. But alongside that there is another system of knowing: impulsive and powerful, if sometimes illogical—the emotional mind . . .
>
> In many or most moments these minds are exquisitely coordinated; feelings are essential to thought, thought to feeling. But when passions surge the balance tips: it is the emotional mind that captures the upper hand, swamping the rational mind. (8–9).

(Goleman, 1995: 8–9).

Goleman also points out how poor emotional coping skills can lead some people to use alcohol, drugs, or other compulsive or addictive behaviors as a dangerous and ineffective form of self-medication for their emotional over-reactivity. Sadly—if they don't really have any other "arrows in their quiver" or "coping tools in their kit"—many emotionally under-skilled users who have reached this point in the early stage of their progression into harmful addiction will often feel subjectively that they have virtually no viable options available except to continue acting out with their harmful compulsive-addictive behavior.

Of course, most people at this stage are still very far from seeing their self-defeating and harmful behavior clearly for what it actually is—no matter how clearly or how strongly this truth may be pointed out to them by family, friends, teachers, counselors, employers, the legal system, and a variety of medical, mental health, or addiction treatment professionals.

There's a traditional recovery slogan which reassures newly clean and sober alcoholics and addicts that:

> "We're not bad people trying to get good. We're just sick people trying to get well"

Without any doubt, most people who've reached this stage and continue to drink or use drugs or engage in other harmful addictive behaviors are good and decent people Unfortunately, some of them are about to pursue a well-traveled path—paved with good intentions mixed liberally with self-medication, self-deception, and poor coping skills—that will soon lead them to leave behind their novice status once and for all.

Sadly, some of our clients who continue unabated with their harmful addictive habits will soon graduate from the early stage of progression and move on into the next, deeper level of self-inflicted pain and trouble on the long slide down the left-hand side of that deadly "U-shaped Curve" that designates the typical *signs, symptoms, and stages of progression* into harmful addiction.

# CHAPTER 5

# Middle Stage Progression

"I live inside a bubble. That's inside a shell. That's inside a box. That's inside a cave. That's under the ocean. Where I am safe. From you. If you really loved me, you'd find me."

—Jules Pfeiffer.

## MIDDLE STAGE

### The "Crucial Phase"

Let's take a moment to consider the logic of the following exchange, which is taken from "The Little Prince" by Antoine de Saint-Exupéry:

"Why are you drinking," demanded the little prince.

"So that I may forget," replied the tippler.

"Forget what?" inquired the little prince, who was already sorry for him.

"Forget that I am ashamed," the tippler confessed, hanging his head.

"Ashamed of what?" insisted the little prince, who wanted to help him.

"Ashamed of drinking!" The tippler brought his speech to an end, and wrapped himself up in an impregnable silence."

There are many distinguishing features that might help us identify when a person has begun to cross the line into the middle stage of a harmful addiction, but a penchant for irrefutable logic is certainly not one of them. As our early stage user begins to move into this new territory, one of the first things that often *will* start to become evident, however, is that their life is becoming

- More and more *centered* around their addictive drinking or using.

He or she will also be very likely to have:

- More family, social, job, school, financial, or legal problems, and more accidents or injuries that harm their health, emotional stability, social roles, and relationships. HD 10. A1. A2. A3. A4. D5. D6.

Harmful addiction is not a static condition, however, and one key distinction that marks the emerging middle stage user is that their problem does not just "stand still." In most cases, therefore, our middle stage user will probably not just experience "more of the same." They have set foot onto a slippery downward slope, and over time they will usually begin to see their problems get progressively worse as they:

- Experience increasingly serious negative consequences and mounting emotional pain directly caused by or made worse by their use. U2. A4. D7.
- Begin to experience a serious deterioration in their overall quality of life. H 11.

Our user's increased tolerance—which is a classic warning sign that a full-blown physical addiction may eventually develop—will continue to grow during the early middle stage. And now—although *it may have already started to emerge much earlier in many cases*—we will see the second classic feature of physical addiction begin to emerge for many users. This distinguishing feature—that will often begin to emerge quite clearly as our user moves firmly into the middle stage—is the onset of:

- Physical Dependence and Withdrawal Symptoms. D2a.

For many people in our popular culture, this is the one true mark of a "real" addiction.

Our emerging middle stage user will often continue to experience many of the early physical signs of a potentially harmful addiction such as:

- Hangovers, headaches, dry mouth, nausea, and vomiting.

But now—in response to their use of a psychoactive substance in large amounts over a long period of time—our user's body and brain has slowly made a biochemical adaptation on a cellular level in order to function normally with a large amount of alcohol or other drug in their system. Therefore, according to

Milam and Ketchum, whenever the alcoholic or addict cuts down or stops using "the addicted cells will suddenly be thrown into a state of acute distress." This acute physical reaction takes place because by this point the user's cells "have become unable to function normally" without a sufficient amount of alcohol or other addictive drug being continually present in the their bloodstream. (Milam & Ketchum, 1981: 64).

With a strictly behavioral addiction—where no psychoactive substance has actually been ingested—the compulsive-addictive activity itself often produces an array of biochemical changes in the body—such as the classic "adrenaline rush." The acute discomfort that many users often feel when this kind of addictive behavior is cut down or stopped seems to closely mimic the experience of physical dependence and withdrawal.

At this point, our user is physically addicted and when their level of use is significantly reduced or stopped they will often experience the onset of an *acute withdrawal syndrome*.

This syndrome may include a number of distressing symptoms—which will often vary widely both in type and severity depending upon which substance has been used, in what amounts, over what period of time.

These uncomfortable withdrawal symptoms could include:

- Sweating or fever.
- Chills or cold sweats.
- Hand tremors or shakes.
- Muscle Aches.
- Dilated Pupils.
- Diarrhea.
- Elevated or reduced heartbeat and pulse.
- Higher or lower blood pressure.
- Increased or reduced appetite.
- Disturbed sleep patterns.
- Insomnia or excessive sleep.
- Vivid dreams or nightmares.
- Fatigue, weakness, or lethargy.
- Yawning and sleepiness.
- Impaired memory.
- Hyperactive central nervous system.
- Nervousness and psychomotor agitation.
- Sluggishness and psychomotor retardation.

- Anxiety and agitation.
- Tension, irritability, and short-temper.
- Moodiness and depression.
- Lacrimation.
- Rhinorrea.
- Piloerection.

I'm not a trained nurse or doctor, and my medical vocabulary is a little sketchy here and there. So, when I saw these last three symptoms listed in the DSM-IV-TR among the diagnostic criteria for symptoms of opioid withdrawal, my first reaction was to say: "What? You've gotta be kidding!" However, I didn't feel it would be very professional or appropriate for me to leave them out just because I had absolutely no idea what they were. So, I looked them up in a medical dictionary, and I'm happy to report in plain English that these three final physical withdrawal symptoms are:

- Crying,
- Runny nose, and
- Hair "standing on end."

Now that our middle stage user has finally developed a full-blown physical addiction—complete with the onset of painful withdrawal symptoms if he or she doesn't continue using up to a certain level—we will usually see them:

- Starting to feel strong cravings and an overwhelming desire to use their preferred addictive substance or activity.
- Drinking or using to relieve or avoid the onset of withdrawal symptoms. D2b.
- Drinking or using earlier in the day in order to maintain an adequate level of the addictive substance in their bloodstream and avoid going into withdrawal. D2b.
- Drinking or using first thing in the morning as an "eye-opener" to steady their nerves, to get rid of a hangover, or to relieve or avoid the onset of painful withdrawal symptoms. CE. AA -4.

So, our user's body and brain has now made a long-term adaptation on a cellular level to the presence of the addictive substance in the bloodstream and his or her cells "have become unable to function normally" without it. It usually takes quite a long time for this adaptation to occur, and in most cases it will also take a long time for these cells to return to normal functioning without the substance being present. As a result, even after the intense physical discomfort and emotional distress associated with an acute withdrawal syndrome is over—

and our user's bloodstream, body, and brain are finally "substance-free"—they are still very far from being "back to normal."

Many physically addicted people will still have to deal with a protracted withdrawal syndrome that can be very unpleasant and uncomfortable. This is a lesser-known but crucially important aspect of physical addiction that often thwarts the best intentions of people who finally decide that they want to stop using completely and permanently. Our user will often remain quite nervous, agitated, anxious, fearful, depressed, or sleepless long after the "acute distress" of their active withdrawal process has ended. In many cases, they will also have some trouble functioning at a normal level cognitively for quite awhile—which might involve difficulty concentrating, thinking clearly, or remembering things.

This *Post Acute Withdrawal Syndrome (PAWS)* can last for several months and some potentially disturbing symptoms might persist for up to a year or two or longer. There's a recovery slogan that describes this overall experience as feeling or being:

### MOCUS—Mentally Out of Focus.

One friend of mine who has been clean and sober for more than 25 years has claimed—only half-jokingly I'm convinced—that:

> "It took me two years to get my brains out of hock—and five years to get them unscrambled."

Most middle stage users, of course, will not have developed their capacity to practice patience, tolerate frustration, or delay gratification sufficiently to endure the discomfort of post acute withdrawal for very long—and this difficulty dealing with discomfort will usually lead to relapse in most cases—sometimes quickly—sometimes more slowly. Very often, this seems to be true even when the user has been educated on the topic and informed very clearly that these agitated and uncomfortable feelings are a normal part of getting clean and sober and will *not* last forever.

Another complicating factor to remember at this point, however, is the possibility that the newly sober user who remains agitated, depressed, or otherwise disturbed, may also be suffering from an undiagnosed or inadequately treated *co-existing psychiatric or mental disorder.*

It may often be premature and inappropriate—or even impossible—to make a definitive diagnosis of a co-existing mental health problem for many users who are still in the earliest stages of physical stabilization and emotional transition from active use into early sobriety. Very often, they are still on an emotional roller coaster—or they are still emotionally blunted—and in either case they usually have not developed any effective emotional coping skills to deal with everyday stresses without self-medicating. For many users at this frag-

113

ile, transitional stage, the subjective experience of getting "sober" is well described by the acronym:

### S.O.B.E.R.—Son of a Bleep! Everything's Real!

However—as we have already discussed—if there actually *is* an undiagnosed or inadequately treated emotional disorder present—then the genuine symptoms of emotional distress involved may undermine or destroy the effectiveness of any addiction treatment or self-help efforts and contribute to a pattern of chronic relapse. Therefore, a careful psychiatric evaluation may be essential in many cases where symptoms of anxiety, depression, mood swings, or other emotional problems persist at abnormal levels for more than a few weeks after abstinence has begun.

Many users with mild to moderate problems will be ready, willing, and able to make permanent healthy changes in their lives at this point if they receive the information and help they need. In many other cases, however, even the best substance abuse education and information—even when combined with appropriate psychotherapy and medication as needed—will accomplish very little or nothing in terms of positive behavior change.

Many middle stage users can be exposed to all of this "help" and still not develop the requisite skills or the needed motivation for change. So these middle stage compulsive-addictive users will keep on using and we will now start to see the emergence of many more signs and symptoms of harmful addiction, which may include the following:

- Increasing loss of control over the frequency and amount of use. A2. D3.
- Increasing unpredictability—as a result—regarding the occasions, duration, amount, and negative outcomes of use. D3.
- The emergence of truly "obsessive-compulsive use" involving extended "binges" and "benders." A2. D3.
- Life becomes more and more centered around drinking or using. A1. D3. D5.
- Much time is spent obtaining or arranging for use of the addictive substance or activity, using it, or recovering from the effects of use. D5.
- Increasing failure to fulfill major role obligations at work, school, or home due to harmful involvement with the addictive substance or activity. A1.
- Obligations to family, children, household, or work are neglected—sometimes for two or more days in a row—because of use. M16.

- Important social, occupational, or recreational activities are given up or reduced due to use. D6.
- Family and friends now complain even more intensely about drinking or use. A4.
- Job, family, and friends are eventually experienced and resented by the user as unpleasant "obstacles" to unfettered drinking or using. A1. A4. D3. D5. D6.

Within the middle stage alcoholic or addicted family system we may now begin to see the emergence of major disruptions. The overall family syndrome during this "crucial phase" may include many of the following features:

- Frequent neglect of household and family responsibilities.
- Stealing money or goods from the home or family members in order to use.
- More complaints, warnings. threats, and bargaining.
- Broken promises and resolutions. A4. D3. D4. D7.
- Creative coping tactics and perpetual compromises.
- Unconscious and dysfunctional "games" develop.
- Controlling behavior and evasiveness.
- Playing "hide and seek, " and "gotcha."
- "Search and destroy missions" looking for hidden stashes.
- Emotional affairs or sexual infidelity.
- Jealousy, suspicion, distrust, and rage.
- Anger, arguments, and fights.
- The evolution of a "closed" family system with rigid, impermeable boundaries; generally inhospitable to new ideas, people, or experiences; and often resistant to any form of outside observation or even visitation inside the home.
- Psychological enmeshment or fusion with weak, poorly defined, porous, or non-existent interpersonal boundaries and a lack of respect for the individual rights, autonomy, wishes, or interests of family members.
- Arbitrary, rigid, and irrational family rules and stereotyped family roles and expectations.
- Authoritarian or dictatorial domination and oppressive control by the user.
- Verbal or physical abusiveness and domestic violence.
- Child abuse or neglect.

- Sexual abuse.
- Emotional and behavioral problems emerge in the children.
- Interventions by police or social service agencies.
- Chronic worry and unhappiness.
- Feelings of guilt, shame, and inadequacy.
- Social withdrawal and isolation.
- A fantasy world of family secrets, lies, and distortions begins to develop.
- Putting up false fronts—looking good, sounding good, and covering up.
- Enabling behavior that allows use and resulting problems to continue and to get worse.
- Over-responsible caretaking behavior to protect or comfort the user.
- Providing material resources and support for the user.
- Trying to help the user stay out of "trouble."
- Making excuses and alibis for the user to employers and others.
- Protecting the user from the negative consequences of their own behavior.
- Rescuing and "bailing out" behavior when the user gets in trouble.
- Increasing denial, delusion, and blindness.
- Avoidance of family problems, personal issues, and potential conflicts.
- Avoidance of genuine communication, confrontation, or concern.
- The "elephant in the living room" syndrome.
- Sweeping problems "under the rug."
- Walking on "eggshells."
- Dysfunctional family values reign—"Don't talk. Don't trust. Don't feel."
- Apathy, fatigue, depression, and repressed or sullen rage toward the user.
- Growing indifference and a loss of respect, love, or affection for the user.
- Gradual loss of interest and concern.
- Loss of self-respect and growing self-neglect.
- Living from crisis to crisis with multiple and multiplying problems.
- Serious financial problems.
- Escalating problems and increasing chaos.

- A sense of impending insanity and doom.
- Chronic anxiety and fear.
- Seeking escape and relief.
- Irrational acting out behavior.
- Seeking answers and outside help.
- Emotional roller coaster—Major ups and downs.
- Dashed hopes and disappointment.
- A continual merry-go-round of hopelessness.
- Emotional numbness, refusing help, and giving up.
- Chronic dishonesty and lies.
- Sadness, remorse, regret, and loss.
- Emotional detachment, better boundaries, and limit setting.
- Separate lives, actual separation, or divorce.

In many ways, the emotional pain of harmful addiction may often be felt much more intensely by the family or loved ones of the user because they are going through all this chaos sober and they are usually not self-medicating themselves or numbing their feelings with alcohol or drugs. In many ways, the family or loved ones of a user may often be more seriously disturbed emotionally than the user—who could conceivably argue: "I act crazy because I'm drunk, high, or stoned half the time—what's your excuse?"

Al-Anon emerged as an offshoot of AA in the 1950s and soon became solidly established as a separate self-help program for the families of active or recovering alcoholics. Since an alcoholic or addict can be described as being "dependent" on alcohol or drugs, it eventually became fashionable in addiction treatment to label their primary partner or spouse as "the co-dependent." This phrase gradually mutated and evolved over the years into the term "codependency." The underlying concept also broadened in scope over the years—much as the generic concept of "addiction" also broadened in our culture. In her book, *Codependent No More,* Melody Beattie defined a "codependent" (which is significantly missing the old hyphen) as

> "a person who has let someone else's behavior affect him or her
> and is obsessed with controlling other people's behavior."

Another classic definition of the term tells us that:

> "A codependent is someone who has *someone else's life* flash
> before their eyes when they are about to die."

Eventually—in popular culture and in some clinical circles—the whole syndrome came to be seen as just another form of harmful addiction in its own right—sometimes referred to as "relationship addiction"—encompassing almost any self-defeating or self-destructive enmeshment in a *dysfunctional primary relationship.*

In the area of work and career, we will also see the development of some very serious negative consequences for the alcoholic, addict, or compulsive-addictive user as they move into the middle stage of a harmful addiction. These problems can include:

- Attempting to function at work while under the influence, hung-over, or going into withdrawal.
- Mental fogginess and decreased problem-solving ability.
- Decreasing enthusiasm or motivation for goal-directed activities.
- Growing passivity and apathy.
- Inattention and lack of concentration at work.
- Frequently poor work quality.
- Repeated minor injuries on and off the job.
- Increasingly frequent lateness for work due to the effects or after-effects of use.
- Frequent days off for vague ailments or implausible reasons.
- Statements at work become undependable.
- Exaggerating work accomplishments.
- Unreasonable resentments toward fellow workers.
- Beginning to avoid coworkers.

In the late middle stage at work, we will often see:

- Job performance far below expected levels.
- Apparent loss of ethical values.
- Frequent time off—sometimes for several days in a row.
- Failure to return to work after lunch or other breaks.
- Grandiose, aggressive, or belligerent behavior.
- Domestic problems interfere with work.
- Complaints or disciplinary actions by employer for using before or during work.
- Employer mandated addiction treatment episodes.
- Job losses due to poor job performance or increasing interpersonal difficulties.

- Frequent job changes.
- Serious financial difficulties.
- Borrowing money from coworkers and others.
- Theft or embezzlement from work to support the costs of addiction.

In the middle stage of a harmful addiction we will also start to see the development of medical problems and observe the first signs that drinking or using is beginning to have some serious negative effects on the physical health and wellness of the alcoholic, addict, or compulsive-addictive user. Hence, this is where we may see:

- Beginning of organ changes, physical damage, medical problems. D7.
- Decreased sexual drive and performance.
- Neglect of nutrition and gradual physical deterioration. D7.
- Hospitalization because of problems related to drinking or using. M21.
- Major accidents and serious physical injuries. A2. D7.
- Deaths by suicide, homicide, accident, or overdose. A2. A3. D2a. D3. D7.

Mentally and emotionally, middle stage compulsive-addictive users will often respond to their own growing lack of control—and to the mounting array of serious problems in their lives—with increasingly intense negative feelings such as:

- Escalating embarrassment.
- Greater guilt, shame, and remorse.
- Plunging self-esteem and deep feelings of inadequacy and inferiority.
- Mounting confusion, fear, insecurity, and anxiety.
- Deeper sadness, depression, or anger.

As our user progresses through the middle stage of harmful addiction, we will often see that the harmful biochemical and physical impact of alcohol or other drugs on the users mind and body is slowly getting worse. The resulting social and family problems and other negative consequences he or she experiences are often becoming even more severe. And the users increasing lack of control frequently becomes even more baffling and frightening for them, In response to all this, we will often see some very serious psychological problems begin to emerge, such as:

- Cognitive impairment and difficulty thinking clearly or remembering things.
- Irrational attitudes and beliefs and distorted thought processes. A4. D7.
- Mood swings and personality changes when using. D7.

- Mood and behavior changes when abstaining.
- Emotional augmentation and personality distortions. D7.
- Grandiose, aggressive, or violent behavior. A2. A3. A4. D7.
- Loss of self-respect and growing self-disgust.
- Self-blaming, self-loathing, and self-hatred.
- Indefinable fears and unreasonable resentments.
- Hopelessness, mental anguish, and despair. D7.

All of this taken together would be more than enough for most "normal" people to "connect the dots" and conclude that it's time to make a commitment to total abstinence. By this point, any "heavy user" or "problem user" would probably have "seen the light" and decided that they need to stop using their preferred substance or activity completely and permanently. Except for one little thing.

> Their problem would never have been allowed to progress to this point because they would have been able to successfully control or limit their use or to stop using completely. They would have been able to either completely eliminate all negative consequences related to their continued use or to successfully contain them at a stable and socially acceptable level.

That—by popular definition—is what makes them a "problem user"—and not an "alcoholic" or an "addict."

What about the user whose problem *has* progressed to this point?

Objectively speaking—and using these informal descriptive terms in the kindest and most compassionate way—I think it would be more than fair to say that they apply:

**This person is clearly an "alcoholic" or an "addict."**

**The shoe fits.**

We are now looking at a compulsive-addictive user who clearly meets all four of the diagnostic criteria for substance abuse and all seven of the diagnostic criteria for substance dependence. Of course, many people who reach this point will be able to recognize, understand, and admit the true nature of their problem. And many of them will be ready, willing, and able to do whatever it takes to stop and to change direction. And yet, mysteriously, many other people who have reached this same point in the progression of a harmful addiction will still not self-identify as an alcoholic or an addict.

Amazingly, even if a skilled clinician were to walk them through this entire list of signs and symptoms point by point—and even if the user had personally provided all of this clinical information in an open, honest manner—they still might not really "get it." Many users who have reached this point are simply not ready, willing, or able to recognize and admit the clear implication of facts drawn directly from their own experience—even when the serious nature of their problem is painfully obvious to an objective clinician and to many of those around them.

A remarkable distinguishing feature of the middle stage compulsive-addictive user who has reached this point—and who is destined to continue further—is that they are still firmly entrenched in the Attempted Common Sense Control Stage on the *Addiction Recovery Learning Curve* (see Chapter 8 for details). They will rarely self-identify as an "alcoholic" or "addict"—or have any accurate understanding of what those terms actually mean—and, most baffling of all to the outside observer, they will still have *virtually no desire to stop.*

In their book *Under the Influence,* James Milam and Katherine Ketchum make two observations that tell us a great deal about the mindset of the middle stage alcoholic, addict, or compulsive-addictive user:

> . . . most alcoholics will make a superhuman effort to *control their drinking* if a return to drinking out of control means jail, mandatory treatment, divorce, or loss of a job. In addition to keeping his marriage, career, and social status intact, however, the alcoholic's most important priority is protecting his *continued freedom to drink . . .*
>
> For the first time, he may realize that he is in *deep trouble* with alcohol. Despite his increasing problems, however, the middle-stage alcoholic rarely considers giving up drinking; he may believe a psychiatrist can help him sort out his 'underlying psychological problems,' but he *cannot believe* that drinking is responsible for those problems.
>
> (Milam & Ketchum, 1981: 103, 109. Emphasis added.)

Why not? This makes no sense. There are a number of recovery slogans that offer a useful perspective on some of the irrational attitudes, addictive beliefs and distorted thinking patterns that are at play here:

"Addiction is a disease of the attitudes."

"We're all here because we're not all there."

"My own best thinking got me here."

"The problem with alcoholism is 90 percent thinking and only 10 percent drinking."

"That's stinking thinking."

"When you take the alcohol out of alcoholism, you still have the 'ism.'"

"That's the disease talking."

"I have a disease that talks to me in my own voice."

"Half of my brain manufactures this *bull*, and the other half *believes* it!"

Some clinicians feel very comfortable using slogans such as "AA Stands for Attitude Adjustment" in their clinical work—because they feel that some of these deeply insightful "catch phrases" will often resonate with their clients more easily—and will therefore mean much more to them—than some of our own clinical jargon. Other clinicians may feel much more comfortable with these pithy aphorisms when it's pointed out that the recoverly slogans and the clinical jargon often mean *virtually the same thing.*

In his chapter entitled "Working with the Preferred Defense Structure of the Recovering Alcoholic" in the book *Practical Approaches to Alcoholism Psychotherapy,* John Wallace observes that "it often seems to be the case that alcoholics are influenced more by the emotional persuasive appeal than the 'rational.' Leadership styles that are likely to work with the alcoholic are often charismatic, inspirational, and spiritual." Thus, while noting that alcoholics are perfectly capable of "logical-analytical" thought, Wallace concludes that "in terms of preference . . . the alcoholic is more drawn to the warmth of magic rather than the cold objectivity of science." (Wallace, 1985: 31)

Hence, it may be good for all of us—clients as well as clinicians—to get on the same page and understand that there is no meaningful difference between the actual change process involved whether we choose to call it an "attitude adjustment" or "cognitive restructuring." It may often be very worthwhile, in fact, for us to help our clients grasp the core concept of "stinking thinking" *before* we try to break that concept down into its two constituent parts and reframe it for them as:

**"irrational beliefs"** and **"distorted thinking patterns."**

In fact, both of these educational steps and communication styles—the informal as well as the formal—may be essential if we want to help our clients really understand what's actually fueling their addictive behavior from the inside out. Both approaches may also be needed, in very practical terms, if we want to help them get a real handle on how to develop more effective coping skills and begin to make some needed changes in their lives.

Now, let's continue our look at the progressive middle stage signs and symptoms of harmful addiction. What we will often see next is a pattern of continued use:

- Despite the user's subjective complaint of loss of control.
- Despite ongoing *social* or *interpersonal* problems likely to have been caused or made worse by use and a strong social contraindication. A4.
- Despite knowledge of ongoing *physical* or *psychological* problems likely to have been caused or made worse by use and an emerging or strong medical contraindication. D7.

In addition to drinking or using to relieve or avoid the onset of physical withdrawal symptoms, our compulsive-addictive user now increasingly:

- Drinks or uses an addictive substance or behavior to relieve anger, insomnia, fatigue, depression, or social discomfort.
- Develops a psychological dependence on using the addictive substance or behavior just to get through routine daily stresses.
- Uses with increasing frequency for emotional relief or escape.
- Uses even more than normal to soothe upset feelings after arguments, frustrations, disappointments, or unusual stresses.
- Feels easily bored when not using and often lacks the skills and/or interests needed to get healthy stimulation and excitement out of life.
- Is unable to discuss his or her feelings, problems, or harmful addiction openly with others.
- Experiences a growing mental obsession with the addictive substance or behavior and increasing preoccupation with use.
- Is having a metaphorical "love affair" with the addictive substance or behavior.
- May be having a literal "love affair" in cases of relationship addictions.
- Often feels an intense craving, desire, or urgency to use.
- Often feels irritable, moody, or depressed when not using.
- Mourns and grieves the loss of the substance or behavior when not using.
- Protects and hides his or her supply as necessary.
- Lies about the frequency and amount of their use.
- Feels uncomfortable in non-using situations.
- Develops a peer support group of fellow users and rejects many nonusers.

- Leads a secret life and often maintains two social identities—a false front for "straight" people and another persona for fellow users.

As this pattern continues to unfold we will see that our user often:

- Begins to use indiscriminately and no longer cares about the time or circumstances or consequences of using.
- Loses conscious awareness of the amount and frequency of his or her use because using has become so routine.
- Develops pathological behaviors such as lying, stealing, cheating, prostituting themselves, and dealing.
- Makes false promises about quitting and deliberately lies and deceives others in order to continue using.
- Begins to experience increasing social alienation, isolation, and withdrawal.
- Quits or loses jobs.
- Devalues and seriously damages personal and family relationships.
- Begins to alienate people and starts to lose sober friends.

At this point, *if it hasn't already happened long before,* outside intervention will seem necessary:

- Family and close friends will try to *make* the user stop.
- Our user often explodes in angry, emotional outbursts when criticized, challenged, or confronted—marked by screaming, yelling, verbal abusiveness, physical destructiveness, or violence.
- Family and friends begin to feel mounting hopelessness and despair.
- Our user continues alienating people and even starts losing friends who use.
- Begins using alone *if he or she hasn't already started to do so long before this.*

Now, let me repeat something here for emphasis that I have already quoted from Milam and Ketchum:

> For the first time, he may realize that he is in *deep trouble* with alcohol. Despite his increasing problems, however, the middle-stage alcoholic rarely considers giving up drinking; he may believe a psychiatrist can help him sort out his 'underlying psychological problems,' but he *cannot believe* that drinking is responsible for those problems.

**How is this possible?** We have already talked about the irrational nature of compulsion and the existence of irrational beliefs and distorted thinking patterns that can fuel harmful addictive behavior. In many cases, however, something even deeper and more subtle is also happening psychologically as the middle stage of a harmful addiction unfolds.

Many users gradually develop a sophisticated array of self-deceptive and often completely unconscious psychological defense mechanisms that protect them from accurately perceiving the more disagreeable aspects of objective reality or from feeling any intense or painful negative emotions. These defenses thus serve to sustain the users growing delusion that continued use will *not* cause even greater pain and mounting problems, but will actually soothe, relieve, excite, or comfort them—which it might still manage to do at times—if only very briefly.

In his chapter on the preferred defense structure of the recovering alcoholic, John Wallace offers a list of some of the most commonly used defenses. These include:

- Denial.
- Projection.
- All-or-Nothing Thinking.
- Conflict Minimization and Avoidance.
- Rationalization.
- Self-Centered Selective Attention.
- Preference for N on-Analytical Modes of Thinking and Perceiving.
- Passivity versus Assertion.
- Obsessional Focusing.

(Wallace, 1985: 27–32)

So now, with an array of sophisticated but very unhealthy defenses quietly at work, our middle stage alcoholic, addict, or compulsive-addictive user manages to sustain their continued use despite mounting negative consequences by:

- Rationalization, minimization, projection, blaming and denial. A4. D7.
- Defining alcoholism or harmful addiction in a way that always excludes themselves—e.g. "I can't be an alcoholic or an addict because . . ."
- Feeling that no one has ever felt the way they do, and that they are "different" from others.
- Developing other forms of "terminal uniqueness."
- Building unreasonable resentments and holding irrational grudges.
- Blaming others for both personal problems and excessive use.

- Manufacturing irrational or semi-plausible alibis and excuses for drinking or using—and then actually believing them much of the time. A4. D7.

One of those Key West tee-shirts I've grown so fond of quoting suggests an interesting perspective that humorously expresses an attitude that our middle stage user now often seems to be embracing at some level as a core value and a virtual philosophy of life.

It offers the following definition:

*"Consciousness—those annoying intervals between naps."*

The same glib but essentially dismal and dysfunctional approach to life is also reflected brilliantly in the following imaginary exchange:

***Question:*** *"What's worse—apathy or ignorance?"*

***Answer:*** *"I don't know, and I don't care."*

Unfortunately, our middle stage user can't afford to play "Rip Van Winkle," "Beautiful Dreamer" or "Sleeping Beauty" indefinitely—without suffering even more dire or deadly consequences.

One day I came across a great bumper sticker that expresses a much different perspective on life and offers some practical wisdom that our user may someday have to wake up and begin to consider.

It declares simply and unequivocally that:

*"Reality is for people who can't handle drugs."*

The natural tendency for repeated irrational acts to produce mounting negative consequences over time seems to be a basic fact of life and an undeniable and inescapable aspect of reality—one that is not greatly influenced by magical or wishful thinking, denial, or delusion. While objective reality may often be rather annoying or inconvenient—most people find that it is very hard to ignore it completely or permanently—no matter how stubbornly or persistently they may try to do so.

As our compulsive-addictive user keeps their head firmly planted in the sand—or elsewhere—and progresses blindly and steadily into the middle stage of harmful addiction—all of the negative consequences, problems, difficulties, damage, chaos, confusion, and insanity in their life will tend to grow progressively worse over time.

Reality will keep pounding on the doors of their perception—screaming a simple message—"Wake up!"—and a desperate warning cry—"Before it's too late!"

Sooner or later—even through the thickest fog of denial and the deepest level of devotion to their chosen addictive substance or behavior—many alcoholics, addicts, or compulsive-addictive users will eventually start to "get" this message. In many cases, however, the terrible truth of their condition will start to seep through their sturdy walls of self-deception only very slowly. The pounding, screaming truth—that is often so loud and clear to those around them —will usually start to echo into their awareness only quite dimly—often in a badly garbled form. The emerging truth that their beloved addiction is not really their friend will be relatively easy to suppress and put down at first.

But, as William Cullen Bryant boldly declares in his 1838 poem "The Battlefield,"

"Truth, crushed to earth, shall rise again . . ."

Sooner or later, our user may begin to develop a truly *desperate* desire to cut down and control their use.

On one level, they may still dream of nothing more than "being able to enjoy it—just a little bit—now and then," while avoiding further negative consequences and they will probably continue to make repeated futile attempts to do so.

On a deeper level, however, they may be starting to realize the truth that, for them at least:

"One is too many, and a thousand are never enough."

Sooner or later, of course, despite any intervals of control or abstinence, this is the grim reality that will assert itself once more. The true middle stage user will lose control again and suffer negative consequences again—and again—and again—and again.

The harsh truth is banging on their door. They don't really hear it very clearly yet. They don't really want to hear it. They just want it to just go away and leave them alone—so they can continue to use in peace. So, in this part of the middle stage of progression in a harmful addiction, we will often see the further development of new "control strategies" and a variety of addiction control "tactics" and "techniques."

This phase is often marked by:

- Repeated attempts to cut down and control use or to abstain temporarily in order to avoid further negative consequences and eventually resume using. A4. D3. D4. D7.
- Making rules, setting limits, and establishing further controls.
- Changing drinking or using patterns.
- Restricting the amount used and the times and places of use.

127

- Switching from one addictive substance or behavior to another.
- Changing the type of drink or the form in which a substance is used.
- Temporary periods of abstinence or controlled use. A4. D3. D4. D7.
- Further broken promises, broken rules, dashed hopes, and failed efforts at controlling the frequency and amount of use. A4. D3. D4. D7.
- Delaying a genuine commitment to permanent abstinence with a variety of excuses.
- Half-hearted or resigned "decisions" to abstain completely and permanently.
- Strong ambivalence, mixed motives, and conflicting desires.
- Wavering motivation between unrestricted use, attempted control, and attempted abstinence.
- Trying to resolve "other" issues that are the "real" problem.
- Changing jobs.
- Changing relationships.
- Attempting geographic cures and escapes.
- Psychiatric treatment.
- Psychotropic medications.
- Doctor's Visits. Prescriptions. Hospitalizations. M20.
- Medical detoxification programs to "sober up" or "clean up."
- A futile "merry-go-round" of failed attempts at control or abstinence.

Some people can go on like this indefinitely and will eventually progress into the late or chronic stage of harmful addiction *without ever getting truly serious at a deep level about wanting to stop.*

In many other cases, however, objective reality will finally break through even the thickest walls of self-deception. Our user will reach the point of "pitiful and incomprehensible demoralization" that the AA Big Book talks about. The terrible truth of their potentially terminal condition will shout in their ear—loud and clear. They will hear it. They will get it. They will embrace the truth, sometimes rejoicing:

"Thank God I finally woke up! Thank God it's not too late!"

Now, our user has finally reached the point where he or she can honestly say:

"I'm sick and tired of being sick and tired!"

Unfortunately, as he or she now moves confidently into the "Attempted Analytical Abstinence" stage on the *Addiction Recovery Learning Curve,* our user is most likely about to experience another round of the "Addiction Control Failure Sequence" that will be discussed further in Chapters 7 and 8.

Completely blind to this prospect, however, our user now:

- makes his or her first sincere, internally motivated, and truly committed effort to abstain completely and permanently.

- Feels quietly confident they can easily abstain—completely and permanently but then they fail to do so in a series of initial, overconfident attempts.

- Makes repeated conscious attempts at abstinence—still assuming in this second round that this should be "easy" to do—but is still unable to abstain permanently.

- Gradually develops a deepening hatred for their harmful addiction and for the damage it causes, begins to understand that abstaining will apparently not be quite as easy or simple a matter as they had imagined—and eventually develops a really serious desire to abstain completely and permanently.

- Continues to relapse and is unable to abstain permanently despite a deepening and increasingly desperate desire to do so as negative consequences continue to mount.

- Voluntarily seeks help by going to an alcohol and drug abuse counselor, or a residential rehab, or some other abstinence-based addiction treatment program, and may dabble sincerely but superficially with AA or another self-help program—but eventually relapses again— and again—and again.

Finally, our user may reach his or her second point of "pitiful and incomprehensible demoralization, " and now—if they don't just give up entirely and resign themselves to a fate of unrestricted, uncontrolled use and grave negative consequences—they may slide unconsciously into a "sincere" but self-deceptive and seemingly endless:

- "Merry-go-round" of *futile, half-hearted,* and *repeatedly failed* attempts at abstinence.

My first job in the mental health and addictions treatment field was on an inpatient substance abuse treatment unit at Hall-Brooke Hospital in Westport, Connecticut, and I've always remembered a small card that had been taped onto the door of one of the rooms on the unit. This *happened* to be the door to the clinical staff room where we held our morning treatment team meetings—but that's *another* story.

The card said:

> "Of all the things I've lost, I miss my mind the most."

With this small pearl of amusing insight and generic self-awareness in mind, let's take another quick look at what the "Big Book" of Alcoholics Anonymous has to say on these matters:

> We know that while the alcoholic keeps away from drink, as he may do for months or years, he reacts much like other men. We are equally positive that once he takes any alcohol whatever into his system, something happens, both in the bodily and mental sense, which makes it virtually impossible for him to stop . . .
>
> These observations would be academic and pointless if our friend never took the first drink, thereby setting the terrible cycle in motion. Therefore, *the main problem of the alcoholic centers in his mind,* rather than in his body. If you ask him why he started on that last bender, the chances are he will offer you any one of a hundred alibis. Sometimes these excuses have a certain plausibility, but none of them really makes sense in the light of the havoc an alcoholic's drinking bout creates . . .
>
> . . . there was always the curious mental phenomenon that parallel with our sound reasoning there inevitably ran some insanely trivial excuse for taking the first drink. Our sound reasoning failed to hold us in check.
>
> The insane idea won out.
>
> (Alcoholics Anonymous, 1976: 22–23, 37)

At this point, our user may begin to sense vaguely that there is a deeper truth still knocking vainly at the doors of their perception. It's been there all along, but even now it's usually buried so deep and it's knocking so patiently and quietly that it can still barely be heard. Many "real" alcoholics, addicts, or compulsive-addictive users—even at this advanced stage of progression into the middle stage of their harmful addiction—still have no idea that it's really there.

Let's go back to the AA Big Book now, and take a closer look at a section that I have already quoted above—but only in part:

> "Once in a while he may tell the truth. And the truth, strange to say, is usually that he has no more idea why he took that first drink than you

have. Some drinkers have excuses with which they are satisfied part of the time. But *in their hearts they really do not know why they do it.* Once this malady has a real hold, they are a baffled lot. There is the obsession that somehow, someday, they will beat the game. But they often suspect they are down for the count.

How true this is, few realize. In a vague way their families and friends sense that these drinkers are abnormal, but everybody hopefully awaits the day when the sufferer will rouse himself from his lethargy and assert his power of will.

The *tragic truth* is that if the man be a real alcoholic, the happy day may not arrive. He has lost control. At a certain point in the drinking of every alcoholic, he passes into a state where *the most powerful desire to stop drinking is of absolutely no avail.* This tragic situation has already arrived in practically every case long before it is suspected.

(Alcoholics Anonymous, 1976: 23–24. Emphasis added.)

# CHAPTER 6

# Late Stage Progression

"Man is not so lost that Eternal Love may not return, so long as Hope retaineth ought of green."

—Dante

"Even in the darkest hour of the night, act as if the dawn has already broken."

—The Talmud

"The moving finger writes, and having writ, moves on. Nor all your piety and wit shall lure it back again to cancel half a line, nor all your tears wash out a word of it."

—Omar Khayyam

"It is always darkest just before the dawn."

♦ ♦ ♦

## LATE STAGE

### The "Chronic Phase"

There is an old saying that will often begin to make some sense to our user by now—no matter how thick their walls of denial, delusion, or self-deception may have been in the past:

First the man takes the drink.

Then the drink takes the drink.

Then the drink takes the man.

By the time our alcoholic, addict, or compulsive-addictive user moves firmly into the chronic late stage of harmful addiction, they will often recognize the "terrible truth" of their condition quite clearly in stark moments of clarity. By this point, however, merely knowing the truth doesn't set them free.

In the past, they may have caught an occasional, frightening glimpse of the true nature of their harmful addiction—like the silent shadow of a ghost passing nearby in the fog at night. Now, however, a clear recognition of their "real problem" will often leap unbidden into their consciousness—ruthlessly, unmistakably, and repeatedly—like a ravenous, blood-thirsty beast that's tearing them apart inside.

For those who prefer to think of the late stage users' subjective experience of harmful addiction in more *clinical terms*—and perhaps a bit less poetically or dramatically—what we often see here is that continued use of their addictive substance or behavior has now become *extremely ego dystonic.*

Unfortunately, the mounting distaste or disgust that they often feel for their behavior doesn't really seem to matter anymore. It just makes their growing awareness of their irrational and irresistible compulsion to continue using all the more painful to bear. In metaphorical terms, we can see that their sane and sober self—what some people would call their "real" self or "true" self—was essentially hijacked and taken hostage by their addictive self—long, long ago.

By now—*if this insight hasn't arrived long before this point*—our user has begun to recognize their own "addictive voice" more and more clearly as something alien, hostile, and seemingly *hell-bent on their destruction.*

By now, however—based on their existing level of knowledge, the development of their emotional coping skills, the array of behavioral change tools they possess, and their conventional will power—it appears that their sane and sober self is often essentially "powerless" to effectively assert its will and act on its healthy desires.

At this stage, our user often feels *scared, hurt, confused, angry, and hopeless* because, after all, doesn't everyone really know?

- This doesn't make any sense!
- This isn't how life is supposed to be!

Unfortunately, in many cases, our user's true heart and sound mind have been held hostage by the addictive self for so long at this stage—and they have been so thoroughly enslaved and brainwashed by the irrational, compulsive power of their harmful addiction—that they barely even know themselves anymore.

They're not just **"hooked"**—they're **"cooked."**

They've been jumping back and forth—"out of the frying pan and into the fire"—and back into the pan again and back out into the fire—over and over and over again. By now, our user has probably played this little game and done this little dance more times than they can possibly remember—so many times, in fact, that they finally begin to *just give up.*

In many cases, they just can't muster the emotional and physical energy it takes to fight back anymore. They begin to realize that they have been engaged in what has finally become a futile struggle with their harmful addiction—a struggle which they have been constantly losing and they are now beginning to *understand* at some deep level that for some mysterious reason this is apparently a struggle that *they will never win.*

By this point, it usually takes far too much emotional energy for our user to even feel any real desperation or despair. They just don't have it anymore. At some point, they've been beaten and defeated and they finally know it—and then true hopelessness and resignation begin to sink in.

**They can see no way out.**

For many users, it often seems by now that the only place where they can feel any comfort at all is in oblivion—buried deep down inside what eventually begins to feel like the soothing warmth of a comfortable womb. "Frying pan? What frying pan?"

For some masters of the art of oblivion their late stage harmful addiction actually begins to feel much more like a slow cooker. I personally would call it a "crock pot" for a number of reasons—not all of which are entirely sympathetic to our poor user.

While there are always some rare and legitimate exceptions—depending upon the particular sad or tragic details of their "story"—many people who really understand the addictive mindset might actually say—even less sympathetically—that our user is now firmly planted on the "pity pot," and is heartily embracing the motto:

"Poor me! Poor me! Pour me a drink!"

Some *really* unsympathetic people—who can see quite clearly what's actually going on in so many cases—and who are honest enough and genuinely caring enough to take the risk of sounding callous or insensitive—may now be so bold as to ask our user:

135

"Would you like some cheese with that whine?"

Of course, the unfolding tragedy of late stage harmful addiction is not really a joking matter anymore. Few people who are intimately involved with our late stage user—who really know them, love them, and care about them—will have much energy left at this stage for levity or mirth. For most of them, the situation will have become far too tragic and sad for any kind of humor to seem appropriate.

Indeed, for some of people who really care about the user, the whole situation will feel almost unbearably painful at times. For many others, however, the most excruciating sense of emotional pain will have passed by now. Not because the painful stimulus isn't there anymore—but simply because many of them have become so desensitized that they can no longer really feel it—or because they have chosen either consciously or unconsciously not to "go there" anymore if they can possibly help it.

Unless the user's close family and friends have learned how to establish strong boundaries—and practice some healthy emotional detachment as embodied in the Al-Anon slogan "detach with love"—many of them will have become so habituated to emotional pain that they can now feel little more than emotional numbness.

In either case, few people will be making any more jokes as their friend or loved one moves inexorably downward into the late stage of harmful addiction. In the same way, few of these people will have much emotional energy left for many more angry complaints, caustic comments, sarcastic remarks, or even any desperate pleas.

### It will often seem like it's too late for all that.

In many cases, this "chronic stage" may drag on for many years, or even decades. But late stage harmful addiction will often reduce the normal life-expectancy of users by many years or decades—and many of them will not survive to enjoy the soothing comfort of the oblivion they crave for very long.

They are sliding into the final depths of a dark abyss that may come to feel much like a bottomless pit for them and for everyone else involved. But it's not. There's one place where our user will always "hit bottom"—sooner or later—if they slide all the way down there without ever getting clean and sober.

Our late stage user is now embarking on the final leg of a long, sad journey that will ultimately lead them only to *the cold, dark oblivion of the grave.*

Continuing with our review of the progressively worsening signs and symptoms of harmful addiction, we will observe that many of our late stage, chronic users will now begin to experience:

- More frequent and severe loss of control over the amount used and the frequency and duration of use. U1.
- Little or no ability to abstain or control their use—even temporarily. D4.
- Increasingly blatant and indiscriminate use of alcohol, drugs, or other compulsive-addictive substances or behaviors.
- Gradual abandonment of all excuses or pretenses to normalcy and the adoption of a totally hopeless and antagonistic attitude that says—sadly or defiantly:

"I don't care anymore. Go shove it."

- Drinking or using that may begin early and continue all day. A1, A2, A4, D2b, D3, D5, D6, D7.
- Prolonged periods of intoxication. A1, A2, D3, D5, D6.
- Benders, binges, or extended runs. A1, A2, D3, D5, D6.

Many users will now start to experience

- Even more severe withdrawal symptoms when their overall amount of use is cut down or completely stopped—some of which are life-threatening and often prove to be fatal.

In addition to the *marked* withdrawal symptoms that generally characterize the middle stage of harmful addiction, our user may now start to experience some of the *later stage symptoms of withdrawal—if they haven't already begun long before this point.*

These include the possibility of:

- Severe shakes.
- Convulsions.
- Seizures.
- Hallucinations.
- DTs—Delirium Tremens. M19.

In many cases, by the time our troubled middle stage user crosses over the invisible line that marks their entry into the chronic late stage of harmful addiction, he or she:

- Feels almost constant emotional pain due to the wide range of steadily growing problems and persistently worsening negative consequences associated with their continued drinking or using. U3.

137

- Is drinking or using just to "survive" emotionally and longs just to "feel normal" again rather than feeling constant emotional pain or numbness. U5.

Under these deteriorating circumstances, we will see that many late stage alcoholics, addicts, or compulsive-addictive users:

- Are unable to feel very much, if any, of the euphoric mood swing they would like to experience when using because of their dramatically increased tolerance. U4.
- Must keep using almost continually in order to avoid or relieve their increasingly severe withdrawal symptoms. D2b.
- Often drink or use well past their tolerance and get drunk or otherwise impaired.
- Find that their drinking or using has become driven, compulsive, and joyless.
- Experience a dramatic decrease in their tolerance level at some point and can no longer "handle" the amount of substance required to keep them from going into major withdrawal.
- Will therefore get drunk or otherwise intoxicated—often to the point of severe incapacitation—with only a small amount of use. D1
- Often drink or use alone—or in the company of "social inferiors."
- Suffer from impaired central nervous system functioning. A2, D7.
- Suffer from diminished cognitive abilities, impaired memory, poor judgment, poor motor coordination, limited sensory acuity, and blunted emotion. A2, D7.
- May begin to suffer irreversible organic brain damage.
- Find simple tasks becoming difficult or impossible to perform. A1, A2, A4, D6, D7.
- Eventually find themselves unable to work or initiate constructive action.
- Suffer serious moral deterioration and experience a growing willingness to violate their own values and to lie, con, cheat, steal, or harm others in order to support their habit.
- Suffer from major alcohol or drug-related medical problems.
- Experience many other progressive physical and medical problems. A2, D7.
- Suffer frequent car accidents and other accidents that often lead to serious physical injury or death for themselves or others.

- Suffer progressive family, social, job, and legal problems. A1, A3, A4. D5, D6.
- Are repeatedly arrested for alcohol or drug-related offenses such as driving while intoxicated, driving with a suspended license, public intoxication, disorderly conduct, illegal possession, dealing, stealing, shoplifting, petty larceny, burglary, robbery, prostitution, assault, rape, domestic violence, child abuse or neglect, or worse.
- Spend time in jails, prisons, hospitals, detox units, psychiatric units, residential treatment programs, halfway houses, homeless shelters, or other institutional settings.
- Make repeated conscious attempts at abstinence that ultimately end in relapse and continued excessive use.
- Sincerely seek outside help to stop using through treatment or self-help programs and will seem to be doing well—for months or even for a few years at a time in some cases—only to be baffled one day by the persistent power of their deeply rooted desire to continue drinking or using and the resilient strength of their irrational ambivalence about permanent abstinence.
- Fall into full-blown relapse soon after their initial use and deteriorate rapidly to find themselves wallowing soon afterward in a pitiful condition that is usually just as bad and oftentimes much worse than anything they had experienced before.
- Continue drinking or using despite strong medical and social contraindications.
- Continue drinking or using despite knowledge of ongoing physical or psychological problems likely to have been caused or made worse by use. D7.
- May suffer the eventual loss of all family, friends, homes, and jobs. A1, A3, A4, D5, D6.
- May eventually sink to a "Skid Row" or equivalent social level.

Within the chronic late stage alcoholic or addicted family system we will tend to see an array of progressively worsening problems. The variables involved in a particular family situation may include some, many, or perhaps even all of the following features:

- Enmeshment, fusion, rigid and arbitrary rules, poor or non-existent boundaries, authoritarian domination and control, disrespect for individual autonomy, stereotyped roles, lies, deception, jealousy, infidelity, and a lack of intimacy, honesty, trust, or communication within a tightly closed and highly secretive family system.

- Continued arguments, fights, chaos, uproar, and domestic disturbances, plus possible verbal or physical abuse, domestic violence, sexual abuse, and child abuse or neglect.
- Serious school, behavioral, or emotional problems in the children.
- Family members seeking counseling, therapy, or psychiatric treatment.
- Serious work and financial problems that affect the family.
- Growing financial dependence on family members by the user and continued stealing of money or goods from the home or family members to support drinking or using.
- Frequent changes of residence for poorly defined reasons.
- Family disorganization and disintegration.
- Family reorganization and major role reversals.
- Further caretaking and enabling behavior that often infantilizes the user.
- Contempt for the user, disgust, loss of respect, and further controlling behavior.
- Parentification of older children who must learn how to take care of themselves, younger siblings, and many adult household responsibilities due to parental distraction, dysfunction, disability, or neglect.
- Continued lies, secrecy, broken promises or resolutions by the user, plus a perpetual game of hiding of bottles or stashes from family members.
- Depression, anxiety, fear, anger, grieving and despair among family members.
- Emotional numbness, distancing, walls, and isolation.
- Nervous breakdowns, severe emotional problems, serious Illnesses, premature deaths, or suicides among family members.

In the area of work and career we will often see a similar pattern of progressively worsening problems for the user who moves into the chronic late stage of harmful addiction. These can include:

- Choosing employment that facilitates drinking or using.
- Frequent lateness for work and early departures.
- Prolonged unpredictable absences from work.
- Increasingly lame excuses for lateness, absences, or other problems at work.

- Drinking or using on the job.
- Warnings, disciplinary actions, or employer mandates to get into an alcohol or drug treatment program and stay clean and sober or be fired.
- Repeated hospitalizations that interfere with work.
- Visible physical or mental deterioration.
- Distractions from work by serious money and family problems or divorce.
- Resentment that a job and work responsibilities interfere with drinking or using.
- Serious interpersonal problems at work involving tension, conflicts, or growing isolation and distancing from coworkers.
- Job performance becomes uneven and generally incompetent.

Eventually, we may see that our chronic late stage user:

- Becomes totally unpredictable and undependable at work.
- Is repeatedly disciplined, demoted, or fired from jobs or starts to quit many jobs before this inevitably happens.
- Is unable to function at the level that their education, experience, training, or vocational skills should allow.
- Often has to take less demanding and lower paid jobs in their chosen field.
- Often becomes unable to hold or be hired for any job in their chosen field and can only attempt to find lower-skilled and lower-paid employment.
- Often finds that he or she is unable to hold any kind of job or to work at all.

There is another valuable recovery slogan that advises us:

"The elevator of addiction only goes down, but you can get off on any floor."

We are now looking at the end-stage user who has taken this ride almost all the way down and doesn't have very much further to go. Let me take a moment here to reiterate some of the key features that often mark the "classic pattern" in chronic late stage harmful addiction. At its worst, this may involve:

The blatant and indiscriminate use of alcohol, drugs, other substances, or other compulsive-addictive behaviors that may begin early and continue all day and night in a 'round the clock pattern

141

of benders, binges, extended runs, and prolonged periods of intoxication leading to the eventual loss of family, friends, jobs, homes, possessions, status, wealth, health, and life itself.

Our alcoholic, addict, or compulsive-addictive user is now nearing the end of what some sources choose to call the

### "Late, Deteriorative Stage."

At this point—according to one of the many progression charts I have collected over the years—while our user may or may not fit the classic "skid row bum" profile, his or her "addiction is now obvious to the most casual observer."

At this advanced stage—while the user is still *actively using* their harmful addictive substance or behavior—it would often be virtually impossible to accurately diagnose or effectively treat any co-existing psychiatric or mental disorder—such as major depression—that might be present and potentially debilitating in its own right. Mentally and emotionally—during this endgame—our user will often:

- Display seriously distorted attitudes, irrational beliefs, and impaired thinking.
- Suffer emotional augmentation, severe mood swings, and personality distortions.
- Overtly express irrational, primitive, or regressive defense mechanisms such as projection, blaming, and denial.
- Have outbursts of rage, terror, grief, or suicidal gestures while drinking or using.
- Feel constant resentments, jealousy, suspicion, and vague indefinable fears.
- Feel vague spiritual or religious desires.
- Continue to isolate, withdraw, and emotionally distance themselves from any intimate, meaningful, or honest interaction with others.
- Fear that he or she is really "losing my mind."
- Engage in anxiety relieving mechanisms such as phone calls at inappropriate times and long, rambling, delusional, self-absorbed monologues.
- Wallow in feelings of inadequacy, self-hatred, self-pity, and helplessness.
- Display classic symptoms of depression such as isolation, immobility, crying, feelings of worthlessness, hopelessness, despair, and suicidal preoccupation.

• Make serious or successful suicide attempts.

Ultimately, for the user who follows the unchecked "course of illness" in harmful addiction "all the way" to its *natural outcome*—and moves all the way through the full range of classic signs, symptoms, and stages of progression—their tragic story will finally come to an end with:

• Incarceration, insanity, dementia, or death by alcohol or drug related overdose, illness, accident, homicide, or suicide. A1, A2, A3, A4, D3, D5, D6, D7

At this point, the only viable alternative to a sad fate of this kind—which actually can and does happen for many people *long before they reach this bitter end*—is described on a number of progression charts as follows:

• Collapse of the alibi system, rationalizations, and denial: treatment and recovery process begins. D4.

## TRUTH OR CONSEQUENCES

Traditional addiction recovery programs have occasionally been criticized—quite unfairly and inaccurately—based on an utterly erroneous assumption that they somehow "require the complete abdication of all rational thought."

In fact, nothing could be further than the truth. Nevertheless, some critics take the following recovery slogan completely out of it's early recovery context—suggesting that the have little genuine understanding of how these programs actually work —and then cite it as evidence:

"Don't think, don't drink, and go to meetings."

Oddly enough, many of these critics not only recognize the impaired capacity for rational thought that characterizes many active addicts, but they actually lay great stress on it. Despite this accurate assessment, however, they apparently fail to appreciate the fact that the slogan *"Don't Think"* is only intended as temporary advice for people who are temporarily incapable of thinking rationally about the pros and cons of further use anyway—because they're still in the earliest stage of trying to make the difficult transition from active progression into lifetime sobriety.

Because this temporary advice is inaccurately assumed to be a permanent prescription to avoid all rational thought, these critics often fail to appreciate the wisdom and ultimate significance of another recovery slogan that's often used in tandem with it:

143

"Bring the body, and the heart and mind will follow."

In fact, traditional addiction recovery programs actually require people in recovery to take complete personal responsibility for staying sober by *learning how to recognize and challenge their addictive beliefs, think clearly, and behave rationally*—as evidenced by a third addiction recovery slogan which urges the newly sober alcoholic—or anyone else who begins to feel an impulse to pick up a drink at any point in their extended recovery process—to

*"Think the Drink Through."*

When anyone takes the time to remember all of the negative conse—quences, pain, suffering, and even death that so often result from the unchecked progression of harmful addiction, and when we take the suggestion offered by Stephen Covey in his book *The 7 Habits of Highly Effective People* and "Begin with the End in Mind," it's very hard for any sane person to put a positive spin on the idea of picking up that drink or drug.

However, it's obvious that many intelligent and well-intentioned people can be innocently fooled into believing and repeating some of the most *subtle, powerful, and seductive self-deceptions* that alcohol, drugs, and other forms of harmful addictive behavior tend to perpetuate.

For example, in his classic book, *The Varieties of Religious Experience*—based on a series of lectures which he delivered at the University of Edinburgh in 1902—the American psychologist, philosopher, and Harvard University professor William James made the following observation which has become quite well-known among people with a special interest in spirituality:

> . . . our normal waking consciousness, rational consciousness as we call it, is but one special type of consciousness, whilst all about it, part-ed from it by the filmiest of screens, there lie potential forms of con-sciousness entirely different. We may go through life without suspect-ing their existence; but apply the requisite stimulus, and at a touch they are there in all their completeness.

> (James, 1961: 305)

It's not widely noted, however, that William James based this celebrated conclusion on observations he'd made in print some years earlier regarding the altered state of consciousness often produced by *"nitrous oxide intoxication."*

Just before this famous passage, James also expressed the following views about the widespread popular appeal of alcohol:

> The sway of alcohol over mankind is unquestionably due to its power to stimulate the mystical faculties of human nature, usually crushed to earth by the cold facts and dry criticisms of the sober hour. *Sobriety*

*diminishes, discriminates, and says no; drunkenness expands, unites, and says yes. It is in fact the great exciter of the Yes function in man.* It brings its votary *(devotee)* from the chill periphery of things to the radiant core. It makes him for the moment one with truth. Not through mere perversity do men run after it. To the poor and the unlettered it stands in the place of symphony concerts and of literature; and it is part of the deeper mystery and tragedy of life that whiffs and gleams of something that we immediately recognize as excellent should be vouchsafed *(become evident)* to so many of us only in the fleeting earlier phases of what in its totality is so degrading a poisoning.

(James, 1961: 304–305. Emphasis added)

The powerful sway of popular myths regarding alcohol and other psychoactive substances—and their remarkable ability to twist our human capacity for common sense—can apparently have a distorting effect on the logical thinking of almost anyone—even a brilliant psychologist, philosopher, and professor like William James (who, presumably, was not under the influence of any intoxicating substances when he wrote these words).

When we look at this statement closely, it's sadly obvious that even such an imposing a figure as William James can manage to get some of the subtle but crucial points that need to be understood about harmful addiction almost completely backwards.

James, of course, is quite right when he concludes that alcohol used in excess is essentially a degrading poison—but he's dead wrong when he romanticizes alcohol's subjective psychoactive effects and suggests that is actually brings a user toward any kind of a "radiant core."

Obviously, readers may accept, reject, or modify whatever I may have to say about all this in the course of reaching their own conclusions. But, in my personal and professional judgment expressing admiration of any kind for any allegedly positive effects of alcohol or other drugs on the human psyche or the human spirit is simply wrong.

By this, I don't mean that expressing direct or indirect praise or implying any respect for the use of alcohol or other drugs as a legitimate means to promote spiritual development or personal growth is just ethically or morally wrong—but that it's just plain wrong—meaning that this kind of positive assessment of what these effects represent is simply mistaken and any intended or unintended praise is undeserved.

The temporary, subjective sensation of stimulation, excitement, enjoyment, or freedom that a drinker often begins to feel as they become intoxicated—and starts "feeling no pain"—has nothing whatsoever to do with the stim-

145

ulation of any "mystical faculties of human nature" as James suggests so mistakenly in the passage above.

As a psychoactive substance, alcohol is a central nervous system depressant, which acts on the human mind, body, and spirit in much the same way as heroin, opiates, sedatives, tranquilizers, barbiturates, and other "downers." None of these substances deserve to be hyped or glorified in any way, and none of them will ever lead anyone to experience any kind of an awakening—spiritual or otherwise.

In fact, when they are used in sufficient quantity, all that these substances will ever really do is bring people down and eventually put them to sleep. In the most tragic cases they can bring a person all the way down into a deep coma or even right up to and through the doors of death—if the deepest part of the brain that controls the user's heartbeat and breathing is ever put to sleep, either accidentally or on purpose.

On the way "down," alcohol or other CNS depressants may give the user a few false, faint, fleeting whiffs and gleams of what *may appear to be* a spiritually awakened state of mind—but it's not.

Similarly, on the way "up" the use of central nervous system stimulants or "uppers" such as cocaine, speed, and other amphetamines, may give the user a sense of elation and some of the same false, fleeting, deceptively spiritual flashes before they eventually flame out, spin out of control, and speed back down to crash and burn—sometimes tragically in a fatal heart attack or stroke.

On the way "out"—or deceptively on the way "in"—the purportedly spiritual effects of hallucinogenic or psychedelic drugs are ultimately just as shallow, deceptive, and delusional, and their use has often lead people into circumstances that can be just as harmful, self-defeating, self-destructive, or even deadly.

Neurochemically, what actually happens as a drinker becomes intoxicated—meaning, in other words, as their brain cells become poisoned by a toxic substance—is that their brain cells are gradually "put to sleep"—to use a very non-technical term—by the sedative psychoactive effects of the drug alcohol.

This numbing and deadening process of putting many brain cells to sleep—while gradually damaging and eventually killing many others—starts out as the frontal and top layer of the brain—the cerebral cortex—is gradually put to sleep. Thus, what is potentially the most rational *and* spiritually sensitive part of the brain routinely gets "knocked out" of commission by the drug alcohol.

## IF IT FEELS GOOD IT MUST *BE* GOOD

Most people, of course, don't actually use this highly evolved portion of their brain very consciously, deliberately, or effectively much of the time in a truly rational, sound, or spiritually sensitive way that would reflect what cognitive-behavioral therapy calls "secondary process' thinking. Rather, in many cases, the conscious and unconscious ego-level mental processes of most normal people tend to be dominated much of the time by deeply-ingrained irrational beliefs and automatic, distorted thought patterns that reflect what cognitive-behavioral therapy calls "primary process" thinking.

Generally speaking, the natural human tendency toward the development of irrational beliefs and distorted thinking patterns seems to be even more dominant and overpowering among people who develop serious harmful addictions.

Under the intoxicating sway of alcohol, what actually happens is that this frequently anxious, negative, and critical portion of the human brain is put to sleep. For many people, having this part of their mental equipment take a little chemically induced "nap" will tend to feel very good at first. Why? Because this most highly evolved part of the human brain—which most people certainly could employ in a rational and deliberate way—tends to operate habitually—much more often than not—in an irrational and generally dysfunctional manner. The resulting stream of passive, automatic "thoughts" or intense, obsessive "self-talk" often amounts to little more than an endless barrage of meaningless mental static. This essentially reactive, non-reflective mental activity is a primary trigger for emotional over-reactivity and mindless chatter of this kind typically leads people to feel overly self-conscious or self-critical—and to become easily and needlessly tense, frustrated, fearful, angry, judgmental or sad.

As a drinker begins to get intoxicated their normal, everyday inhibitions and self-consciousness begin to fade because these are controlled by the part of the brain that is being sedated. Likewise, their normal tensions, anxieties, and resentments are relaxed; their normal awareness, preoccupation, or obsession with life problems or difficulties begins to recede; and their more carefree and fun-loving emotional nature is temporarily released from its normal restraints as the more primitive level of their brain that controls their emotions begins to dominate their behavior.

Some people would call the varied assortment of negative personality traits that tend to dominate many people their "addictive self," or their "addictive voice." This is the part of the personality that wants to get wasted, stoned, bombed, trashed or smashed because on one level it can't cope with reality in a healthy way, and, on a deeper, subconscious level, it may also be riddled with shame, guilt, and self-hatred, and driven by an impulse toward self-punishment, self-harm, or self-destruction.

It's certainly *not* motivated by the liberating power of unconditional love.

For many people it's very true that their natural, playful, kind, and loving self—which is sometimes called their "inner child"—is often "crushed to earth" by the unhealthy, irrational, and compulsive part of our ego structure which usually operates at a shallow, primitive, and immature level of awareness that I like to call our "fearful angry confused ego."

It's also true that this automatic, negative, and normally dominant part of our personality routinely oppresses and defeats the best intentions and sincere efforts of a positive, healthy assortment of rational ego-level personality traits that some people would call our "inner adult" or "sober self"—while our deeper, fully rational, and truly spiritual level of awareness—that I like to call our "fully awakened compassionate energy"—remains hidden, dormant, and untapped.

Artificially altering their brain chemistry by drinking, using any other kind of drugs, ingesting any mood-altering substances, or engaging in any form of harmful compulsive, addictive, or escapist behavior, may temporarily feel good for the user, but these activities do absolutely nothing to help a person tap into the deepest spiritual core of their being and experience the life-transforming power of unconditional love that can only be found there.

So, let me review, clarify, and conclude this critique of the passage quoted above from William James, and end our detailed review of the signs, symptoms, and stages of progression in harmful addiction, by stressing my personal views on the following *crucial points* that I believe we as clinicians will need to help our clients understand:

- The use of alcohol and other drugs does absolutely nothing to stimulate "the mystical faculties of human nature" or anything else associated with true spirituality.

- On the contrary, the use of alcohol and others drugs can only provide false, fleeting flashes of feeling good and "feeling no pain" that *may sometimes appear* to reflect a spiritually awakened state of mind—but do not.

- In fact, the persistent or excessive use of alcohol and others drugs can only serve to keep a person in perpetual bondage and may permanently block their potential to experience any kind of genuine spiritual awakening or true happiness.

- "The mystical faculties of human nature," the freedom of our "natural, playful, kind, and loving self," and our potential for true spiritual development and personal growth are not "crushed to earth" by anything associated with true sobriety.

- On the contrary, these natural and healthy human potentials are inhibited primarily by an array of irrational beliefs and distorted thinking patterns and "by the cold facts and dry criticisms" that usually dominate the frequently foolish and illogical mentality of our fearful, angry, confused, ego.

- This powerful, selfish, and self-perpetuating part of our personality tends to keep us trapped in a shallow, primitive, and immature ego-level of awareness; to keep us cut off from any direct contact with the deepest spiritual core of our being; and to prevent us from having any direct experience of the life-transforming power of unconditional love which can only be found there.

- "The sway of alcohol over mankind is unquestionably due to its power" to help people find a way, however briefly, to "feel good" and "forget their cares" by temporarily sedating the part of our brain where these negative, unhealthy, irrational, and compulsive aspects of our personality hold sway.

- Drunkenness or intoxication does not expand, unite, or say yes to anything that is truly healthy or worthwhile in life.

- Drunkenness or intoxication is absolutely not "the great exciter of the *Yes* function in man."

- On the contrary, drunkenness or intoxication ultimately damages, diminishes, defeats, or destroys any potential a person may have for true health, happiness, or any genuine spiritual experience.

- Drunkenness or intoxication ultimately shouts "No" to all good things in life.

- Drunkenness or intoxication can never bring anyone "from the chill periphery of things to the radiant core."

- On the contrary, drunkenness or intoxication will ultimately block a person from the true experience of any genuine warmth or love in their life, and will only lead people—either gradually or quickly—toward the cold, dark, silence of the grave.

- Drunkenness or intoxication will never allow anyone to experience even one moment of genuine oneness or truth.

- On the contrary, drunkenness or intoxication can only lead people into a perpetual nightmare of falsehood, lies, minimization, rationalization, self-deception, denial, and death.

- People "run after" drunkenness or intoxication "not through mere perversity," but in a misguided and futile attempt to fill their spiritual emptiness and satisfy their deepest needs as human beings for an unshakable sense of meaning and purpose in life.

- True sobriety does not "diminish, discriminate, or say no" to anything that is truly healthy or worthwhile in life.

- On the contrary, true sobriety is an essential prerequisite for true health, happiness, or any genuine spiritual experience, and it enthusiastically says "Yes" to all good things in life.

- True inner peace, inner power, personal freedom, and enduring joy of this kind can never come to us artificially from anyone or anything outside of ourselves.

- On the contrary, all truly good things in life can only come to people through the direct personal experience and practice of the life-transforming power of unconditional love when they allow it to flow freely through the deepest spiritual core of their being as a blessing into their lives and the lives of others.

It's a deep mystery and a genuine tragedy that anyone could ever be so foolish as to believe the monumental lie that the faint *whiffs and gleams* of something that *appears* to be excellent in a state of drunkenness or intoxication could ever be anything other than what it really is—the start of *a degrading process of self-poisoning* than can only lead a persistent, excessive user right up to or through the doors of futility, failure, insanity, disability, or death.

# PART THREE

# RECOVERY

# CHAPTER 7

# The Face to Face Unified Addiction Recovery Model

"Be sure to keep a mirror always nigh,
in some convenient handy sort of place,
and now and then look squarely in thine eye,
and with thyself keep ever face to face."

—John Kendrick Bangs.

"He has the greatest blind side who thinks he has none."

—Dutch Proverb.

"No matter how far you have gone down the wrong path, turn back!"

—Turkish Proverb.

♦ ♦ ♦

Let's take a moment to recall that the full title and subtitle of this book is:

**Addiction, Progression, & Recovery: Understanding the Stages of Change on the Addiction Recovery Learning Curve.**

Now that we've concluded our comprehensive examination of the signs, symptoms and stages of progression in harmful addiction, it's time for us to move on and tackle what has traditionally been one of the most difficult and perplexing questions faced by clinicians working in the addiction treatment and recovery field:

> How can we most effectively help our clients make *the difficult transition from active progression into active recovery?*

We've just seen rather graphically how the *progression* of harmful addiction will often take place gradually but inexorably over a period of many years. Now, we will begin to explore why *making the transition into recovery* is so often an extended and complex process as well.

Before moving on, however, I'd like to reiterate briefly that it's far beyond the intended scope of this book to present a fully detailed discussion of the *long-term, lifetime addiction recovery process* itself—or to review the well-established traditional models that describe the normal stages of recovery and the developmental tasks that have been most strongly linked to the achievement of permanent recovery at each stage.

As clinicians trying to help our clients understand, accept, and make the *gradual transition* from the active progression of harmful addiction into a lifestyle of sustained sobriety, recovery, and personal growth, there's one unalterable fact of life that we must always remember:

> In this extended developmental learning process that is both experiential and experimental, there is simply no "silver bullet," no "magic pill," and no "overnight cure."

In the first chapter of this book, I noted that:

> Some of your clients will not be ready, willing, or able to face this issue honestly—or to self-disclose openly—or to make significant changes in their lives. Nevertheless, when you can effectively communicate the information that follows to your clients you may be able to gently plant some seeds of knowledge, self-awareness, and motivation that could make it much more difficult for them to continue avoiding the issue indefinitely.

> The seeds that you plant during one treatment episode with a client may not bear fruit until many years later during a later treatment episode with another clinician. Therefore, when you consider the vastly oversimplified concept of "treatment outcomes," I hope you'll understand the crucial role that your own episode of "treatment failure" may have played on the client's long journey through the addiction recovery learning curve toward their eventual destination of "treatment success" and lifetime sobriety.

As clinicians addressing the problem of harmful addiction *realistically*, we usually won't be expecting or demanding immediate results in most cases. Indeed, we'll probably have to develop and expand our own capacity to practice the healthy coping skills of patience, improved frustration tolerance, and delayed gratification that we'll be trying to promote in our clients.

Our *primary treatment goal* in most cases will not be overnight success, but to help our clients gradually build the firm foundation of knowledge, insight, motivation, and skill that they'll need in order to permanently change their harmful addictive behavior much *sooner* than they might otherwise have been able to do without our assistance.

To accomplish this, we need to understand *the actual long-term process of internal change* that many people with serious harmful addictions will usually have to go through in order to successfully make the vital transition into sustained recovery.

The core concept of learning through repeated trial and error is the theoretical foundation for a *unified addiction recovery model* I've developed. This longitudinal model is designed to promote the overall process of making permanent change more effectively by helping our clients:

- *understand* the irrational and compulsive nature of harmful addiction more thoroughly,
- *recognize* the signs, symptoms, and progression of harmful addiction in their personal history more accurately,
- *make sense* of their own past, present, and *future* experiences more fearlessly,
- *identify* any problem they may have—or may be developing—with harmful addiction more clearly, and
- *begin to change* their most harmful, self-destructive, or self-defeating addictive behaviors more promptly.

I call this new perspective:

**The Face to Face Unified Addiction Recovery Model.**

"Face to Face" is an acronym that stands for:

***"Formal Addiction Control Experiments"***

and

***"Failed Addiction Control Experiments."***

This system offers a practical way for clinicians to *simultaneously:*

- **Assess,**

155

- **Educate,**
- **Motivate,** and
- **Empower**

clients who may need our help in order to

- **Recognize,**
- **Understand,** and
- **Change**

a pattern of harmful compulsive or addictive behavior.

The notion of gradually learning what works and what doesn't work by repeated trial and error is grounded in the wisdom of a traditional addiction recovery slogan that tells us:

> "Insanity is repeating the same behavior and expecting a different result."

Most of us are probably familiar with the old saying:

> "If at first you don't succeed: try, try again."

Many of us may have also heard the joke:

> "If at first you don't succeed, just *redefine success*!"

For anyone who's really trying to change a harmful addictive or compulsive behavior, and continues to experience persistent failure—no matter what method or approach they are currently attempting—this process of continual re-evaluation is not a joke.

### It's essential.

Eventually, if they ever get really serious, or perhaps even desperate about wanting to control or completely stop their harmful addiction, a person with a proven track record of persistent failure will have to take a good look in the mirror one day, face themselves honestly, and ask one simple question:

> "If I fail, and fail, and fail again, maybe it's time to try something else?"

Then, if they're willing to make new choices, accept new goals, try again and again, and take further corrective actions as needed—in an ongoing experimental process of trial and error—they may eventually learn how to produce more reliable, acceptable, and satisfying results.

The *Face to Face Unified Addiction Recovery Model* outlines an **Addiction Recovery Learning Curve** that describes five stages of change that many people with the most serious compulsive or addictive behaviors will often have to go through on their long road to real and lasting recovery.

These five *naturally-occurring* and *easily-observable* stages are formally identified in this model as follows:

1. Uncontrolled Use with Consequences
2. Attempted Common Sense Control
3. Attempted Analytical Abstinence
4. Attempted Spiritual Sobriety
5. Rational Spiritual Sobriety.

The five different approaches in this *unified* addiction recovery model are *not* included because of any *prediction* or *expectation* that the particular methods employed at each stage will necessarily "work." Nor are they included because of any abstract, academic, or theoretical hypothesis—or any dogmatic philosophical conviction—that one particular approach is intrinsically superior to all the others or *should* be successful in all cases.

Rather, the five stages on the *Addiction Recovery Learning Curve* are each included in this model—as a simple matter of readily observable fact—because people who develop the most serious harmful addictions will usually have to go through each of these stages and *find out for themselves*—through their own *direct personal experience*—whether or not a given approach will actually work for them before they will *ever* be ready—usually after many repeated and increasingly painful failures—to move on to the next stage.

Let me immediately stress two crucial points about this approach:

1. Learning through painful personal experience is *not* a personal or clinical recommendation.
2. This *learning curve concept* merely reflects a realistic understanding of *how* most people actually change harmful addictive behaviors and *what* most clients are actually going to do in real life—regardless of what may be recommended to them clinically.

As Groucho Marx once asked:

"Who are you going to believe? Me or your own two eyes?"

Embedded within each of the five major stages of change on the *Addiction Recovery Learning Curve* there is an **Addiction Control Failure Sequence** consisting of five successive *levels of motivational intensity and effort* that the many users will have to go through at each stage.

Why?

Because going through this whole learning process is often necessary before most people will ever be completely convinced—based on their own painful and repeated personal experience of failure—that they must move on to the next stage.

In formal terms, the five levels in the *Addiction Control Failure Sequence* that might have to be experienced at *each* stage on the *Addiction Recovery Learning Curve* are called:

1. Initial Attempts.
2. Secondary Attempts.
3. Serious Attempts.
4. Desperate Attempts.
5. Futile Attempts.

In simpler terms, this process involves a sequence of unsuccessful efforts at control or abstinence that reflect:

1. sublime overconfidence,
2. uneasy concern,
3. serious, focused efforts,
4. desperate efforts, and
5. persistent failure and futility.

For users with serious harmful addictions, this natural process of failed attempts at control or abstinence often resembles the internal dynamics of going up to the plate for a turn at bat in baseball and experiencing *"three strikes and you're out!"*

In the real life-or-death game of harmful addiction, however, as reflected in the five-level *Addiction Control Failure Sequence*, there's simply no limit on the total number of strikes allowed—and no cap on the total amount of pain that has to be experienced—before a person honestly decides to give up and move on to the next stage where they can finally

• try a different method, or
• pursue a different goal.

Let me clarify that using the term "failure" in this model—in the formal term the "*Addiction Control Failure Sequence*"—is not meant to be at all harsh, critical, or judgmental. It's meant to provide an honest, accurate, and description of an observable and measurable objective reality.

Using the word "failure" moreover, does *not* indicate any prior *expectation* or *prediction* of failure for a particular individual who is working through a particular stage in the process.

In fact, for any individual client or user, there's simply no prior expectation or prediction of success or failure in this model—just an objective framework in which to make observations, keep score, and see what happens—or to base reasonably solid clinical expectations or predictions on a client's established, recorded, or self-reported prior history and experience.

There is such a thing as "success" in the *Addiction Control Failure Sequence* on the *Addiction Recovery Learning Curve*—but it's not a loosely defined, fleeting, or temporary thing.

If serious efforts at any stage on the Addiction Recovery Learning Curve were to result in *complete, permanent, lifetime success* in maintaining controlled use or total abstinence—with no exceptions and no further negative consequences whatsoever—then that particular user would be able to *successfully drop out* of the whole "learning curve" process.

Using the word "failure" so *persistently* in this model is certainly *not* intended as a *prescription* for "learned helplessness," nor is it used as a *prediction* of what *will* happen.

The word "failure" is merely used as a reasonable and accurate *description* of what *may happen* in the future—or as an honest and realistic *explanation* for what may have *already happened* repeatedly in the past in many cases.

Obviously, many users who are involved in the *active progression* of a serious harmful addiction will repeatedly fail to achieve anything even remotely like "complete, permanent, lifetime success." Indeed, this very pattern of repeated failure to control or stop their use and avoid further negative consequences will be the *most important single element* in helping most users to identify the existence of a harmful addiction and understand the deeply irrational and compulsive nature of their problem.

In this model, a skilled clinician will explicitly challenge clients to enter into a long-term "learning process." He or she will introduce clients to the notion of honestly reframing their past, present, and future experience as a series of *Formal Addiction Control Experiments*. Then, by suggesting the possibility that these efforts might turn into—or might already represent—a series of *Failed Addiction Control Experiments*—we may be able to successfully encourage and empower many of these clients to "get real," "get honest," "cut their losses" and move on to the next stage *sooner* rather than later.

Let me emphasize once more that this may be achieved by helping clients recognize the true significance of their personal experience of repeated failure—both retrospectively—by looking *back* at the signs, symptoms, and consequences they have *already experienced* in the past—and prospectively—by looking *ahead* as they move into the future—hopefully with open eyes, an open mind, and a brave heart—for the *eventual development* of signs, symptoms, and negative consequences they have not yet experienced.

One of our major treatment goals—as we work with clients who are painfully passing through the *Addiction Control Failure Sequence* at any stage on the *Addiction Recovery Learning Curve*—will be to help them *reduce* or *eliminate* their need to pass through the *desperate* or *futile* attempts at each stage.

## THE PROCESS OF CHANGE

In harmful addictions, an internalized motivation for change may sometimes appear suddenly and strongly in dramatic situations where there's been a traumatic shock of some kind—such as an accident, an arrest, a death, a serious injury, or a frightening "close call."

In most cases, however, a serious desire for change *doesn't magically appear overnight.*

In fact, it's *far* more common in most people with harmful addictions to see a genuine, internalized motivation for change develop quite slowly in *a logical sequence of stages*.

As clinicians, one of our primary therapeutic goals will be to motivate, educate, and empower clients with harmful addictions to recognize the severity of their problem and then to accept and actively embrace their own personal responsibility for changing their most self-defeating or self-destructive attitudes and behaviors.

To do this effectively, we will need to understand the key features of the *Face to Face Unified Addiction Recovery Model* and the five stages of change on the *Addiction Recovery Learning Curve*. Before doing that, however, we will need to understand the fundamentals of how most people actually go about making *any* major changes in their lives.

Psychologists James Prochaska, Carlo DiClemente, and John Norcross have developed a comprehensive "Transtheoretical Model" of change that describes *six generic stages in the process of change.*

These six stages can be summarized as follows:

1. **Pre-Contemplation**—The user often has no subjective perception that any problem exists, no concern about any related consequences, and no thoughts about changing their behavior—often despite the fact that others may have seen a real problem and may have expressed their concern about it to the user quite strongly.

2. **Contemplation**—The user now recognizes clearly that a problem exists, has become concerned about the consequences, and begins to actively consider the possibility of changing their behavior. This process usually involves weighing the predictable costs of continued use against the likely benefits of change.

3. **Preparation**—The user has made a definite decision to change, and begins to gather whatever information, support, or resources they believe will be needed to begin changing their behavior.

4. **Action**—The user takes any active steps that they think are needed—depending on what their personal goal may be—to change, cut down, control, or completely stop their self-identified problem behavior.

5. **Maintenance**—The user takes any active steps that they think are needed to continue their new behavior patterns and prevent relapse—and continues to do so for as long as these active steps are necessary.

6. **Termination**—The user experiences no temptations, cravings, or urges to return to their harmful addictive behavior. He or she never even thinks about using, and no further conscious actions are required to maintain permanent change because:

### "The problem has been solved."

(Prochaska & DiClemente, 1984; Prochaska, Norcross & DiClemente, 1994)

The *first five* of these six generic stages of change have been adapted and embedded into the fabric of the *Addiction Recovery Learning Curve,* as we shall see below.

Why only the first five?

In the traditional disease model of harmful addiction, full recovery from the most serious forms of harmful compulsive or addictive behavior—such as alcoholism or drug addiction—is seen as a lifetime process because serious harmful addiction is seen as *a chronic condition with no permanent "cure."*

Regardless of whether a clinician accepts or rejects basic the terms and concepts of the traditional "disease model" per se, one thing seems to be very clear to most experienced professionals working in the addiction treatment field:

> people who develop the most serious harmful addictions seem to face a *recurrent lifetime risk of serious relapse* if they take no active ongoing steps to prevent it.

This powerful reality has been widely recognized and accepted almost across the board among professionals working in the addiction treatment field—

by the social learning theorists and cognitive-behavioral therapists who first developed an extensive repertoire of "relapse prevention" skills and by many clinicians and counselors who eagerly try to teach these principles and skills to their clients while working comfortably within the philosophical framework of traditional addiction treatment programs that warmly embrace the disease-model of harmful addiction and the twelve-step spiritual approach to addiction recovery

Within the generic six stage change model, therefore, the Termination Stage would *not* seem to apply for most people recovering from serious harmful addiction.

Most of these people would probably have to remain active in the Maintenance Stage—consciously pursuing a sober lifestyle—one day at a time—for the rest of their life. This means that they would most likely need to take active steps to monitor and manage their chronic and "incurable" condition on a daily basis—in much the same way that many diabetics must carefully monitor their blood sugar level and inject themselves with insulin as needed.

In harmful addiction, however, there is one significant difference that is repeatedly demonstrated by the addict's apparent inability to abstain. This crucial difference is pointed out by the "Big Book" of Alcoholics Anonymous when it asserts:

> . . . the *main* problem of the alcoholic centers in his *mind*, rather than in his body.

> (Alcoholics Anonymous, 1976: 23. Emphasis added.)

Therefore, the twelve-step model for maintaining permanent lifetime recovery from harmful addiction suggests that a recovering person will need to take proactive steps on a daily basis to monitor their mental, emotional, physical, *and* spiritual condition on a fairly deep and meaningful level and strive to maintain a healthy balance in order to *"protect their sobriety"* and *"prevent relapse."*

In this model, which is congruent in many ways with cognitive-behavioral principles and practices, the maintenance of lifetime sobriety would also require a recovering person to identify and change any irrational beliefs, distorted thinking patterns, selfish motives, dysfunctional personality or character traits, and grandiose or self-defeating attitudes that would otherwise tend to fuel their harmful addiction and leave them *perpetually vulnerable to relapse.*

This is a very tall order since most people who eventually develop harmful addictions usually start out with no conscious awareness that they even have a problem—and no idea that they may eventually need to contemplate making major changes in the way they live. Therefore, naturally, they also tend to have virtually no motivation or desire to change.

Furthermore, even during the middle and late stages of progression in harmful addiction, the common tendency toward rationalization, minimization, self-deception, denial, and ambivalence about the relative costs and benefits of use will often diminish a user's *insight and motivation for change.*

As clinicians working with people coping with harmful addictions it will be our job to help *improve* our client's *insight* and *increase* their *motivation for change.*

William Miller and Stephen Rollnick have adapted Prochaska's generic change model and have made it into a cornerstone of their book, *Motivational Interviewing: Preparing People to Change Addictive Behavior.* They describe "motivational interviewing" as "an approach designed to help clients build commitment and reach a decision to change," and state that "It represents something of a polar opposite from an authoritarian, confrontational style." They believe that ". . . the therapist need only offer three critical conditions to prepare the way for natural change: accurate empathy, non-possessive warmth, and genuineness," and they link the therapist's tasks to their paraphrased adaptation of the generic stages of change in the following way:

### Stages of Change and Therapist Tasks

#### Pre-contemplation

Raise doubt—Increase the client's perception of risks and problems.

#### Contemplation

Tip the balance—Evoke reasons to change, and risks of not changing.

#### Determination

Help the client determine the best course of action to follow.

#### Action

Help the client take active steps toward change.

#### Maintenance

Help the client identify and use relapse prevention strategies.

#### Relapse

Help the client renew the cycle of change without becoming stuck or demoralized.

(Miller & Rollnick, 1991: 18)

Motivational Interviewing and the generic stages of change provide the foundation for *Motivational Enhancement Therapy* which, as we will see below, is a core element in the eclectic blend of therapeutic approaches that have been incorporated philosophically into the *Addiction Recovery Learning Curve* approach for promoting permanent change.

## THE COMPLEXITY OF CHANGE

Let's take a moment to quickly review the six generic stages of change in Prochaska's *Transtheoretical Model* as discussed above:

1. Pre-Contemplation
2. Contemplation
3. Preparation
4. Action
5. Maintenance
6. Termination

When we consider these six generic stages of change alone it's often very easy—and perhaps even tempting—to take a simplistic "all or nothing" view that fails to appreciate the actual complexity involved in the overall process of learning how to control or stop harmful addictive behavior.

When we fail to recognize the strong ambivalence and mixed motives, and the fluctuating goals and methods that are usually involved in this messy process, it can also become very easy or tempting to ask naive "black or white" questions, such as:

- Are you thinking about stopping, or not?
- Are you ready to stop, or not?
- Are you trying to stop, or not?
- Are you staying stopped, or not?

By contrast, when we fully integrate the generic stages of change and the principles of motivational interviewing with the different client goals and methods involved in the five stages of change on the *Addiction Recovery Learning Curve,* we can then begin to appreciate the more complex reality that's involved in the *actual process of change* in harmful addiction more fully and begin to intervene with specific clients in a more individualized, targeted, meaningful, and effective way.

As already noted, *many of our clients will simply not be ready for major change and therefore won't be dissuaded from continued use by our well-reasoned clinical recommendations, even when these are factually supported by a detailed individual symptom checklist.* Even so, we may still be able to help some of them understand the real nature of their condition and begin to change their harmful addictive behavior more "quickly" when we encourage them to honestly adopt the core concept of conducting *Formal Addiction Control Experiments and Failed Addiction Control Experiments*—even if this painful learning process ultimately involves multiple relapses and has to take place during the course of multiple treatment episodes over an extended period of time.

In reality, the lengthy process of change that's typically involved in successfully making the transition from harmful addiction into sustained recovery is very natural, human, organic, imperfect, irrational, frustrating, erratic, and messy—and it usually involves:

- ambivalent and fluctuating motives;
- inconsistent and irrational behavior;
- persistent and progressive loss of control and inability to abstain;
- progressively worsening signs and symptoms;
- progressively worsening negative consequences;
- temporary periods of "successful" control or abstinence;
- repeated failures, relapses, and eventual re-evaluation;
- gradually evolving goals;
- different targets of change; and
- countless methods of change that may be attempted over time.

When we begin to use the *Addiction Recovery Learning Curve* model to structure and make sense of the overall process and evaluate where an individual client stands, we are no longer limited to using rather blunt and crude assessment instruments such as asking:

**"So, do you really want to stop or not?"**

Rather, we can begin to ask an array of *much more sophisticated, sensitive, individualized, timely, and pertinent questions.*

This might help our client's begin to see—much more quickly and accurately—where they actually stand in this extended, overlapping process of

- attempted change,

165

- repeated failure, and
- continued harmful progression.

For example?

At any stage on the *Addiction Recovery Learning Curve*—as we'll see below when we examine the *Addiction Progression and Recovery Evaluation Process* that's included as a part of the model—we can work with our clients to evaluate where they seem to stand with regard to each of the following critical factors—from both the clinician's point of view and the client's point of view:

- The client's imagined and actual level of use, degree of problem severity, and stage of progression into harmful addiction.
- The client's imagined and actual action stage of change on the *Addiction Recovery Learning Curve* and their imagined and actual level of motivational intensity in the *Addiction Control Failure Sequence.*
- The next method, goal, and stage of change that the client currently contemplates, if any.
- The next method, goal, and stage of change that the client needs to contemplate.
- The next method, goal, and stage of change that the client needs to prepare for.
- The next method, goal, and stage of change on which the client needs to take action.
- Future methods, goals, or stages of change on the *Addiction Recovery Learning Curve* that are still in the pre-contemplation stage for the client.

## SUMMARY AND OVERVIEW

Before we move on to discuss the philosophical premises underlying the *Face to Face Unified Addiction Recovery Model*, examine the different goals and learning processes involved at each stage on the *Addiction Recovery Learning Curve*, and review the eclectic blend of psychotherapeutic approaches and self-help models involved, let's take some time right now to look at a summary and overview of the entire *Face to Face model* in outline form as it is presented in a clinical training seminar handout that I've developed:

166

## THE FACE TO FACE UNIFIED ADDICTION RECOVERY MODEL

### *Formal Addiction Control Experiments and Failed Addiction Control Experiments*

> *"Be sure to keep a mirror always nigh,*
> *in some convenient handy sort of place,*
> *and now and then look squarely in thine eye,*
> *and with thyself keep ever face to face."*

> —John Kendrick Bangs.

## *THE ADDICTION RECOVERY LEARNING CURVE*™

**Five Stages of Change** that people with the most serious harmful addictive behaviors will usually have to go through on the long road to lasting recovery:

1. Uncontrolled Use with Consequences.
2. Attempted Common Sense Control.
3. Attempted Analytical Abstinence.
4. Attempted Spiritual Sobriety.
5. Rational Spiritual Sobriety.

### *The Addiction Control Failure Sequence*

**Five Levels of Motivational Intensity** that people with the most serious harmful addictive behaviors will often have to go through at each stage on the *Addiction Recovery Learning Curve* before they will be ready to admit failure and move on to the next stage:

1. Initial Attempts.
2. Secondary Attempts.
3. Serious Attempts.
4. Desperate Attempts.
5. Futile Attempts.

### *The Addiction Control Change Process*

**Five Generic Steps** adapted from Prochaska, et al, that people with the most serious harmful addictive behaviors will have to take at each stage on the *Addiction Recovery Learning Curve* before they will be ready move on to the next stage:

A. **Action**—Active attempts at control or abstinence at this stage.

B. **Maintenance**—Permanently successful control at this stage.

C. **Pre-Contemplation**—Failing but not thinking about the next stage.

D. **Contemplation**—Actively thinking about moving to the next stage.

E. **Preparation**—Preparing to take action at the next stage.

# GOALS, TREATMENT APPROACHES, & SELF-HELP MODELS

## *THE ADDICTION RECOVERY LEARNING CURVE*™

### *Foundation Stage: Personal Responsibility and Motivation*

**Client Goals:**

Relieve personal problems, comply with treatment mandate, and/or get out of treatment.

**Treatment Goals:**

The client will:

- Accept complete personal responsibility for their own life; for their own beliefs, attitudes, motives, desires, thoughts, feelings, words, and deeds; and for all positive results or negative consequences that may ensue.

- Recognize that many of their daily thoughts, feelings, words, and deeds are habitually reactive, negative, self-defeating, or harmful because they are driven compulsively by unexamined or unconscious:
  - negative attitudes;
  - shallow motives;
  - selfish desires;
  - irrational beliefs;
  - distorted thinking patterns;
  - immature or overly critical ego-states; or
  - corrupt core values, ethics, or principles.

- Make a decision to identify and change all of their negative ego-level traits.

**Primary Treatment Approach:**

Reality Therapy, Transactional Analysis, Rational-Emotive, & Cognitive-Behavioral Therapy.

**Self-Help Models:**

7 Habits of Highly Effective People, The Voice Dialogue Method, & Emotional Intelligence.

## *Stage One—Uncontrolled Use With Consequences*

**Client Goal:**

Continue to use their preferred addictive substance or behavior—as often and as much as they wish—while making *no* changes and experiencing *no* further negative consequences.

**Treatment Goals:**

The client will achieve:

- Improved insight, motivation, and skills for more responsible coping, and
- Complete permanent avoidance of any further negative consequences associated with the addictive substance or behavior—or
- Move on to the next stage:

  **Attempted Common Sense Control.**

**Primary Treatment Approach:**

Motivational Enhancement Therapy

(+ Reality Therapy, Transactional Analysis, Rational-Emotive & Cognitive-Behavioral).

**Self-Help Model:**

7 Habits of Highly Effective People, The Voice Dialogue Method, & Emotional Intelligence.

## *Stage Two—Attempted Common Sense Control*

**Client Goal:**

Attempt controlled use and moderation to avoid further negative consequences.

**Treatment Goals:**

The client will achieve:

- Improved insight, motivation, and skills for more responsible coping, and

- Permanent lifetime moderation as manifested by completely successful controlled use—with *no* further episodes of loss of control and *no* further negative consequences—or
- Move on to the next stage—Attempted Analytical Abstinence.

**Primary Treatment Approach:**

Motivational Enhancement Therapy.

(+ Reality Therapy, Transactional Analysis, Rational-Emotive & Cognitive-Behavioral).

**Self-Help Model:**

Moderation Management (+ 7 Habits, Voice Dialogue, Emotional Intelligence).

## *Stage Three—Attempted Analytical Abstinence*
**Client and Treatment Goals:**

The client will:

- Maintain complete permanent abstinence from their harmful addictive substance or behavior by learning and employing sound rational-emotive and cognitive behavioral self-management skills—or
- Move on to the next stage:
  **Attempted Spiritual Sobriety.**

**Primary Treatment Approach:**

Relapse Prevention, Rational-Emotive & Cognitive-Behavioral Therapy.

(+ Reality Therapy, Transactional Analysis & Motivational Enhancement).

**Self-Help Model:**

Rational Recovery—SMART Recovery (+ 7 Habits, Voice Dialogue, Emotional Intelligence).

## *Stage Four—Attempted Spiritual Sobriety*
**Client and Treatment Goals:**

The client will:

- Continue to learn, practice, and improve rational-emotive and cognitive-behavioral coping skills, and
- Achieve a spiritual awakening and maintain complete permanent abstinence through active participation in a twelve-step self-help

recovery program and practice of the traditional spiritual principles involved—or

• Move on to the next stage—Rational Spiritual Sobriety.

**Primary Treatment Approach:**

Twelve Step Facilitation Therapy, Transpersonal Psychology, and Logotherapy.

> (+ Reality Therapy, Transactional Analysis, Rational-Emotive, Cognitive-Behavioral & Motivational Enhancement).

**Self-Help Model:**

Alcoholics Anonymous—or another appropriate twelve-step program.

> (+ 7 Habits, Voice Dialogue, Emotional Intelligence).

## *Stage Five—Rational Spiritual Sobriety*

**Client and Treatment Goals:**

The client will:

• Develop integrated rational, emotional, and spiritual living skills by blending rational-emotive and cognitive-behavioral coping skills with a practical translation of twelve-step program principles—and other universal spiritual principles—into clear, simple, modern terms and effective self-management techniques they can easily understand, accept, and begin to practice, and

• Maintain complete permanent abstinence from their harmful addictive substance or behavior.

**Primary Treatment Approach:**

"Transpersonal Cognitive Therapy"

> (An eclectic and adapted blend of principles and techniques drawn from Reality Therapy, Transactional Analysis, Rational-Emotive and Cognitive-Behavioral Therapy, Motivational Enhancement Therapy, Twelve-Step Facilitation Therapy, Transpersonal Psychology, Logotherapy, and Rational Spirituality—plus any other compatible approaches—as needed).

**Self-Help Model:**

Rational Spirituality.

> (+ 7 Habits, Voice Dialogue, Emotional Intelligengce—**within** existing self-help & support programs).

## INTEGRATED OUTLINE—STAGES, LEVELS, & STEPS

### *THE ADDICTION RECOVERY LEARNING CURVE*™

## *Foundation Stage:*
## *Personal Responsibility and Motivation*
### *Addiction Control Failure Sequence:*

Level 0 — No motivation or willingness to accept personal responsibility for your own life.

**Goal:** To accept and embrace complete personal responsibility for your own life.

### *Addiction Control Change Process:*

Step 0A — Action—Attempting to avoid accepting personal responsibility for your own life.

Step 0B — Maintenance—Permanently successful in avoiding personal responsibility.

Step 0C — Pre-Contemplation—Failing but not thinking about accepting responsibility.

Step 0D — Contemplation—Thinking about accepting personal responsibility for your own life.

Step 0E — Preparation—Preparing to accept full personal responsibility for your own life.

Step 0F — Action—Attempting to accept complete personal responsibility for your own life.

Step 0G — Maintenance—Permanently successful embrace of personal responsibility.

## *Stage One—Uncontrolled Use With Consequences*
### *Addiction Control Failure Sequence:*

Level 1 — Initial Attempts to avoid the consequences of uncontrolled use.

Level 2 — Secondary Attempts.

Level 3 — Serious Attempts.

Level 4 — Desperate Attempts.

Level 5 — Futile Attempts.

**Goal:** To reduce or eliminate the need for desperate or futile attempts before moving on to the next stage.

**Addiction Control Change Process:**

Step 1A — Action—Attempting uncontrolled use with no consequences.

Step 1B — Maintenance—Permanently successful uncontrolled use with no consequences.

Step 1C — Pre-Contemplation—Failing but not thinking about attempting controlled use.

Step 1D — Contemplation—Thinking about attempting controlled use.

Step 1E — Preparation—Preparing to attempt common sense control over use.

## Stage Two—Attempted Common Sense Control

**Addiction Control Failure Sequence:**

Level 6 — Initial Attempts to control use and avoid further consequences.

Level 7 — Secondary Attempts.

Level 8 — Serious Attempts.

Level 9 — Desperate Attempts.

Level 10 — Futile Attempts.

**Goal:** To reduce or eliminate the need for desperate or futile attempts before moving on to the next stage.

**Addiction Control Change Process:**

Step 2A — Action—Attempting common sense control over use.

Step 2B — Maintenance—Permanently successful controlled use with no consequences.

Step 2C — Pre-Contemplation—Failing but not thinking about any need for total abstinence.

Step 2D — Contemplation—Thinking about possible need for permanent total abstinence.

Step 2E — Preparation—Preparing to attempt permanent total abstinence.

## Stage Three—Attempted Analytical Abstinence

**Addiction Control Failure Sequence:**

Level 11 — Initial Attempts to abstain completely & permanently using rational coping skills.

Level 12 — Secondary Attempts.

Level 13 — Serious Attempts.

Level 14 — Desperate Attempts.

Level 15 — Futile Attempts.

**Goal:** To reduce or eliminate the need for desperate or futile attempts before moving on to the next stage.

*Addiction Control Change Process:*

Step 3A — Action—Attempting total abstinence with rational coping skills.

Step 3B — Maintenance—Permanently successful abstinence with rational coping skills.

Step 3C — Pre-Contemplation—Failing but not thinking about possible need for a spiritual solution.

Step 3D — Contemplation—Thinking about possible need for a spiritual solution.

## Transition Stage—From Hopeless to Wholeness

*Addiction Control Failure Sequence:*

Level 16 — "Step Zero"—Persistent failure to control or stop use.

Level 17 — "Step One"—Recognition of compulsion and "powerlessness."

*Addiction Control Change Process:*

Step 3E — Preparation—Preparing to attempt a traditional spiritual approach to sobriety.

## Stage Four—Attempted Spiritual Sobriety

*Addiction Control Failure Sequence:*

Level 18 — Initial Attempts to abstain permanently using traditional spiritual approaches.

Level 19 — Secondary Attempts.

Level 20 — Serious Attempts.

Level 21 — Desperate Attempts.

Level 22 — Futile Attempts.

**Goal:** To reduce or eliminate the need for desperate or futile attempts before moving on to the next stage.

*Addiction Control Change Process:*

Step 4A — Action—Attempting a traditional spiritual approach to sobriety.

Step 4B — Maintenance—Permanently successful traditional spiritual sobriety.

Step 4C — Pre-Contemplation—Failing but not thinking about need for rational spirituality.

Step 4D — Contemplation—Thinking about possible need for rational spiritual sobriety.

Step 4E — Preparation—Preparing for active pursuit of rational spiritual sobriety.

## Stage Five—Rational Spiritual Sobriety

**Addiction Control Failure Sequence:**

Level 23 — Initial Attempts to abstain permanently through rational spiritual sobriety.

Level 24 — Secondary Attempts.

Level 25 — Serious Attempts.

**Hypothesis:** Rational Spiritual Sobriety will not fail when fully understood and seriously attempted.

**Addiction Control Change Process:**

Step 5A — Action—Actively pursuing rational spiritual sobriety.

Step 5B — Maintenance—Permanently successful achievement of rational spiritual sobriety.

# THE ADDICTION PROGRESSION & RECOVERY EVALUATION PROCESS

### A) Client's Opinion     B) Clinician's Observation

For all potentially harmful addictive substances or behaviors, please identify, discuss, and evaluate all credible reasons—and all known or suspected facts—supporting both the client's opinion and the clinician's observations in each of the following ten areas:

1. Client's current *Level of Use*—and past highest *Level of Use*.
2. Client's current *Problem Severity Level*—and past highest *Severity Level*.
3. Client's current *Stage of Progression* into Harmful Addiction.
4. Client's current *Stage* on the *Addiction Recovery Learning Curve*.
5. Client's current *Level* in the *Addiction Control Failure Sequence*.
6. Client's current *Action* or *Maintenance Step* in the *Addiction Control Change Process*.

7. *Learning Curve Stage* and *Action Step* Client currently Contemplates, if any.
8. *Learning Curve Stage* and *Action Step* Client *needs* to Contemplate Next.
9. *Learning Curve Stage* and *Action Step* Client *needs* to Prepare for Next.
10. *Learning Curve Stage* and *Action Step* Client *needs* to Move To Next.

- - - - - - - - - - - - - - - - - - - - - - - - - - - - - - - - - - - - - - - - -

## Levels of Use

1. Abstinence.
2. Experimental Use.
3. Rare, Minimal, or Occasional Use.
4. Normal, Social, Recreational, or Moderate Use.
5. Heavy or Frequent Use.
6. Excessive or Problem Use.
7. Abuse.
8. Dependence.

## Range of Problem Severity

1. None.
2. Mild.
3. Moderate.
4. Serious.
5. Severe.
6. Grave.

## Stages of Progression into Harmful Addiction

1. No Signs or Symptoms.
2. Problem Use.
3. Warning Stage.
4. Early Stage.
5. Middle Stage.
6. Late Stage.

- - - - - - - - - - - - - - - - - - - - - - - - - - - - - - - - - - - - - - - - -

## LEARNING FROM EXPERIENCE

Many years ago, long before he became the holistic health guru you may know about from public television and the shelves of your local bookstore, Andrew Weil wrote a book about addiction with the fascinating title:

*From Chocolate to Morphine.*

When we think about the compulsive nature of harmful addiction—and about all of the signs, symptoms, and mounting negative consequences that we have seen in our detailed review of the *stages of progression*—we always need to remember that most people start out on this treacherous path rather innocently by "using" a particular addictive substance or behavior in order to help themselves *"feel good" or "feel better" in some way.*

In 1929, Ogden Nash observed that:

"Candy is dandy, but liquor is quicker."

Each of these substances—the dandy candy, the quicker liquor, the chocolate, or the morphine—clearly starts out subjectively doing something beneficial "for" the user, and not just something objectively harmful "to" them.

Unfortunately, in a harmful addiction, a gradual loss of control over use of the chosen addictive substance or behavior eventually starts to produce unintended negative consequences that are clearly harmful or destructive for the user or for others.

Strangely, however, even after they have started to complain about many negative consequences and the mounting costs of use, many people will continue to feel quite strongly that there are still many important ongoing benefits of use.

As the negative consequences associated with their harmful addiction continue to get progressively worse over time, most users will begin to "experiment"—over and over again—trying to find a *magic formula* that will somehow allow them to continue reaping the benefits of use while avoiding the negative consequences.

One of the central identifying characteristics of a harmful addiction will be the persistent *failure* of these attempts at control and *continued use* despite the ongoing experience of negative consequences.

And yet, many users who find themselves in this unhealthy and dangerous predicament will persist in acting as if they believed—in the memorable words of Mae West—that:

"Too much of a good thing is . . . wonderful!"

Obviously, this kind of faulty "logic" is pure nonsense. In fact, the addictive beliefs that are so fervently held by most harmful users are often virtually incomprehensible to rational people who have no problems in this area—until we recall the *irrational* and *irresistible* nature of compulsion and remember the words of Alcoholics Anonymous:

> The idea that somehow, someday he will control and enjoy his drinking is the great obsession of every abnormal drinker. The persistence of this illusion is astonishing. Many pursue it to the gates of insanity or death.

> (Alcoholics Anonymous, 1976: 30)

In their book, *Staying Sober: A Guide to Relapse Prevention,* Terence Gorski and Merlene Miller offer a useful overview of the basic stages of change and growth in the overall addiction recovery process—and the developmental tasks linked to achieving permanent recovery at each stage.

Let's take a quick look at this model for a moment:

## THE RECOVERY PROCESS

### *Developmental Stages, Primary Tasks, and Treatment Goals*

1. **Pre-Treatment—Recognition of Addiction**

   Learning by the consequences that you cannot safely use addictive chemicals.

2. **Stabilization—Withdrawal and Crisis Management**

   Regaining control of thought processes, emotional processes, memory, judgment, and behavior.

3. **Early Recovery—Acceptance and Non-Chemical Coping**

   Accepting the disease of addiction and learning to function without drugs and alcohol.

4. **Middle Recovery—Balanced Living**

   Developing a normal, balanced lifestyle.

5. **Late Recovery—Personality Change**

   Development of healthy self-esteem, spiritual growth, healthy intimacy, and meaningful living.

6. **Maintenance—Growth and Development**

   Staying sober and living productively.

   (Gorski & Miller, 1986: 83–102)

The crucial first step on the path toward changing any problem behavior is simply for the person with the problem to

- recognize *that* a problem actually exists, and to
- clearly identify *what* the problem actually is.

As clinicians, we will see that many of our clients in the warning stage or early stage of developing a harmful addiction aren't even *thinking* about making any changes in their attitudes or behavior.

Why?

*Because at this early stage most clients really don't feel that there is any problem.*

Therefore, as we begin to work with our clients in a concurrent and mutually reinforcing psychoeducational assessment and counseling process we will initially need to help them

- **learn** about the many signs and symptoms of harmful addiction,
- **identify** which signs, symptoms, and negative consequences they have already experienced personally,
- **understand** the true nature of *compulsion*,
- **correctly interpret** the actual *meaning* of their own experience— past, present, and future,
- make an **accurate self-diagnosis** of their own condition, and
- **honestly face** the question:

### "Am I really in control of my own behavior?"

For many people who develop the most serious harmful addictions, answering this vital question will not be an easy, quick, or simple matter.

Indeed, the *presumably simple stage of recovery* that Gorski and Miller almost seem to dismiss by calling it "pre-treatment"—with its deceptively simple goal—"learning by the consequences that you cannot safely use addictive chemicals"—often takes *many years* for some people to complete.

In many cases, this extended learning process—which has also been called the "transition stage" of recovery—may involve

- many "treatment failures,"
- multiple relapses,
- repeated loss of control,
- mounting negative consequences, and
- a great deal of painful trial and error.

Whether we like it or not, most of this is almost completely *unavoidable*. Why?

Because—as we've already seen in our detailed examination of the signs, symptoms, and stages of progression—a serious problem with harmful addiction often develops quite slowly and it is sometimes very difficult—for the user and for others—to distinguish the signs of an emerging problem from some of the effects of so-called "normal use."

As the signs of a serious problem begin to surface more clearly, many users will also feel strong ambivalence and mixed motives about either controlled use or permanent abstinence, and many of them will gradually develop unconscious or semi-conscious patterns of excuses and alibis reinforced by rationalization, minimization, self-deception, or denial—that seriously obstruct their ability to recognize or address the emerging problem.

Even after the user finally sees and admits that a real "problem" actually exists, another complicating factor often emerges:

> In most cases—at this early point in the transition process—most users with a harmful addiction haven't even *begun* to contemplate the *possibility* that they might not be *able* to easily control and safely continue their use if they really wanted to do so.

Sadly, it seems that very few people are wise enough to have any real ability to learn much from the painful experience or example of others—and even less so from their warnings—no matter how well-informed or well-intended these warnings may be.

Most people will usually need to be firmly convinced—by *their own personal experience* of repeatedly trying and failing to control their use—that they "cannot safely use" the addictive substance or behavior that has become a problem for them.

As Alfred, Lord Tennyson, has written:

> "Others' follies teach us not,
> Nor much their wisdom teaches;
> And most, of sterling worth, is what
> Our own experience preaches."

For most people, it's only after the mounting costs of continued use have finally come to *far outweigh* the perceived benefits of use that they begin to develop any deeply internalized motivation for change.

Ultimately, we must recognize that the two processes of *active progression* and *gradual transition to recovery* will almost always have to *overlap*.

We need to appreciate how some people can actually be "getting better" over an extended period of time—paradoxically and often almost imperceptibly—in terms of developing the knowledge, insight, and motivation they will eventually need in order to produce permanent change—even as they are also quite obviously and often dramatically "getting worse" in terms of readily observable signs, symptoms, and negative consequences.

How can this possibly be so? Because this is how most people with harmful addictions actually do change. The *direct personal experience* of getting worse over time, reinforced by the *increasingly painful* negative consequences involved, eventually proves to be *convincing,* and finally allows them to truly *recognize* their problem, *understand* it's severity, *admit* the failure of all their past and present efforts to achieve control or abstinence, *accept* their personal responsibility to *take more effective action* and finally become willing to *try to do something different about it.*

## A PRAGMATIC APPROACH

Thomas Edison has been quoted as saying:

> "Genius is one percent inspiration and ninety-nine percent perspiration."

With this attitude toward life and work, he would probably agree that:

> "The only place where "success" comes before "sweat" is in the dictionary."

True recovery from any harmful compulsive-addictive behavior is an active process. It involves learning from our own past, present, and *future* experiences — and from those of others whenever possible. Then, making our own choices, taking further action, making more mistakes, evaluating results, and thus learning more about the nature and severity of the problems we may face and what we can or cannot do about them.

Edison reportedly had to experiment with about a thousand different types of filaments before he was finally able to produce an electric light bulb that would last long enough to be commercially viable. One after another, the various materials and coatings he tried to use would burn out too quickly. So he kept changing his approach, over and over again, each time trying something slightly or radically different, until he found the combination of materials and coatings that would work.

One day, many years later, or so I've heard anecdotally, someone asked him how he was able to keep on trying, over and over again, after so many failures?

Edison looked at him, apparently rather confused, and said:

> *"What you mean by failure*? Every one of those experiments eliminated a method that wouldn't work, and they were all *suc-*

*cessful* in bringing me another step closer to finding one that would."

In Chapter Three of this book—during our discussion of "willpower" and "powerlessness" in the section focused on understanding "The Addiction Cycle"—we have seen how painful personal experience is often the most effective teacher for many people suffering from harmful addiction—and perhaps the only teacher for most people that will *ever* make a deep or lasting impression.

We have also seen how many people who are now successfully maintaining long-term sobriety in AA initially experienced one or more serious relapses before they "finally" got sober. These people will often jokingly refer to their last binge or extended relapse as *"the convincer."* Similarly, many people who have returned to AA after "going back out" and failing one more time to control their drinking—or those who have made the same unsuccessful experiment without ever leaving the meeting rooms of AA—will often joke:

"I was out there in the 'research division.'"

As an informal metaphor, this sort of humorously pragmatic and objective approach actually represents a fact-based, semi-scientific attitude—that is essentially experiential, experimental, and empirical—that could someday bode well for the bottom-line in a user's long-term recovery process."

As clinicians, I believe we can help shorten the typically extended addiction recovery learning process for some of our voluntary clients—those who genuinely want to change their harmful compulsive or addictive behavior—simply by making it more explicit—even when they remain deeply ambivalent about making any permanent change. Likewise, I believe we can also help motivate some of our involuntary clients toward the development of an internalized desire for change simply by introducing them to the concept of an *Addiction Recovery Learning Curve.*

This unified five stage model could be especially useful if clients were introduced to it in early treatment episodes that typically might take place during the warning stage or early stage of progression into harmful addiction. Ideally, it might give these clients *a conceptual framework* that could help them make sense of their *future* experiences more quickly—and help them recognize that healthy and rewarding alternatives really exist for them more easily—almost in spite of themselves.

Even when they're initially resentful and resistant—and have little or no conscious desire to change—many people who have been legally mandated or otherwise pressured into treatment could *eventually* benefit from receiving good information about the irrational, compulsive, and progressive nature of harmful addiction.

Of course, this *general information* can be even more valuable when it is accompanied by detailed feedback about the specific signs and symptoms of harmful addiction that the client may have already experienced personally. Ultimately, this individualized feedback could then be even more useful over the long-run when presented with *a detailed early warning about future signs, symptoms, and negative consequences that the client may eventually experience—and should start to watch out for*—if they plan, quite understandably and predictably, to carry on with their "field research" and continue using.

Those clients who are in fact destined to develop more serious problems with harmful addiction will thus have been given a set of baseline concepts to consider in their initial treatment episodes—and will have provided some baseline data for themselves to recall and for the clinical record to reflect should they present for future treatment episodes. In that event, of course, they will undoubtedly have much more relevant data to report and many more salient experiences in their harmful addiction history to process and try to understand—and most likely many more advanced signs, symptoms, and negative consequences to consider as well.

## AN HONEST APPROACH

Most importantly, the *Face to Face Unified Addiction Recovery Model* proposes that clients can benefit from an informed combination of general knowledge that's presented concurrently with individualized assessment and feedback processes when both are coupled with a genuinely caring therapeutic engagement and an uncompromising challenge for clients—at any age or stage of progression—to stop and think seriously about the fundamental realities of life and *get honest with themselves.*

In many cases, of course, mandated or otherwise coerced clients may feel that they can't be—or just don't *want* to be—completely honest with anyone about the true facts of their experience. In my view, the near certainty that some clients will be deliberately lying or withholding information should be openly and non-judgmentally discussed and realistically acknowledged with all clients—both individually and when working together in psychoeducational or psychotherapeutic groups.

Then, in both settings, I believe that a simple request should be made in roughly the following terms:

> "I understand why you might feel that you have to lie to me about all this. And that's okay, if that's the best you can do for right now.

I don't take it personally, and I'd only admire your courage and your wisdom when and if you ever came clean with me.

But I do have *one* request:

Please try to take all of this information in as best you can, and try to take all of these questions very seriously, and try to answer them for yourself as honestly as you possibly can.

Please do yourself a big favor and take some time to look at yourself in the mirror—*face to face*—and just try your best to get real.

In other words, you can lie to me—if you feel you really have to—but *please don't lie to yourself.*"

This heartfelt request is reflected in the unofficial "motto" of the *Face to Face Unified Addiction Recovery Model:*

> *"Be sure to keep a mirror always nigh,*
> *in some convenient handy sort of place,*
> *and now and then look squarely in thine eye,*
> *and with thyself keep ever face to face."*

> —John Kendrick Bangs.

## A DESCRIPTIVE AND VALID APPROACH

Before proceeding any further, let's take a few moments here to briefly consider the "empirical foundation" for the *Face to Face Unified Addiction Recovery Model* and explore the "theoretical validity" of the *Addiction Recovery Learning Curve* concept.

In their book *Research in Social Work,* William Reid and Audrey Smith discuss the essential difference between naturalistic, qualitative research methodology—where a researcher often acts as a "participant observer"—and experimental, quantitative research methods—where "the researchers role is that of the objective observer whose involvement with the phenomena being studied is limited to what is required to obtain necessary data." They describe quantitative research as "the extension to the social sciences of the methodology of the natural sciences," and they contrast this approach with qualitative research designs where:

Stress would be placed on understanding the system from the perspective of the actors involved rather than through imposition of the researchers' theoretical views.

Reid and Smith indicate that "qualitative methodology rests on the assumption that valid understanding can be gained through accumulated knowledge acquired firsthand by a single researcher."

They also stress the view that

*essential validity* is accorded the researcher's understanding gained through variable methods of *data collection* and through the use of his or her own capacity for *analysis* and *synthesis* of complex events.

(Reid & Smith, 1981: 87–89. Emphasis added.)

In this regard, let me stress that *the five stages of change on the Addiction Recovery Learning Curve are purely descriptive and are not merely theoretical.*

By this, I mean that these five stages are *not* based on an experimental, quantitative research study designed to test some abstract academic theory or scientific hypothesis about how people *might* or *should* be able to produce permanent change in their most harmful compulsive or addictive behaviors. Rather, these five stages are merely a retrospective "synthesis and description" of an empirical reality that is readily observable and widely repeated in the personal experience of many users. My original contribution in this book is merely to structure and present a new conceptual framework that accurately describes this reality with some newly-minted and easiliy understandable clinical terminology.

This descriptive "learning curve" model is based solidly on the foundation of countless direct personal observations that I have made over a period of 23 years during personal and professional interactions that I've had with thousands of people dealing with very serious harmful addictions.

My own views on addiction and recovery are based in part on my professional education and clinical training as a licensed clinical social worker and a licensed alcohol and drug abuse counselor—and even more extensively on my direct clinical experience working thousands of clients in the mental health and addictions treatment field since 1987.

My views are also drawn from my own personal experience in recovery from compulsive overeating and morbid obesity since 1981—at which time I weighed more than 300 pounds—plus my unusual experience maintaining a normal weight and a weight loss of about 140 pounds since 1983. During this time, I've had countless personal interactions with thousands of peers in recovery and have made innumerable direct observations that have helped shape my perspective during more than two decades of active participation in a self-help recovery program.

Finally, in addition to the insight gained through my education, training, and thousands of empirical observations, the theoretical framework for the *Face to Face Unified Addiction Recovery Model* and the *Addiction Recovery Learning Curve* concept has also evolved through a long process of personal study and reflection—carefully assimilating and slowly synthesizing a wide range of diverse views on *addiction, recovery, rationality, and spirituality.*

The sum total of all the data that I have gathered during the past 23 years of "naturalistic, qualitative field research" has made it very clear to me that this is how *most* people who develop serious harmful addictions actually *do* change or ultimately *fail* to change such behavior over the long run.

In essence, let me reiterate that this new "model" merely *describes* and *structures* observable reality in a systematic way with some newly coined technical terms and innovative clinical concepts. The experiential reality of this long-term process of personal change has been widely recognized and openly discussed in different ways for decades by many people who are active in the addiction treatment field and in various self-help recovery programs. It has also been widely recognized that this *basic learning process* is often—and perhaps even universally—repeated among those people who eventually develop and then struggle to overcome the most serious harmful addictions.

What has been sadly missing—thus far—has been any widespread recognition of the powerful underlying unity that binds all of the superficially "competing" addiction treatment and recovery philosophies together into the seamless whole that this new model merely seeks to explain and formalize.

We will begin to examine the integrated philosophical principles underlying the *Addiction Recovery Learning Curve* model in the next chapter.

At this early point in its formal development, I make no apology for the fact that there is no published empirical research establishing the reliability of the *Face to Face Unified Addiction Recovery Model,* nor any documented "scientific" evidence supporting the validity and clinical soundness of *the Addiction Recovery Learning Curve* concept.

In this regard, Reid and Smith point out that:

> qualitative methodologists ascribe an *essential validity* to the firsthand, holistic knowledge acquired by the researcher. Quantitative methodologists, on the other hand, are basically skeptical about knowledge gained in this way, objecting to its imprecision, its vulnerability to bias, and lack of rigor in investigating causal sequences. As a result, they tend to view qualitative methodology as a form of exploratory-formulative research, useful primarily as a precursor to more definitive, quantitative investigations. *Rejecting this subordinate role, qualitative*

> *researchers believe that their methods are quite capable of acquiring definitive knowledge.*

They also make the following points that are central to understanding and accepting the "essential validity" of the *Face to Face Model*:

> It may be true that the knowledge gained by the qualitative researcher may be skewed by the biases of the investigation, but at the same time it may reveal *a richness and depth of understanding of complex situations* that is simply beyond the capacity of quantitative research, no matter how rigorously and artfully applied . . .

> A holistic viewpoint and the gradual synthesis of data from many sources can result in *a grasp of relationships* that might never emerge in fragmented quantitative analysis . . .

> Even if quantitative research is taken as the epitome of the scientific method, it must be recognized that *many facets of social phenomena do not lend themselves to quantitative study*. With all their limitations, *qualitative investigations may often have greater payoff in usable knowledge.*

> (Reid & Smith, 1981: 89–91. Emphasis added.)

Now, let's begin to take a look at some of the *philosophical premises* underlying the *Face to Face Unified Addiction Recovery Model*.

## THE "EITHER-OR" FALLACY

Here is a quick POP QUIZ:

**Question 1:**  How many therapists does it take to change a light bulb?
*Answer A:*  *One. But the light bulb has to really want to change.*
*Answer B:*  *None. A therapist can help, but the light bulb has to change itself.*
*Answer B:*  *Ten. One therapist helps the light bulb change, and nine of them try to finish the paperwork!*

**Question 2:**  How many alcoholics does it take to change a light bulb?
*Answer:*  *Two. One of them holds the light bulb, and the other one drinks until the room starts to spin.*

**Question 3:**  How many Al-Anon members does it take to screw in a light bulb?
*Answer:*  *None. The Al-Anon members detach with love, and the light bulb screws itself.*

**Question 4:**  How many academic intellectuals does it take to change a light bulb?

> ***Answer:***   *Two. One to change the light bulb, and a second one to kick the chair out from under him.*

Historically, the addiction treatment and recovery field has been marked by a number of "serious" and often heated philosophical disagreements, and this sad tendency shows little or no sign of abating.

As we have just seen, I believe that the *Face to Face Unified Addiction Recovery Model* and the *Addiction Recovery Learning Curve* simply reflect the observable reality of how most people actually change seriously harmful compulsive or addictive behaviors over an extended period of time.

Nevertheless, there are specific principles and practices that are "put to the test" in each of the five different stages of change in this model that some highly partisan or dogmatic advocates of other philosophical approaches would probably scorn as being *heretical—or possibly even hateful.*

When considering the comparative validity of various "controversial approaches" to addiction and recovery issues it is often quite useful to bear in mind the following two pearls of wisdom:

- "Beware of hardening of the categories.
- "A conclusion is what you reach when you get tired of the effort of thinking."

For any reader who is already involved in the addiction treatment and recovery field—if you find yourself feeling *seriously offended* by any part of this *unified addiction recovery model* —it may also be useful to take a close look at yourself in the mirror and consider the sobering words of George Santayana:

> "Fanaticism consists in redoubling your effort when you have forgotten your aim."

The three most significant areas of toxic misunderstanding, misinformation, disagreement, and debate in the addiction treatment and recovery field—for which an open mind and a decent sense of humor are often a good antidote—involve:

- Social learning models of addiction "versus" the disease model,
- Controlled use or moderation based models of recovery "versus' the total abstinence approach, and
- Cognitive-behavioral, "rational," or "secular" recovery models "versus" the twelve step "spiritual" model.

We will be considering the contending philosophical and practical issues involved in each of these approaches in some detail in the next chapter, so we'll just take a quick overview of the topic for now.

In an effort to bring some clarity to these muddy adversarial waters—strictly within the context of various total abstinence approaches—the National Institute on Alcohol Abuse and Alcoholism (NIAAA) conducted Project MATCH over an eight-year period starting in 1989. This multi-site research project—which has been described as "the largest and most expensive treatment research study ever conducted in the alcoholism field"—tried to determine scientifically whether or not there were any identifiable patient characteristics that could be used to predict greater treatment success.

It attempted to accomplish this by psychologically testing a large pool of patients—all of whom had been previously diagnosed with alcohol dependence—and then randomly assigning them to participate in a standardized, manual-based outpatient treatment program consisting of either:

- Cognitive-Behavioral Coping Skills Therapy,
- Motivational Enhancement Therapy, *or*
- Twelve Step Facilitation Therapy.

(Marlatt, 1999)

In December, 1996, prior to the publication of the full-research report in 1997, the NIAAA issued a news release announcing the researchers' principle conclusion, that:

"patient-treatment matching does not substantially alter outcomes."

(NIAAA, 1996)

However, I would challenge a faulty premise underlying the entire research design for Project MATCH which is:

the *mistaken* assumption that it is either necessary or wise to make an exclusive treatment choice of this kind.

This initial "either-or" fallacy is a fundamental flaw in the choice of experimental variables that Project MATCH was designed to test—which essentially invalidates the usefulness of entire undertaking.

With all due respect, thinking so narrowly "inside the box" in this manner seems to reflect the sort of adversarial and erroneous "hardening of the categories" that has tended to dominate the conventional wisdom of *all* of the "opposing camps" in the addiction treatment field to some degree over the past three or four decades.

When we thoughtfully and holistically consider the universal principles underlying cognitive-behavioral coping skills therapy, motivational enhancement therapy, *and* twelve step facilitation therapy, it should become quite clear in short order to anyone with an unbiased, open mind that in reality almost *all* clients could benefit from an eclectic combination of *all* three approaches.

Taking an "either-or" stance toward these *three powerful approaches* is nonsensical. It is very much like conducting a research program that would deprive one ill-fated experimental group of air, and a second unlucky group of water, and a third hapless group of food—in order to test whether people need air, water, *OR* food to survive—when all human beings obviously *need all three*.

After all, can anyone really dispute that improved cognitive-behavioral coping skills could potentially benefit almost anyone who is helped to develop them? And don't virtually all people need an objective assessment, constructive feedback, and some strong motivational encouragement at certain times to help them move on to the next stage of change in the addiction recovery process? And wouldn't a deeper understanding of many sound universal spiritual principles—such as those found in the twelve step recovery program and elsewhere—benefit almost anyone who could really grasp them and effectively incorporate them into their daily life in a rational, meaningful, and practical way?

## A UNIFIED APPROACH

When we take a look at the three core philosophical disagreements that often dominate conventional thinking in the addiction treatment and recovery field it can easily appear at first glance that the different positions taken on key questions—like the classic dispute over moderation or abstinence for instance—must inevitably clash with each other quite strongly.

However, as I've already pointed out in the Introduction to this book, when we look more closely at the deeper underlying principles involved in each approach we will begin to see how these apparent conflicts are largely *semantic, superficial, unfortunate, and unnecessary.*

The *Face to Face Unified Addiction Recovery Model* and the *Addiction Recovery Learning Curve* concept are designed to help people reconcile many of the *apparent philosophical "differences"* which seem to be so glaring when the overall process of harmful addiction, progression, recognition, and recovery is seen shortsightedly in a *superficial, partial, and fragmented manner.*

190

There is, in fact, a powerful underlying unity and coherence that binds all of the apparently "competing" addiction treatment and recovery philosophies together into a *seamless whole.*

This essential unity can be recognized quite clearly when we take the time to look at *all* of the different philosophical approaches holistically. In fact, we can easily see how well they all fit together and complement each other when we start to look at them in *a logical sequence on a simple continuum of change.*

My ultimate aim as a writer, speaker, trainer, and seminar leader dealing with addiction and recovery issues is to help more clinicians and clients achieve *a clear understanding of this deeper unity.*

### Why do I call this approach the Face to Face *Unified* Addiction Recovery Model?

Because all of the different philosophical approaches to addiction treatment and recovery can fit easily and comfortably into this model and all of them are accepted and understood as being *legitimate* and *clinically appropriate* for *certain* people when they are dealing with *different* issues at *particular* stages in the overall process of change on the *Addiction Recovery Learning Curve.*

Indeed, for many people, fully mastering the fundamentals of each approach in a logical sequence—including the knowledge base and practical skills involved—will often prove to be essential in the process of achieving permanent recovery and sustained personal growth.

As we will see, the insights and skills clients can learn at each stage will often represent crucial developmental tasks and essential building blocks for change that they will eventually need as they move forward through the overall process of change.

Let me stress once more, however, that this is *not* because the particular approach employed at a particular stage is expected to "work" for them.

Rather, as we have seen, it is simply because most people will have to *find out for themselves*—through their own *direct personal experience*—whether or not a given approach will work for them before they will *ever* be ready—usually after repeated, painful failures—to move on to the next stage.

For example?

- Most people will usually have to experience the negative consequences of unrestricted use repeatedly before they would ever be seriously motivated to consistently attempt controlled use.

- Most people will usually have to fail miserably and repeatedly at controlled use before they would ever be seriously motivated to attempt complete abstinence through the consistent use of rational coping skills.

- Most people will usually have to fail miserably and repeatedly at this kind of "rational-secular" sobriety before they would ever imagine that they might need or be seriously motivated to attempt any kind of "spiritual solution."

- And, finally, many people will often have to "fail" at a vaguely defined and hence poorly understood attempted spiritual solution as well before they would ever be seriously motivated to personally identify and persistently practice a set of universal spiritual principles that they can easily understand and express in *clear, simple, modern, rational terms.*

Happily—if they have given all of the recommended approaches a *serious and open-minded effort* at each stage —many users will eventually be able to use the enhanced insight and improved coping skills gained in the process quite constructively at some point in the future. This will often be so despite the fact that they may have had to admit defeat at that particular stage on the *Addiction Recovery Learning Curve* and then move on to try a different set of addiction recovery methods or goals in the next.

## AN ECLECTIC APPROACH

The psychologist Abraham Maslow may be best known for his famous "Hierarchy of Needs." However, he is also the original source for a very well-known saying:

> "When the only tool you own is a hammer, every problem begins to resemble a nail."

This notion may offer a partial explanation for the ineffectual "either-or" approach that some people seem to take when dealing with addiction treatment and recovery issues.

Sadly, many theorists and practitioners seem to be much too firmly attached to one particular addiction recovery philosophy and to one corresponding treatment method. This often leads them to adopt a "one size fits all" approach toward addiction treatment which they will tend to employ consistently—regardless of a particular client's individual needs, abilities, and circumstances, level of insight, motivational goals, stage of progression, and stage of change.

By contrast, the *Face to Face Unified Addiction Recovery Model* incorporates an eclectic and cumulative blend of different therapeutic interventions and self-help models that complement and reinforce each other significantly over time and can empower some clients much more effectively in the long-run than would any single approach.

Ideally, each of these therapeutic approaches—which will be identified and discussed in the next chapter—should be custom tailored and intuitively blended with the others by a skilled clinician to meet the individual learning needs of a particular client and help them accomplish the distinct developmental tasks that are found at each stage on the *Addiction Recovery Learning Curve*.

I have already stressed my conviction that this new model merely *describes* observable reality in a systematic way with some newly coined technical terms and concepts. On another level, however, the model is *unique* and *original* in recommending a *fairly specific, eclectic blend* of treatment approaches and self-help models.

There is, however, one important caveat that I need to mention here:

While the underlying principles and practical goals that apply at each stage on the *Addiction Recovery Learning Curve* are of central importance, my own personal recommendations regarding the treatment methods and self-help models to be employed are intended to be illustrative of general principles and thus suggestive only.

Therefore, I believe it could be perfectly appropriate and highly effective in many cases for an experienced and knowledgeable clinician to blend in other therapeutic approaches, methods, or techniques—and to recommend other self-help programs—as long as these are philosophically consistent with the core principles and key developmental goals of each particular stage on the overall learning curve model

Now that we've taken an overview of the entire *Face to Face Unified Addiction Recovery Model*, let's turn to our attention to the next chapter, where we will examine the philosophical premises underlying the five stages of change on the *Addiction Recovery Learning Curve* in more detail, explain the different goals and learning processes involved at each stage, and review the eclectic blend of psychotherapeutic approaches and self-help models involved.

# CHAPTER 8

---

# The Addiction Recovery Learning Curve

"Assume a virtue, if you have it not . . . Refrain tonight, and that shall lend a kind of easiness to the next abstinence; the next more easy; for use almost can change the stamp of nature."

—William Shakespeare.

"The path of excess leads to the palace of wisdom."

—William Blake.

"Life is a succession of lessons which must be lived to be understood."

—Ralph Waldo Emerson.

◆ ◆ ◆

In the previous chapter, we've taken a look at the five basic stages of change and twenty-five possible levels of motivational intensity involved in the overall process of change on the *Addiction Recovery Learning Curve*.

This new model offers a conceptual framework for understanding a natural developmental learning process that's readily observable in the experience of many users and easily understandable when the overall process of change in addiction, progression, and recovery is considered objectively as a whole.

This model tries to explain this natural learning process in fairly clear and systematic terms that may be easily misunderstood by some readers. Let me stress, therefore, that this model should not be interpreted as an overly rational, rigid, and linear attempt to neatly compartmentalize what amounts to a very human, imperfect, irrational, and painful personal experience for many users.

In fact, this model is designed to help clinicians and clients make some sense of where they may stand—and where they may be headed—in a naturally nonlinear, illogical, repetitive, and circular learning process. Therefore, all of the concepts and terms proposed by this new model to describe this natural process must be understood and used in an adaptive, flexible, and pragmatic way that recognizes this ultimate reality.

Whether we like it or not, it's vital to understand and accept the fact that many people with the most serious harmful addictions will probably have to go through a slow, frustrating, confusing, scary, messy, disorganized, and occasionally agonizing learning process in order to successfully make *the difficult transition from active progression into a viable and enduring recovery.*

In the previous chapter, we've taken a quick look at this new model in a fairly simple outline form. Now, we can begin a more detailed discussion of the philosophical premises underlying the *Face to Face Unified Addiction Recovery Model,* review the different goals, learning processes, and methods of change involved at each stage on the *Addiction Recovery Learning Curve*, and highlight some of the key principles found in each of the psychotherapeutic approaches and self-help models included in this eclectic approach.

Let's start with the:

## FOUNDATION STAGE: PERSONAL RESPONSIBILITY AND MOTIVATION

A client who enters treatment with unresolved issues or serious doubts about their need to accept complete personal responsibility for their own life may already be sincerely motivated to abstain completely and permanently from all harmful addictive substances or behaviors. Hence, they could be seen as working through *Stage Three* or *Four* on the *Addiction Recovery Learning Curve*—which are *Attempted Analytical Abstinence* or *Attempted Spiritual Sobriety*. However, they could just as easily be starting out in *Stage One*—which is *Uncontrolled Use with Consequences*—blissfully unaware that any harmful addictive problem even exists, or may eventually develop, and completely unmotivated to even contemplate the idea of making any changes in their own attitudes or behavior.

### Philosophical Premise:

Regardless of their current level of motivation for change, or their apparent stage of change on the *Addiction Recovery Learning Curve*, anyone hoping to change any kind of deeply rooted behavioral habit must eventually come to terms with the *Foundation Stage* –which addresses the fundamental issues of *Personal Responsibility and Motivation.*

Why is that? Because most people will have little or no chance of success at any stage if they have not truly learned, understood, accepted, and started to practice the basic principles found in *Reality Therapy, Transactional Analysis, Cognitive-Behavioral Therapy*—and in many other sound models for personal change and growth—that all stress the vital importance of realism, rationality, and responsibility in one way or another.

President Harry S. Truman was often subjected to harsh criticism and merciless ridicule by his political opponents—who coined the phrase: "To err is Truman." Nevertheless, apart from occasionally turning a blind eye to the misdeeds of some friends, he was rarely criticized for ducking his own personal responsibility, as America's Chief Executive Officer, for making tough choices and taking the blame as necessary when things went wrong. In fact, Truman liked to remind himself—and anyone else involved in decision-making at the highest level—that he alone was ultimately responsible for making the really hard choices on the most important and difficult issues coming to him from all over the country and all over the world.

To stress this point, he had a small sign sitting on his desk in the White House which said simply:

"The buck stops here."

There's a bit of bumper sticker humor that expresses a far more common attitude that many people seem to embrace, which says:

"The buck doesn't even slow down here."

They also seem to remain blissfully unaware of a simple but significant anatomical fact:

"Whenever I point a finger at someone else, there are always three fingers pointing back at me."

If there is one fundamental point about addiction treatment—and the overall addiction recovery process—that must be clearly understood by anyone who would like to be helpful to others—or to recover personally—it is this simple fact:

There is
*no* technique or treatment,
*no* method or medication, and
*no* procedure, program, or philosophy
that can help anyone *permanently change*

any *serious* harmful addiction
without *deeply* engaging
and *consistently* sustaining
their own *passionate motivation* to do so
as their *single most important personal priority.*

In the long-run—even when the overall recovery process is supported by various treatments, techniques, methods, medications, procedures, programs, or philosophies—the recovering person must always remember that true lifetime recovery from harmful addiction will ultimately have to be something done *"by" them because it can never be done "for" them or "to" them.*

Many clinicians, however, work in treatment settings where we have a formal therapeutic relationship with people who are cast into the social role of being a "patient." This stereotyped label often implies that the person playing the patient role will be seen as the passive recipient of some kind of *outside intervention, treatment, medication, or procedure.*

Over the past few decades, however, there has been a growing awareness in medicine of a holistic *mind-body-spirit* connection and a growing recognition of the vital role that the patient *must* play in their own healing.

The old-fashioned "medical model" for defining the roles and responsibilities of the "patient" and the "healer" has been slowly falling out of favor—even in traditional medicine. This archaic approach is now seen by many as overly paternalistic, occasionally authoritarian, and often ineffective—*especially in the realm of behavioral health.* Hence—except in some rare cases of extreme disability or impairment—many healthcare providers now stress the fact that the "patient" must

- take complete personal responsibility for their own wellness, and
- play an active role in their own healing.

While this is true for modern healthcare, prevention, wellness, and fitness programs in general—and for enlightened mental health, self-help, and personal growth programs in particular—in the process of addiction treatment and recovery it's especially true that:

Passivity is a formula for disaster.

Indeed, the need for people to take personal responsibility and persistent action is so central to the addiction recovery process that I deliberately avoid using the relatively passive word "patient" in my professional writing or speaking as much as possible. Instead, I strongly prefer to use the more active word "client" to describe the people we serve in addiction treatment—regardless of our clinical role or practice setting.

True recovery from harmful addiction is a very active, lifelong process, and I vividly recall *a small decal* that had been placed *on every bathroom mirror* in the Guenster Rehabilitation Center—a residential alcohol and drug abuse treatment center located in Bridgeport, Connecticut—which flatly declared:

> "You are looking at the person who is responsible for your sobriety."

Edgehill Newport, a nationally renowned substance abuse treatment center once located in Newport, Rhode Island, awarded *a small medallion* to every client who had successfully completed the residential treatment program there. This medallion had an engraving of the Newport Bridge on one side, and on the other side it presented a powerful reminder that emphasized the same vital point with the simple slogan:

> "I am responsible."

Thus, clinicians working with people struggling with any form of harmful addiction must constantly stress the need for them to accept personal responsibility for improving and maintaining their own well-being. We must also stress the imperative need for them to develop both their willingness and ability to take sustained action if they hope to be successful in the difficult process of long-term addiction recovery.

## Learning Process:

There's a well-known recovery slogan that urges patience and persistence by describing the subjective experience of a recovering person in this way:

> First, it gets real.
> Then, it gets worse.
> Then, it gets better.

As clinicians, we need to help our clients get over any immature longing for "instant gratification," and abandon any hopeless yearning to find some kind of a "quick fix," a "magic pill," or a "silver bullet."

We need to help our clients understand that the overall process involved in addiction and recovery can probably be grasped more usefully in these terms:

> First, it gets *worse*—while I'm using.
> Then, it gets *real*—when I stop.
> Then, I *feel* worse.
> Then, I take *action*.
> Then, it *gets* better.

Then, I *feel* better.

Just like the "Law of Gravity," the "Law of Karma" seems to be an inescapable fact of life. This universal principle can be expressed in Western terms by the phrase:

*"What you sow is what you reap."*

Anyone embracing a dogmatic belief system that insists this isn't really so will eventually find out otherwise—just as surely as if they had confidently walked off the edge of a cliff on the strength of an absolute philosophical conviction that they could fly.

This is the true meaning of the bumper sticker which laments sadly that:

"My karma ran over my dogma."

In addiction recovery, the "law of personal responsibility" works in the same inexorable way.

It has often been pointed out that:

"A decision *not* to make a decision is still a decision."

When someone facing a potentially serious problem decides to "wait and see," "do nothing," "hope for the best," or just "give up all hope"—or when they blindly ignore, willfully neglect, or just try to forget important personal matters—we must remember that these are all autonomous personal *choices* that they are actually making—either consciously or unconsciously—and that they will have to live or die with the positive results or negative consequences that follow.

We need to let our clients know that while they can choose to either neglect or embrace their personal responsibility for how they live their own lives—their ultimate personal responsibility can never be truly abandoned or transferred. This is another basic fact of life—a universal principle—and perhaps even a fundamental law of nature:

> Except *perhaps* in cases of severe psychiatric disability or major cognitive impairment—regardless of whether they like the job or want the job—the fact is that no one can ever really abdicate their personal responsibility or resign from their role as *chief executive officer of their own life.*

> Even if someone actually tries to "delegate" the responsibility for making their choices to others—consciously or unconsciously—they are still *ultimately responsible* for making *that* choice and for dealing with the positive results or negative consequences that follow.

There is a fundamental point about the essential nature of life and reality that we as clinicians must help our clients begin to understand and accept:

> We are *all* personally responsible for our own lives—for our own beliefs, attitudes, motives, and desires; our thoughts, feelings, words, and deeds; our my goals, priorities, work, and relationships; our mistakes, lapses, failures, and flaws; and ultimately for our own joys, successes, health, harmony, and happiness..

In this regard, there's an interesting philosophical question that asks us to consider:

> "If ignorance is bliss, why aren't more people happy?"

Let me reframe that question in another way:

> Why do you suppose that most people will have little or no chance of achieving any *meaningful* success or finding any *true* happiness in life if they never learn or apply the *universal principles* and *core values* underlying so many sound models for personal change and growth—including *Reality Therapy, Transactional Analysis,* and *Cognitive-Behavioral Therapy* among others?

Most people simply don't understand how often they react emotionally, automatically, and unconsciously—and act out immaturely or hypercritically in so many shallow, negative, harmful or self-defeating ways. They simply don't recognize how their mental and emotional states and their everyday behavior is so often determined by unconscious or unexamined factors such as internalized parent or child ego-states, shallow motives, selfish desires, irrational beliefs, and distorted thinking patterns.

Nor do they truly understand how they alone are completely responsible for their own *thoughts, feelings, words, and deeds.*

Through sheer ignorance in most cases, many people still blame their own negative feelings, self-defeating behaviors, and personal problems or disappointments on the attitudes, words, and deeds of other people; on frustrating daily events; on difficult, demanding, or stressful situations; or perhaps even on some truly tragic or traumatic life circumstances.

Therefore—being mentally, emotionally, and spiritually blinded—they simply can't grasp how their emotional reactivity can *only* be triggered through the filter of their *own* personal values, beliefs, attitudes, motives, desires, and thinking style.

Because their thinking is not grounded in any consistently rational techniques or empowering foundational principles, most people who are functioning at this low level of awareness and insight simply cannot recognize—as yet—how they *alone* are ultimately responsible for *any* and *all* emotional *frustration* or *distress* they may feel.

This means, of course, that they also remain powerless—for the time being at least—to fully grasp the bright and promising implications of another simple but profound fact of human nature—that *they alone are ultimately responsible* for their own health, harmony, and happiness as well.

A fundamental goal during the *Foundation Stage* on the *Addiction Recovery Learning Curve* will be to help our clients accept and embrace complete personal responsibility for their own lives; for their own beliefs, attitudes, motives, desires, thoughts, feelings, words, and deeds; and for all positive results or negative consequences that may ensue.

## Treatment Approaches:

At the outset, the *Face to Face Unified Addiction Recovery Model* is grounded in the therapeutic principles and techniques found in *Reality Therapy, Transactional Analysis,* and *Cognitive-Behavioral or Rational-Emotive Therapy.*

As I've already indicated, it's far beyond the intended scope of this book to offer a detailed summary—or even a complete outline—of the various treatment and self-help approaches highlighted in the *Addiction Recovery Learning Curve* model. With that caveat in mind, here is a very brief sketch introducing some **fundamental principles** found in each approach:

**Treatment Approach:**

### Reality Therapy—William Glasser

> Developing a *therapeutic involvement* may take anywhere from one interview to several months . . . Once it occurs, the therapist begins to insist that the patient *face the reality of his behavior.* He is *no longer allowed to evade* recognizing what he is doing or his responsibility for it. When the therapist takes this step . . . the relationship deepens because now someone *cares* enough about the patient to make him face a truth that he has spent his life trying to avoid: *he is responsible for his behavior . . .*

> . . . the patient is *desperate for involvement* and suffering because he is *not able to fulfill his needs* . . . this desperation is often hard to see . . . The ability of the therapist to get *involved* is the major skill in doing Reality Therapy, but it is most difficult to describe . . . and when the patient does not *want* to be in therapy . . . the task is particularly difficult.

We emphasize *the morality of behavior*. We face the issue of *right and wrong* . . . in contrast to conventional psychiatrists who do not make the distinction between right and wrong . . .We teach patient *better ways* to fulfill their needs . . . (and develop) more satisfactory patterns of behavior. Conventional therapists do not feel that teaching *better behavior* is a part of therapy.

(Glasser, 1975: 33, 26, 54. Emphasis added.)

## Treatment Approach:

### Transactional Analysis—Eric Berne

. . . an *ego state* may be described as . . . a system of feelings accompanied by a related set of behavior patterns. Each individual seems to have available a limited repertoire of such ego states, which are *not roles but psychological realities* . . . (1) ego states which resemble those of *parental figures,* (2) ego states which are autonomously directed toward *objective appraisal of reality,* and (3) . . . ego states which were *fixated in early childhood* . . . Colloquially: 'Everyone carries his parents around inside' . . . 'Everyone has an adult' . . . (and) 'Everyone carries a little boy or girl around inside' . . .

Parents, deliberately or unaware, teach their children from birth how to behave, think, feel, and perceive. *Liberation* from these influences is no easy matter, since they are *deeply ingrained* and are necessary during the first two or three decades of life for biological and social survival . . . For certain fortunate people there is something that transcends all classifications of behavior, and that is *awareness*; something which rises above the programming of the past, and that is *spontaneity*; and something that is more rewarding than games, and that is *intimacy*.

(Berne, 1964: 23–24, 182, 184. Emphasis added.)

## Treatment Approach:

### Cognitive Therapy—Aaron Beck
### Rational-Emotive Therapy—Albert Ellis

It is often useful to make a distinction . . . between *'two types of thinking.'* The first type is the *higher-level* type of thinking that involves judgment, weighing of the evidence and consideration of alternative explanations *(secondary process)*. The *lower-level* form of cognition, in contrast, tends to be relatively rapid and does not seem to involve any complicated logical processes *(primary process)* . . . One of the characteristic of the lower-level cognitions is that they tend to be *auto-*

*matic.* They arise as if by *reflex* and are generally not the result of deliberation or careful reasoning.

(Beck, et al, 1967: 323. Emphasis added).

Although negative life events are likely to be accompanied by negative emotional states, these *events do not directly cause our emotional reactions* . . . According to the ABC Model . . . negative life events we often confront are called *Activating Events*, or As, and the emotions and behaviors that subsequently accompany these events are called the *Consequences*, or Cs . . . Whereas people traditionally argue that negative Activating Events in their lives (or in their pasts) actually cause their current distress . . . it is their *thoughts* and *Beliefs* or Bs, about Activating Events that primarily and more directly *cause their disturbances*.

(Ellis, et al., 1988: 2. Emphasis added.)

## Self-Help Model:

*The Seven Habits of Highly Effective People.*

During the *Foundation Stage* on the *Addiction Recovery Learning Curve,* which focuses on *Personal Responsibility and Motivation* and a bit later on as well in *Stage One* which involves *Uncontrolled Use With Consequences,* many clients are deeply invested in maintaining the illusion—inside and out—that "all is well." Therefore, they will tend to resist any labeling that might "diagnose," "pathologize," or "stigmatize" them or directly challenge the rigid façade which they always try to maintain that is masking their essentially fragile inner sense of self. They will also be likely to turn a deaf ear to any interventions that tend to overtly "therapize" them. Hence, they will often resist any self-help model that suggests there might be a need for any kind of recovery, rehabilitation, or remediation. Because of this, it may often be much more appropriate and effective to engage clients at this early stage with a solid, success-oriented self-help model that is essentially provocative but still non-threatening.

*The Seven Habits of Highly Effective People*—which offer exactly this kind of a challenging, positive, optimistic, and principle-centered focus on personal growth and achievement—may be paraphrased as follows:

1) Take personal responsibility and initiative for creating positive changes in your life.
2) Identify your core values and develop a personal vision, a clearly defined mission, and a set of meaningful and energizing goals for your life.

3) Focus attention and energy on your larger goals as the top priority in how you manage your time and plan your activities.

4) Avoid selfishness, competition, or conflict and work cooperatively with others for the mutual benefit of all.

5) Listen and genuinely care about the needs of others in all of your interactions.

6) Enhance your personal vision, energy, skills, and efforts by blending them with the vision, energy, skills, and efforts of others.

7) Take good care of yourself and continue to actively learn, grow, and improve as a person.

*Seven Habits of Highly Effective People*—Stephen Covey

> The Character Ethic . . . things like integrity, humility, fidelity, temperance, courage, justice, patience, industry, simplicity, modesty, and the Golden Rule . . . taught that there are *basic principles of effective living,* and people can only experience true success and enduring happiness as they learn and integrate these principles into their basic character . . .

> The Character Ethic is based on the fundamental idea that there are principles that govern human effectiveness—*natural laws in the human dimension* that are just as real, just as unchanging and (just as) unarguably 'there' as laws such as gravity are in the physical dimension . . . These principles are not esoteric, mysterious, or "religious" ideas . . . unique to any specific faith or religion . . . (They) are a part of every major enduring religion, as well as enduring social philosophies and ethical systems. They are self-evident and can easily be validated by any individual.

> (Covey, 1989: 18, 32. Emphasis added.)

## Self-Help Model:

*The Voice Dialogue Method.*

Most clients at this stage on the *Addiction Recovery Learning Curve* will not be ready for any kind of self-help program that is directly focused on changing potentially harmful compulsive or addictive behavior. However, they may benefit from exposure to a self-help model that focuses on raising their level of self-awareness and insight by increasing their ability to recognize the sometimes elusive fact that the "voice" that they "hear" or "use" on a daily basis in their continual process of internalized "self-talk" is *not necessarily their own.*

Most people can probably relate to the metaphorical notion of a rowdy "committee" that is continually *meeting inside their head,* and many of us can also appreciate the humor of the bumper sticker which confesses:

"I do what the voices in my head tell me to do."

A client in this initial *Foundation Stage* must be introduced to the concept that their negative feelings and harmful compulsive or addictive behavior most likely has some deep roots in unconscious or unexamined aspects of their own psyche and personality structure. They must gradually learn how irrational beliefs, distorted thought patterns, selfish desires, shallow motives, and emotionally reactive parent or child ego-states often operate automatically and semi-autonomously to drive their feelings and behavior in an irrational or compulsive manner. They must also learn that there are many sound cognitive-behavioral techniques for *rationally disputing* their own addictive beliefs and automatic thoughts.

Above all, it will be essential for clients who may or may not yet have any desire to accept personal responsibility for their own life, or to change any harmful addictive behavior, to begin to recognize that they possess—or may often be possessed by—an internalized *"addictive voice"* and *"addicted self"*—as opposed to their *"sane and sober self."*

There are three addiction recovery slogans that can powerfully reinforce this basic concept:

- "That's the disease talking."
- "I have a disease that talks to me in my own voice."
- "Half of my brain manufactures this *bull*, and the other half *believes* it!"

(Fingarette, 1988: 104–105)

As noted previously, Herbert Fingarette would clearly have to stretch the limits of his verbal comfort zone to utter the phrase "That's the disease talking," but he acknowledges the reality of a powerful inner force that he might feel comfortable calling "the addictive voice," when he declares that:

> For most of us, it is only when we are contemplating a serious change in some central activity that we come to consciously realize the momentum the activity has acquired . . . the change suddenly seems far more disruptive than we could have imagined. At this point, we may feel in the grip of some alien opposing power that is trying to prevent us from doing what we rationally want to do. But the obstacle is not in truth an alien power. It is our deeply-rooted habit-bound self opposing

the fragile reed of a new desire to be other than who or what we have been. And the more genuine our desire to change, the more tense and intense the conflict.

(Fingarette, 1988: 104–105).

Henry David Thoreau published his classic book *Walden* in 1854 at a time when slavery still flourished in the southern United States. In this book, he commented brilliantly on the internalized state of psychological bondage that many people have experienced throughout much of recorded history when he observed that:

It is hard to have a Southern overseer; it is worse to have a Northern one; but worst of all when you are the slave-driver of yourself.

(Thoreau, 1960: 10)

Edward Deci echoes this theme is his book *Why We Do What We Do: Understanding Self-Motivation*, when he notes that

A master-slave relationship exists to some degree within everyone.

Deci emphasizes the crucial difference between inner-directed autonomous behavior reflecting true freedom of choice, and "externally" controlled behavior which can also be internalized or "introjected" into our psyche in an unhealthy way. In this vein, he observes that "People can regulate themselves in quite autonomous and authentic ways, or alternatively in quite controlling and dictatorial ways, pressuring and criticizing themselves," and he adds that: "many people find this idea easy to comprehend in the case of, say, an addict, who is a slave to her addiction . . . but the dynamics are the same for many other behaviors."

Deci speaks of people who are "controlled by strong introjects" which he describes as "internalizations that take the form of 'shoulds' and 'oughts' . . . voices in one's head so to speak that . . . issue orders—sometimes like mean-spirited drill sergeants and sometimes like loving and well-meaning (but nonetheless intrusive) aunts." He says that true freedom and authenticity can never be found through any conscious or unconscious reaction to the demands of our introjects—regardless of whether our reaction takes the form of "rigid, dutiful compliance," or "half-hearted adherence," or "outright rebellion"—because any of these reactions ultimately cause people to "suppress their inner self" and when this occurs he states that "a mature, true self has never developed." (Deci, 1995: 11, 94–95, 111)

Finally, let's briefly consider a psychodynamic interpretation of these same inner realities. "From the point of view of the ego," according to Charles Brenner in his book *An Elementary Textbook of Psychoanalysis*, "the establishment of the identifications that form the superego is a very great aid to its defensive efforts against id impulses which it is struggling to master." Thus, Brenner notes "the parental prohibitions have been permanently installed in the mind, where they can keep an ever watchful eye on the id." However, he adds that "from the point of view of the egos independence and its freedom to enjoy instinctual gratifications the superego identifications are a very great disadvantage . . . The ego has acquired not merely an ally in the superego, it has acquired a master."

Of particular relevance to our emerging theme of "inner voices," Brenner notes that it is through the repeated experience of "verbal commands or scolding" that most children internalize parental controls. "The consequence of this," he then observes, "is that the superego bears a close relationship to auditory memories and in particular to memories of the spoken word. Some intuitive perception of this fact is probably responsible for the common figure of speech which refers to the 'voice of conscience.'" (Brenner, 1973: 124–125)

The *Voice Dialogue Method* offers a useful framework for achieving a better understanding of our own *inner voices* and *self-talk*. On the negative side, its basic concepts are compatible philosophically with the lower-level experience of *automatic thoughts, primary process thinking,* and *emotional reactivity* as described in *Cognitive-Behavioral* and *Rational-Emotive Therapy,* and with the autonomous activity of *unconscious parental or child ego-states* as described in *Transactional Analysis.* It is also quite compatible philosophically with the notion of the *addicted self* in addiction recovery, and the *Id, superego, shadow self* or *demonic self* as described in various psychoanalytic or spiritual traditions.

On the positive side, this model also suggests how people can achieve conscious access to an *aware ego* that is compatible philosophically with the notion of the *sober self* in classic addiction recovery and the higher-level practice of *rational disputation* and deliberative *secondary process thinking* found in *Cognitive-Behavioral* and *Rational-Emotive Therapy.* This healthy level of awareness is also comparable to the *conscious adult ego-state* in *Transactional Analysis* and the development of a *mature, responsible, adult personality that* is a primary goal in *Reality Therapy.* The *aware ego* in this model also has some similarity with the concept of the *soul,* the *spirit,* the *real self, true self, authentic self,* or an *awakened self* as this universal notion is expressed in various ways across a wide range of different spiritual traditions.

**Voice Dialogue Method**—Hal & Sidra Stone

. . . the ego has been referred to as the *executive function* of the psyche, or the choice maker. Someone has to run the operation, and the ego does the job . . . As our consciousness evolves, our ego becomes *a more aware ego*. As a more aware ego, it is in a better position to make *real choices* . . . However, very early . . . it becomes clear that the ego has *succumbed* to a combination of different *sub-personalities* that have *taken over* its executive function. Thus, what is functioning as the ego may, in fact, be a combination of the *protector/controller, pusher, pleaser, perfectionist, and inner critic.* This unique combination of sub-personalities, or energy systems, *perceives* the world in which we live, *processes* this information, and then *directs our lives* . . . Most people believe that they have *free will* because *they* choose to do a particular thing and they think that this is really choosing. We have discovered, however, that there is *remarkably little choice in* the world. Unless we *awaken the consciousness process*, the vast majority of us are *run* by the energy patterns with which we are identified or by those which we have disowned.

. . . development of an *awareness level* that can *witness* and an *aware ego* that can *embrace* both power and vulnerability is one of the central goals of transformational work.

(Stone & Stone, 1989: 21–22, 191. Emphasis added).

## Self-Help Model:

## *Emotional Intelligence*

Trying to "self-mediate" painful or distressing emotions is a central feature of harmful addiction in many cases and helping our clients learn how to identify and express feelings in a healthy and effective way is perhaps the most vital task in the addiction treatment process. In his book, Emotional Intelligence, Daniel Goleman discusses the nature of "multiple intelligences"—a concept pioneered by Harvard psychologist Howard Gardner—and he notes the critical fact that "Academic intelligence has little to do with emotional life." With this in mind, he observes that "The brightest among us can founder on the shoals of unbridled passions and unruly impulses," and he cites the work of Yale psychologist Peter Salovey, who identifies five main domains of "emotional intelligence" that any truly healthy person will eventually need to master:

1) Knowing one's emotions,
2) Managing emotions,
3) Motivating oneself,
4) Recognizing emotions in others, and

209

5) Handling relationships.

*Emotional Intelligence*—Daniel Goleman

> . . . the design of the brain means that we often have little or no control over *when* we are swept by emotion, nor over *what* emotion it will be. But we can have some say over *how long* an emotion will last.
>
> Though the predisposition to substance abuse may, in many cases, be brain-based, the feelings that drive people to 'self-medicate' themselves through drink or drugs can be handled without recourse to medication, as Alcoholics Anonymous and other recovery programs have demonstrated for decades. Acquiring the ability to handle those feelings—soothing anxiety, lifting depression, calming rage—removes the impetus to use alcohol or drugs in the first place. These basic emotional skills are taught *remedially* in treatment programs for alcohol and drug abuse. It would be far better, of course, if they were *learned early in life,* well before the habit became established.
>
> (Goleman, 1995: 33-34, 43, 57, 255. Emphasis added).

**PERMANENT SUCCESS** in dealing with harmful addiction while functioning at this otherwise irresponsible level would mean consistently controlling or completely and permanently stopping any potentially harmful compulsive or addictive behavior—with *no* exceptions.

This, of course, would indicate that the client involved is *not* a problem user or abuser and would suggest that they are actually capable of normal, social, or recreational use.

However, their long-term chances of achieving any genuine emotional balance or any true life satisfaction while remaining stuck at this fundamentally shallow, emotionally reactive, and chronically immature level of awareness and motivation would seem to be virtually nil—with or without the negative impact of a harmful addiction thrown in for good measure.

**REPEATED FAILURE** at this level to successfully control or stop their harmful addictive behavior may eventually convince a client—perhaps with the help of a clinician, teacher, mentor, sponsor, coach, spiritual advisor, family member, or friend—that they must accept and embrace complete personal responsibility for their own lives and become willing to take persistent, constructive action before they can ever hope to succeed *at any stage* on the *Addiction Recovery Learning Curve.*

# STAGE ONE:
# UNCONTROLLED USE WITH CONSEQUENCES

A client in treatment at this stage on the *Addiction Recovery Learning Curve* may actually want to get some counseling or other help in order to relieve some personal problems—or they may just want to comply with the requirements of a treatment mandate. Most mandated clients at this stage, however, will want nothing more than to keep right on using and get out of treatment as soon as possible by any means necessary—honest or dishonest—compliant or non-compliant. One way or another, all clients at this stage share one motivational trait in common—they have *absolutely no desire* to cut down, control, or stop using their preferred addictive substance or behavior *in any way, shape, or form*.

Instead—although this may involve some truly magical or wishful thinking on their part—they would like to continue using exactly as they have before—but they want to be able to do so *without* experiencing any negative consequences.

## Philosophical Premise:

Thus far, as we have examined the signs, symptoms, and stages of progression in harmful addiction, we have tended to focus on the question of how to *identify* and *counsel* those people who have developed—or who may be in the process of developing—the most serious problems.

Let's recall some important material from Chapter Two of this book which focused on Assessment and Diagnosis:

Regardless of the addictive substance or compulsive behavior involved, or the reasons for using it, there can be a wide range of potential Levels of Use and it can be helpful for us to think of these levels as occurring on a progressively serious scale as follows:

**LEVELS OF USE**

1. Abstinence.
2. Experimental Use.
3. Rare, Minimal, or Occasional Use.
4. Normal, Social, Recreational, or Moderate Use.
5. Heavy or Frequent Use.
6. Excessive or Problem Use.
7. Abuse.
8. Dependence.

It is important to remember that most people who are engaged in potentially harmful addictive or compulsive behaviors—such as eating, drinking, drug use, gambling, sex, relationships, or work—will never experience *any* negative consequences from their use. Therefore, they will never even reach the level of "problem use" on this scale, even though they may be heavily involved with a particular substance or behavior. Indeed, many *positive addictions* are often marked by frequent and heavy involvement with a healthy behavior or beneficial activity.

We must always remember that many people with less severe problems *will actually be successful* without too much real fuss or effort—once they *really get serious* about it –in changing what may only amount to *a "bad habit" or a "problem behavior."*

By contrast, one of the key indicators that a client may be in the process of developing a harmful addiction—or at least a pattern of problem use—is that they will not be *able* to continue using exactly as they have before without experiencing negative consequences.

## Learning Process:

As a user continues to experience episodic, periodic, or continuous "loss of control" over the use of their preferred addictive substance or behavior—and experiences the unwanted negative consequences that ensue—he or she will eventually realize that such consequences will be *inevitable* unless they are willing to make a conscious, deliberate effort to *limit or control* their use.

## *Treatment Approach:*

At this stage, a skilled eclectic therapist would continue using *Cognitive-Behavioral Therapy, Rational-Emotive Therapy, Transactional Analysis,* and *Reality Therapy* as needed. Technically, of course, even in the earlier *Foundation Stage* the therapist would already have started using motivational principles and techniques—simply in order to *engage* a client in a therapeutic alliance and begin to *motivate* them toward change. Now, however, since we have a specific behavioral target of change in mind for the client—to attempt controlled use rather than continue completely unrestricted use—our treatment emphasis will need to shift towards "Motivational Enhancement Therapy."

**Motivational Interviewing**—Miller & Rollnick

As we have already seen, William Miller and Stephen Rollnick describe "Motivational Interviewing" as "an approach designed to help clients build commitment and reach a decision to change" and they identify the *essential tasks for the therapist* as follows:

• Raise doubt—Increase the client's perception of risks and problems.

- Tip the balance—Evoke reasons to change, and risks of not changing.
- Help the client determine the best course of action to follow.
- Help the client take active steps toward change.
- Help the client identify and use relapse prevention strategies.
- Help the client renew the cycle of change in the event of relapse without becoming stuck or demoralized.

(Miller & Rollnick, 1991: 18)

## *Self-Help Model:*

At this early stage on the *Addiction Recovery Learning Curve*, it is appropriate to continue orienting the unmotivated client toward the achievement of better insight and try to encourage the development of an internalized desire for self-improvement by continuing to emphasize the basic self-help principles and practices found in *The Seven Habits of Highly Effective People* and *The Voice Dialogue Method.*

***PERMANENT SUCCESS*** for a user at this stage would mean the *complete absence* of *any* negative consequences associated with their continued unrestricted use.

This would establish factually that this client apparently has *no problem* with harmful addiction—when dealing with the presenting substance or behavior—and is *not* a problem user or abuser. This kind of *permanent* track record—with no exceptions—would establish by history that they are probably capable of continued normal, social, or recreational use.

***REPEATED FAILURE*** to continue using as much and as often as they wish while permanently avoiding *any* unwanted negative consequences will usually be enough to persuade most people—sooner or later—that they actually *do* have some kind of a problem.

It is only at this point—when they have become completely convinced by their own experience that there really *is* something wrong—no matter how much they may minimize or trivialize it—that most people will really want to make some changes. No matter how long it may take, it is only when this inner shift finally happens—and not before—that they will finally be ready to move on to the next stage on the *Addiction Recovery Learning Curve—Attempted Common Sense Control.*

## STAGE TWO:
## ATTEMPTED COMMON SENSE CONTROL

A client at this stage on the *Addiction Recovery Learning Curve* clearly recognizes that their excessive use of a preferred addictive substance or behavior consistently leads to many unwanted negative consequences and that it cannot be allowed continue unchecked. They will have a strong desire to continue using their addictive substance or behavior—and to receive all of the perceived benefits of use—but they are now internally motivated to learn how to successfully cut down and control their use.

At this point, they really want to avoid any further negative consequences and they are often highly motivated to do so. They are also firmly convinced in most cases that they *will be able* to do so—or that they "should" be able to do so easily—with little or no effort or serious difficulty.

At this stage, however, they still have no desire whatsoever to abstain completely and permanently from all further use.

## Philosophical Premise:

In our discussion of the either-or fallacy, I indicated that we would be considering the contending philosophical and practical issues involved in three significant areas of disagreement and debate that have existed historically in the addiction treatment and recovery field:

- The Social Learning Model "versus" the Disease Model
- Moderation "versus" Total Abstinence
- Secular "versus" Spiritual Recovery

I also promised to discuss how all of the different "competing" approaches can fit easily and comfortably into the *Face to Face Unified Addiction Recovery Model*—because they are all understood and accepted as being legitimate and clinically appropriate for *certain* people at *certain* stages in the overall process of change.

Let's begin by taking a look at some issues related to:

### The Social Learning Model "versus" the Disease Model

Advocates for the *"social learning model"* of harmful addiction contend that it is essentially a "learned behavior that can be unlearned."

In the Preface to their classic 1985 book *Relapse Prevention: Maintenance Strategies in the Treatment of Addictive Behaviors,* Alan Marlatt and Judith Gordon state that the "overarching theoretical orientation" of the Relapse

Prevention (RP) model is that "addictive behaviors are conceptualized as over-learned habit patterns rather than addictive diseases."

They go on to indicate that:

> A key assumption underlying the RP approach is that addictive habit patterns can be changed through the application of self-management or self-control procedures. The role of the therapist is to teach the client to be his or her own 'maintenance man' in the habit-change process.

In his overview of the RP model, Marlatt adds:

> . . . the overall aim is to teach the individual how to achieve a *balanced lifestyle* and to prevent the development of unhealthy habit patterns . . . A balanced lifestyle is one that is centered on the fulcrum of moderation (in contrast with the opposing extremes of either excess or restraint).

(Marlatt and Gordon, 1985: xii, 4).

Proponents of the *"disease model,"* as we have already seen in Chapter One, tend to define harmful addiction as a "bio-psycho-social-spiritual illness" that is primary, chronic, progressive, incurable, and potentially fatal—characterized by inability to abstain, inevitable loss of control over use, and the experience of significant negative consequences as a result.

These are not mutually exclusive concepts, and in the *Addiction Recovery Learning Curve* model there are no real grounds for any philosophical dispute between them.

One core misunderstanding here involves a peculiar failure by some social learning advocates to recognize that merely identifying a harmful addiction as "a disease" is *not* an automatic or fatalistic "death sentence" that must inevitably produce false but powerful and self-fulfilling feelings of hopelessness, doom, despair, and apathy.

On the contrary, merely identifying harmful addiction as a disease—just like informing a client that they have a diagnosis of cancer, kidney or heart disease, or diabetes—does not magically absolve the user from their need to accept complete personal responsibility for their own health and wellness and to play an active role in their own treatment or recovery program.

In fact, as we've already established very clearly, assuming complete personal responsibility and taking persistent constructive action is essential to the addiction recovery process, and *passivity is a formula for disaster.*

There is a closely related failure by some social learning advocates to understand that the first step concept of powerlessness in the twelve-step program does *not* sanction any abdication of personal responsibility and is *not* a formula for learned helplessness.

In fact, the first step in the twelve step recovery program is very clearly written in the *past tense*:

> "We admitted we *were* powerless over alcohol—and that our lives had become unmanageable."

Indeed, this is merely the *first* of *twelve active steps*, which absolutely *require* the user with a harmful addiction to accept full personal responsibility for *doing* something about it.

In fact, the sometimes sadly or savagely misunderstood twelve-step program actually suggests a way of life that is firmly grounded in the warm embrace of full personal responsibility for all aspects of a person's inner and outer life. For example, consider how clearly the following quotation taken from a basic AA text entitled *Twelve Steps and Twelve Traditions* insists on the need for a sober alcoholic to maintain a rather extraordinary, persistent, and healthy daily level of self-monitoring, self-awareness, and calm self-corrective action:

> A *continuous* look at our assets and liabilities, and a real desire to learn and grow by this means, are *necessities* for us. We alcoholics have learned this the hard way. More experienced people, of course, in all times and places have practiced unsparing self-survey and criticism. *For the wise have always known that no one can make much of his life until self-searching becomes a regular habit, until he is able to admit and accept what he finds, and until he patiently and persistently tries to correct what is wrong.*

> (Alcoholics Anonymous, 1952: 88. Emphasis added.)

Now, let's take a quick look at the second area of unfortunate misunderstanding and unnecessary disagreement in the addiction treatment and recovery field:

### Moderation "versus" Total Abstinence

In the *Addiction Recovery Learning Curve* model, there are also no real grounds for disagreement or dispute between advocates of "total abstinence" as the only sound method for dealing with a *serious harmful addiction* and those who strongly insist that "moderation" or "controlled use" will be possible for many *problem users*.

The core misunderstanding here involves a failure—by some of the more dogmatic advocates for either approach—to recognize the existence of a natural learning curve which most users will *have* to follow in order to *determine for themselves* whether or not they can safely control and enjoy their use.

Some strong advocates of "total abstinence for everyone" fail to accept the simple fact that many clients—perhaps even *most* of them in early treatment episodes—will continue trying to control their use—in many cases *long after* they have received a strong clinical recommendation for total abstinence.

Some clinicians also seem to be inclined to take an inappropriate "one size fits all" approach to assessment and diagnosis, and therefore seem to be unable or unwilling to recognize the simple fact that many people with milder problems *will* be able to permanently and successfully control their use.

Similarly, some die-hard advocates of "moderation for all"—or "controlled-use for everyone"—strongly insist that *anyone* can learn how to control their use—no matter how severe or advanced their harmful addiction may have become. Therefore—despite a massive amount of clinical experience, mounds of anecdotal evidence, and multiple research findings reported over many decades in literally tens of thousands of cases—they either cannot or will not concede the simple fact that *controlled use appears to be functionally "impossible" in many cases.*

Let me reiterate that there are no grounds for any philosophical dispute here and both approaches are valid elements in an integrated model like the *Addiction Recovery Learning Curve.* Indeed, we need to recognize very clearly how well all of these apparently "competing" philosophical approaches actually complement each other when we look at them all together holistically in *a logical sequence on a simple continuum of change.*

For example?

We have already seen that the "Big Book" of Alcoholics Anonymous—which is adamant about the need for "real alcoholics" to abstain completely from alcohol—does not insist that total abstinence will be necessary for all problem drinkers.

In fact, the Big Book states—in a rather common sense matter of fact way—that most "real" alcoholics will only become convinced of the true nature of their condition through a long process of repeated experimentation involving much trial and error in their "countless vain attempts" at "controlled drinking."

Specifically, as previously noted, the AA Big Book declares that:

> We do not like to pronounce any individual as alcoholic, but you can quickly diagnose yourself. Step over to the nearest barroom and try some controlled drinking. Try to drink and stop abruptly. Try it more than once. It will not take long for you to decide, if you are honest with yourself about it. It may be worth a bad case of the jitters if you get a full knowledge of your condition.

> (Alcoholics Anonymous, 1976: 31–32).

The basic text of the Moderation Management self-help program expresses complete agreement on this basic point and states flatly that:

> Moderation is *not* for everyone, and MM considers it a *success* when people discover in the program that they need to move on to total abstinence.

(Kishline, 1994: 79. Emphasis added.)

Of course, no ethical clinician would ever "endorse" or recommend an approach that seems—in their best clinical judgment—to be doomed to failure, and there is no fundamental conflict between the tenets of the "disease model" of addiction and the "social learning model" on this point.

*By definition*—according to the disease model—no "real" alcoholic or addict would ever have the ability to consistently control their use over the long-run. Some social learning theorist condemn this notion as a *self-fulfilling prescription* for "learned helplessness," but it is actually nothing of the kind.

In fact, it is merely a *retrospective description* of an *established track record* in a particular case.

Similarly, any user who demonstrates the ability to consistently and permanently control their use, *by definition*, should not be described as a "real" alcoholic or addict.

## Learning Process:

In order to help *educate, motivate,* and *empower* unmotivated clients for eventual change—any serious treatment recommendation needs to be made within the overall context of *an integrated psychoeducational assessment, feedback, and counseling process.*

Our most crucial task as clinicians—as we have already seen—will be to help our client's understand the true nature of compulsion, correctly interpret the actual *meaning* of their own experience—past, present, *or* future—and make an accurate self-diagnosis of their own condition.

In all of this, at *any* stage on the learning curve, we must consistently nudge our clients toward the next appropriate contemplation stage of change by gently and persistently challenging them to honestly face the question:

"Am I really in control of my own behavior?"

Ideally, a clinician would work with a client individually in this process in order to identify all of the signs and symptoms that the client has experienced personally—and is willing to admit to—plus *all* negative consequences and each of the diagnostic criteria that they meet as well. Then, working from this detailed and individualized symptom checklist, all of the reasons for making a particular assessment, diagnosis, and treatment recommendation should be clearly explained to the client, thoroughly reviewed, and openly discussed.

In many cases—after a thorough individualized assessment process is completed—more than enough solid clinical data will be available to factually establish the existence of a serious harmful addiction. If it appears that "the shoe fits" in a particular case, then the only responsible recommendation for that particular client would be *total abstinence.*

Under these circumstances, however, even a strong clinical recommendation for total abstinence will often fail to be truly persuasive or convincing to a die-hard user. This will often be true even when the recommendation comes from a highly skilled and caring clinician who has developed a solid therapeutic relationship of good rapport and trust with the client.

Therefore—to use the vernacular—since so many clients are "gonna do what they're gonna do"—no matter what has been recommended—it may be necessary for them to *seriously try* and *repeatedly fail* at one or more moderation-based programs *as a part of their treatment plan*—in a truly open-minded and honest spirit of experimentation if possible—before they can ever be truly "convinced" of their need to abstain completely and permanently and thus become internally motivated to do so.

## Treatment Approach:

At this stage, an eclectic therapist would continue using *Cognitive-Behavioral Therapy, Rational-Emotive Therapy, Transactional Analysis, Reality Therapy,* and *Motivational Enhancement Therapy* as needed—all of which have been described above.

## Self-Help Model:

At this stage, our user recognizes and admits that a problem exists and they are internally motivated to resolve it. However, they are not prepared to make any commitment to complete abstinence from their preferred addictive substance or behavior. This is because—overall—they still experience their use subjectively as a positive and beneficial part of their life.

Clients who are at this stage should certainly continue using the basic principles and practices of the *Seven Habits* and *Voice Dialogue* just as before, but now they might also benefit from active participation in *Moderation Management,* or some other controlled-use support group.

One note of caution is needed here:

From my book-knowledge, and subsequent news accounts, I know that MM—like any human enterprise—has certainly had its fair share of tragic flaws and harsh critics. Many people are well aware that the founder of MM herself rather courageously resigned from the group some years ago when she finally realized that she could not successfully control her drinking and needed to commit herself to total abstinence from alcohol—which she then found difficult to do, with tragic consequences. I am not personally endorsing *Moderation Management* as an organization, or making any specific recommendation for or against participation in the MM program at this time. Frankly, I'm not in a position to do so because I have had no direct personal experience with the group to date.

In this context, the phrase self-help "model" refers primarily to the underlying goal of "attempted control" and not to the particular organization named—which I cite here merely as a well-known example. In any case, MM is a self-help organization focused solely on meeting the needs of problem *drinkers*, and it would therefore not be appropriate for people dealing with other forms of harmful addictive behavior.

Generally speaking, there seem to be very few viable self-help groups around for people at the *Attempted Common Sense Control* stage. Except for MM—and perhaps a small handful of support groups established by some controlled use treatment programs—the notion of a "self-help group" for people at this stage on the *Addiction Recovery Learning Curve* is largely an abstract idea.

### Moderation Management—Audrey Kishline

> The purpose of Moderation Management is to provide a supportive environment in which people who have made the healthy decision to reduce their drinking can come together to help each other change . . . You should NOT start this moderation-based program if . . . you are now abstaining from alcohol after a history of alcohol dependence.
>
> (Kishline, 1994: 25, 70–72)

### Preface—Frederick Glaser

> Because there are so many more problem drinkers than alcoholics, the burden of alcohol problems on society derives largely from the problem drinkers . . . Unfortunately, virtually the entire treatment effort in the United States is directed at those with the most severe problems, and not at the problem drinkers . . . In this context, the development of Moderation Management (MM) takes on great significance . . . it is directed at *problem drinkers* . . . While some of these individuals will resolve their problems without assistance, the majority are in need of help. Yet neither the standard treatment programs nor the existing self-help groups are likely to be congenial to them . . . It should, of course, be understood that to advocate for assistance for those with less than the most severe problems is *not* to advocate against assisting those with severe problems.
>
> (Glaser, 1994: xvi–xvii)

**PERMANENT SUCCESS** at this stage would mean the establishment of a *lifetime track record* of successful moderation and controlled use—with *no* exceptions, *no* loss of control, and *no* negative consequences.

This would establish that this person may have been a problem user or abuser at one point, but they are *not* a "real alcoholic or addict"—as those terms are conventionally used in the disease model of harmful addiction.

> By this *complete consistency*, he or she would empirically demonstrate the ability to continue using their preferred addictive substance safely at a normal, social, or recreational level.

**REPEATED FAILURE** to successfully control their use and avoid any further negative consequences—which will often take place over the course of many years and will usually involve increasingly serious loss of control and mounting negative consequences—will eventually convince most people that they

> *must abstain completely and permanently* from their harmful addictive substance or activity.

By the time they reach this "moment of truth" most users will have experienced many signs and symptoms of harmful addiction, and many of them will have progressed far into the middle stage of alcoholism or drug addiction.

Whether they really like it or not, many of these people will now be able self-identify clearly as an "alcoholic" or "addict." They may begin to apply these stereotyped labels to themselves—with relatively few reservations—whether or not they really understand what these terms actually mean at any deep level or truly appreciate how deadly and serious their condition may actually be.

Most people who reach this point are already stuck quite firmly in the grip of a powerful and progressive compulsion. However—because they have never seriously tried to stop and failed—many of them will only *begin* to accurately perceive and truly appreciate the powerful nature of this compulsion long after they have moved well into the next stage on the *Addiction Recovery Learning Curve—Attempted Analytical Abstinence.*

## STAGE THREE:
## ATTEMPTED ANALYTICAL ABSTINENCE

A client at this stage on the *Addiction Recovery Learning Curve* is now convinced that they have a serious problem with harmful addiction. They understand that they must abstain completely and permanently from their preferred addictive substance or behavior and they are internally motivated to do so. If they have had a problem with alcohol or drugs, they will usually be able to self-identify as an "alcoholic" or "addict" with little or no minimization or denial.

If they are truly in the grips of a progressive, harmful addiction, of course, they will also feel a great deal of ambivalence about permanent abstinence and will continue to wish deep down inside that they could somehow manage to use in moderation or even somehow enjoy uncontrolled use with no consequences if that were possible.

## Philosophical Premise:

Now, let's take a look at the third area of unfortunate misunderstanding and unnecessary disagreement in the addiction treatment and recovery field:

### Secular "versus" Spiritual Recovery

It is a common practice in most traditional addiction treatment programs to recommend active participation in Alcoholics Anonymous or another twelve-step program. In many cases, this recommendation will be made on the basis of an objective clinical assessment and a sound diagnosis. In many other cases, however, it will be made as a general recommendation for *all* clients regardless of their individual symptom profile.

In either case, this recommendation is often made long before a client actually reaches this point on the *Addiction Recovery Learning Curve*—where he or she self-identifies as an alcoholic or addict and has finally developed an internalized motivation for total abstinence.

Moreover, in many cases where there *is* a sincere, internalized motivation for total abstinence, the traditional clinical recommendation for active participation in a twelve-step program is often made long before the user has any clue that purely secular approaches for changing harmful attitudes and behavior *might not work for them*.

The twelve-step self-help recovery program was first developed by Alcoholics Anonymous in the mid-1930s, and it offers an explicitly spiritual approach for dealing with the problem of internalized compulsion—which is a central feature that all harmful addictions have in common.

For many people struggling with harmful addiction, the recommendation to get involved in a twelve-step program will prove to be life-saving, transformational, and relatively easy to accept. This will often be especially true for those clients who are already philosophically inclined toward a religious or spiritual approach to life but have lacked any practical or effective spiritual program to follow.

At this stage on the *Addiction Recovery Learning Curve*, however, many people will see *little or no need* for any kind of "spiritual solution."

This will be especially true for people who are confused about the vital distinction that must always be made between "conventional religion" and "true spirituality," and even more so for people who start out with *a negative or hostile attitude toward religion.*

Two leading critics of the disease model of harmful addiction are Stanton Peele, author of, *The Diseasing of America: How We Allowed Recovery Zealots and the Treatment Industry to Convince Us that We Are Out of Control* and Herbert Fingarette, the author of *Heaving Drinking: The Myth of Alcoholism as a Disease.* They are both also significant critics of the spiritual solution for harmful addiction suggested in the twelve-step program first developed by Alcoholics Anonymous.

In his book *The Soul of Recovery: Uncovering the Spiritual Dimension in the Treatment of Addictions,* however, Christopher Ringwald, notes that: "Much of what they fault is outside the realm of Twelve-Step fellowships or spiritual solutions. Groups such as AA and NA are easy targets for the sins of the 'recovery industry.'" Ringwald observes that "Often AA or NA is held accountable for misrepresentations by treatment professionals. These often adapt the Twelve Steps for their own purposes. But then their patients graduate, attend meetings, and repeat these messages as AA truths," and he concludes with the observation that:

> Basically, what both Peele and Fingarette propose as radical alternatives are remarkably similar to the Twelve-Step approach.

> (Ringwald, 2002: 21–23).

## Learning Process:

In many cases, clients at this stage on the *Addiction Recovery Learning Curve* have already started to understand how often they use their harmful addictive substance or behavior as

> an ineffective "coping mechanism" in an unsuccessful and self-defeating attempt to "self-medicate," "relieve," "escape," or "forget" their daily stress, emotional discomfort, or larger problems in life.

Hence, at this point many of these people will start to accept the idea—either grudgingly or readily—that if they really want to stay clean and sober they will need to develop *a more effective and satisfying way of thinking, feeling, and living.*

Many people at this stage will be sincerely motivated to "analyze" some of their more vexing *personal problems* and distressing *negative emotions.* They will often try to "figure out" *why* they think, feel, and act the way they do, and they will often be quite anxious to learn *what* they can do about changing it.

223

In essence, at this point many people will sincerely want to understand their own emotional reactivity more clearly and learn how to control it more effectively.

They will be especially eager to learn how to make themselves "feel better" or "feel good" in a healthy way—without indulging in harmful addictive behavior that always ends up, sooner or later, producing exactly the opposite result.

Therefore, when they are offered the opportunity, many people at this stage on the *Addiction Recovery Learning Curve* will be quite eager to learn how to use sound rational-emotive and cognitive-behavioral approaches to change their own

- negative attitudes,
- irrational beliefs,
- distorted thoughts,
- agitated feelings, and
- harmful behaviors.

Most people who are gradually working through this stage will tend to remain firmly convinced—often despite mounting evidence to the contrary—that these approaches will work for them to produce complete, permanent abstinence—or that they "should" work with little or no difficulty.

As we have seen, many real "alcoholics" or "addicts"—who self-identify as such without reservation and have become genuinely committed to total abstinence—might still be quite wary, confused, or reflexively belligerent when it comes to the idea of embracing any sort of "spirituality."

Even without any initial bias or hostility against a spiritual approach, however, very few users will embark on their *first serious commitment to total abstinence* already convinced of their *need* for a "spiritual solution" to their problem.

Why?

Because anyone who has never seriously and sincerely *tried* to abstain will simply have no direct personal experience to indicate that they may not be *able* to do so.

Therefore, it would be more than merely "appropriate" for people at this stage to pursue a strictly rational-emotive, cognitive-behavioral or "secular" approach to achieve and maintain total abstinence—in many cases it would be *almost inevitable* that they would do so, and almost impossible for them to grasp that they may actually *need* a spiritual solution.

If this kind of a purely secular approach really works for them consistently—meaning not just for weeks, months, or years, but for life—then that's *wonderful*.

Case closed.

For many users, of course, this kind of permanent success will not be their experience. For some baffling reason, even many users who actually take the time to learn and make the effort to practice sound rational-emotional coping skills will find, nevertheless, that they just *can't*, *won't*, or *don't* successfully achieve or maintain complete and permanent abstinence.

For most of these users, the strange idea that they might actually *need* to find some kind of a "spiritual solution" in order to achieve and maintain sobriety can only begin to make some sense *after* they have learned—from their own repeated experience—that they apparently "can't" stay clean or sober—control their emotional reactivity—or even think in a consistently rational manner—without first calming their minds and centering themselves spiritually.

## *Treatment Approach:*

At this stage, the eclectic therapist would continue using *Transactional Analysis, Reality Therapy,* and *Motivational Enhancement Therapy* as needed, but they would begin to put a special emphasis on helping the client develop and practice many of the proven rational and emotional coping skills found in *Cognitive-Behavioral* and *Rational-Emotive Therapy*—which should have been at least introduced to all clients in the initial *Foundation Stage* as we have already discussed above.

This would be especially true for any clients who are initially resistant or antagonistic toward any kind of a spiritual approach because they will often need to be thoroughly convinced that they have really "tried everything" before they can even begin to consider moving on to the next stage of *Attempted Spiritual Sobriety.*

Philosophically, of course, many clients may be ready, willing, able, and perhaps even eager to "skip ahead"—forget about *attempted analytical abstinence* altogether—and begin to participate in a twelve-step spiritual recovery program immediately without any serious reservations.

Certainly, they should not be discouraged from doing so, but we must also remember that in the *Face to Face Unified Addiction Recovery Model* it will be vital for clients not to skip any essential steps in the *addiction recovery learning process.*

You may recall from Chapter Five of this book—which focused on understand the middle stage signs and symptoms of progression in harmful addiction—that John Wallace has identified a "preference for non-analytical modes of thinking and perceiving" as a commonly used unconscious psychological defense mechanism among clients making the transition into recovery.

It is often true that working "with" a client's maladaptive emotional defenses may be necessary in early stages of treatment and recovery—rather than trying to challenge or restructure them too quickly—because many clients will start out with few healthy rational or emotional coping skills to employ as an effective alternative.

In the long-run, however, maintaining an inherent bias against deliberative thinking will leave a client highly vulnerable to emotional over-reactivity and eventual relapse if it is not successfully overcome.

We must always remember that fully mastering the *fundamentals* of each treatment approach in a logical sequence—including the *knowledge base* and *practical skills* involved—will often prove to be *essential* in the long-term process of change for many people. The *insights* and *skills* that clients can learn at each stage—or in each treatment approach—will often represent crucial *developmental tasks* and essential *building blocks* for change that they will eventually need as they move forward through the *Addiction Recovery Learning Curve*.

Horace Walpole once observed with considerable accuracy that:

> "Life is a comedy for those who think, and a tragedy for those
> who feel."

Therefore, in this *unified addiction recovery model*, even clients who are predisposed to "leap ahead to a spiritual solution" should be helped to understand that it will be crucial in the long-run for them to learn and practice the fundamental skills of *clear thinking* that are found in

## Cognitive-Behavioral and Rational-Emotive Therapy.

Similarly, clients who are already firmly committed to *Stage Four* on the *Addiction Recovery Learning Curve—Attempted Spiritual Sobriety*—but who are still struggling with relapse when you begin to work with them– should be helped to understand that learning these essential skills—and then integrating them fully into an effective spiritual approach to life—represents a core principle and practice of

### *Stage Five—Rational Spiritual Sobriety.*

## *Self-Help Model:*

Clients who are making the transition into *Stage Three* on the *Addiction Recovery Learning Curve—Attempted Analytical Abstinence*—should continue using the basic principles and practices of the *Seven Habits of Highly Effective People* and the *Voice Dialogue Method*. At this point, however, continued participation in *Moderation Management,* or any other controlled-use support group would no longer be appropriate. This is because our user has finally realized that they cannot safely control their use of their preferred addictive substance or behavior and that they must abstain completely and permanently.

By now, as we have already seen, many clients will have started to understand their need to develop sound rational and emotional coping skills—but they will usually feel no need for any kind of a "spiritual solution"—unless their prior belief system predisposes them in that direction. Hence, they will often be receptive to a self-help model such as *Rational Recovery, SMART Recovery, SOS—Secular Organizations for Sobriety (also known as "Save Our Selves), Men for Sobriety,* or *Women for Sobriety,* all of which are based on exclusively "secular" or "rational" principles.

While any of these approaches may be helpful for clients at this stage, let's take a quick look at some features of what may be the best-known of these programs:

### Rational Recovery—Jack Trimpey

#### The Addictive Voice Recognition Technique (AVRT)

*Alcohol-and drug-dependent people hear voices.* But then, so does everyone else. . . . In the normal human consciousness, there are voices, usually sounding like our own. In our 'mind's ear,' we can literally hear ourselves talking to ourselves . . .

*Living as we do in a largely irrational society, our inner voices take on ideas and beliefs that we accept, because of their prevalence and popularity, without much critical analysis.* . . . disturbed unhappy people can help themselves greatly by disputing their own irrational ideas and then replacing them with rational ideas that, *by definition*, are objectively true and serve one's enlightened self-interest . . .

While nondrugged persons harbor a balance of rational and irrational ideas, *addicted persons are profoundly irrational, or unreasoning, when it comes to the continued use of the addictive substance* . . . Almost all pleasure becomes associated with the intoxicant, even though the toxin is also the chief cause of the underlying pain . . .

In fact, *there is an animal, or beastly, quality to the addict's dominant inner voice* . . . 'It' drowns out the other voices . . . and takes over its host's decisions and judgments almost as if he or she had been hijacked . . . *The Beast* listens to your rational voices, which sometimes challenge its firm control over you, and then plays word games to destroy any decisions just made.

(Trimpey, 1989: 57, 59–61. Emphasis added.)

Another note of caution:

In this context, the phrase self-help "model" refers once again only to the underlying goal—which is "attempted analytical abstinence" at this stage—and does not reflect a personal endorsement of this particular program—which I cite here primarily because it is widely known in the addiction treatment and recovery field as a prototypical example of the type.

*In particular, while I would not actively recommend against clients using the Rational Recovery model. I also could not endorse it in good conscience without expressing some serious reservations.*

My first concern is that the basic literature of the *Rational Recovery* program often takes what seems to be an *irrational, emotional,* and almost automatically *belligerent* position *against* any participation in the twelve-step spiritual recovery program.

Indeed, on one level, the entire *Rational Recovery* program can be seen as a negative "reaction" *against* the spiritual nature of the twelve-step recovery program. This is clearly reflected in the title of the original text for the *RR program*—"The small book"—which was chosen to reflect the program's deliberate positioning of itself as a "rational alternative" to the twelve-step spiritual recovery program which was originally presented in the "Big Book" of Alcoholics Anonymous.

There is an even deeper problem that prevents me from personally recommending participation in the *Rational Recovery* program at this time. This stems from the sad fact that all of this *negativity* and *hostility*—which actually seems to be well-intentioned and sincere—is based on a *complete misunderstanding* of how the twelve-step spiritual recovery process actually works and what it actually requires.

We will examine the nature of this misunderstanding in our upcoming discussion of *Stages Four and Five* on the *Addiction Recovery Learning Curve—Attempted Spiritual Sobriety* and *Rational Spiritual Sobriety,*

A fundamental goal of the *Face to Face Unified Addiction Recovery Model*—as I have previously stated—is to help people understand the powerful underlying unity that actually binds all of the superficially "competing" philosophies in the addiction treatment and recovery field together into a seamless whole that becomes readily apparent when we look at all of them holistically and see how well they actually complement each other when they are understood and applied in a logical sequence on a simple continuum of change.

In this regard, I have suggested that an open mind and a decent sense of humor are crucial traits for anyone who would like to resolve many of the unfortunate areas of toxic misunderstanding, misinformation, disagreement, and debate in this field and find the common ground on which well-meaning people can join together in harmony.

Sadly, both of these crucial qualities seem to be in somewhat short supply in the *"official dogma"* of the *Rational Recovery* program at this time.

I am basically optimistic about the prospect of entering into a constructive and healing dialogue—based on the clarity and simplicity of the universal spiritual principles identified in the *Rational Spirituality* self-help system—which we will begin to examine in the next few sections. At this time, however, despite all the good that it might otherwise have to offer, I genuinely fear that anyone participating in the *Rational Recovery* program could wind up being seriously limited or even potentially harmed by exposure to so many angry feelings and distorted views about the rational validity and ultimate wisdom of seeking to live by a set of universal spiritual principles.

Now, let's get back on track and conclude our discussion of *Stage Three* on the *Addiction Recovery Learning Curve—Attempted Analytical Abstinence.*

**PERMANENT SUCCESS** at this level would mean the establishment of a *lifetime track record* of complete abstinence—with no exceptions—using cognitive-behavioral and rational-emotive coping skills alone. This would indicate that while this person may have been legitimately diagnosable as being alcohol or drug dependent, he or she is *not* a *"real* alcoholic"—as this term is used informally in the "Big Book" of Alcoholics Anonymous. Nor could they be considered a *"real* addict" on similar grounds.

This crucial verbal distinction has been stressed a number of times in this book. Let me reiterate that this concept is *not* reflected anywhere in our official diagnostic, clinical, or technical vocabulary—but it is, nevertheless, a very useful construct when we need some way to identify those people with *the most severe and stubborn forms of harmful addiction.*

While the person who is *permanently successful* at this stage may have had a serious problem with harmful addiction—actually meeting the diagnostic criteria for psychoactive substance "dependence"—their ability to abstain completely and permanently using conventional, secular coping skills would exclude them, by definition, from this final category, the "real" alcoholic or addict.

**REPEATED FAILURE** to abstain permanently and completely at this stage—using rational coping skills alone—and the resulting experience of continued use, increasing loss of control, and steadily worsening negative consequences—will often bring people to a point of complete desperation.

Many people who reach this point will begin to understand that their harmful addiction has become a matter of life or death. Nevertheless, the irresistible and irrational compulsion they feel inside will be so overpowering that they will still be *unable to stop using permanently.*

Now—regardless of any previous antagonism, ambivalence, confusion, or reservations they may have felt about religion or spirituality—many people who reach this point of utter hopelessness and despair will finally become convinced by their own painful, baffling, and frightening loss of control over their own behavior that they *must* move onto the next stage on the *Addiction Recovery Learning Curve—Attempted Spiritual Sobriety.*

## TRANSITION STAGE:
## FROM HOPELESS TO WHOLENESS

Before they can truly enter the next learning stage of *attempted spiritual sobriety,* most clients will have to *personally experience* what I have chosen to call:

> **"STEP ZERO"**—Persistent failure to control or stop their harmful compulsive-addictive behavior despite their *deep, sincere,* and often *desperate* desire to do so.

Even in cases where people may have already been actively involved in a twelve-step recovery program—and thought they already understood it quite well—it is only *now* that they can truly begin to understand the irrational and irresistible nature of compulsion and start to grasp the full implications of the concept of "powerlessness" as expressed in:

> **"STEP ONE"**—We admitted we were powerless over our addiction—that our lives had become unmanageable.

Now, let's take a look at:

## STAGE FOUR:
## ATTEMPTED SPIRITUAL SOBRIETY

Many users who are successfully abstaining from their harmful addictions in twelve-step spiritual recovery programs may have been favorably predisposed toward following a principled, spiritual way of life before "hitting a high bottom" at an early age and entering a twelve-step program rather easily and painlessly—without having to go through all of the agony that is usually a prerequisite to reaching "Step Zero" as described above.

This doesn't necessarily mean that these users didn't have to pass through the first three stages on the *Addiction Recovery Learning Curve—Uncontrolled Use with Consequences, Attempted Common Sense Control,* and *Attempted Analytical Abstinence.* It would simply suggest that they didn't have to spend a great deal of time repeatedly failing in their *serious attempts* at control at each of these stages before becoming "convinced" that they had to move on to the next.

In many of these cases, it's entirely possible that they never even had to reach the level of making *desperate attempts* at any point in the learning process before "getting it" and moving on. Almost by way of definition, those users who could be accurately described as "high bottom" cases probably never became mired in a seemingly endless round of *futile attempts* at control at any of the three earlier stages in the *addiction recovery learning process.*

Most people who reach this stage on the *Addiction Recovery Learning Curve*, however, are not nearly this fortunate. They are much more likely to represent "low bottom" cases—people who have had to go through a long and painful process before reaching the point where they are finally prepared to make their *initial attempts* at spiritual sobriety.

Sadly, for many of them, their long and painful series of "learning experiences" may be destined to continue for quite some time.

The "Big Book" of Alcoholics Anonymous poses the fundamental question facing people at this stage on the *Addiction Recovery Learning Curve* in the following way:

> If, when you honestly want to, you find you cannot quit entirely, or if when drinking, you have little control over the amount you take, you are probably alcoholic. If that be the case, *you may be suffering from an illness which only a spiritual experience will conquer.*
>
> Our human resources, as marshaled by the will, were not sufficient. They failed utterly.
>
> Lack of power, that was our dilemma. *We had to find a power by which we could live, and it had to be a Power greater than ourselves.*
>
> (Alcoholics Anonymous, 1976: 44–45. Emphasis added.)

At this stage, the delusional walls of rationalization, minimization, self-deception, and denial—that may have been slowly cracking and crumbling for years—will often seem to disappear altogether at times, and most people will have intervals of *terrifying clarity* when they are *starkly aware* of their desperate need to find some kind of a "spiritual solution" for a life-or-death problem—even if they're not quite sure what that would mean or how it might actually work.

At this point, many people will begin to recognize their genuine need for practical and effective help from "God" or a "Higher Power" of some kind—to use conventional twelve-step terminology. This will be true for some people who might sincerely describe themselves as spiritual seekers—even if they're not really sure what these terms actually mean to them. This recognition of a real need for help or strength from some kind of "God" or "Higher Power" will often exist quite strongly even in people who may tend to choke on these terms in disgust whenever they utter them—people who might describe themselves variously as atheists, agnostics, skeptics or critics—or as traumatized survivors of religious abuse—or as people recovering from religious addiction—or perhaps as intellectuals, scientists, humanists, existentialists, realists, or rationalists—or perhaps simply as dedicated hedonists.

Oddly enough, for the person who comfortably describes themself as a religious "believer," a clear recognition of their desperate need for genuine access to a "power greater than ourselves"—as a literal matter of life-or-death—may pose even more difficult problems than it does for committed nonbelievers. They may feel hurt, disappointed, betrayed, baffled, or enraged because they have been "praying like crazy" and it hasn't helped. They will often feel lost and confused because "God" has apparently been unwilling or unable to relieve or remove their increasingly powerful compulsion to continue using—despite their deep and sincere faith that "praying for help" *should* work.

As they *truly* make the transition into *attempted spiritual sobriety,* there is one question that points toward a common ground for all users, regardless of their prior spiritual or religious orientation, and that is:

How badly will a person really *want* recovery?

According to the basic literature of Alcoholics Anonymous, for those who truly grasp the essential life-or-death significance of their predicament, they will probably have to want recovery:

- "with all the desperation of drowning men," and
- "with all the fervor with which the drowning seize life preservers."

(Alcoholics Anonymous, 1976: 28 & 1953: 22)

Under these circumstances, even those chronic relapsers who have been quite belligerent toward *any* kind of spirituality—and have repeatedly voiced the classic complaint of the twelve-step program dropout— "I just can't *stand* all that 'God' stuff"—may finally be ready to drop that tired old refrain and sincerely *try* to grasp the true meaning of:

**"STEP TWO"**—Came to believe that a Power greater than ourselves could restore us to sanity.

Eventually, despite their initial distaste for the "G-word"—or their sincere confusion or disappointment about it—most people who genuinely reach this stage of baffled and frightened desperation will also be ready to wrestle with the practical meaning of:

232

**"STEP THREE"**—Made a decision to turn our will and our lives over to the care of God, *as we understood Him.*

## Philosophical Premise:

Now, let's continue our look at the third area of philosophical misunderstanding and disagreement in the addiction treatment and recovery field:

### Secular "versus" Spiritual Recovery.

As strange at it may seem, there are basically no real grounds for dispute between the advocates of so-called "rational-emotive, cognitive-behavioral, or secular" approaches to addiction treatment and recovery and those who offer *"a spiritual solution."*

First of all, there is no philosophical "requirement" in the *Face to Face Unified Addiction Recovery Model* for anyone to seek a spiritual solution if they find that pursuing a purely "rational-secular" approach really works for them— on a permanent basis. If so, they can successfully drop out of the whole *Addiction Recovery Learning Curve* process at Stage Three if they wish to do so.

The "Big Book" of Alcoholics Anonymous—which is often referred to as the "Bible" of the twelve-step spiritual recovery program—certainly doesn't insist in any way that a spiritual approach will be necessary for all problem drinkers.

Rather, as we have recently noted, it merely offers the *suggestion* that many alled *"real"* alcoholics *"may* be suffering from an illness which only a spiritual experience will conquer."

Secondly, in advanced cases where some kind of a spiritual solution seems to be desperately needed—but the client is totally baffled by the idea, or strongly biased against it—it would then be entirely appropriate for us as clinicians— in good conscience and with considerable accuracy—to reframe and redefine the experience of "a spiritual awakening" as a *deep form* of "cognitive restructuring."

People who are philosophically inclined to favor a "rational-secular" approach to sobriety—and even those who feel very negative about any kind of spiritual approach—will find that the last two stages on the *Addiction Recovery Learning Curve—Attempted Spiritual Sobriety* and *Rational Spiritual Sobriety*—are actually compatible with their views on two separate grounds:

> **First,** they don't even *have* to seek a spiritual solution unless they find that they really need one, and

> **Second,** if they really do need to find "a spiritual foundation for rational living," it will be entirely possible to formulate "a rational foundation for spiritual living."

So, how can we reframe and redefine the experience of "a spiritual awakening" as a *deep form* of "cognitive restructuring?"

This process is fairly simple, and it essentially involves helping a person enlarge their basic "cognitive schema"—meaning their overall perception and understanding reality—by helping them begin to consciously experience the reality of the spiritual dimension of their being. For many people—as we will begin to see more clearly in the next section and in the next chapter—this may often be done most easily and simply by deliberately tapping into and expressing the life-transforming power of unconditional love on a daily basis as the most important personal priority in life.

## Learning Process:

Sadly, some professionals in the addiction treatment and recovery field—and many clients as well—are quite dogmatic about the necessity of pursuing *a purely "rational-secular" approach.*

They fail to appreciate how the practice of sound spirituality can greatly enhance a person's capacity to develop:

- more rational thinking,
- greater peace of mind,
- better emotional balance,
- improved self-control,
- healthier behavior,
- more satisfying relationships, and
- much more effective living skills.

Consciously or unconsciously, many people who "voluntarily" begin to attend AA, or any other twelve-step self-help recovery meetings, are still essentially resistant, reluctant, resentful, and filled with serious reservations.

They seem to have a great deal of difficulty understanding or accepting the power and validity of the universal principles involved in a spiritual recovery process.

Chronic relapsers will often return to treatment saying:

> *"I've been to those twelve-step meetings, and they don't work!"*

Of course, this sounds very much like someone who might go to a gym to get in shape and spends most of their time socializing in the steam room or sitting in the sauna—and then complains:

> *"I've been to those gyms, and they don't work!"*

As clinicians, we must help our clients understand that *recovery from harmful addiction is not a spectator sport.*

We need to stress the fact that passively sitting around and waiting for some kind of a *"miracle"* to occur spontaneously—with or without fervent prayers for help—is *a sure-fire formula for relapse.*

Many people, of course, will sincerely approach the *Attempted Spiritual Sobriety* stage with no conscious resistance and no overt antagonism.

Indeed, many people will be philosophically and emotionally *eager* to find an effective spiritual solution.

Even so, many of these open-minded and willing people have discovered that the universal spiritual principles embedded within the traditional terminology of the twelve-step program can still be quite confusing and difficult for them to fully grasp—and even harder for them to put in to practice.

Naturally, this difficulty can be even more pronounced for people who have had to overcome their initial resistance or antagonism toward a spiritual approach just to get this far.

Therefore, even many people who are sincerely trying to "work" the twelve-step program will continue to struggle vainly with the powerful compulsion that lies at the root of their harmful addiction and will continue to suffer serious relapses.

So, what's the problem?

Many people who enter the *Attempted Spiritual Sobriety* stage on the *Addiction Recovery Learning Curve* may actually be "stuck" in an

> immature, concrete, skeptical, rebellious, or hypercritical *stage of faith development.*

> (Fowler, 1981)

This kind of "arrested spiritual development" can be a real problem for people who identify themselves as religious "believers" *or* "unbelievers." We will examine James Fowler's model for the *stages of faith development* in more detail in the next section. For now, let's consider one core misunderstanding that often results from this arrested development which seems to be especially common among the more dogmatic advocates for strictly "rational" or "secular" approaches for addiction recovery. This involves a persistent failure to recognize the crucial difference that exists between individual (internalized) spirituality and conventional (organized) religion.

This confusion then leads to their somewhat stunning failure to grasp a simple matter of objective and observable fact:

> Working a twelve-step spiritual recovery program does *not* require anyone to join *any* organized religion or religious denomination, or insist that anyone must accept or practice *any* specific religious or theological creeds, doctrines, dogmas, devotions, or disciplines.

After many years of puzzled reflection, I have finally come to see what I believe to be the primary reason for this misunderstanding:

> While the twelve-step program does offer a simple "spiritual" solution, *it is expressed in "religious" terminology* that unquestionably makes it more difficult for many people to understand, accept, or practice the universal spiritual principles involved.

A significant number of people react to explicitly religious language quite sincerely in a negative or bewildered way—for a wide range of possible reasons that may be good or bad, accurate or inaccurate, informed or uninformed, logical or illogical, and mature or immature. Regardless of the reasons for their negativity or confusion, however, many of these people will eventually *need* to find and use more universal, understandable, and acceptable "spiritual" terms that are clearly practical, applicable, and transformational for them.

Despite a repeated emphasis in official twelve-step program literature on the healthy, positive, caring, and forgiving nature of "a loving God," many people will experience *any* kind of religious or theological language as something *intolerably irrational or threatening*. Because of an arrested or immature stage of faith development, excessively concrete or literal thinking, past negative or growth-limiting experiences with religious people or institutions, open-minded and tolerant personal or political values, rigidly held and reassuring "rational" beliefs—or perhaps through pure ignorance, bias, or lack of interest—they will often react almost viscerally to *any* religious ideas, images, symbols, or terms.

Any form of religious ideation or terminology, therefore, might trigger an automatic, negative reaction in these people—sometimes based on a foundation of unthinking assumptions and unconscious projections—that may lead them to perceive *whatever* is being said as:

- emotionally childish, silly, superstitious, and magical;
- intellectually foolish, irrational, illogical, and indefensible:
- completely abstract, academic, theoretical, and impractical;

- hopelessly obscure, mysterious, nonsensical, and confusing;
- unacceptably authoritarian, abusive, stern, judgmental, and harsh;
- painfully narrow, intolerant, bigoted, biased, tribal, and exclusive;
- mindlessly fanatical, fundamentalist, extremist, cruel, or violent; and therefore
- fundamentally flawed, dangerous, and deeply offensive.

By contrast, when we examine the fifth and final stage on the *Addiction Recovery Learning Curve—Rational Spiritual Sobriety*—we will learn how people can begin to "translate" the universal spiritual principles involved in the twelve-step program into clear, simple, modern terms and effective self-management techniques that they can easily understand, accept, and begin to practice in their daily life.

In the meantime, however, let's look at a few more widely held misconceptions about the spiritual recovery process:

Some advocates for strictly "secular" approaches to recovery—and, frankly, many people who are active in twelve-step recovery programs and getting poor results because they don't really grasp the spiritual principles involved —seem to be almost fixated on the completely false idea that seeking to live in harmony with universal spiritual principles means accepting a permanent prescription for "learned helplessness" that *must* involve:

- a complete **abdication** of *all* personal responsibility,
- the passive **surrender** of *all* free-will, and
- the complete **suspension** of *all* common sense and rational thought
- to the mysterious machinations of some **external power.**

Hence, naturally, these people fail to recognize the fundamental reality that seeking to live by spiritual principles simply means nurturing a willingness to

- tap into a deep source of *inner wisdom and strength,* and *then*
- be guided by their *own conscience and compassion* on a daily basis.

Above all, they fail to recognize that seeking to live in harmony with universal spiritual principles—perhaps more than any other way of life—actually *requires* that people become willing to accept complete personal responsibility for all of their own:

- beliefs,
- attitudes,
- motives,
- desires,

237

- thoughts,
- feelings,
- words, and
- deeds.

There's a central tenet of the traditional disease model of harmful addiction—and of the twelve-step spiritual recovery program that's become so closely associated with it in most people's minds—that's been repeated so often that it's become a virtual slogan or mantra.

It states flatly that:

> You're not responsible for being an alcoholic or an addict, but now that you know you have this problem you're completely responsible for taking whatever steps are necessary to achieve and maintain your own sobriety.

The depth of misunderstanding that has existed historically about the undeniable fact that following the twelve-step program requires the rigorous practice of personal responsibility is almost unbelievable. This misunderstanding is clearly reflected in a 1982 article on "Models of Helping and Coping" that was cited favorably in the introductory chapter to the classic cognitive-behavioral text *Relapse Prevention* published three years later.

This article described four contrasting models for attributing personal responsibility for the onset and resolution of a problem:

1) The Moral Model—People are responsible for problems and solutions.
2) The Compensatory Model—People are not responsible for problems but are responsible for solutions.
3) The Medical Model—People are not responsible for problems or solutions.
4) The Enlightenment Model—People are responsible for problems but are not responsible for solutions.

Although the disease model of harmful addiction and the twelve-step spiritual recovery program clearly reflect the basic assumptions of the Compensatory Model—that alcoholics and addicts are not responsible for causing their addiction but are fully responsible for finding an effective solution for their sobriety—this article and the prominent book that cited it both embraced the mistaken view that the twelve-step program is an example of the Enlightenment Model.

How did they manage to get this so completely wrong?

First, the undisputed fact that active alcoholics and addicts can no longer blame circumstances or other people for their problem but must "see the light" and recognize that they hold deeply irrational addictive beliefs and attitudes that must be changed if they are to ever get sober and stay sober is taken to mean that they are personally responsible for becoming alcoholics or addicts in the first place because they held these faulty attitudes and beliefs.

In fact, in the twelve-step model it is precisely this past history of "diminished capacity" for rational thought that "absolves" active alcoholics and addicts from the onus of genuine personal responsibility or moral culpability for originally "causing" their problem with harmful addiction. The legitimacy of this informal "insanity defense" that protects the user from blame and shame for causing their problem and the reality of their personal responsibility for future change are both clearly reflected in the language of Step Two—"Came to believe that a Power greater than ourselves could restore us to sanity."

Secondly, the undisputed fact that active alcoholics and addicts can't be expected to change problem behavior until they learn how to recognize and change the faulty attitudes and beliefs that empower it—and must therefore acquire and internalize the knowledge, skills, and personal power that they lack at the beginning of this learning process—is taken to mean that they are not responsible for solving their problem because they will almost certainly have to seek some outside educational help and emotional support in order to learn how to do so.

Concluding that a person is not *responsible* for solving a problem just because they initially lack the knowledge and skills needed to do so on their own is nonsensical because it's just like saying a first grader isn't responsible for learning how to read, write, and do arithmetic because they can't acquire these skills on their own without going to school.

The emphasis on personal responsibility in the twelve-step program is actually so strong that I can barely grasp the line of faulty logic that would lead anyone to think that it tells people with harmful addictions that they are not personally responsible for solving their problem—regardless of how or why the problem may have been originally caused.

This misunderstanding seems to be based on a flawed assumption that twelve-step program is actually a one-step program that seriously requires people to reach the following string of absurd conclusions:

> Now that I've admitted I'm powerless over this problem that I've caused, I can see very clearly that that I'm not responsible for doing anything whatsoever about it and I don't actually have to do anything about it—other than ask God to magically solve it for me—because nothing that I could ever do would ever work anyway.

(Brickman, et al., 1982: 369–374; Marlatt and Gordon, 1985: 12–15)

In our final chapter focused on Rational Spirituality, we will learn how to translate universal spiritual principles into clear, simple, rational terms that most people can easily understand, accept, and learn how to practice within the framework of existing self-help programs. We will see how many people are able to gracefully dispense with the word "God"—and even the traditional idea of God—if either the word or the idea ultimately serve as an obstacle that blocks them from experiencing and practicing the life-transforming power of unconditional love that lives in the heart and soul of the twelve-step program.

In the meantime, two well-known sayings are quite pertinent here:

"God works through people."

"God helps those who help themselves."

Another core misunderstanding already mentioned briefly involves a widespread failure to recognize that many people are apparently unable to control their emotional reactivity well enough to effectively use sound rational-emotive or cognitive-behavioral coping skills without making a conscious effort to *calm their minds and center themselves spiritually.*

Hence, many people also fail to recognize that the practice of true spirituality actually *requires* that people learn how to slow down, pause, and tap into a deep source of

- inner peace,
- inner power,
- personal freedom, and
- enduring joy

that is natural, healthy, and powerfully *enhances* their capacity for

- clear thinking and rational living.

Many people working their way through the *Attempted Spiritual Sobriety* stage on the *Addiction Recovery Learning Curve* will tend to flounder and fail at first—until they find some way to successfully resolve whatever spiritual confusion or antagonism they may initially feel.

Hence, in one way or another, they must try to make practical and applicable sense of the universal spiritual principles and powerful self-help techniques found in the twelve-step recovery process.

In most cases, as noted above, this means that they will eventually have to "translate" the deeper meaning of many of the "religious" terms used in the twelve steps into clear, simple, modern terms that express the universal spiritual principles involved in a meaningful way that they can easily understand, accept, and begin to practice.

## Treatment Approaches:

At this stage, an eclectic therapist would continue using *Reality Therapy, Transactional Analysis, Cognitive-Behavioral* and *Rational-Emotive Therapy,* and *Motivational Enhancement Therapy* as needed, but they would begin to put a special emphasis on helping the client

- *awaken* to the dynamic reality of the spiritual dimension of their being, and
- *engage* effectively in *Alcoholics Anonymous* or another appropriate twelve-step spiritual recovery program.

*To accomplish these tasks, Twelve-Step Facilitation Therapy, Transpersonal Psychology,* and *Logotherapy* are three psychotherapeutic models that are consistent with our new holistic emphasis on helping our clients successfully integrate the *mental, emotional, physical,* and *spiritual* dimensions of their being.

Up to this point, the treatment approaches and self-help models we have emphasized have generally embraced two common themes:

**First,** in one way or another, they have all stressed the need for clients to develop a greater conscious awareness of the hidden factors at work in their mental and emotional life so that they can achieve more consistent control over their own thoughts, feelings, words, and deeds.

**Secondly,** they have all had a pragmatic and utilitarian focus on the pursuit of enlightened self-interest—helping clients learn how to behave in a more rational way in order to successfully meet their genuine human needs and avoid being victimized any further by their own most compulsive, harmful, or self-defeating attitudes and behavior.

Now, the primary focus of treatment and self-help efforts will be to help clients begin to transcend their primary pursuit of everyday self-interest, and start to focus on fulfilling our deepest human need—which may be expressed in rational-spiritual terms as our fundamental need to develop a strong sense of *meaning, mission, passion, and purpose in life.*

This is vitally important because, as John Wallace has observed:

The sober member of AA *needs* his ideological base. He can ill-afford the dispassionate, disinterested, and, indeed, almost casual play upon words and ideas of the inquiring academic intellectual. The alcoholic recognizes intuitively that he needs a stable and enduring *belief system* if he is to stay sober.

(Wallace, 1978: 21)

In essence, as we begin to facilitate an explicitly spiritual approach to recovery in this stage and in the one that follows, our primary focus as clinicians will now shift toward enhancing our client's willingness and ability to develop a deep devotion to a *positive addiction* dedicated to promoting the unity and welfare of all people through their daily commitment to the practice of *Love and Service*.

## Treatment Approach:

### Twelve-Step Facilitation—NIAAA

The overall goal of this program is to facilitate patient's *active participation* in the fellowship of AA. It regards such active involvement as the primary factor responsible for sustained sobriety ('recovery') and therefore as *the desired outcome of participation* in this program . . . The treatment program has two major goals, which relate directly to the first three Steps of Alcoholics Anonymous . . . *Acceptance* by patients that they suffer from the chronic and progressive illness of alcoholism . . . that they have lost the ability to control their drinking . . . (and) that, since there is no effective cure for alcoholism, the only viable alternative is complete abstinence from the use of alcohol . . . (and) *Surrender* . . . (meaning) . . . acknowledgement on the part of the patient that there is hope for recovery . . . but only through accepting the reality of loss of control and by having faith that *some Higher Power* can help the individual whose willpower has been defeated by alcoholism . . . (and) acknowledgment by the patient that the fellowship of AA has helped millions of alcoholics to sustain their sobriety and that the patient's *best chances for success* are to follow the AA path.

(Nowinski et al., 1995: 1–3. Emphasis added.)

## Treatment Approach:

### Transpersonal Psychology—Abraham Maslow

I should say that I consider Humanistic, Third Force Psychology to be transitional, a preparation for a still "higher" Fourth Psychology, *transpersonal* . . . going beyond . . . identity, self-actualization, and the like . . . These new developments may very well offer a tangible, . . . effective satisfaction of the *'frustrated idealism'* of many quietly desperate people, especially young people. These psychologies give promise of developing into the *life-philosophy,* . . . the *value-system,* the *life-program* that these people have been missing. Without the *transcendent* and the *transpersonal,* we get sick, violent, and nihilistic, or else hopeless and apathetic. We need something 'bigger than we are' . . . to commit ourselves to.

(Maslow, 1968: iii–iv. Emphasis added.)

**Treatment Approach:**

**Logotherapy**—Viktor Frankl

We who lived in concentration camps can remember the men who walked through the huts comforting others, giving away their last piece of bread. They may have been few in number, but they offer sufficient proof that

> *everything can be taken from a man but one thing: the last of the human freedoms—to choose one's attitude in any given set of circumstances, to choose one's own way . . .*

*It is this spiritual freedom—which cannot be taken away—that makes life meaningful and purposeful.*

What man actually needs is not a tensionless state but rather the *striving and struggling for a worthwhile goal*, a *freely chosen task.* What he needs is not the discharge of tension at any cost but *the call of a potential meaning* waiting to be fulfilled by him.

One should not search for an *abstract meaning* of life. . . . Ultimately, man should *not* ask what the meaning of his life is, but rather he must recognize that *it is he who is asked.* In a word, each man is questioned by life; and he can only answer to life by *answering for* his own life; to life he can only respond by being *responsible.*

(Frankl, 1984: 86–87, 121, 127, 131. Emphasis added.)

## *Self-Help Model:*

At this stage, clients should continue using the basic principles and practices of the *Seven Habits of Highly Effective People* and the *Voice Dialogue Method,* but further participation in *Rational Recovery*—or any other "rational-secular" self-help support group—may no longer be helpful. This is because our user has finally realized that they apparently cannot abstain completely and permanently on the basis of using sound rational and emotional coping skills alone and they must now begin to seek some kind of a "spiritual solution."

Continued participation in a strictly "rational-secular" self-help program might be counter-productive at this point because the leaders and other members may misunderstand and contradict the practice of spiritual principles or be overtly hostile to the pursuit of any kind of a spiritual approach.

Unless they were already favorably predisposed toward taking a spiritual approach, before they really "had to," our user should now be at a point of desperation or hopelessness where they are finally ready—whether they really like it or not —to participate actively in *Alcoholics Anonymous* or some other appropriate twelve step-program.

### The Twelve-Step Program—Alcoholics Anonymous.

> We have shown how we got out from under. You say, 'Yes, I'm willing. But am I to be consigned to a life where I shall be stupid, boring and glum, like some righteous people I see? I know I must get along without liquor, but how can I? Have you a sufficient substitute?
>
> Yes, there is a substitute, and it is vastly more than that. It is a fellowship in Alcoholics Anonymous. There you will find release from care, boredom, and worry. Your imagination will be fired. *Life will mean something at last.* The most satisfactory years of your existence lie ahead . . . You are going to meet new friends in your own community . . . Among them you will make lifelong friends. You will be bound to them with new and wonderful ties, for you will escape disaster together and you will commence shoulder to shoulder your common journey. Then *you will know what it means to give of yourself* that others may survive and rediscover life. You will learn the *full meaning* of '*Love thy neighbor as thyself.*'

(Alcoholics Anonymous, 1976: 152–153. Emphasis added.)

**PERMANENT SUCCESS** at this stage would mean the establishment of a *lifetime track record* of complete abstinence—with no exceptions—and the ongoing development of personal growth, emotional balance, health, harmony, happiness, and true life satisfaction.

This would indicate that a person has been able to understand and practice the basic spiritual principles of the twelve-step recovery program on its own terms—with little or no need for any *"rational spiritual translation."*

**REPEATED FAILURE** to stay clean and sober at this stage —or to achieve the deep sense of inner peace, inner power, personal freedom, and enduring joy that are "promised" as a result of working the twelve-step program—will eventually convince many people that they must begin to define the vague notion of "some Higher Power" much more specifically and functionally as they move on to the final stage on the *Addiction Recovery Learning Curve—Rational Spiritual Sobriety*.

## STAGE FIVE:
## RATIONAL SPIRITUAL SOBRIETY

During the final stage on the *Addiction Recovery Learning Curve* a recovering person successfully resolves any theoretical, abstract, theological, or semantic confusion they may have had about the universal spiritual principles found in the twelve-step recovery program.

During this stage—regardless of the specific terminology they may ultimately choose to employ—they finally learn how to "translate" the language used in the twelve-step program in a way that is both meaningful and useful for them and to describe the underlying spiritual principles in practical, applicable, and transformational terms that they can easily understand, accept, and begin to practice in their daily life.

### Philosophical Premise:

Developing what some people would comfortably call "a mature faith"—which adds up to an unshakable confidence in the ultimate value, meaning, and purpose of our own life —is the primary task to be accomplished during the fifth and final stage on the *Addiction Recovery Learning Curve—Rational Spiritual Sobriety*. In his Foreword to the book *When God Becomes a Drug,* by Father Leo Booth, John Bradshaw makes the following useful observations on the question of mature versus immature faith:

> As Freud pointed out in 'The Future of an Illusion,' one of the assumptions of dysfunctional faith is that one loses faith by questioning faith. It takes courage to go against the terrors of hell and judgment that our wounded child fears. Only by questioning our faith can we emerge with a mature faith.

> (Booth, 1993: x)

In his book *The Art of Loving*—while he is not explicitly referring to the process of spiritual development—Erich Fromm points out a very widely believed fallacy that is typical of an immature and insecure level of faith when he observes that:

> Most people see the problem of love primarily as that of being loved, rather than that of loving, of one's capacity to love. Hence, the problem to them is how to be loved, how to be lovable.

Fromm defines "Love" as "the active concern for the life and the growth of that which we love," and he offers a crucial insight into an aspect of personal growth that is also directly relevant to the overall process of spiritual development with the following formula:

- Infantile love follows the principle: *'I love because I am loved.'*
- Mature love follows the principle: *'I am loved because I love.'*
- Immature love says: *'I love you because I need you.'*
- Mature love says: *'I need you because I love you.'*

(Fromm, 1956: 1, 22, 34)

This astute observation echoes the central theme that runs throughout twelve-step program principles which we can see reflected in the "Big Book" of Alcoholics Anonymous when it states without any hesitation or ambiguity:

- "Helping others is the foundation stone of your recovery. A kindly act once in awhile isn't enough. You have to act the Good Samaritan every day if need be."
- "Our very lives` as ex-problem drinkers, depend upon our constant thought of others and how we may help meet their needs."
- ". . . if an alcoholic failed to perfect and enlarge his spiritual life through work and self-sacrifice for others he could not survive the certain trials and low spots ahead."

(Alcoholics Anonymous, 1976: 97, 20, 14–15)

In his book, *Stages of Faith—The Psychology of Human Development and the Quest for Meaning,* James Fowler outlines six stages of faith development that can be linked in sequence over the human life span to three other widely respected models of human development:

- Jear Piaget's **Stages of Cognitive Development,**
- Lawrence Kohlberg's **Stages of Moral Development,** and
- Erik Erikson's **Stages of Psychosocial Development.**

It's far beyond the intended scope of this book to examine each of these developmental models in detail and explore the links that exist between them and the most common stages of spiritual development. However, it's important to note the fact that as we help our clients begin to understand and move through a gradual process of learning and spiritual growth in *Stages Four and Five* on the *Addiction Recovery Learning Curve—Attempted Spiritual Sobriety* and *Rational Spiritual Sobriety*—what we'll actually be doing is to help them move into a more *mature, age appropriate,* and *functional* stage of faith development.

With this in mind, let's take a quick overview of the

# Stages of Faith Development

### Stage One—The Innocent—Intuitive-Projective Faith
This stage of faith is typical in preschool children, and it is usually filled with a great deal fantasy, imagination, powerful images, and play.

### Stage Two—The Literalist—Mythic-Literal Faith
This stage of faith is typical from age six through eleven. Religious images and stories are taken literally and interpreted concretely.

### Stage Three—The Loyalist—Synthetic-Conventional Faith
This stage of faith typically appears in adolescence. Conformity with a peer group and a sense of belonging and identification are of paramount importance.

### Stage Four—The Critic—Individuative-Reflective Faith
This stage of faith typically develops in the late teens and early twenties. The young adult begins to ask serious questions about the ultimate meaning of life—often challenging or rejecting traditional assumptions.

### Stage Five—The Seer—Conjunctive Faith
This stage of faith typically appears after the age of thirty since maturity is required for its development. The adult gradually develops an individual belief system and a core set of personal values by integrating a wide range of different views and influences through the prism of their own experience.

### Stage Six—The Saint—Universal Faith
A person at this stage of faith is motivated by their devotion to practicing a set of universal spiritual principles in all aspects of their daily life. Their faith involves a total commitment to the conscious experience of wholeness and is often marked by a deep devotion to the practice of patience, kindness, tolerance, and unconditional love for themselves and all others.

The *lifelong process of spiritual growth* through these six stages of faith development doesn't resemble anything like "climbing a spiritual ladder," but tends to evolve in a gradual, natural, organic way that usually isn't very direct, linear, or calculated.

As a person gradually moves through the stages over a period of many years, they will not necessarily abandon the traditional images, beliefs, practices, or relationships that were meaningful and important for them at earlier stages, but they will often be able to truly appreciate and experience their deeper spiritual meaning and power in a dynamic way that had never been possible before. (Condensed, paraphrased, and adapted from Fowler, 1981 & Stokes, 1989).

## RELIGIOUS ADDICTION AND RELIGIOUS ABUSE

Many sincerely religious people clearly radiate a deep sense of inner peace, power, purpose, passion, and joy and they are truly compassionate, gentle, tolerant, understanding, forgiving, and flexible people—because their religious experience and practice is a deeply rooted expression of true spiritual experience and practice.

On the other hand, many conventionally "religious" people seem to share few if any of these truly spiritual traits and anyone with an open-mind can appreciate the sad kernel of truth expressed in the bumper sticker that exclaims:

"Dear Lord, Save Me—From Your Followers!"

Father Leo Booth is an author, speaker, and ordained Episcopal Priest who specializes in addiction recovery and treatment issues, and he has coined the highly accurate and valuable terms "religious addiction" and "religious abuse" to describe a widespread problem that has stunted true spirituality and seriously harmed many people over many centuries—both perpetrators and victims.

In his book *When God Becomes a Drug,* he writes:

> Religious addiction entails using God, a religion, or a belief system as a means both to escape or avoid painful feelings and to seek self-esteem. It involves adopting a rigid belief system that specifies only one right way, which you feel you must force onto others by means of guilt, shame, fear, brainwashing, and elitism. Thus religious addiction almost always results in the abuse of someone in the name of your beliefs.

"In the name of God," according to Father Booth, both the victims and perpetrators of religious addiction and religious abuse will often:

- "have been made to feel fear, guilt, shame, and anger."
- "emotionally, physically, or sexually abused themselves or others."
- "brought themselves or others to the edge of financial ruin."
- "judged and condemned themselves or others as worthless and inherently bad."

Father Booth notes that religious addiction and religious abuse are equal-opportunity problems, and he reports that victims and perpetrators alike are "people from all walks of life: lay people, clergy, fundamentalist and mainstream Christians, Orthodox Jews, atheists, agnostics, Buddhists, Muslims, New Age disciples, and Twelve Step junkies."

Nevertheless, Booth identifies a common theme that can be observed repeatedly on a personal level across a wide range of superficially contrasting belief systems, and he describes a typical perpetrator of religious abuse in the following way:

> Their unhealthy beliefs about themselves and God poison their lives. They use religion as a means to acquire power and control, especially to gain money or sex, or both. Their only means of gaining self-respect or self-control is to lock themselves into rigid, intolerant perfectionism, harshly judgmental of others who don't follow their rules. They use God, religion, or their beliefs not to liberate themselves spiritually, but to escape emotional pain. Such behavior creates an insurmountable barrier to authentic spirituality and worse, to a healthy, creative relationship with that inner Power I call God.

> (Booth, 1998: 2, 16–17)

As clinicians, we will certainly need to consider the possibility that many clients who seem to be stuck in an immature, reactive, or rebellious stage of faith development may actually have some past or present history of involvement with religious addiction or religious abuse—as victims or perpetrators or both.

As part of our ongoing psychoeducational assessment and feedback process, we will need to help our clients carefully explore this history and try to determine for themselves how it may manifest itself in recurring post-traumatic emotional reactions to a wide variety of everyday stressors, unusual challenges, and difficult enduring life circumstances.

Then, as part of our treatment approach, we will need to help our clients

- begin to **explore** how they may be trying to self-medicate their emotional over-reactivity with their harmful addictive behavior,
- **move on** toward a more mature stage of faith development by considering how they may be inappropriately trying to defend themselves emotionally by their reflexive antagonism toward anything "spiritual,"
- begin to **recognize** how their understandable defensiveness and hostility on the topic of spirituality may actually have been shaped and determined by their past negative experiences, and

- **appreciate** how their negative reactions may actually be triggered by their seriously distorted and inaccurate belief systems and their essential ignorance about the deeply beneficial and healthy nature of true spirituality.

## Learning Process:

During the *Rational Spiritual Sobriety* stage, we will need to help our clients learn how to "translate" the universal spiritual principles found in the twelve-step program into clear, simple, modern terms that they can easily understand, accept, and begin to practice in their daily life.

How does this work?

The phrase "Higher Power" is perhaps the most widely used example of a term that is preferred by people who are confused or antagonized by the actual terminology found in the twelve steps—which is "God, as we understood Him."

In fact, the phrase "as we understood Him" is itself an early example of this "translation" process at work. It was originally adopted as part of the twelve-step program of Alcoholics Anonymous—and first published in the AA "Big Book" in 1939—in an attempt to avoid unnecessarily alienating and losing potential members for whom achieving sobriety could be a matter of life and death.

After seeing many people reject their "simple spiritual solution" because of an automatic reaction of hostility toward anything that smacked of organized religion, the phrase "as we understood Him" was added in order to clarify the crucial distinction that exists between the direct personal experience of true spirituality and the superficial embrace of conventional religious doctrines, dogmas, creeds, images, rituals, or belief systems.

Dr. Bob Smith, one of the co-founders of Alcoholics Anonymous, made an even greater contribution to this early spiritual "translation" process—and helped make the essential spiritual values of the twelve-step program much easier for anyone to understand and apply—when he declared:

> Our twelve steps, when simmered down to the last, resolve themselves
> into the words: love and service.

There are many ways that people can accomplish this "rational-spiritual translation" task—and a wide array of meaningful words, symbols, images, ideas, and practices that can successfully point people toward the inner path that leads to direct spiritual experience.

Hence, there is no need for anyone in recovery to engage in an endless struggle trying to "understand" or "make sense" out of spiritual concepts, theoretical abstractions, theological doctrines, or religious terms that strike them as confusing, bogus, meaningless, or mysterious.

Based on thousands of direct personal observations over the past 23 years, however, it's become very clear to me that achieving a healthy personal transformation toward wholeness in mind, body, and spirit will often prove to be the *final* and *most critical* challenge that many people will need to overcome on their long journey through the *Addiction Recovery Learning Curve.*

Hence, it is often essential—in one way or another—for people who are dealing with the most serious and deadly forms of harmful addiction to identify and practice a valid set of *universal spiritual principles.*

Tragically, however, this essentially simple and natural task is often falsely perceived as something complicated or difficult to grasp—by people who are functioning intellectually on a rather superficial level.

The conceptual problem that some people have in understanding the essential reality and transforming power of some simple universal spiritual principles such as "love" and "service" is roughly similar to the difficulty that some overly "rational" people often seem to have in grasping the motions of *multiple intelligences* in general and *emotional intelligence* in particular. (Goleman, 1995)

Sadly, this conceptual difficulty can become a fatal stumbling block that some people dealing with serious harmful addictions never become fully ready, willing, or able to surmount.

## *Treatment Approach:*

At this stage, an eclectic therapist would continue using an individualized blend of interventions drawn from *Reality Therapy, Transactional Analysis, Cognitive-Behavioral* and *Rational-Emotive Therapy, Motivational Enhancement Therapy, Twelve Step Facilitation, Transpersonal Psychology, Logotherapy* and other appropriate therapeutic models as needed.

By now, however, they might also begin to feel the need for a simple phrase to *clearly identify* and *accurately describe* the essence of an integrated approach that would synthesize the core principles and practices found in *all* these treatment models into a unified whole.

I believe that a new, integrated approach of this kind could legitimately and accurately be called:

### *"Transpersonal Cognitive Therapy."*

This is a technical term that I have coined to describe the theoretical approach underlying **RS—Rational Spirituality**®—a self-help system that I have developed and will introduce in the next chapter.

It consists of an eclectic blend of proven tools for rational change currently found in *rational-emotive, cognitive-behavioral,* and other therapies with a practical translation of *universal spiritual principles*—including those found in the twelve step recovery program—into clear, simple, modern terms and effective self-management techniques that most people can easily understand, accept, and begin to practice.

## Self-Help Model:

At this stage, clients should continue using the basic principles and practices of the *Seven Habits* and *Voice Dialogue,* and continue their active participation in *Alcoholics Anonymous* or any other appropriate twelve-step *program.*

At this point, however, or *perhaps even much earlier in their overall change process,* they might also benefit by beginning to learn about the core principles and practices of a new self-help system I have developed—and mentioned just above—which is called *"Rational Spirituality."*

I will discuss some of the basic principles and practices of this integrated self-help model very shortly in the next chapter.

### HYPOTHESIS:

*Rational Spiritual Sobriety* will not fail when fully understood and seriously attempted.

**PERMANENT SUCCESS** at this level would mean the establishment of a *lifetime track record* of complete abstinence—with no exceptions—and the ongoing development of personal growth, emotional balance, health, harmony, happiness, and true life satisfaction.

This would indicate that a person has been able to understand and practice the universal spiritual principles found in the twelve-step spiritual recovery program by successfully "translating" them into clear, simple, modern terms that they can easily understand, accept, and begin to practice in their daily life.

**REPEATED FAILURE** to stay clean and sober at this stage —or to achieve the deep sense of inner peace, inner power, personal freedom, and enduring joy that are "promised" as a result of working the twelve-step program—would suggest that a person has not fully learned, understood, accepted, or practiced the numerous lessons for healthy living that may be found throughout the various stages on the *Addiction Recovery Learning Curve.*

If so, this suggests that they may need to get more help—and do some serious thinking and careful soul-searching—in order to identify their most crucial learning needs and the essential developmental tasks that they may have neglected, avoided, or misunderstood.

Otherwise, they may need to seriously consider looking for another recovery model altogether that might offer them whatever it is that they think they really need or want.

# CHAPTER 9

# RS–Rational Spirituality®

"Knock, knock."
"Who's there?"
"No one."
"No one who?"
"No one's there."

"I come from a mixed family: My mother is Jewish and my father is Catholic. One of them invented guilt, and the other one perfected it!"

"Your vision will become clear only when you can look into your own heart. Who looks outside, dreams; who looks inside, awakes."

—Carl Jung.

"To put more faith in lies and hate than truth and love is the true atheism."

—James Russell Lowell.

♦ ♦ ♦

Over the past 23 years, I've had professional and personal interactions with literally thousands of people who were struggling with serious harmful addictions.

I've been participating in a self-help recovery program personally since 1981 in order to deal with a life-or-death problem that I gradually developed during my late teens and twenties with compulsive overeating and morbid obesity. Fortunately, because of my ongoing, daily commitment to practice the sane, sensible, and healthy way of life suggested by this recovery program, I've been able to maintain a normal weight—and a weight loss of about 140 pounds—since 1983.

I've also been working professionally in the mental health and addictions treatment field since 1987 because of the serious interest I had developed in addiction, recovery, and spirituality during the first six years of my own recovery process. During this time, I went back to graduate school for a master's degree in clinical social work, completed an intensive year-long training program in alcoholism and chemical dependency counseling, and went on to earn my current credentials as a licensed clinical social worker and a licensed alcohol and drug abuse counselor.

During all of this time, I've repeatedly observed that many people seem to be driven into virtually unbreakable patterns of harmful addiction by their compulsive obedience to the dictatorial demands of an insatiable, internalized *"addictive self."* I've seen how their unsteady willpower—and their struggling *"sober self"*—can be dominated and defeated repeatedly by some of their most shallow desires, selfish motives, unreasonable resentments, exaggerated fears, irrational beliefs, and distorted thinking patterns.

Over and over again—even when they aren't dealing with an identifiable harmful addiction—I've seen how a person's emotional reactivity can persist at an intense and overpowering level—either blatantly or rather quietly—even when they've learned a number of sound cognitive-behavioral coping skills and are seriously trying—sometimes almost desperately—to *stop and think rationally* before they begin acting out again.

On the other hand, I've also seen many apparently "hopeless" people who have gradually learned how to successfully manage their overpowering emotional reactivity by the sincere, persistent application of twelve-step spiritual principles and practices in their daily lives.

All of my personal and professional experience—and everything that I've learned in my professional education, clinical training, and independent study over the years—has led me to reach one central conclusion:

> Many people are apparently *unable* to use sound rational and emotional coping skills without first calming their minds and centering themselves spiritually.

I've personally seen so many sad or even tragic consequences unfold because people have lacked an effective "spiritual foundation for rational living" that I've become convinced there is an urgent need for clinicians to learn how to offer their clients a simple and effective way to understand, integrate, and practice sound *rational and spiritual* principles in a fully unified and consistent manner.

In order to provide people with a clear example, an ideal model, and a simple vocabulary illustrating how a *"rational-spiritual" integration* of this kind can be accomplished, I've developed a self-help system called:

### *RS—Rational Spirituality*®.

The *Rational Spirituality* model was initially crafted to help people who are working through the fifth and final stage on the *Addiction Recovery Learning Curve*—which I have chosen to call:

### *"Rational Spiritual Sobriety."*

However, as the *Rational Spirituality model* has gradually evolved and developed over the past few years it is now intended to be used for the potential benefit of anyone who may be interested in learning how to

- *calm* their mind,
- *center* themselves spiritually,
- *tap into* a deep source of inner peace, inner power, personal freedom, and enduring joy,
- *control* their own thoughts, feelings, words, and deeds more consistently,
- *successfully manage* their emotional reactivity,
- *achieve* better emotional balance, and
- gradual*y learn* how to live a healthier, happier, more rational, rewarding, and meaningful life.

In our discussion of *Stages Three, Four and Five* on the *Addiction Recovery Learning Curve*—which are *Attempted Analytical Abstinence, Attempted Spiritual Sobriety* and *Rational Spiritual Sobriety*—we've already seen how some strong advocates for purely "rational-secular" approaches to addiction and recovery often fail to appreciate how the practice of sound spirituality can produce many of these benefits.

We've also seen how some people will tend to automatically resist or resent the idea of seeking any kind of a spiritual solution—and how many others may find themselves sincerely baffled or confused once they get to a point of hopelessness and desperation so deep that only an equally deep and effective spiritual solution can apparently help them.

Additionally, we've noted that many of the people in either of these categories may actually be "stuck" in an immature stage of faith development or—more accurately—how they may be in *an arrested stage of spiritual development* that leads them to react to spiritual ideas in dysfunctional ways that may be a bit too *concrete, literal, skeptical, cynical, defensive, rebellious, hostile, or hypercritical.*

Finally, we've seen how many people who are dealing with or struggling against dealing with these vital questions simply fail to understand the crucial difference between conventional "religion" and true spirituality. We've also observed how this essentially semantic confusion often results in a serious mis-understanding of what true spirituality, the twelve-step spiritual recovery pro-gram, and the natural process of spiritual growth and development are really all about.

Many people experience conventional religious terminology as obscure, mysterious, confusing, archaic, annoying, or objectionable.

Successfully making the transition from *"Attempted Spiritual Sobriety"* to *"Rational Spiritual Sobriety"* on the *Addiction Recovery Learning Curve* requires that a person eventually comes to understand a simple set of universal spiritual principles in a logical way—*using any terms that really make sense to him or her* —and then begins to put them into practice as guiding principles in their life on a daily basis—if they should freely choose to do so.

The *Rational Spirituality* self-help system suggests a set of clear, simple, modern terms to accurately describe some of these universal spiritual principles in a practical and easily understandable way. It is thereby intended to offer peo-ple "a rational foundation for spiritual living" that might be more helpful than the conventionally religious terms that are so often used—rather dogmatically and counter-productively in many cases—when serious spiritual issues are being discussed in an abstract, theoretical, or theological way.

## OUTLINE AND SUMMARY

As I write this book on *"Addiction, Progression, & Recovery"*—which is intended primarily for a professional audience—I'm also developing two addi-tional books intended for general readers. The first will discuss *The Addiction Recovery Learning Curve* that has been introduced in this volume, and the sec-ond book will describe and discuss the closely related *Rational Spirituality* self-help system in depth.

It's far beyond the intended scope or purpose of this book to discuss all of the features of the *"RS model"* in detail, but I believe it would be quite helpful for clinicians working with clients who are struggling with harmful addictions to explore and understand some of the basic philosophical premises underlying the model.

Before doing so, however, it would also be important for us to review a outline and summary of the entire *Rational Spirituality* model.

The *Rational Spirituality* self-help system suggests some clear, simple, modern language to describe a set of universal spiritual principles or practices in each of the following areas:

- One Ultimate Authority
- One Primary Power
- One Primary Purpose
- One Common Problem
- One Personal Code
- One Personal Vow
- Two Levels of Awareness
- Two Golden Rules
- Three Fundamental Skills
- Four Eternal Truths
- Four Essential Practices
- Four Personal Rewards
- Five Stages of Change
- Seven Simple Steps
- Twelve Core Principles
- Twelve Translated Steps

Here is an overview of the entire model as it is presented in my seminar handouts, including some quotations that also appear on the handouts:

## RS—Rational Spirituality®

**A spiritual foundation for rational living
and a rational foundation for spiritual living.**

How to find inner peace, inner power, personal freedom,
and enduring joy through the practice of patience, kindness,
tolerance, and unconditional love.

**A practical pathway out of our ego and into our soul.**

- Bonding people and principles.
- Boosting our bottom line by devoting our lives to service.
- Becoming more values-centered and socially responsible.
- Doing our business or work as a blessing to ourselves and others.

- Blending spiritual development with proven tools for rational change.

**Rational Spirituality** is a self-help system that seamlessly blends the proven tools for rational change currently found in rational-emotive and cognitive-behavioral therapy with a practical translation of twelve-step program principles—and other universal spiritual principles—into clear, simple, modern terms and effective self-management techniques that most people can easily understand, accept, and begin to practice.

## ONE ULTIMATE AUTHORITY

Inner Truth, as we honestly seek to understand it, expressed through our own intuition, compassion, conscience, discernment, and deeper consciousness.

## ONE PRIMARY POWER

The life-transforming power of unconditional love flowing through the deepest spiritual core of our being.

## ONE PRIMARY PURPOSE

Always to add whatever we can to the stream of goodness and light in our sometimes dark and troubled world, and to help others do likewise.

## ONE COMMON PROBLEM

Many people are apparently unable to use sound rational and emotional coping skills without first calming their minds and centering themselves spiritually.

## TWO LEVELS OF AWARENESS

1. Fearful Angry Confused Ego.
2. Fully Awakened Compassionate Energy.

## TWO GOLDEN RULES

1. Always seek to know and do that which is right and good for you.
2. Always seek to know and do that which is right and good for others, too!

## THREE FUNDAMENTAL SKILLS

1. Learn how to care more deeply.
2. Learn how to think more clearly.
3. Learn how to act more wisely.

## FOUR ETERNAL TRUTHS

1. True happiness will never be found by seeking it.
2. True happiness is always a by-product of a good and meaningful life.
3. A good life will be focused more on what I can give than on what I can get.
4. A meaningful life requires a personal mission, values, vision, purpose, passion, acceptance, and action.

## FOUR ESSENTIAL PRACTICES

1. Patience.
2. Kindness.
3. Tolerance.
4. Unconditional Love.

## FOUR PERSONAL REWARDS

1. Inner Peace.
2. Inner Power.
3. Personal Freedom.
4. Enduring Joy.

## FOUR DEAD-END DISTRACTIONS

Trying to:
1. KNOW the Unknowable.
2. DO the Undoable.
3. CONTROL the Uncontrollable.
4. AVOID the Unavoidable.

## FIVE STAGES OF CHANGE

1. Conflict and Consequences.
2. Attempted Common Sense Control.
3. Attempted Analytical Awareness.
4. Attempted Spiritual Solution.
5. Rational Spiritual Solution.

**"If our true nature is permitted to guide our life, we grow healthy, fruitful, and happy."**

—Abraham Maslow.

## SEVEN SIMPLE STEPS

1. SENSE—Something is wrong inside or out.
2. STOP—Before I make it worse.
3. CENTER—Myself in heart, mind, body, and soul.
4. THINK—What really happened and what really counts?
5. FEEL—Unconditional love and understanding for one and all.
6. CHOOSE—A right, good, sane, and healthy course.
7. ACT—As wisely and compassionately as I possibly can.

## TWELVE CORE PRINCIPLES

1. Patience, kindness, tolerance, and love are universal principles that always lead to inner peace and inner power when properly understood and practiced.
2. How we feel and what we do flows from what we care about and how rationally we think.
3. Rational thinking is a skill that can be developed in an active learning process.
4. We are all both human and spiritual beings.
5. The human intellect can promote or obstruct our spiritual growth.
6. True spirituality is natural, healthy, and enhances our rational thinking.
7. True spirituality cannot be fully comprehended by the mind or expressed in words.
8. True spirituality does not contradict or require the practice of religion.
9. There are many sound spiritual disciplines we can learn and practice.
10. Rational and spiritual development occur in natural stages that cannot be rushed, but can be blocked, delayed, or permanently avoided.
11. Life has all the meaning and purpose we choose to give it.
12. Unconditional love is the most peaceful, powerful, and practical spiritual energy in the universe.

### Rational Spirituality

is a new way of thinking, feeling, living, and working that is profoundly satisfying and effective.

It allows us to tap deep roots of inner wisdom from the head, the heart, the body, and the soul.

It is a practical program for people who want to deepen their spiritual awareness and build a better life, better relationships, a better workplace, and a better world.

## ONE PERSONAL CODE

I am honest with myself and others, and I take complete personal responsibility for my own life:

- my beliefs, attitudes, motives and desires;
- my thoughts, feelings, words and deeds;
- my goals, priorities, work and relationships;
- my mistakes, lapses, failures and flaws;
- my joys, successes, health, harmony and happiness.

## ONE PERSONAL VOW

Today, I dedicate myself to a pure and noble cause:

To center myself within the deepest spiritual core of my being and devote my life to the intelligent practice of patience, kindness, tolerance and unconditional love for myself and for all others.

Today, I will continue to learn and grow as I become the wonderful and caring person I am meant to be.

I will not stay asleep or stuck in a shallow ego-centered box where I am driven by selfishness, pride, shame, greed, fear, anger, sadness, sloth, striving, stress, or success—because this would obstruct my ability to practice unconditional love and prevent me from fulfilling my primary purpose in living today.

Today, I will let go of all shallow motives, selfish desires, irrational beliefs, or distorted thinking patterns that trigger any ego-level emotional distress or difficulty.

And I will allow my victory over these illusions to inspire others to seek the same deep source of inner peace, inner power, personal freedom, and enduring joy that I have found through my daily devotion to the practice of unconditional love.

I will do my best to remember and to practice this vow today in all that I think, feel, say, and do.

> This is the true joy in life, the being used for a purpose recognized by yourself as a mighty one; the being thoroughly worn out before being thrown on the scrap heap; the being a force of nature instead of a fever-

ish selfish clod of ailments and grievances, complaining that the world will not devote itself to making you happy.

—George Bernard Shaw.

I don't know what your destiny will be, but one thing I know: the only ones among you who will be really happy are those who have sought and found how to serve.

—Albert Schweitzer.

## TWELVE TRANSLATED STEPS

1. I admit that I have a problem dealing with compulsion—irresistible impulses to perform irrational acts that produce negative consequences in my life.

2. I believe that by tapping into the life-transforming power of unconditional love flowing through the deepest spiritual core of my being I can find the inner peace and the inner power I need to control my own thoughts, feelings, words, and deeds more consistently.

3. Therefore, I will breathe slowly and deeply, calm my mind, center myself within the deepest spiritual core of my being and devote my life to the intelligent practice of patience, kindness, tolerance, and unconditional love for myself and for all others.

4. While centered within the deepest spiritual core of my being, I will take an objective and compassionate look at my ego-level personality and character traits—and I will identify in writing all self-defeating or negative attitudes, shallow motives, selfish desires, irrational beliefs, and distorted thinking patterns that may obstruct my ability to practice unconditional love.

5. While centered within the deepest spiritual core of my being, I will gently accept complete personal responsibility for resolving all of my ego-level attitude and thinking problems — and I will discuss them openly with one trusted person.

6. I am entirely ready to let go of all of my self-defeating or harmful ego-level traits, negative attitudes, shallow motives, selfish desires, irrational beliefs, and distorted thinking patterns.

7. Whenever I sense that any of my negative ego-level traits are active and causing emotional distress for myself or others I will immediately stop and re-center myself spiritually—and I will promptly rededicate my life to the intelligent practice of patience, kindness, tolerance, and unconditional love for myself and for all others.

8. While centered within the deepest spiritual core of my being, I will make a list of all persons I have harmed and I will let go of all negative ego-level traits that might prevent me from making amends to them all.

9. While centered within the deepest spiritual core of my being, I will make direct amends to such persons, wherever possible, except when to do so would injure them or others.

10. Whenever I sense that any of my negative ego-level traits are active and causing emotional distress for myself or others I will immediately stop and re-center myself spiritually. I will identify the problems involved specifically, discuss them openly with at least one trusted person, and promptly rededicate my life to the intelligent practice of patience kindness, tolerance, and unconditional love.

11. I will continue to center myself within the deepest spiritual core of my being through my daily devotion to the intelligent practice of patience, kindness, tolerance and unconditional love—and I will seek to improve my ability to function from this deeper level of awareness more consistently during all of my waking hours.

12. As I experience a healthy personal transformation toward wholeness as the result of these steps, I will center my attention and focus my energy daily on trying to fulfill my primary purpose in living today:

> *Always to add whatever I can to the stream of goodness and light in our sometimes dark and troubled world, and to help others do likewise.*

## RS—TWELVE TRANSLATED STEPS

A translation of the Twelve Step Program into "Rational Spiritual Terminology"

### The Twelve Steps:

1. We admitted we were powerless over *our addiction*—that our lives had become unmanageable.

   I admit that I have a problem dealing with compulsion—irresistible impulses to perform irrational acts that produce negative consequences in my life.

2. Came to believe that a power greater than ourselves could restore us to sanity.

   I believe that by tapping into the life-transforming power of unconditional love flowing through the deepest spiritual core of my being

I can find the inner peace and the inner power I need to control my own thoughts, feelings, words, and deeds more consistently.

3. Made a decision to turn our will and our lives over to the care of God—as *we understood Him.*

   Therefore, I will breathe slowly and deeply, calm my mind, center myself within the deepest spiritual core of my being and devote my life to the intelligent practice of patience, kindness, tolerance, and unconditional love for myself and for all others.

4. Made a searching and fearless moral inventory of ourselves.

   While centered within the deepest spiritual core of my being, I will take an objective and compassionate look at my ego-level personality and character traits—and I will identify in writing all self-defeating or negative attitudes, shallow motives, selfish desires, irrational beliefs, and distorted thinking patterns that may obstruct my ability to practice unconditional love.

5. Admitted to God, to ourselves, and to another human being, the exact nature of our wrongs.

   While centered within the deepest spiritual core of my being, I will gently accept complete personal responsibility for resolving all of my ego-level attitude and thinking problems — and I will discuss them openly with one trusted person.

6. Were entirely ready to have God remove all these defects of character.

   I am entirely ready to let go of all of my self-defeating or harmful ego-level traits, negative attitidues, shallow motives, selfish desires, irrational beliefs, and distorted thinking patterns.

7. Humbly asked Him to remove all our shortcomings.

   Whenever I sense that any of my negative ego-level traits are active and causing emotional distress for myself or others I will immediately stop and re-center myself spiritually—and I will promptly rededicate my life to the intelligent practice of patience, kindness, tolerance, and unconditional love for myself and for all others.

8. Made a list of all persons we had harmed and became willing to make amends to them all.

   While centered within the deepest spiritual core of my being, I will make a list of all persons I have harmed and I will let go of all negative ego-level traits that might prevent me from making amends to them all.

9. Made direct amends to such persons, wherever possible, except when to do so would injure them or others.

   While centered within the deepest spiritual core of my being, I will make direct amends to such persons, wherever possible, except when to do so would injure them or others.

10. Continued to take personal inventory, and when we were wrong promptly admitted it.

    Whenever I sense that any of my negative ego-level traits are active and causing emotional distress for myself or others I will immediately stop and re-center myself spiritually. I will identify the problems involved specifically, discuss them openly with at least one trusted person, and promptly rededicate my life to the intelligent practice of patience kindness, tolerance, and unconditional love.

11. Sought through prayer and meditation to improve our conscious contact with God, as we understood Him, praying only for knowledge of his will for us and the power to carry that out.

    I will continue to center myself within the deepest spiritual core of my being through my daily devotion to the intelligent practice of patience, kindness, tolerance and unconditional love—and I will seek to improve my ability to function from this deeper level of awareness more consistently during all of my waking hours.

12. Having had a spiritual awakening as the result of these steps, we tried to carry this message to others who share our addiction, and to practice these principles in all our affairs.

    As I experience a healthy personal transformation toward wholeness as the result of these steps, I will center my attention and focus my energy daily on trying to fulfill my primary purpose in living today:

    *Always to add whatever I can to the stream of goodness and light in our sometimes dark and troubled world, and to help others do likewise.*

(The original Twelve Steps are from the AA "Big Book", Pages 59–60)

> **"When you are good to others, you are best to yourself."**
>
> —Benjamin Franklin.

> **"All who joy would win must share it—happiness was born a twin."**
>
> —Lord Byron.

> **"Those who bring sunshine to the lives of others cannot keep it from themselves."**
>
> —Sir James Matthew Barrie.

> **"We can do no great things—only small things with great love."**
>
> —Mother Teresa.

> **"My religion is simple. My religion is kindness."**
>
> —Dalai Lama.

> **"Our twelve steps, when simmered down to the last, resolve themselves into the words: love and service."**
>
> —AA Co-founder Dr. Bob Smith.

## RS—ONE PERSONAL VOW

A translation of the "Third Step Prayer" from the Twelve Step Program into "Rational Spiritual Terminology."

**The Third Step Prayer:**

God, I offer myself to Thee—

Today, I dedicate myself to a pure and noble cause:

To center myself within the deepest spiritual core of my being and devote my life to the intelligent practice of patience, kindness, tolerance and unconditional love for myself and for all others.

. . . to build with me and to do with me as Thou wilt.

Today, I will continue to learn and grow as I become the wonderful and caring person I am meant to be.

Relieve me of the bondage of self, that I may better do Thy will.

I will not stay asleep or stuck in a shallow ego-centered box where I am driven by selfishness, pride, shame, greed, fear, anger, sadness, sloth, striving, stress, or success—because this would obstruct my ability to practice unconditional love and prevent me from fulfilling my primary purpose in living today.

Take away my difficulties . . .

Today, I will let go of all shallow motives, selfish desires, irrational beliefs, or distorted thinking patterns that trigger any ego-level emotional distress or difficulty.

. . . that victory over them may bear witness to those I would help of Thy Power, Thy Love, and Thy Way of life.

And I will allow my victory over these illusions to inspire others to seek the same deep source of inner peace, inner power, personal freedom, and enduring joy that I have found through my daily devotion to the practice of unconditional love.

May I do Thy will always!

I will do my best to remember and to practice this vow today in all that I think, feel, say, and do.

(The Third Step Prayer is from the AA "Big Book", Page 63).

A human being is part of a whole, called by us the 'Universe,' a part limited in time and space. He experiences himself, his thoughts and feelings, as something separated from the rest—a kind of optical delusion of his consciousness. This delusion is a kind of prison for us, restricting us to our personal desires and to affection for a few persons nearest to us. Our task must be to free ourselves from this prison by widening our circle of compassion to embrace all living creatures and all of nature in its beauty.

—Albert Einstein.

The life-transforming power of unconditional love is like a chisel in the hands of a sculptor—it only works when we tap it.

—Dale Kesten.

## PHILOSOPHICAL PREMISES: WHAT PEOPLE REALLY NEED

There's a wonderful story I heard many years ago about a recovering compulsive overeater who had placed a sign inside his refrigerator. Whenever he opened the refrigerator door, the sign would remind him:

"Whatever you're looking for, it's not in here."

Whatever it is that we're "really looking for" as human beings, I think it's fair to say that we'll never be able to find it in a refrigerator—or on a plate, in a bag, in a bottle, in a glass, or a can, a needle, a cigarette, a joint, a pipe, or a pill. More significantly, we will never be able to find what we really need at our deepest core level as human beings in any dependent, domineering, or dysfunctional relationships; nor in any fleeting sensual pleasures, superficial fun, excitement, or escapism; nor in any social roles, recognition, outside approval, or love; nor in any amount of worldly wealth, power, possessions, prestige, status, or conventional "success."

So, what do we really need? What are we really looking for?

To refresh your memory, let me reiterate what I've already said about this in the preface to this book:

> Above all else, when we finally see the futility of approaching life like a vacuum cleaner—vainly trying to fill our *spiritual emptiness* with anything or anyone we can find outside ourselves—and when we make a *conscious* and *deliberate decision* to allow the *life-transforming power of unconditional love* to flow freely through our daily lives from a hidden wellspring deep inside ourselves—like water through a garden hose—to refresh, nourish, and brighten our days and the days of all those whose lives we are privileged to touch—then we will come to understand why the principles of *rational spirituality* would suggest that the *one primary purpose* of a *good and meaningful life* could be:
>
> *"Always to add whatever we can to the stream of goodness and light in our sometimes dark and troubled world, and to help others do likewise."*

G. Alan Marlatt is a cognitive-behavioral theorist who criticized "the influence of untested myths and the rhetoric of dogma that have held a tight grip on the addictions field for the past several decades" in the ground-breaking book *Relapse Prevention* which he co-edited in 1985.

In the same work, however, Marlatt also observed that:

> Spiritual pursuits and addictive behaviors often share a common element in that they are frequently associated with an altered state of con-

sciousness that is quite different from the ordinary waking state of mind. For some clients, the need to experience this altered state with drugs or other addictive activities may mask an underlying need for a deeper and more satisfying spiritual life.

(Marlatt and Gordon, 1985: 18–19, 298)

In the previous chapter, we briefly examined some basic principles found in *Transpersonal Psychology* and *Logotherapy* as we reviewed the *Attempted Spiritual Sobriety* and *Rational Spiritual Sobriety* stages on the *Addiction Recovery Learning Curve.* In doing so, we have seen how these models not only recognize but stress our deep human need for something much more significant that a mere "altered state of consciousness"—they also stress our fundamental need for wholeness, a sense of spiritual identity, idealism, meaning, and purpose in life.

Viktor Frankl explored this basic theme in his book *Man's Search for Meaning*—which introduced *Logotherapy*—and he relates this need directly to the issue of harmful addiction.

Frankl declares flatly that:

> Such widespread phenomena as depression, aggression, and *addiction* are not understandable unless we recognize the *existential vacuum* underlying them.

Frankl clarifies this statement by adding:

> . . . there are various *masks* and *guises* under which the *existential vacuum* appears. Sometimes the *frustrated will to meaning* is vicariously compensated for by a *will to power,* including the most primitive form of the will to power, the will to money. In other cases, the place of frustrated will to meaning is taken by the *will to pleasure.*

(Frankl, 1984: 128–130. Emphasis added.)

In their book *Spiritual Diversity in Social Work Practice: The Heart of Helping,* Edward Canda and Leola Furman also stress the crucial importance of helping clients find a deeper meaning and purpose for living. Moreover, they emphasize the importance of clinicians developing their ability to identify and discuss universal spiritual principles with clients using a diverse array of clear, understandable, and mutually acceptable terms.

They strongly assert that:

> Spirituality is *the heart of helping.* It is the heart of empathy and care, the pulse of compassion, the vital flow of practice wisdom, and the driving force of action for service. Social Workers know that our professional roles, theories, and skills become rote, empty, tiresome, and

finally lifeless without this heart, by whatever names we call it. *We know that the people we serve seek spirituality, by whatever names they call it,* to help them thrive, to succeed at challenges, and to infuse whatever materials and relationships we assist them with to have *meaning* beyond mere survival value.

(Canda & Furman, 1999: xv. Emphasis added.)

This therapeutic emphasis on the development of sound spirituality as a key element in mental, emotional, and physical health is hardly new. In 1933, Carl Jung identified what he believed people really need in the very title of his book: *Modern Man in Search of a Soul,* where he made the bold declaration that:

Among all my patients in the second half of life—that is to say, over thirty five—there has *not been one* whose problem in the last resort was not that of finding *a religious outlook on life.*

"It is safe to say that *every one of them* fell ill because he had lost that which the living religions of every age have given to their followers, and none of them has been really healed who did not regain his religious outlook.

This of course has *nothing* whatever to do with a particular creed or membership in a church.

(Jung, 1933: 229. Emphasis added.)


## THE EITHER-OR FALLACY REVISITED

Naturally, many people fail to understand or simply disagree with the basic premises underlying the quest for any sort of a spiritual or religious approach to life.

In many cases, sadly, this is because they are sincerely confused about the crucial differences that exist between conventional religion and true spirituality which—according to one of the *Twelve Core Principles of Rational Spirituality* as noted above—neither contradicts nor requires the practice of religion.

Many people, of course, sincerely prefer to follow a materialistic path through life based solely on the vigorous or hapless pursuit of personal pleasure and self-interest, and many of these people may become quite successful and feel quite happy with themselves and with their lot. Many people, obviously, will never feel *any* strong impulse or need to seek a deeper sense of meaning or purpose in their lives.

The *Rational Spirituality* self-help system is intended to promote a deeper understanding and more effective practice of twelve-step program principles—and other universal spiritual principles—among people who are not generally feeling quite so smug, self-satisfied, or successful: first, among those people who simply fail to understand the true nature of basic spiritual principles and practices because of the fog of semantic confusion that so often surrounds them, and then, especially, among those who may only disagree with taking a spiritual approach to life because they wrongly assume that doing so must contradict many core values and principles that they already hold dear.

The basic text of the *Rational Recovery* self-help program was published in 1989, and offered what was described as "a revolutionary new approach" to alcoholism based solely on the principles and practices of rational-emotive and cognitive-behavioral therapy.

Reflecting an often bitter controversy that has existed historically in the addiction treatment and recovery field between advocates of so-called "secular" versus "spiritual" approaches, this volume was actually called "The small book" in order to draw a sharp and deliberate contrast between its supposedly "rational" approach and the allegedly irrational "spiritual solution" found in the twelve-step recovery program as presented in the 1939 "Big Book" of *Alcoholics Anonymous*

In strictly logical terms, however, it might be quite difficult for many intelligent, down-to-earth people to decide which approach theoretically makes "less sense." After all, the purportedly "rational" recovery program as presented in "The small book" has its own "fairy tale" flavor when it seriously suggests thinking of the "Addictive Voice" in symbolic terms as a ravenous, powerful, and self-destructive "Beast" lurking deep within the psyche of the alcoholic—whether they are actively drinking or sober.

This admitted fantasy would have to be contrasted with the self-described "uncommon sense" of the "Big Book" which seriously suggests thinking of "God, as we understood Him" in symbolic terms as a powerful, liberating, and loving life-force—or as a "Higher Power"—that can restore people to sanity and reason but can only be found by those who are willing to look for this "Great Reality" deep within themselves and then consistently use all of their natural intelligence and reason to "test (their) thinking by the new God-consciousness within."

However biased it may be concerning the reality of the spiritual dimension of our being, I do have to thank the *"Rational Recovery"* self-help program for providing me with the initial inspiration many years ago for the name of the *"Rational Spirituality"* self-help system.

The basic idea of *"Rational Spirituality"* first occurred to me one day when I was reading the "small book" and first understood how the very *name* of the *Rational Recovery* program seems to be based on an automatic and deeply

271

irrational assumption that *any* kind of explicitly spiritual approach to life—almost by definition—must be somehow intrinsically and hopelessly *irrational*.

By contrast, another one of the *Twelve Core Principles* of *Rational Spirituality* noted above strongly asserts that:

> True spirituality is natural, healthy, and *enhances* our rational thinking.

There's an old aphorism I enjoy which tells us:

> There are two types of people in the world—those who divide everything into two types—and those who don't.

The "small book" of *Rational Recovery* asserts quite strongly that:

> . . . there are *two kinds of people: believers and thinkers*. Yes, we all do both, but we tend toward one personal style or another. And we also tend to approach our lives and problems as ones who either have *faith* in *unchanging principles* or as ones who *think things through* and use *reason* as the light that shows the way . . . When push comes to shove, either way will do, but *we cannot have it both ways* on the *central issues* of recovery from chemical dependence.

> (Trimpey, 1989: xxvii. Emphasis added.).

With all due respect, I believe that this assertion is sadly mistaken and reflects a deep misunderstanding of some essential unifying principles that actually exist in the addiction treatment and recovery field—but are often obscured by an unfortunate fog of semantic confusion.

Let me stress one fundamental point that I believe we must help our clients understand—above all else—whenever they are thinking about pursuing a spiritual solution to their problems with harmful addiction:

> There is *absolutely no contradiction whatsoever* between being guided by "unchanging principles" and using our natural intelligence and our rational thinking skills to carefully analyze situations and make saner, wiser, healthier, and more rewarding behavioral choices.

> This is *not* a question of "either-or."

> In fact, we *must* have it both ways.

We all *need* to be guided by some simple, logical, universal principles of *right and wrong*—whether or not we choose to think of them as "spiritual" principles—*and* by the logical application of *reason* if we ever hope to have lives that are not merely "successful" or "happy" but also truly sane, sound, sober, and meaningful.

## WHAT'S IN A NAME?

Many people obviously have a great deal of conceptual or emotional difficulty seriously entering into the *Attempted Spiritual Sobriety* stage on the *Addiction Recovery Learning Curve*. Many others find that they are able to do so without too much trouble, but then they repeatedly fail to make the crucial transition from this level of growth into the final stage of *Rational Spiritual Sobriety.*

In countless cases, I've observed that many of these people seem to have one fundamental trait in common: they seem to share a negative or confused reaction to the term "God, as we understood Him" that is so central in the life-philosophy and core principles of the twelve-step spiritual recovery program.

In this regard, it's very important for us as clinicians to help our clients grasp the profound implications of the following thoughts from the basic text of the twelve-step program—the AA "Big Book":

> To us, the Realm of Spirit is broad, roomy, all inclusive; never exclusive or forbidding to those who earnestly seek. It is open, we believe, to all men.

> When, therefore, we speak to you of God, we mean *your own conception of God.* This applies, too, to other spiritual expressions which you find in this book. *Do not let any prejudice you may have against spiritual terms deter you from honestly asking yourself what they mean to you.*

> (Alcoholics Anonymous, 1976: 46–47)

In a similar vein, Oliver Wendell Holmes, Jr., once observed that:

> We must think things not words, or at least we must constantly *translate* our words into the facts for which they stand, if we are to keep to the real and the true.

The phrase "Higher Power" is a classic example of a term that is often preferred by people who are either confused or antagonized by the actual terminology found in the Twelve-Step program—which is "God, as we understood Him"—and let's remember that the deliberate use of the phrase "as we understood Him" in the text of the twelve-step program is itself an early example of a spiritual "translation" process at work.

For anyone struggling to grasp the real meaning of the Third Step in practical terms, I'd like to suggest that you can think of this step quite reasonably as saying "Made a decision to turn our will and our lives over to the care of God as we understood Him, Her, or It"—if that language might be more helpful for you. Then, I'd also suggest that if the idea that "God is Love" makes any sense as a starting point, it would perhaps be more accurate, understandable, and practical to start thinking of the actual spiritual power at work in this step as an "It" rather than as a "Him" or a "Her."

Of course, the "rational spiritual translation" of the Third Step in the Rational Spirituality model seeks to resolve the confusion that many people feel over the idea that some mysterious external power has to be involved by suggesting that the most practical way to "take" this step involves making a simple but profound decision to devote our lives to "the intelligent practice of patience, kindness, tolerance, and unconditional love for ourselves and for all others.

Informally, I would make the following suggestion to anyone who ever feels a little confused when scratching their chin and looking up at the ceiling or the sky while contemplating the real meaning of the phrase "Higher Power?"

> Start thinking in terms of your "deeper power" and you will probably be turning your heart and your mind in the right direction—which is toward the life-transforming power of unconditional love flowing through the deepest spiritual core of your being.

> Stop thinking so much about being "powerful" or "powerless" and start thinking in terms of turning this extraordinary "power on," or keeping this awesome "power off."

To anyone who has ever felt puzzled—or offended—by the oft-repeated term "powerless," therefore, it may be helpful to start thinking in terms of having a "deeper power" that you can either remember to turn "on"—by pausing and centering yourself spiritually in times of agitation or distress—or else forget about and leave turned "off."

Many people who limit themselves to thinking in simplistic, concrete, all-or-nothing terms of being merely "powerful" or "powerless" will often continue to suffer from their emotional reactivity because they remain intellectually "stuck"—or spiritually "asleep"—operating on a shallow, fearful, angry, or confused ego-level of awareness and are apparently unable or unwilling to tap into and fully awaken their own deeper level of compassionate energy and awareness.

However, once people have learned how they can begin to do this— through a simple devotion to the intelligent daily practice of patience, kindness, tolerance, and unconditional love for themselves and for all others—then they are much more likely to remember that they have a healthy and powerful alternative to emotional reactivity that is always available.

They are much more likely to remember that they *always* have another choice—a powerful option to take a moment to stop, breathe deeply, calm their mind, center themselves spiritually, think rationally and clearly, and tap into a deep source of inner peace, inner power, personal freedom, and enduring joy that's always there deep within and will never run dry.

Some of our clients will eventually reach a point in their mental, emotional, and spiritual development where they are ready to ask sincerely how this is done?

When that happens, we can respond by *repeating* what we may have just finished saying a few moments before—but they were unwilling, unable, or just not ready to hear or truly understand—by telling them:

> You *learn* how to do it—*slowly*—over a long period of time in natural stages that cannot be rushed—by thinking in terms of having your deeper "power on" or your "power off"—rather than in terms of being "powerful" or "powerless."
>
> Then, you'll gradually begin to remember—much more often and much more promptly with practice as time goes by—that you can *always* find your freedom from emotional reactivity—in the time it takes for one deep breath—by tapping into the life-transforming power of unconditional love flowing freely through the deepest spiritual core of your being.
>
> And you can do this, very simply, through your persistent daily devotion to the intelligent practice of patience, kindness, tolerance, and unconditional love for yourself and for all others.
>
> So, all you have to do is to become ready, willing, and able to remember four simple words—patience, kindness, tolerance, and love—the next time you're feeling agitated, angry, anxious, fearful, sad, stressed, or upset by anyone or anything—and then decide—right there and then in that moment—whether or not you're willing to give them a try.
>
> And once you begin to see how much better that usually works for you—compared to how you were reacting before—you'll gradually learn how to do it better by choosing to practice, practice, practice, and keep on practicing—until responding with patience, kindness, tolerance, and love becomes almost automatic and it really takes a lot to throw you off balance emotionally.

In Part One of this book, which focused on understanding addiction, we considered the widespread use of the popular but clinically meaningless terms "alcoholism" or "addiction"—versus official diagnostic terminology which speaks of substance "abuse" or "dependence."

In doing so, we also briefly pondered an important philosophical point raised by William Shakespeare when he asks:

> "What's in a name? A rose by any other name would smell as sweet."

Love and Service? God? Wholeness? Higher Power? Deeper Power? Unconditional Love? Does it really matter what we call it?

Carl Jung touched on this point in his book *Answer to Job* when he observed:

> "I am quite conscious that I am moving in a world of images and that *none of my reflections touches the essence of the Unknowable.*"

For many reasons, however, I think it's crucially important that skeptics, doubters, and critics eventually concede to their innermost selves that "God" is not a four-letter word—because this simple level of spiritual open-mindedness, perception, and discernment is an essential step toward achieving an even more important, subtle, and mature understanding which recognizes that:

> the authentic life-transforming power of unconditional love flowing through the deepest spiritual core of our being—which is the most peaceful, powerful and practical spiritual energy in the universe—and is sometimes called "God"—is *not a three-letter word either*.

Whenever I think of the difficulty that many people have coming to terms with the deepest meaning of the word "God," I am reminded of the following humorous but profound question:

> "Did you hear about the dyslexic, agnostic, insomniac who stayed up all night wondering if there really is a Dog?"

The absurdity of this question, of course, rather poignantly reflects the wisdom of another one of the *Twelve Core Principles* of *Rational Spirituality* of Rational Spirituality which reminds us all that

> "True Spirituality cannot be fully comprehended by the mind or expressed in words."

There's a profoundly meaningful recovery slogan which tells us that:

> "The longest journey in recovery is the eighteen inches from your head to your heart."

True spirituality is not *an idea* but *an action*. True spirituality involves the *direct personal experience of* a *living inner reality* that must eventually manifest itself in daily thoughts, feelings, words, and deeds of *unconditional love* for both ourselves and others. Therefore, discussing true spirituality in mere words, or trying to reduce it to a comprehensible set of *ideas*—without ever *experiencing it directly*—is quite fruitless. Indeed, it's much like trying to compare apples and oranges by looking up their definitions in the dictionary—or looking at color photos of each—or examining a sample of each sitting on a plate—or picking them up and handling them—or dissecting them and examining them under a microscope—or conducting a chemical analysis of their makeup in a laboratory—or identifying all of the vitamins, minerals, and nutrients they contain—and so on and so forth—without ever having *tasted* either one.

## PUTTING SPIRITUALITY INTO PRACTICE

In their book *A Spiritual Strategy for Counseling and Psychotherapy,* P. Scott Richards and Allen Bergin note that:

> In recent years, there has been a resurgence of spiritual interest and faith within the American population and an explosion of popular and professional literature on the subject . . . This spiritual energy has created a powerful cultural demand for psychotherapists to be more aware of and sensitive to religious and spiritual issues . . . recent professional literature suggests that *many clients can be successfully treated only if their spiritual issues are addressed sensitively and capably* . . . Despite the impressive amount of work that has been done to develop a spiritual strategy for psychotherapy, this body of theory, research, and clinical techniques is currently somewhat fragmented and incoherent . . . *Many therapists would like to incorporate spiritual perspectives and interventions into their work, but they do not understand how to do so.*

(Richards & Bergin, 1997: 5–6, 9. Emphasis added).

The *Rational Spirituality* self-help system is intended to address this problem by offering clinicians and clients "a spiritual foundation for rational living and a rational foundation for spiritual living."

In other words, *Rational Spirituality* offers people a simple and straightforward model for *a new way of thinking, feeling, living, and working* that is *spiritually centered, profoundly satisfying, and highly effective* precisely because it is also reality-based and rationally sound.

What does this actually mean?

First, that the *Rational Spirituality* model is intended to help people gradually tame their overpowering ego-level emotional reactivity in a very practical way by learning how to calm their minds and center themselves spiritually—and thus build a spiritual foundation for rational living.

Secondly, that the *RS* model can also help people by suggesting some simple language and sensible ideas that can help them unblock their arrested spiritual development by resolving their semantic confusion regarding deeper spiritual realities—and thus build a rational foundation for spiritual living.

## LOST IN TRANSLATION

In a 1961 letter to Alcoholics Anonymous co-founder Bill Wilson, Carl Jung expressed a profound insight into the deepest needs of one of his former patients in this way:

> His craving for alcohol was the equivalent on a low level of the spiritual thirst of our being for *wholeness*, expressed in medieval language: *the union with God.*

With these reasonably simple and straightforward words I believe that Carl Jung has pointed us directly at the deepest root cause of serious harmful addiction and most forms of self-defeating or destructive compulsive behavior—at least in those cases that do not involve any severe psychopathology or organicity.

Unfortunately, however, his profoundly insightful and eloquent words are *not simple and straightforward enough.*

No matter how beautiful, meaningful, or deeply moving this kind of "medieval language" may be for many people—myself included—it is also very clear to me—based on thousands of personal interactions and observations over the past 23 years—that this sort of religious terminology will be experienced by many other people as little more than nonsensical or vaguely threatening babble.

For many people, this kind of religious language will *not* provide a useful channel for improved understanding but will actually pose a significant obstacle to the development of any mature spiritual insight or practical spiritual experience.

Therefore, in order to "translate" what this profound insight actually means in practical terms—for those people who will only be confused or offended by this particular choice of words—the *Rational Spirituality* model suggests that we may have to gracefully dispense with the "medieval language"—or any other explicitly "religious" terminology—when we consider the ultimate question:

"What *are* we really looking for?"

Translating Jung's insight in this way—using strictly modern terms out of deference and respect for the needs of all—the *Rational Spirituality* model suggests that we may confidently identify *"the deepest need of our being"* as the conscious daily practice of our essential

> **WHOLENESS**—meaning the functional, balanced, and harmonious integration of the mental, emotional, physical, and spiritual dimensions of our being.

Unfortunately, while this particular definition of the word "wholeness" may "make sense"—in strictly logical terms—to more people than the more obscure and mysterious notion of achieving "union with God," it is still expressed in terms that are quite abstract and complex.

In the interest of simplicity, clarity, and common sense, therefore, the *Rational Spirituality* model seeks as often as humanly possible to avoid using any concepts or terms that are essentially *theoretical, abstract,* or *theological* in favor of alternative terms that are *practical, applicable, and transformational.*

Thus, before we even *try* to help our clients begin to contemplate moving toward the crucial goal of "wholeness," we will need to go another step deeper and ask ourselves what does the "functional, balanced, and harmonious integration of the mental, emotional, physical, and spiritual dimensions of our being" actually *mean* in practical, applicable, transformational terms?

Dr. Bob Smith was a co-founder of Alcoholics Anonymous and he made a great contribution to this spiritual "translation" process—and helped make the essential spiritual principles of the twelve-step program much easier for anyone to understand and apply—when he declared:

> "Our twelve steps, when simmered down to the last, resolve themselves into the words: love and service."

We now have a very simple and powerful "formula" to work with that should be relatively easy for most people of reasonable intelligence and goodwill to intellectually understand, philosophically accept, and functionally begin to practice.

In essence, this simple formula for living asserts that a life seriously devoted to the practice of love and service will generally be healthier, happier, more meaningful, and more rewarding than a life spent drifting aimlessly or a goal-oriented life dedicated primarily to the relentless or lackadaisical pursuit of more shallow motives and selfish desires.

The *Rational Spirituality* self-help system takes the simple and powerful formula proposed by "Dr, Bob" a few steps further by providing a detailed and practical translation of twelve-step program principles—and other universal spiritual principles—into clear, simple, modern terms and effective self-management techniques that most people can easily *understand, accept, and begin to practice.*

The *Rational Spirituality* model suggests that our deepest needs—as human and spiritual beings—are:

- the direct personal experience of the life-transforming power of unconditional love flowing from the deepest spiritual core of our being, and
- the intelligent practice of patience, kindness, tolerance, and unconditional love for ourselves and for all others—flowing from this deep source of inner peace and inner power—as the practical expression of this transforming power in our daily lives.

In a nutshell—in the simplest possible terms—the *Rational Spirituality* self-help system is intended to teach people:

> How to find inner peace, inner power, personal freedom, and enduring joy through the intelligence practice of patience, kindness, tolerance, and unconditional love.

*The Rational Spirituality* model is based on a well-founded conviction—based on my 23 years of direct personal experience and thousands of direct personal observations—that making a decision to follow this sort of spiritually centered and principled path actually represents an entirely *rational* approach to life.

The intrinsic wisdom of following *a rational spiritual path* of this kind becomes painfully obvious when contrasted with the foolish notion of taking a directly opposite approach to life:

> How to find inner chaos, inner weakness, perpetual bondage, and enduring pain through the ignorance practice of impatience, meanness, intolerance, and unconditional hostility.

## PRINCIPLES VERSUS PUNISHMENTS

Many thoughtful people are sincerely disturbed or confused by the paradoxical, controversial, and apparently contradictory concept so easily embraced by so many conventionally religious people of a simultaneously kind, loving, forgiving, cruel, vengeful, and punishing "God." There's an aphorism that's popular among some people who recognize the basic moral logic reflected in the Eastern "Law of Karma"—and therefore accept the rough Western equivalent that "What you sow is what you reap"—which addresses the apparent contradiction that clearly exists when this issue is considered superficially in terms that may be too concrete and literal to reveal the underlying reality of the universal spiritual principles at work.

This aphorism suggests:

"We are not punished *for* our sins: we're punished *by* our sins."

Consider the case of a preoccupied person who manages to fall off the edge of a cliff and hurt themselves badly because they were in a hurry and weren't paying enough attention while running along a cliffside trail. In purely physical terms, does it really matter whether this person was in a hurry to save a child or to murder a rival? Quite clearly, one way or another, he or she was not being "punished" by "Law of Gravity." On the contrary, they are simply "reaping the natural negative consequences" of violating the and generally immutable laws of nature that seem to operate with no moral condemnation or judgment and to make no exceptions for good or bad intentions.

In the spiritual realm, likewise, there are a number of universal spiritual principles at play that seem to operate in a similar natural and nonjudgmental fashion.

Therefore, it's simply not necessary in spiritual terms to think of people having to "obey" a set of "authoritarian laws" or "restrictive rules" or risk being "judged," "condemned," or "punished," for their "rebellion" or "disobedience" when they violate or ignore these universal spiritual principles—either consciously or unconsciously.

The actual reality involves freely choosing whether or not to live in harmony with a set of positive, healthy, universal spiritual principles that often immediately embody their own reward or reap the natural negative consequences that that sooner or later seem to follow when we make essentially foolish or selfish choices.

The moral logic reflected in *Rational Spirituality,* simply turns the whole "punishment paradigm" around 180 degrees and proposes a "positive paradigm" which confidently asserts that:

> We are not rewarded *for* our practice of patience, kindness, tolerance, and unconditional love: we're rewarded *by* our practice of patience, kindness, tolerance, and unconditional love.

The polar opposite of this altruistic approach to life—and its critical relationship to the development and progression of harmful addiction—has been described in the AA Big Book in the following way:

> *Selfishness, self-centeredness! That, we think, is the root of our troubles.* Driven by a hundred forms of fear, self-delusion, self-seeking, and self-pity, we step on the toes of our fellows and they retaliate. Sometimes they hurt us, seemingly without provocation, but we invari-

ably find that at some time in the past we have made decisions based on self which later placed us in a position to be hurt.

*So our troubles, we think, are basically of our own making.* They arise out of ourselves, and the alcoholic is an extreme example of self-will run riot, though he usually doesn't think so.

*Above everything, we alcoholics must be rid of this selfishness.*

We must, or it kills us!

(Alcoholics Anonymous, 1976: 62. Emphasis added)

## IMMEDIATE VERSUS IMAGINARY REWARDS

In his book *The Art of Loving,* as we have already noted, Erich Fromm begins by making a wise observation that points toward a root cause of much human selfishness and self-seeking:

> Most people see the problem of love primarily as that of *being loved,* rather than that of *loving,* of one's capacity to love. Hence, the problem to them is how to be loved, how to be lovable.

Fromm clearly states his own view that ". . . love is an action, the practice of a human power, which can be practiced only in freedom and never as a result of compulsion." He then points out a corresponding reality—rarely recognized by most people—that *"Love is an activity, not a passive affect."* Then he continues with a statement that echoes a universal truth reflected in the *Rational Spirituality* model—that devotion to the practice of unconditional love carries it's own immediate, intrinsic rewards—by making the powerful observation that:

> In the most general way, the active character of love can be described by stating that *love is primarily giving, not receiving* . . . The most important sphere of giving . . . is not that of material things, but lies in the specifically human realm. What does one person give to another? He gives of himself, of the most precious he has, he gives of his life . . . *He does not give in order to receive; giving is in itself exquisite joy.*

> (Fromm, 1956: 1, 18, 20. Emphasis added.)

In *Rational Spirituality,* the crucial process of pursuing a unified personal goal that reflects a meaningful and important purpose in life is very simple, immediate, and down to earth. It's true, of course, that the development of a greatly increased capacity for the delayed gratification of selfish desires is a natural by-product of following this way of life—along with the growth of a much higher tolerance for the inevitable frustrations faced by most human beings on a daily basis—but this model does not primarily seek to promote the practice of self-denial in the pursuit of long-term goals that may or may not eventually be achieved. Rather, *Rational Spirituality* calls for a consistent focus on *the immediate daily practice of the central goals involved*—not as a means to an end, but as a worthy and rewarding end in itself.

In a nutshell, once again, these goals are:

> Always to add whatever we can to the stream of goodness and light in our sometimes dark and troubled world, and to help others do likewise—and find a deep source of inner peace, inner power, personal freedom, and enduring joy—through our daily devotion to the intelligent practice of patience, kindness, tolerance, and unconditional love for ourselves and for all others.

Regardless of how well or how imperfectly a person may be able to practice these principles at any given moment, most people can easily recognize how, nevertheless, he or she will immediately begin to change the emotional tone and content of any situation or any human interaction for the better by the mere fact that they are trying to do so.

By this means, especially when dealing with difficult or distressing people, events, or circumstances, a person who is practicing these principles may or may not become a part of a hoped-for solution—if a conventional "solution" is even possible in some situations—but they will certainly not be an aggressive, self-seeking, or improperly self-sacrificing part of the problem.

Whenever we speak of truly practicing "unconditional love," however, it's also very important to remember, as M. Scott Peck states in his book *The Road Less Traveled: A New Psychology of Love, Traditional Values and Spiritual Growth,* that:

> . . . real love does not have its roots in *a feeling of love.* To the contrary, real love often occurs in a context in which the feeling of love is lacking, when *we act lovingly despite the fact that we don't feel loving.*

> (Peck, 1978: 88. Emphasis added.)

In fact, when a person develops a conscious intention to avoid the pitfalls of shallow ego-level emotional reactivity by continually centering and re-centering themselves spiritually as they go through the day—and when they make persistent, deliberate attempts to do so to the best of their ability—they will have found a way to tap into a deep source of spiritual power that will always be available to them—regardless of how well or how badly external events may be unfolding and regardless of how well or how badly they may be feeling superficially on the typically fearful, angry, confused ego-level of awareness.

When a person learns by persistent practice how to tap into the life-transforming power of unconditional love flowing through the deepest spiritual core of their being—and when they allow that most peaceful, powerful, and practical spiritual energy in the universe to flow freely through their lives, their thoughts, their feelings, their words, and their deeds in a harmonious and almost effortless way—as a blessing for themselves and for all those whose lives they are privileged to touch—then their fully awakened compassionate energy will have found a powerful purpose for living that is deeply meaningful, truly rewarding, and almost completely independent of the potentially negative influence of difficult people or disturbing outside circumstances or events.

For many people in our fast-paced modern world, of course, outside circumstances or events can feel very disturbing, stressful, or even overwhelming at times. This widespread problem is reflected in the humorous lament:

> "God put me here on Earth to accomplish a certain number of
> tasks—and right now I'm so far behind I'll never die!"

For many people, the most common response to this dilemma will be to try to *do more, do it better, and do it faster*—or to feel internally pressured or guilty by an irrational belief that they "should" or "must" be a hard-working "human doing" rather than a healthy "human being." But this emotionally reactive response ignores the wisdom expressed by Carl Jung when he observed that:

> "Hurry is not *of* the Devil—it *is* the Devil!"

M. Scott Peck begins his book *The Road Less Traveled* with the simple observation that

> Life is difficult . . . This is a great truth, one of the greatest truths. It is
> a great truth because once we truly see this truth , we transcend it.
> Once we truly know that life is difficult—once we truly understand
> and accept it—then life is no longer difficult. Because once it is accept-
> ed, the fact that life is difficult no longer matters.

> (Peck, 1978: 15)

The core principles and practices of *Rational Spirituality* can help people gradually begin to achieve a deeper level of awareness and a more effective way of life that can become increasingly "Happy, Joyous, and Free"—to use a wonderful recovery slogan drawn directly from the AA "Big Book" (1976: 133). This is because they are so deeply grounded in the universal wisdom that Scott Peck and so many others all point toward—which amounts to a realistic perception, a deep understanding, and a mature acceptance of *life as it actually is*.

This highly-adaptive attitude is expressed in the vernacular of traditional twelve-step recovery groups by the recommendation to:

"Accept life on life's terms."

In his book *Flow: The Psychology of Optimal Experience,* Mihaly Csikzentmihalyi (whose name, I believe, is pronounced mee-holly chick-zent-mee-holly) describes "a theory of optimal experience based on the concept of flow—the state in which people are so involved in an activity that nothing else seems to matter." He notes that in a state of flow "the experience itself is so enjoyable that people will do it even at great cost, for the sheer sake of doing it," and states very clearly that

> Because optimal experience depends on the ability to control what happens in consciousness moment by moment, each person has to achieve it on the basis of his own individual efforts and creativity.

William Glasser directly identifies the entire notion of achieving a "positive addictive state" with the achievement of this psychological state of flow and optimal experience in his book *Positive Addiction,* and Csikzentmihalyi points out a very common difficulty that is directly related to the problem of harmful addiction:

> The only authority many people trust today is instinct. If something feels good, if it is natural and spontaneous, then it must be right. But when we follow the suggestions of genetic and social instructions without question we relinquish the control of consciousness and become helpless playthings of impersonal forces. The person who cannot resist food or alcohol, or whose mind in constantly focused on sex, is not free to direct his or her psychic energy.

Csikzentmihalyi also makes the remarkably insightful and valuable observation that "A thoroughly socialized person . . . *may encounter thousands of potentially fulfilling experiences, but he fails to notice them because they are not the things he desires,"* and he goes on to suggest that "The most important step in emancipating oneself from social controls is the ability *to find rewards in the events of each moment."*

*Rational Spirituality,* of course, goes beyond the original concepts of flow, optimal experience, and positive addiction by proposing the additional ideas of transcending our normal, shallow, ego-level of awareness by learning how to function more consciously and consistently at a deeper level of spiritual awareness for a deeper and more meaningful set of motives. However, the Rational Spirituality model "transcends and includes" these earlier concepts—to use a concept elaborated by Ken Wilber in his book *The Marriage of Sense and Soul: Integrating Science and Religion*—and the notion of achieving "immediate rewards" is described perfectly by Csikzentmihalyi in the following discussion of the state of flow:

> If a person learns to enjoy and find meaning in the ongoing stream of experience, in the process of living itself, the burden of social controls automatically falls from one's shoulders. Power returns to the person when rewards are no longer relegated to outside forces . . . Instead of forever straining for the tantalizing prize dangled just out of reach, one begins to harvest the genuine rewards of living. But it is not by abandoning ourselves to instinctual desires that we become free of social controls. We must also become independent from the dictates of the body, and learn to take charge of what happens in the mind . . . What counts is not so much whether a person actually achieves what she has set out to do; rather, it matters whether effort has been expended to meet the goal, instead of being diffused or wasted . . . When an important goal is pursued with resolution, and all one's varied activities fit together into a unified flow experience, the result is that *harmony* is brought into consciousness.

> (Csikzentmihalyi, 1990: 3–5, 17–18, 217)

## CONSIDER THE ALTERNATIVES

I'm currently engaged in the process of writing two books for general readers describing the *Addiction Recovery Learning Curve* model and the *Rational Spirituality* self-help system. I'm also developing clinical training seminars and personal growth workshops in order to present this material to interested professionals and others. I'd be very happy to send news about these evolving projects to anyone who may be interested, and I'd also be delighted to hear from any readers who may have any questions or comments on either model.

For now, let me conclude this brief and partial introduction to the *Rational Spirituality* self-help system by making the following observations:

In 1997, as noted above, P. Scott Richards and Allen Bergin reported that

> recent professional literature suggests that many clients can be successfully treated only if their spiritual issues are addressed sensitively and capably.

A well-known aphorism suggests that it is often quite *pointless and futile* for people to ponder the question:

"What is the meaning of life?"

Rather, it's always much more *productive* for us to ask the question:

"What gives my life meaning?"

In attempting to answer this vital question for themselves, many of our clients will undoubtably come up with viable and healthy alternatives that are more meaningful and sensible to them as individuals than any of the specific terms or ideas suggested by the *Rational Spirituality* model.

One of our most important tasks as clinicians, however, will always be to gently and persistently challenge our clients to begin the serious task of developing their own rational answer to this crucial question:

"What gives my life a vital sense of value, meaning, purpose, passion, and satisfaction?"

In doing so, I believe we should encourage all of our clients to use both their creative imagination and reality-testing as vividly as possible to actively consider the full range of their alternative choices—both positive and negative—since finding a viable answer to this question will literally be a matter of life-or-death for some of them.

Please recall that we began Part One of this book—which focused on understanding addiction—by noting that many people who drink or use other kinds of drugs will often find themselves seriously asking the question:

"How do I really *know* if I have an alcohol or drug abuse problem?"

We also noted that some of these people can't answer this question accurately because their ability to perceive the truth of the matter has become lost in an unconscious fog of *minimization, rationalization, self-deception, or denial.*

Stumbling rather blindly and unconsciously through life is by no means a harmful habit that is found only among those people who are struggling with serious harmful addictions.

On the contrary, many people in our modern world seem to travel through their allotted days on earth reacting rather automatically and unthinkingly to whatever life throws their way—while functioning on a rather superficial and mechanical level—according to the impractical principles of a philosophical system that could be called:

### ER—Emotional Reactivity.

Over many years, I've observed repeatedly that many angry, frustrated, fearful, or unhappy people, who are metaphorically "walking in darkness," seem to be suffering from a widespread but rarely disgnosed disorder that I have chosen to call:

### CRDD—*Cranial Rectal Displacement Disorder.*

One of my favorite cartoons shows a man floating serenely about four or five feet off the ground. He's smiling down at another man who has both feet planted firmly on the ground. This other fellow seems to be very tense and agitated as he wags his finger accusingly at the man floating calmly in mid-air and complains:

"You don't understand the gravity of the situation!"

I firmly believe that we must try to help our clients actively bring their **sense of humor and absurdity** to bear on all of the **serious questions** we are addressing in order to avoid developing a potentially **life-threatening** or **life-deadening** case of:

### ETSS—the *Entirely Too Serious Syndrome.*

Tapping into a deep source of enduring joy and enhancing our ability to appreciate the absurd or amusing aspects of life under *all* circumstances—no matter how stressful, sad, or tragic they may actually be or merely seem to be—does *not* require that we abandon all common sense or neglect our personal responsibility for rational thinking. In fact, developing a truly healthy sense of humor—and effectively exercising our emotional autonomy and our capacity for more consistent self-control—demands a *high degree of deliberate devotion* to the consistent practice of rational thinking blended with an unusual depth of "uncommon sense" that is truly insightful, intuitive, and compassionate.

Let's take a moment to recall Horace Walpole's provocative observation that:

"Life is a comedy to those who think, and a tragedy to those who feel."

In this spirit, I believe many clients could benefit from seriously pondering the actual wisdom or foolishness of our hypothetical *"ER self-harm system"* which would probably suggest the following:

## ONE PRIMARY PURPOSE

Always to get whatever I want, whenever I want it,
in this often frustrating and annoying world,
and to have others do things my way as often as possible.

Our clients should also be encouraged to consider the core practice of *"Emotional Reactivity"*—reflecting the harmful habits of a life unintentionally devoted to the ignorant practice of impatience, meanness, intolerance and unconditional hostility—which might productively be called the:

## SEVEN STUPID STEPS

1. SENSE—Something feels bad or rubs me the wrong way.
2. GO—With my most shallow, selfish, and negative ego-traits.
3. REACT—Automatically, emotionally, and impulsively.
4. LEAP—To the first foolish conclusion that crosses my mind.
5. DENY—My desperate desire to feel no pain at any cost.
6. RUSH—Into a wrong, bad, insane, and unhealthy course.
7. ACT OUT—As stupidly and selfishly as I possibly can.

By contrast, I believe it would also be appropriate and potentially quite beneficial for us to encourage our clients to ponder the possible wisdom of the core practice of *Rational Spirituality*—clearly reflecting the healthy habits of a life intentionally devoted to the intelligent practice of patience, kindness, tolerance, and unconditional love—which consists of:

## SEVEN SIMPLE STEPS

1. SENSE—Something is wrong inside or out.
2. STOP—Before I make it worse.
3. CENTER—Myself in heart, mind, body, and soul.
4. THINK—What really happened and what really counts?
5. FEEL—Unconditional love and understanding for one and all.
6. CHOOSE—A right, good, sane, and healthy course.
7. ACT—As wisely and compassionately as I possibly can.

As clinicians, if we feel that it would be appropriate for us to recommend that some of our clients seriously consider adopting or adapting some of the core concepts suggested by the *Rational Spirituality* model as a way of life, then I believe we should also suggest that these clients take a look at the appendix in the AA "Big Book" which addresses the topic of "Spiritual Experience"—where Herbert Spencer is quoted as saying:

> There is a principle which is a bar against all information, which is proof against all arguments and which cannot fail to keep a man in everlasting ignorance—that principle is contempt prior to investigation.

> (Alcoholics Anonymous, 1976: 569)

With this sage advice in mind, we can then gently challenge our clients once more to face the ultimate question:

"What gives my life value, meaning, passion, and purpose?"

If some of our clients haven't yet formulated a healthy answer to this question that they can practice in their everyday life, then we can remind them that the *Rational Spirituality* model proposes a simple formula for living a *good* and *meaningful* life—and seriously challenge our most open-minded clients to give this attitude and approach toward life a serious try for awhile—unless they can come up with something better that will really work and make more sense for them.

So, what was that simple formula again?

How to find inner peace, inner power, personal freedom, and enduring joy through the intelligent practice of patience, kindness, tolerance, and unconditional love, for ourselves and for all others.

♦ ♦ ♦

## ONE PRIMARY PURPOSE

Always to add whatever we can
to the stream of goodness and light
in our sometimes dark and troubled world,
and to help others do likewise.

♦ ♦ ♦

# CONCLUSION

# All's Well that Ends Well

"Our twelve steps, when simmered down to the last, resolve themselves into the words: love and service."

—Dr. Bob Smith.

◆ ◆ ◆

In this book, we've explored the basic nature of harmful addiction and have examined the signs, symptoms and stages of progression in considerable detail.

We have also considered how we as clinicians can best help our clients make the difficult transition from *active progression into active and sustained recovery.*

In doing so, we've explored the new *Face to Face Unified Addiction Recovery Model* and the *Addiction Recovery Learning Curve* which is based on thousands of direct personal observations I've made over the past 23 years and describes how people with the most serious and stubborn harmful addictions usually make the difficult transition into permanent recovery over an extended period of time in *five naturally-occurring stages.*

This model recognizes that since so many clients are *"gonna do what they're gonna do"* during or after treatment anyway, they might as well be encouraged to do so in an honest, open-minded spirit and try to reframe their past, present, and future experiences as a series of:

*Formal Addiction Control Experiments*

*and*

*Failed Addiction Control Experiments.*

291

We've seen that when we help clients begin to honestly take this kind of an approach—seriously evaluating the results of their own choices—they may be able to dramatically reduce the total number of negative consequences needed and significantly shorten the overall amount of time required for them to learn the lessons that can only be taught—in most cases—by their own painful personal experience.

Hopefully, this book has offered some useful ideas and information suggesting how concerned clinicians might help clients begin to make wiser choices by teaching them how to use this five-stage conceptual structure to evaluate the lessons to be learned from their own past, present, and future experiences more quickly and easily.

We've also explored the idea that many people struggling with the most serious harmful addictions will often need to find a new and compelling positive addiction in order to replace their most harmful, self-defeating, and self-destructive attitudes and behavior with *a healthy and deeply satisfying alternative.*

How does this work in actual practice?

In Part One of this book, we defined some **key terms** and **core concepts** as follows:

> **Addiction**—To habitually devote oneself—or give oneself up—to a particular behavior or activity.
>
> **Devotion**—To dedicate, consecrate, give up, or apply oneself to some purpose, activity, or person.
>
> **Compulsion**—An irresistible impulse to perform an irrational act—the core element in all harmful addictions.
>
> **Harmful Addiction**—An unhealthy form of self-defeating addictive behavior that is based on compulsion, produces unwanted negative consequences for the addicted person, diminishes or destroys their strength and wellness, and ultimately sabotages their success and satisfaction in life.
>
> **Positive Addiction**—A healthy form of self-enhancing addictive behavior that is based upon personal commitment and freedom of choice, maximizes the strength and wellness of the addicted person, and ultimately contributes to greater success and satisfaction in life.

We have seen how the root definition of the word "addiction" is central to making the distinction between a harmful addiction and a positive addiction because as we go through our day it asks each of us to consciously consider the vital question:

"What purpose, activity, or person has become the object of my devotion?"

Let's recall for a moment Mark Twain's humorous but profound observation about the difficulty many people encounter while trying to change compulsive-addictive behavior:

"It's easy to give up smoking. I've done it a thousand times."

I wonder if he kept trying the *same thing* over and over again?

**Will power. Just do it. Just say no?**

For most people with the more serious forms of harmful addiction this approach just doesn't work in the long-run.

Rather, they will need to find something much better—a substitute—a meaningful new way of life that is genuinely satisfying and truly meets their deepest human needs—to which they can joyfully and unconditionally:

**"Just say yes!"**

## DEEP PURPOSE AND PASSION

The central theme of this book proposes that developing a passionate devotion to a healthy, positive addiction—to which they can cheerfully "Just say Yes!"—is often the only viable alternative for many people struggling with the most serious and stubborn harmful addictions.

As I mentioned at the beginning of this book, I have been maintaining a normal weight since 1983—after a weight loss of about 140 pounds that commenced in 1981when I weighed more than 300 pounds. In that year, I joined a self-help recovery program to address my compulsive overeating and morbid obesity and found a powerful solution that really works. I've been working professionally in the mental health and addictions treatment field since 1987, and my interest in this field developed during my first six years in recovery when I became deeply involved in voluntary service as part of my recovery program. I had suffered a huge relapse toward the end of my first year in recovery, and I had decided at that point that this was truly a matter of life and death for me. I was 31 years old and I seriously doubted if I would live to see 40 if this sad situation didn't turn around. I finally had my priorities straight, and I was able to make the following resolution:

"Don't even *think* about what you're going to *do* with your life, Dale. Let's just see if you can manage to *save* your life first."

For the next five years, I literally couldn't even bear to think about making a meaningful career choice and I devoted my time and attention to my recovery, to recovery meetings, to voluntary service, and to a down-to-earth, rather mundane "recovery job" which I clearly thought of as "basic training" and "practice"—to see if I could actually manage to be "average" rather than impatiently leaping ahead of myself trying to do something "special."

My voluntary service work and my growing focus on helping others gradually led to the development of a deep desire to find something that I could do professionally that would allow me to explicitly practice the principles I was learning in recovery in the vocational dimension of my life as well.

This deepening desire was continually reinforced by a small poster I had on my office wall—which featured a colorful cartoon portraying an ethnically and racially mixed group of smiling people of all ages—framed above and below by some powerful words constantly reminding me that:

"Love is where it's at—people are what it's for!"

The *Rational Spirituality* self-help system suggests that passionately devoting one's daily life to the intelligent practice of patience, kindness, tolerance, and unconditional love for ourselves and for all others represents a powerful, healthy, positive alternative to harmful addiction that is completely consistent with a wide range of universal spiritual principles—including those found in the twelve-step program and in the core values of most of the world's enduring religious traditions and spiritual paths.

Why is it so crucial that a recovering person develop a passionate devotion to practicing a healthy, positive addiction that adequately addresses some of the most fundamental questions regarding the ultimate meaning and purpose of life?

Well, to be honest, for many people this isn't crucial—never has been and never will be.

There's another small and colorful wall poster that I have in my office that declares flatly:

"Your life. Your responsibility."

So, if a shallow, materialistic, or purely hedonistic solution really works for some people, and if a superficial and self-seeking way of life really satisfies them—so be it. That's fine. Ultimately, that's really their business and their choice. But many of us want, need, and *demand* more out of life.

My father's name is Art Kesten, and for his 60th Birthday, now many years ago, I gave him a small plaque to hang on the wall that says:

"Youth is a gift of nature, but age is a work of art."

As clinicians, if we are truly devoted to promoting the optimal growth and development of our clients as human beings through every age and stage of the human life span, then we will need to help them grasp the fundamental truth that they are responsible for their own lives and that they will have to eventually decide for themselves what really matters to them most of all in life—if they want to become wiser and more mature as they get older in age, and if they want to develop a life that is healthier, happier, and more meaningful for them.

In *The Art of Loving,* Erich Fromm clearly states his view that "love is an art, just as living is an art."

And yet, he observes that for most people

> in spite of the deep-seated craving for love, almost everything else is considered to be more important than love: success, prestige, money, power—almost all our energy is used for the learning of how to achieve these aims, and almost none to learn the art of loving.

Then, Fromm firmly declares that "if we want to learn how to love we must proceed in the same way we have to proceed if we want to learn any other art, say music, painting, carpentry, or the art of medicine or engineering." Later, he makes another vital point—which is directly relevant to the need for our clients to develop a passionate devotion to their primary, healthy, positive addiction—when he states unequivocally that beyond mastering the theory and practice of any art, there is yet another essential factor involved:

> the mastery of the art must be a matter of ultimate concern; there must be nothing else in the world more important than the art.

> (Fromm, 1956: 4–5.)

In the same way, if we truly decide that, for us, "Love is where it's at and people are what it's for," then we will realize that *nothing* is ultimately more important than our daily devotion to the intelligent practice of unconditional love for ourselves and for all others.

Some serious critics of the spiritually-centered process of personal change embodied in the twelve-step program seem to misunderstand how this spiritual approach to addiction recovery actually works while at the same time advocating solutions that are fundamentally similar to this model in many important ways.

In many significant respects, the alternative approaches to sober living that they propose only seem to differ from a "spiritual" approach semantically and quite superficially. In fact, when we consider the universal principles that are actually involved, the broad common ground on which these supposedly "inconsistent" approaches actually stand becomes increasingly obvious.

In his book *Heavy Drinking: The Myth of Alcoholism as a Disease,* for example, Herbert Fingarette points out quite rightly that:

> To focus only on the drinking behavior, in isolation from all else, is to miss the point that a central activity reverberates throughout a person's way of life. Thus, for a heavy drinker to make a major change in his drinking patterns requires *a reconstruction of his way of life.* The drinker must learn over time to see the world in different terms, to cultivate new values and interests, to find or create new physical and social settings, to develop new relationships, to devise new ways of behaving in those new relationships and settings.

Even after criticizing the coercive aspects of some traditional addiction treatment programs that require AA attendance—and expressing some significant misconceptions about key aspects of the twelve-step model—Fingarette nevertheless notes quite favorably that:

> . . . while the group's doctrine holds that alcoholism is a disease, the practice of AA is entirely nonmedical. *AA is not a treatment, but a new way of life for those who choose to become involved.* Members join a community that fosters intense emotional bonds, provides an integrated set of values and priorities, with powerful symbols and rituals, and offers frequent social activities and an active network of communication. For regular members . . . AA . . . comes to replace drinking as an activity central to their lives and identity.

> (Fingarette, 1988: 90–91, 110. Emphasis added.)

In their book *The Truth About Addiction and Recovery*—to cite another example of common ground—Stanton Peele and Archie Brodsky identify a number of "personal resources and skills" that they believe people "must have in order not to be addicted." They included as central elements in this vital mix:

- intimacy and supportive relationships,

- new activities and interests, and

- larger, more meaningful goals.

"Addiction" according to Peele and Brodsky, "is largely a matter of misplaced energy, in both a physical and a moral sense." They note that some people involved in harmful addictions are ". . . so busy trying to get their needs met through a futile compulsion that they missed obvious opportunities to redirect their energy more constructively." They also state their strong conviction that ". . . the activities that most decisively reduce addictive diversions to irrelevancy are those that express a *true engagement with others and a higher moral purpose.*"

In this regard, Peele and Brodksy state that *"AA is right that a higher vision direction provides a direction and an energy for living and a major bulwark against addiction."* Then they point out the undisputed truth that "passively buying the AA doctrine does not provide as energizing a vision as does voluntarily committing yourself to some larger goal in life [which could include] helping people in any way."

(Peele and Brodsky, 1991:219-220. Emphasis added.)

As we have already noted repeatedly, passivity is indeed a sure-fire formula for disaster and a virtual prescription for relapse for those suffering from the most serious harmful addictions. However, this highly commendable, principled, values-centered and generally accurate statement by Peele and Brodksy obviously misses one crucial point:

> The twelve-steps are a truly gentle and tolerant program of inner change that ultimately leads people to pursue *a vigorous lifestyle of patient and persistent action* devoted to the intelligent practice of unconditional love for ourselves and for all others.

> This mature, responsible, spiritually-centered, and action-oriented way of life actually empowers people to transcend the selfish anxieties and emotionally reactive tensions that habitually dominate our shallow ego-level of awareness.

> This kind of joyful liberation is possible because this way of life intentionally abandons self-seeking as the primary or exclusive goal of our everyday activities and it is consciously dedicated to the higher (or deeper) purpose of helping others on a daily basis in every dimension of our lives through caring relationships and unselfish acts of service.

In *The small book* of Rational Recovery, Jack Trimpey clearly validates the central importance of *unconditional love and service* in the addiction recovery process—although he chooses to express these universal principles in slightly different terms:

> RR clients learn that they can make themselves *feel good at will just by thinking lovingly of themselves,* and that they need not change in any way in order to do so. We do not remain sober in order to think well of ourselves; it is because *we like and value ourselves* that we do not drink. We think well of ourselves, ironically, for the same reason that we used to drink—to feel good. Self-worth reminders simply express *unconditional self-acceptance* and the idea that to drink would be poisoning *a friend, oneself.*

> If you should have a lapse of judgment and drink or use drugs, you will be acutely aware that you have violated *a covenant with yourself that is next to sacred.* All right, let's call it sacred. You can say that *your life is sacred* if nothing else is.
>
> *Now certain of my inherent worth, I can take the risks of loving, for loving is far better than being loved.*
>
> (Trimpey, 1989: 69, 108, 274 Emphasis added).

Now, in order to more fully appreciate the deep underlying unity that genuinely exists between all of these supposedly contradictory approaches to addiction recovery—which collectively stress the universal need for new values and interests, new relationships, true engagement with others, voluntary commitment to a higher moral purpose, unconditional self-acceptance, love for others, and the need for some kind of an alternative, healthy positive addiction that is truly happy, joyous, and free—please consider the following snapshot description of the fundamental nature of full recovery and true sobriety from "A Vision for You"—the final chapter of the AA Big Book:

> These men had found something brand new in life. Though they knew they must help other alcoholics if they would remain sober, that motive became secondary. It was transcended by the happiness they found in giving themselves for others.
>
> So our fellow worker will soon have friends galore . . . When a few men in this city have found themselves, and have discovered the joy of helping others to face life again, there will be no stopping until everyone in that town has had his opportunity to recover—if he can and will.
>
> (Alcoholics Anonymous, 1976: 159,163–164).

## WHAT REALLY COUNTS?

If you briefly browse through the books in the "Addiction and Recovery" section of any large bookstore, you'll quickly see that a virtual cottage industry of "AA-bashing" books has developed in the world of publishing in recent decades. Some of these critical volumes are quite thoughtful and valuable. Others are quite misleading and off base. Some of these books virtually reek with irrational resentment and others seriously propose absurdly immature and concrete all-or-nothing ideas. Many of the critical books in this backlash phenomena present a fascinating blend of all these features—the good, the bad, and the ugly—and they can all be found sitting right there on the shelves—alphabetically by author—side-by-side with more conventional books that warmly and uncritically embrace the traditional disease concept of harmful addiction and the twelve-step spiritual recovery program.

In his famous essay on *Self-Reliance,* Ralph Waldo Emerson offers some stirring advice that would undoubtedly warm the heart of many critics who routinely disparage any spiritual approach to effective living as inherently passive, dependent, and irrational:

> "Trust thyself: every heart vibrates to that iron string."

Many of these critics would almost certainly enjoy and endorse one of Emerson's most widely quoted sentiments—which also comes from this well-known but rarely read 19th Century essay:

> "A foolish consistency" says Emerson, "is the hobgoblin of little minds, adored by little statesmen, philosophers and divines."

In one-way or another, most of these critics seem to embrace the notion of "self-reliance" quite warmly. Therefore, if they're inclined to take Emerson as a potential authority for this point of view, I suppose they'd want to heed his warning and carefully watch out for any hint of bias, prejudice, thoughtless conformity, or "foolish consistency" that might contaminate their own belief system and perhaps blind them to the following truths that are so self-evident to so many others:

> A spiritually-centered life involves the personal exercise of true authenticity, personal autonomy, and genuine freedom of choice expressed through a voluntary decision to obey the dictates of our own conscience and the ultimate authority of Inner Truth, as we honestly seek to understand it.

> When it is truly and deeply genuine, this transformational spiritual decision will be followed by a vigorous course of persistent action—inside and out—and the gradual acceptance of complete personal responsibility for all aspects of our own life—including all of our beliefs, attitudes, motives, desires, thoughts, feelings, words, and deeds and all positive results and negative consequences that these may produce.

If these critics of twelve-step spirituality as a valid and effective way of life have any serious philosophical doubts or questions about any of this, they need only look at two additional statements made by Emerson right smack in the middle of his essay on Self-Reliance, which, we should remember, virtually fathered the enduring prominence of this ideal in the public mind:

1) The power which resides in him is new in nature, and none but he knows what that is which he can do, nor does he know until he has tried . . . We but half express ourselves, and are ashamed of the divine idea that each of us represents.

2) We lie in the lap of immense intelligence, which makes us receivers of its truth and organs of its activity. When we discern justice, when we discern truth, we do nothing of ourselves, but allow a passage to its beams.

(Emerson, 1993:20, 24, 27)

It's crucial for anyone who wants to live a sane and sober life that's solidly grounded on personal responsibility and self-reliance—or help others learn how to do so—to fully understand that there truly are some universal spiritual principles that are not merely "consistent" with living this kind of a good life—they are actually essential and foundational features of such a life.

In our final chapter on "Rational Spirituality," we've clearly seen that it's not necessary to use any abstract or explicitly religious terminology—such as "the divine idea" or "immense intelligence" or "God"—in order to help clients learn how to tap the deep "power that resides within us all" and begin to practice these universal spiritual principles.

In fact, we've seen how these principles can always be "translated" into clear, simple, modern terms and perhaps we've begun to appreciate how these principles are often expressed most helpfully when they are personally embraced and role-modeled by a would-be helper in this flexible and open-minded way.

At the beginning of his Pulitzer Prize winning book *The Denial of Death*, Ernest Becker favorably quotes an observation made in 1902 by William James in *The Varieties of Religious Experience* that:

"mankind's common instinct for reality," says James, "... has always held the world to be essentially a theatre for heroism."

Becker therefore suggests that "our central calling, our main task on this planet, is the heroic," and then he adds:

In childhood, we see the struggle for self-esteem at its least disguised. The child is unashamed about what he needs and wants most. His whole organism shouts the claims of his natural narcissism . . . for the prerogatives of limitless self-extension, what we might call 'cosmic significance.

The urge to heroism is natural, and to admit it honest. . . . The question that becomes then the most important one that man can put to himself is simply this: how conscious is he of what he is doing to earn his feeling of heroism?

(James, 1961: 288; Becker, 1971; Becker, 1973: 1, 3–5. Emphasis added.)

There are two well-known concepts that are widely accepted as fundamental "facts of life" and both are highly relevant to the addiction recovery process:

- "Nature abhors a vacuum," and

- "You can't replace something with nothing."

As clinicians, we will need to gently but persistently challenge our clients to consciously identify or decide what is really meaningful and important in life for them. We will need to help them honestly face some ultimate questions about what they really want and need in life, what they are doing to achieve it, and what really works or doesn't work in the long run to help them achieve it.

H. L. Mencken once wrote:

An idealist is one who, on noticing that a rose smells better than a cabbage, concludes that it will also make better soup.

In this book, we've talked about providing essential nourishment for the human heart, mind, body, and soul; about roses that would smell as sweet by any other name; about conclusions being what you reach when you get tired of the effort of thinking; about the limitations of the scientific method; about the clumsiness of quantitative, experimental research designs for testing complex human processes; about the foolishness of contempt prior to investigation; and about the wisdom of beginning with the end in mind.

Mencken also wrote that:

For every human problem, there is a neat, simple solution, and it is always wrong.

At the risk of violating this general principle—while abandoning the concept of a control group and any quest for a scientifically "valid" test—the essence of the therapeutic approach recommended in this book could be reduced to two simple questions that we might begin asking *all* of our clients right from the very start:

- Did you try to practice patience, kindness, tolerance, and love?

- Are you willing to practice patience, kindness, tolerance, and love?

Nothing in this book should be taken on faith. Any principles or practices that I've proposed can only be proved valid or valuable through the direct personal experience of uniquely individual human beings who are ready, willing, and able to give them a try.

And to try again, and again, and again—patiently and persistently in a life-long process of learning and personal growth—with just enough faith on tap to recognize that:

"Practice makes progress, not perfection."

When a person becomes totally committed to their ongoing recovery process they will also be completely ready—mentally, emotionally, physically, and spiritually—to devote themselves to a new way of life that will consistently promote their personal growth, health, and true happiness—perhaps because it is built on a healthy, natural foundation that is solidly grounded in the enduring and truly heroic principles of *Love and Service*

And when they are finally prepared to see their new clean and sober lifestyle as a consciously chosen and persistently practiced positive addiction—they will often be ready to get thoroughly *"hooked on wholeness."*

And, when that happens, we may have the deep satisfaction of seeing them turn an apparently endless string of failures into *a pattern of permanent sobriety and lifetime success.*

# Addiction Recovery Self-Evaluation Questionnaire

**The FACE to FACE Unified Addiction Recovery Model**

**ADDICTION RECOVERY
SELF-EVALUATION QUESTIONNAIRE**

**WHAT REALLY COUNTS?**

## DIRECTIONS:

Please indicate which of the five phrases immediately below best describes how you would begin versions A, B, and C of each statement listed below:

1. I agree completely that . . .
2. I agree very much that . . .
3. I agree somewhat that . . .
4. I disagree that . . .
5. I disagree completely that . . .

## STATEMENT:

In order to fulfill my deepest needs as a human being, and lead a healthier, happier, and more meaningful life . . .

- A) I *need* to
- B) I *want* to
- C) I am *willing* to

## Hypothetical Example 1—Item 23—Full Statements:

- A. I agree completely that—in order to fulfill my deepest needs as a human being, and lead a healthier, happier, and more meaningful life—I *need* to—identify for myself what my deepest needs as a human being really are. (1)
- B. I agree somewhat that—in order to fulfill my deepest needs as a human being, and lead a healthier, happier, and more meaningful life—I *want* to—identify for myself what my deepest needs as a human being really are. (3)
- C. I disagree that—in order to fulfill my deepest needs as a human being, and lead a healthier, happier, and more meaningful life—I *am wiling* to—identify for myself what my deepest needs as a human being really are. (4)

## Hypothetical Example 1—Item 23—Coded Responses:

23 A–1
23 B–3
23 C–4

## Hypothetical Example 2—Item 41—Full Statements:

- A. I agree completely that—in order to fulfill my deepest needs as a human being, and lead a healthier, happier, and more meaningful life—I *need* to—monitor my thoughts, feelings, words, and deeds more consistently and make changes more promptly when something is wrong. (1)
- B. I agree that—in order to fulfill my deepest needs as a human being, and lead a healthier, happier, and more meaningful life—I *want* to—monitor my thoughts, feelings, words, and deeds more consistently and make changes more promptly when something is wrong. (2)

C. I agree completely that—in order to fulfill my deepest needs as a human being, and lead a healthier, happier, and more meaningful life—I *am willing* to—monitor my thoughts, feelings, words, and deeds more consistently and make changes more promptly when something is wrong. (1)

## *Hypothetical Example 2—Item 41—Coded Responses:*

41 A–1

41 B–2

41 C–1

## QUESTIONNAIRE ITEMS:

In order to fulfill my deepest needs as a human being, and lead a healthier, happier, and more meaningful life . . .

1)  1 2 3 4 5  A    Recognize how I may be using harmful addictive substances
    1 2 3 4 5  B    or behaviors in a doomed attempt to manage my emotional
    1 2 3 4 5  C    reactivity and satisfy my deepest human needs?

2)  1 2 3 4 5  A    Become familiar with the full range of signs, symptoms,
    1 2 3 4 5  B    negative consequences, and stages of progression in harmful
    1 2 3 4 5  C    addiction?

3)  1 2 3 4 5  A    Identify all personal signs, symptoms, and negative conse-
    1 2 3 4 5  B    quences of harmful addiction that I have ever experienced in
    1 2 3 4 5  C    my life and especially those I am experiencing presently?

4)  1 2 3 4 5  A    Monitor my future experience for the appearance of more
    1 2 3 4 5  B    signs, symptoms, or negative consequences of harmful
    1 2 3 4 5  C    addiction?

5)  1 2 3 4 5  A    Identify my present stage of progression into harmful
    1 2 3 4 5  B    addiction?
    1 2 3 4 5  C

6) 1 2 3 4 5  A   Learn the diagnostic criteria for substance abuse or
   1 2 3 4 5  B   dependence?
   1 2 3 4 5  C

7) 1 2 3 4 5  A   Identify all criteria that I currently meet for an official
   1 2 3 4 5  B   diagnosis of substance abuse or dependence?
   1 2 3 4 5  C

8) 1 2 3 4 5  A   Monitor my future experience for the emergence of more
   1 2 3 4 5  B   diagnostic criteria for substance abuse or dependence that I
   1 2 3 4 5  C   may meet?

9) 1 2 3 4 5  A   Continue to drink or use drugs as before, but avoid negative
   1 2 3 4 5  B   consequences?
   1 2 3 4 5  C

10) 1 2 3 4 5  A   Control and moderate my drinking or drug use to avoid
   1 2 3 4 5  B   negative consequences?
   1 2 3 4 5  C

11) 1 2 3 4 5  A   Abstain from my drugs-of-choice and control any other
   1 2 3 4 5  B   drinking or drug use?
   1 2 3 4 5  C

12) 1 2 3 4 5  A   Abstain completely from all drinking or drug use to avoid
   1 2 3 4 5  B   negative consequences?
   1 2 3 4 5  C

13) 1 2 3 4 5  A   Understand my relapse triggers, high-risk situations, and
   1 2 3 4 5  B   relapse warning signs?
   1 2 3 4 5  C

14) 1 2 3 4 5  A   Develop and practice a structured daily recovery program
   1 2 3 4 5  B   and relapse prevention plan?
   1 2 3 4 5  C

15) 1 2 3 4 5  A   Find clean and sober ways to deal with stress, difficult
   1 2 3 4 5  B   people, problems, and feelings?
   1 2 3 4 5  C

16) 1 2 3 4 5 A  Find clean and sober ways to relax, enjoy myself, socialize,
    1 2 3 4 5 B  and meet my real needs?
    1 2 3 4 5 C

17) 1 2 3 4 5 A  Recognize when I need help and emotional support from
    1 2 3 4 5 B  others?
    1 2 3 4 5 C

18) 1 2 3 4 5 A  Ask for help and emotional support from others when I need
    1 2 3 4 5 B  it?
    1 2 3 4 5 C

19) 1 2 3 4 5 A  Have a sponsor, mentor, coach, counselor, clergy member, or
    1 2 3 4 5 B  good friend with whom I talk frequently?
    1 2 3 4 5 C

20) 1 2 3 4 5 A  Seek to understand, encourage, and help others dealing with
    1 2 3 4 5 B  problems like my own?
    1 2 3 4 5 C

21) 1 2 3 4 5 A  Attend and participate openly and fully in self-help-mutual
    1 2 3 4 5 B  support group meetings?
    1 2 3 4 5 C

22) 1 2 3 4 5 A  Develop a devotion to a meaningful, healthy, positive addiction
    1 2 3 4 5 B  in order to manage my emotional reactivity and satisfy my
    1 2 3 4 5 C  deepest human needs?

23) 1 2 3 4 5 A  Identify for myself what my deepest needs as a human being
    1 2 3 4 5 B  really are?
    1 2 3 4 5 C

24) 1 2 3 4 5 A  Define for myself what true health, happiness, and success
    1 2 3 4 5 B  really mean to me?
    1 2 3 4 5 C

25) 1 2 3 4 5 A  Become more open and honest with myself?
    1 2 3 4 5 B
    1 2 3 4 5 C

26) 1 2 3 4 5 A    Think more clearly and rationally?
     1 2 3 4 5 B
     1 2 3 4 5 C

27) 1 2 3 4 5 A    Act more wisely and compassionately?
     1 2 3 4 5 B
     1 2 3 4 5 C

28) 1 2 3 4 5 A    Take complete personal responsibility for my own life?
     1 2 3 4 5 B
     1 2 3 4 5 C

29) 1 2 3 4 5 A    Take complete personal responsibility for my own beliefs,
     1 2 3 4 5 B    attitudes, motives, and desires?
     1 2 3 4 5 C

30) 1 2 3 4 5 A    Take complete personal responsibility for my own thoughts,
     1 2 3 4 5 B    feelings, words, and deeds?
     1 2 3 4 5 C

31) 1 2 3 4 5 A    Take better care of myself mentally, emotionally, physically,
     1 2 3 4 5 B    spiritually, and socially?
     1 2 3 4 5 C

32) 1 2 3 4 5 A    Identify and express my true feelings and my real needs in a
     1 2 3 4 5 B    healthy and constructive way?
     1 2 3 4 5 C

33) 1 2 3 4 5 A    Be more positive, optimistic, constructive, and effective
     1 2 3 4 5 B    pursuing personal plans and goals?
     1 2 3 4 5 C

34) 1 2 3 4 5 A    Communicate with others more openly, honestly, directly
     1 2 3 4 5 B    and assertively?
     1 2 3 4 5 C

35) 1 2 3 4 5 A    Set appropriate limits with others more clearly and firmly?
     1 2 3 4 5 B
     1 2 3 4 5 C

36) 1 2 3 4 5  A   Become more structured, disciplined, and responsible in my
    1 2 3 4 5  B   daily habits and routines?
    1 2 3 4 5  C

37) 1 2 3 4 5  A   Become less rigid, demanding, critical, or perfectionistic in
    1 2 3 4 5  B   my daily habits and routines?
    1 2 3 4 5  C

38) 1 2 3 4 5  A   Become more flexible, accepting, and forgiving of human
    1 2 3 4 5  B   imperfection in myself and others?
    1 2 3 4 5  C

39) 1 2 3 4 5  A   Become more calm, easy-going, and relaxed?
    1 2 3 4 5  B
    1 2 3 4 5  C

40) 1 2 3 4 5  A   Learn how to control stress and emotional reactivity by
    1 2 3 4 5  B   practicing sound rational and emotional coping skills?
    1 2 3 4 5  C

41) 1 2 3 4 5  A   Monitor my thoughts, feelings, words, and deeds more
    1 2 3 4 5  B   consistently and make changes more promptly when
    1 2 3 4 5  C   something is wrong?

42) 1 2 3 4 5  A   Become aware more quickly when something feels wrong
    1 2 3 4 5  B   inside or out?
    1 2 3 4 5  C

43) 1 2 3 4 5  A   Stop and think whenever something upsets me rather than
    1 2 3 4 5  B   immediately reacting or acting out emotionally?
    1 2 3 4 5  C

44) 1 2 3 4 5  A   Recognize how many of my automatic thoughts and emotional
    1 2 3 4 5  B   reactions are triggered by my own irrational self-talk,
    1 2 3 4 5  C   unexamined parent or child ego states, and unconscious
                        game playing?

45) 1 2 3 4 5 A    Identify deeply ingrained personal wants, needs, beliefs,
     1 2 3 4 5 B    attitudes, values, and desires that have been socially-
     1 2 3 4 5 C    programmed into me and are not really my own?

46) 1 2 3 4 5 A    Identify and change all self-defeating or harmful ego-level
     1 2 3 4 5 B    traits, negative attitudes, shallow motives, selfish desires,
     1 2 3 4 5 C    irrational beliefs, and distorted thinking patterns that make
                     me feel unsettled, unhealthy, unhappy, unfulfilled, or
                     unsuccessful?

47) 1 2 3 4 5 A    Develop a deep sense of meaning and purpose in life and a
     1 2 3 4 5 B    clear set of guiding principles?
     1 2 3 4 5 C

48) 1 2 3 4 5 A    Be led more consistently by my own compassion, conscience,
     1 2 3 4 5 B    and my deepest sense of right and wrong?
     1 2 3 4 5 C

49) 1 2 3 4 5 A    Recognize and reject the fallacy that I must feel loved in
     1 2 3 4 5 B    order to feel good and worthwhile?
     1 2 3 4 5 C

50) 1 2 3 4 5 A    Become less self-absorbed and less obsessed with my own
     1 2 3 4 5 B    problems and desires?
     1 2 3 4 5 C

51) 1 2 3 4 5 A    Care more deeply about the feelings, needs, wants, and well-
     1 2 3 4 5 B    being of others?
     1 2 3 4 5 C

52) 1 2 3 4 5 A    Identify and change behavior that violates my own deepest
     1 2 3 4 5 B    values and principles?
     1 2 3 4 5 C

53) 1 2 3 4 5 A    Identify a set of universal spiritual principles that I can that I
     1 2 3 4 5 B    can easily understand, accept, practice, and explain rationally
     1 2 3 4 5 C    in clear, simple, modern, practical terms?

54) 1 2 3 4 5 A    Learn how to calm my mind and center myself spiritually in
    1 2 3 4 5 B    order to practice sound rational and emotional coping skills
    1 2 3 4 5 C    more effectively?

55) 1 2 3 4 5 A    Respect my fundamental need to practice patience, kindness,
    1 2 3 4 5 B    tolerance, and unconditional love for myself and for all
    1 2 3 4 5 C    others?

56) 1 2 3 4 5 A    Learn how to tap into a deep inner source of serenity,
    1 2 3 4 5 B    acceptance, courage, action, and wisdom?
    1 2 3 4 5 C

57) 1 2 3 4 5 A    Learn how to tap a deep source of inner peace, inner power,
    1 2 3 4 5 B    personal freedom, and enduring joy?
    1 2 3 4 5 C

58) 1 2 3 4 5 A    Learn how to practice patience, kindness, tolerance, and
    1 2 3 4 5 B    unconditional love for myself and for all others?
    1 2 3 4 5 C

59) 1 2 3 4 5 A    Devote my life to the intelligent practice of patience,
    1 2 3 4 5 B    kindness, tolerance, and unconditional love for myself and
    1 2 3 4 5 C    for all others?

60) 1 2 3 4 5 A    Always seek to add whatever I can to the stream of goodness
    1 2 3 4 5 B    and light in our sometimes dark and troubled world, and help
    1 2 3 4 5 C    others do likewise?

## ADDICTION PROGRESSION & RECOVERY EVALUATION PROCESS

**Directions:** For all potentially harmful addictive substances or behaviors, please indicate where you believe you stand in each of the following ten areas:

    1) My **current** Level of Use—and **past highest** Level of Use
    2) My **current** Problem Severity Level—and **past highest** Severity Level
    3) My **current** Stage of Progression into Harmful Addiction
    4) My **current** Stage on the *Addiction Recovery Learning Curve*
    5) My **current** Level in the *Addiction Control Failure Sequence*

6) My **current** <u>Action</u> or <u>Maintenance Step</u> in the *Addiction Control Change Process*

7) *Learning Curve* <u>Stage</u> and <u>Action Step</u> I **currently** Contemplate, if any

8) *Learning Curve* <u>Stage</u> and <u>Action Step</u> I *need* to **Contemplate Next**

9) *Learning Curve* <u>Stage</u> and <u>Action Step</u> I *need* to **Prepare for Next**

10) *Learning Curve* <u>Stage</u> and <u>Action Step</u> I *need* to **Move to Next**

# APPENDIX 2

# Individualized Addiction History

These are the basic elements that should be included in a thorough diagnostic assessment and psychoeducational feedback interview:

*Lifetime Overview of Compulsive or Addictive Behaviors:*

**Preferred Primary & Secondary Substances or Behaviors**

"Drugs of Choice"

**List All Other Substances or Compulsive-Addictive Behaviors Ever Used**

*History of Use for EACH Substance or Behavior:*

**Age at First Use**
**Age at First Regular Use.**
**Age at First Problem Use.**

**Evaluate Current Use. Past Month. Past Year. Lifetime.**

(Note Significant Patterns, Trends, or Changes Over Time).

**Use Patterns**

None. Episodic. Periodic. Continuous.

**Typical Amounts Used per Day of Use**

**Routes of Administration**

Oral, Nasal, Smoking, IV, Behavioral.

**Typical Intoxication Levels**

None. Mild. Moderate. Serious. Severe.

**Frequency of Use**

Days per Week, Month, or Year.

**Duration of Use Episodes**

Hours per Typical Day of Use.

**Significant Variations in Use Patterns**

Weekends, Holidays, Special Occasions, Unusual Stressors.

**Signs and Symptoms of Problem Use, Abuse, or Dependence**

**Perceived Benefits of Use**

**Negative Consequences of Use**

**Attempts at Control**
  **Individual Efforts.**
  **Self-Help Programs**
  **Treatment Episodes**

**Periods Of Controlled Use**

**Periods Of Abstinence**

**Primary Relapse Warning Signs and Triggers**

*Client and Clinician Ratings for Each Substance or Behavior:*

**Evaluate Current Use. Past Month. Past Year. Lifetime.**
(Note Significant Patterns, Trends, or Changes Over Time).

**Level of Use or DSM-IV-TR Diagnosis**

None. Experimental Use. Occasional Use. Social Use.
Heavy Use. Problem Use. Abuse. Dependence.

**Problem Severity**

None. Mild. Moderate. Serious. Severe. Grave.

**Current Stage of Progression**

None. Warning Stage. Early Stage. Middle Stage. Late Stage.

### Current Stage on the Addiction Recovery Learning Curve

1. Uncontrolled Use with Consequences.
2. Attempted Common Sense Control.
3. Attempted Analytical Abstinence.
4. Attempted Spiritual Sobriety.
5. Rational Spiritual Sobriety.

### Current Level in Addiction Control Failure Sequence for this Stage

1. Initial Attempts
2. Secondary Attempts
3. Serious Attempts
4. Desperate Attempts
5. Futile Attempts

### *Current Intoxication and Potential Withdrawal Risk:*

Date, Time, and Amount of Last Use for Each Substance or Behavior

Frequency and Amount of Use in Past Week
History of Withdrawal Symptoms

### *Current Bio-Psycho-Social-Spiritual Status:*

### Assess Impact of Problems on Compulsive or Addictive Behaviors

### Assess Impact of Compulsive or Addictive Behaviors on Problems

Emotional, Behavioral, Cognitive, or Spiritual Problems.
Medical Problems or Physical Conditions.
Social, Family, or Relationship Problems.
Work, School, Financial, Housing, Transportation, or Legal Problems.
Other Significant Environmental Problems or Stressors.
Overall Level of Current Functioning, Strengths, or Impairments.

### Current Motivation for Change

None. Mild. Moderate. Serious. Desperate. Futile.

### *Next* Appropriate Action Stage

Attempted Common Sense Control.
Attempted Analytical Abstinence.

Attempted Spiritual Sobriety.
Rational Spiritual Sobriety.

## Current Stage of Change for Next Appropriate Action Stage

Pre-Contemplation. Contemplation. Preparation.

## Current Recovery Environment.

Excellent. Very Good. Good. Fair. Poor. Bad.

## Current Risk for Relapse or Continued Problem Use.

None. Mild. Moderate. Serious. Severe. Grave.

# REFERENCES AND RESOURCES

Alcoholics Anonymous. (1953). *Twelve Steps and Twelve Traditions*. New York, NY: Alcoholics Anonymous General Service Office.

Alcoholics Anonymous. (1973). *Is AA for You? Twelve Questions Only You Can Answer*. (Pamphlet). New York, NY: Alcoholics Anonymous General Service Office.

Alcoholics Anonymous. (1976). *Alcoholics Anonymous: The Story of How Many Thousands of Men and Women have Recovered from Alcoholism*. Third Edition. New York, NY: Alcoholics Anonymous General Service Office.

American Psychiatric Association. (2001). *Diagnostic and Statistical Manual of Mental Disorders*. (Fourth Edition—Text Revision). Washington, DC: American Psychiatric Association.

ASAM. (2001). *ASAM Patient Placement Criteria for the Treatment of Substance-Related Disorders*. (Second Edition-Revised—ASAM PPC-2R) Chevy Chase, MD: American Society of Addiction Medicine.

Barrett, Richard. (1998). *Liberating the Corporate Soul: Building a Visionary Organization*. Boston, MA: Butterworth—Heinemann.

Beattie, Melody. (1987). *Codependent No More*. Center City, MN: Hazelden.

Beck, Aaron. (1967). *Depression: Causes and Treatment*, Philadelphia, PA: University of Pennsylvania Press.

Beck, Aaron; Wright, Fred; Newman, Cory; and Liese, Bruce. (1993). *Cognitive Therapy of Substance Abuse*. New York, NY: Guilford Press.

Becker, Ernest. (1971). *The Birth and Death of Meaning*. (Second Edition). New York, NY: The Free Press.

Becker, Ernest. (1973). *The Denial of Death*. New York, NY: The Free Press.

Becvar, Dorothy. (1997). *Soul Healing: A Spiritual Orientation in Counseling and Therapy*. New York, NY: Basic Books.

Benson, Herbert. (1996). *Timeless Healing: The Power and Bilogy of Belief*. New York, NY: Fireside.

Berne, Eric. (1964). *Games People Play: The Psychology of Human Relationships*. New York, NY: Grove Press, Inc.

Blanton, Brad. (1994). *Radical Honesty: How to Transform Your Life by Telling the Truth*. New York, NY: Dell Trade Paperbacks.

Boorstein, Seymour. (Ed.) (1996). *Transpersonal Psychotherapy*. (Second Edition). Albany, NY: State University of New York Press.

Booth, Leo. (1998). *When God Becomes a Drug: Understanding Religious Addiction and Abuse*. (Book I). Long Beach, CA: SCP Limited.

Booth, Leo. (1998). *The God Game—It's Your Move: Healing the Wounds of Religious Addiction and Abuse*. (Book II). Long Beach, CA: SCP Limited.

Branden, Nathaniel. (1994). *The Six Pillars of Self-Esteem*. New York, NY: Bantam Books.

Brenner, Charles. (1973). *An Elementary Textbook of Psychoanalysis*. (Revised Edition) Madison, CT: International Universities Press, Inc.

Brickman, Phillip, et al. (1982). "Models of Helping and Coping." *American Psychologist*. April 1982. Vol. 37, No. 4, Pages 368–384.

Brown, Stephanie. (1985). *Treating the Alcoholic: A Developmental Model of Recovery*. New York, NY: John Wiley & Sons.

Burnett. Bill. (2001). "As I See It: On the Disease of Addiction." *The Counselor*. October. Vol. 2, No. 5, Page 7.

Burns, David, D. (1980). *Feeling Good: The New Mood Therapy.* New York, NY: Avon Books.

Canda, Edward, R. and Furman, Leola, D. (1999). *Spiritual Diversity in Social Work Practice: The Heart of Helping.* New York, NY: The Free Press.

Carnes, Patrick. (1991). *Don't Call It Love: Recovery from Sexual Addiction.* New York, NY: Bantam Books.

Cloninger, C.R.; Sigvardsson, S.; Bohman, M. (1996). "Type I and type II alcoholism: An update." *Alcohol Health and Research World. 20.* (1),18–23.

Cook, D.R. (1985). "Craftsman versus Professional: Analysis of the Controlled Drinking Controversy." *Journal of Studies on Alcohol. 46.* (5), 433–442.

Covey, Stephen, R. (1989). *The 7 Habits of Highly Effective People: Restoring the Character Ethic.* New York, NY: Fireside.

Csikzentmihalyi, Mihalyi. (1990). *Flow: The Psychology of Optimal Experience.* New York, NY: Harper Perennial.

Deci, Edward, L. (1995). *Why We Do What We Do: Understanding Self-Motivation.* New York, NY: Penguin Books USA, Inc.

Edwards, Griffith, et al. (1979). *Alcohol and Alcoholism. Report of a Special Committee of the Royal College of Psychiatrists.* London: Tavistock.

Ellis, Albert; McInerney, John; DiGuiseppe, Raymond; and Yeager, Raymond. (1988). *Rational-Emotive Therapy with Alcoholics and Substance Abusers.* New York. NY: Pergamon Press.

Ellis, Albert, and Velten, Emmett. (1992). *When AA Doesn't Work for You: Rational Steps to Quitting Alcohol.* Fort Lee, NJ: Barricade Books.

Elkin, Michael. (1984). *Families Under the Influence: Changing Alcoholic Patterns.* New York, NY: W.W. Norton & Company.

Emerson, Ralph, Waldo. (1993). *Self-Reliance and Other Essays.* New York, NY: Dover Publications.

Fingarette, Herbert. (1988). *Heavy Drinking: The Myth of Alcoholism as a Disease. Berkeley,* CA: University of California Press.

Fowler, James, W. (1981). *Stages of Faith: The Psychology of Human Development and the Quest for Meaning*. San Francisco, CA: Harper San Francisco.

Frances, Richard, J., and Miller, Sheldon, I. (1998). "Addiction Treatment: Overview." in Frances, Richard, J., and Miller, Sheldon, I. (Eds.) *Clinical Textbook of Addictive Disorders*. (Second Edition). New York, NY: Guilford Press.

Frankl, Viktor. (1984). *Man's Search for Meaning*. (Revised and Updated). New York, NY: Washington Square Press.

Fromm, Erich. (1947). *Man for Himself: An Inquiry into the Psychology of Ethics*. New York, NY: Holt, Rinehart & Winston, Inc.

Fromm, Erich. (1956). *The Art of Loving*. New York, NY: Harper & Row Publishers.

Galanter, Mark & Kleber, Herbert. (Eds.) (1999). *Textbook of Substance Abuse Treatment*. (Second Edition). Washington, DC: American Psychiatric Press, Inc.

Glaser, Frederick, B., "Preface," in Kishline, Audrey, (1994). *Moderate Drinking: The Moderation Management Guide for People Who Want to Reduce Their Drinking*, New York, NY: Crown Trade Paperbacks.

Glasser, William. (1975). *Reality Therapy: A New Approach to Psychiatry*. New York, NY: Harper and Row Publishers.

Glasser, William. (1976). *Positive Addiction*. New York, NY: Harper and Row.

Goleman, Daniel. (1995). *Emotional Intelligence: Why It Can Matter More Than IQ*. New York, NY: Bantam Books.

Gorski, Terence, and Miller, Merlene. (1986). *Staying Sober: A Guide for Relapse Prevention*. Independence, MO: Herald House/Independence Press.

Gorski, Terence. (1989). *Passages Through Recovery: An Action Plan for Preventing Relapse*. San Francisco, CA: Harper/Hazelden.

Graham, A.W.; Schultz, T.K. & Wilford, B.B. (Eds.) (1998). *Principles of Addiction Medicine*. (Second Edition). Chevy Chase, MD: American Society of Addiction Medicine.

James, William. (1961). *The Varieties of Religious Experience: A Study in Human Nature*. New York, NY: Collier Books.

John-Roger, and McWilliams, Peter. (1990). *Life 101: Everything We Wish We Had Learned in School—But Didn't*. Los Angeles, CA: Prelude Press.

Johnson, Vernon. (1980). *I'll Quit Tomorrow: A Practical Guide to Alcoholism Treatment*. New York, NY:Harper & Row.

Jung, Carl. (1933). *Modern Man in Search of a Soul*. New York, NY: Harcourt, Brace, Jovanovich.

Kabat-Zinn, Jon. (1994). *Wherever You Go There You Are: Mindfulness Meditation in Everyday Life*. New York, NY: Hyperion.

Kadden, Ronald, et al. (1995). *Cognitive-Behavioral Coping Skills Therapy Manual: A Clinical Research Guide for Therapists Treating Individuals with Alcohol Abuse and Dependence*. Project Match Monograph Series. Volume 3. Washington, DC: National Institute on Alcohol Abuse and Alcoholism.

Katz, Stan, and Liu, Aimee. (1991). *The Codependency Conspiracy: How to Break the Recovery Habit and Take Charge of Your Life*. New York, NY: Warner Books.

Kesten, Dale. (1988). *The Recovery Evaluation Process (REP): First Draft of a rapid assessment instrument to evaluate recovery and prevent relapse in recovering outpatient substance abusers*. (Unpublished Paper). New York, NY: Columbia University School of Social Work.

Kesten, Dale. (2001). *Understanding the Stages of Change in Addiction and Recovery*. (Seminar Manual). Eau Claire, WI: PESI Healthcare.

Kesten, Dale. (2004). *The Addiction Recovery Learning Curve*. (Seminar Handout). Westport, CT: The Highlight Zone Personal Growth Programs.

Kesten, Dale. (2004). *RS—Rational Spirituality*. (Seminar Handout). Westport, CT: The Highlight Zone Personal Growth Programs.

Kinney, Jean and Leaton, Gwen. (1982). *Understanding Alcohol: A Complete Guide to Alcohol Problems and Their Treatment.* New York, NY: New American Library.

Kishline, Audrey. (1994). *Moderate Drinking: The Moderation Management Guide for People Who Want to Reduce Their Drinking*, New York, NY: Crown Trade Paperbacks.

Mack, Avram H.; Franklin, John R., Jr.; and Frances, Richard, J. (2001). *Concise Guide to Treatment of Alcoholism & Addictions.* (Second Edition). Washington, DC: American Psychiatric Publishing, Inc.

Marlatt, G. Alan and Gordon, Judith. (Eds.) (1985). *Relapse Prevention: Maintenance Strategies in the Treatment of Addictive Behaviors.* New York, NY: Guilford Press.

Marlatt, G.A. and Tapert, S.F. (1993). Harm Reduction: Reducing the Risks of Addictive Behaviors." (243–273). in Baer, J.S., Marlatt, G.A., and McMahon, R.J. (Eds.) *Addictive Behaviors Across the Life Span: Prevention, Treatment, and Policy Issues.* Newbury Park: Sage Publications.

Marlatt, G.A. (1999). "From Hindsight to Foresight: A Commentary on Project MATCH." in Tucker, Jalie, A, Donovan, Dennis, M., Marlatt, G. Alan. (Eds). *Changing Addictive Behaviors: Bridging Clinical and Public Health Strategies.* New York: NY: Guilford Press.

Maslow, Abraham, H. (1968). *Toward a Psychology of Being.* (Second Edition). New York, NY: VanNostrand Reinhold.

McCrady. B.S. et al. (1985). "The Problem Drinkers' Project: A Programmatic Application of Social-Learning based Treatment." In Marlatt, G.A. & Gordon, R. (Eds.). *Relapse Prevention: Maintenance Strategies in Treatment of Addictive Behaviors.* New York, NY: Guilford Press.

Metzger, Lawrence. (1988). *From Denial to Recovery: Counseling Problem Drinkers, Alcoholics, and Their Families.* San Francisco, CA: Jossey-Bass Publishers.

Milam, James and Ketcham, Katherine. (1981). *Under the Influence: A Guide to the Myths and Realities of Alcoholism.* New York, NY: Bantam Books.

Milkman, Harvey and Sunderwirth, Stanley. (1987). *Craving for Ecstasy: The Consciousness & Chemistry of Escape*. Lexington, MA: Lexington Books.

Miller, William, R. (Ed.). (1999). *Integrating Spirituality into Treatment: Resources for Practitioners*. Washington, DC: American Psychological Association.

Miller, William, and Rollnick, Stephen. (1991). *Motivational Interviewing: Preparing People to Change Addictive Behavior*. New York, NY: Guilford Press.

Miller, William, R., Rollnick, Stepehn, and Conforti, Kelly. (2002). *Motivational Interviewing, Second Edition: Preparing People for Change*. (2nd Edition). New York, NY: Guilford Press.

Miller, William; Zweben, Alan; DiClemente, Carlo, and Rychtarik, Roberto. (1995). *Motivational Enhancement Therapy Manual: A Clinical Research Guide for Therapists Treating Individuals with Alcohol Abuse and Dependence*. Project Match Monograph Series. Volume 2. Washington, DC: National Institute on Alcohol Abuse and Alcoholism.

Mooney, Al; Eisenberg, Arlene; and Eisenberg, Howard. (1992). *The Recovery Book*. New York, NY: Workman Publishing.

National Council on Alcoholism. Criteria Committee. (1972). "Criteria for the Diagnosis of Alcoholism." *American Journal of Psychiatry*. (129:2).

NIAAA. (1992). "Moderate Drinking." *Alcohol Alert. Number 16*. April, 1992. Washington. DC: National Institute on Alcohol Abuse and Alcoholism.

NIAAA. (1996). "NIAAA Reports Project MATCH Main Findings." *News Release*. December 17,1996. Washington, DC: National Institute on Alcohol Abuse and Alcoholism.

Nowinski, Joseph; Baker, Stuart; and Carroll, Kathleen. (1995). *Twelve Step Facilitation Therapy Manual: A Clinical Research Guide for Therapists Treating Individuals with Alcohol Abuse and Dependence*. Project Match Monograph Series. Volume 1. Washington, DC: National Institute on Alcohol Abuse and Alcoholism.

Ogilvie, Heather. (2001). *Alternatives to Abstinence: A New Look at Alcoholism and the Choices in Treatment*. New York, NY: Hatherleigh Press.

Peck, M. Scott. (1978). *The Road Less Traveled: A New Psychology of Love, Traditional Values, and Spiritual Growth*. New York, NY: Simon & Schuster.

Peele, Stanton. (1991). *The Truth About Addiction and Recovery*. New York, NY: Fireside Books.

Peele, Stanton. (1989). *Diseasing of America: Addiction Treatment Out of Control*. Boston, MA: Houghton Mifflin Company.

Prochaska, James and DiClemente, Carlo. (1984). *The Transtheoretical Approach: Crossing Traditional Boundaries of Therapy*. Homewood, IL: Dow Jones/Irwin.

Prochaska, James; Norcross, John; and DiClemente, Carlo. (1994). *Changing for Good*. New York, NY: William Morrow.

Reid, William, and Smith, Audrey. (1981). *Research in Social Work*. New York, NY: Columbia University Press.

Richards, P. Scott and Bergin, Allen E. (1997). *A Spiritual Strategy for Counseling and Psychotherapy*. Washington, DC: American Psychological Association.

Ringwald, Christopher D. (2002). *The Soul of Recovery: Uncovering the Spiritual Dimension in the Treatment of Addictions*. New York, NY: Oxford University Press.

Rogers, Ronald L. and McMillin, Chandler Scott. (1988). *Don't Help: A Guide to Working with the Alcoholic*. Seattle. WA: Madrona Publishers.

Rotgers, Frederick. "Preface." In Ogilvie, Heather. (2001). *Alternatives to Abstinence: A New Look at Alcoholism and the Choices in Treatment*. New York, NY: Hatherleigh Press.

Schaler, Jeffrey. (2000). *Addiction is a Choice*. Chicago, IL: Open Court.

Seligman, Martin E.P. (1990). *Learned Optimism: How to Change Your Mind and Your Life*. New York, NY: Pocket Books.

Siegel, Bernie S. (1986). *Love, Medicine & Miracles: Lessons Learned about Self-Healing from a Surgeon's Experience with Exceptional Patients*. New York, NY: Harper & Row, Publishers.

Silva, Won, Lee; Calkins, Richard S.; and Rafferty, Ann P. (1993). "Alcohol Use," in *Health Risk Behaviors, 1992: Results of Michigan's Behavioral Risk Factor Survey*, Lansing, MI: Department of Public Health. pp. 49–61.

Smith, David E., and Seymour, Richard. (2001). *Hazelden Clinician's Guide to Substance Abuse*. Center City, MN: Hazelden.

Steiner, Claude. (1971). *Games Alcoholics Play: The Analysis of Life Scripts*. New York, NY: Ballantine Books.

Steinglass, Peter. (1987). *The Alcoholic Family*. New York, NY: Basic Books.

Stokes, Kenneth. (1989). *Faith is a Verb: Dynamics of Adult Faith Development*. Mystic, CT: Twenty-Third Publications.

Stone, Hal and Stone, Sidra. (1989). *Embracing Ourselves: The Voice Dialogue Manual*. Novato, CA: Nataraj Publishing.

Tart, Charles. (Ed.) (1975). *Transpersonal Psychologies*. New York, NY: Harper Colophon Books.

Thoreau, Henry, David (1960). *Walden or, Life in the Woods.* (1854). New York, NY: Signet Classics.

Trimpey, Jack. (1989). *The small book: A Revolutionary Alternative for Overcoming Alcohol and Drug Dependence*. New York, NY: Delacorte Press.

Trimpey, Jack. (1996). *Rational Recovery: The New Cure for Substance Addiction*. New York, NY: Pocket Books.

Tucker, Jalie. (1999). "Changing Addictive Behavior: Historical and Contemporary Perspectives." in Tucker, Jalie A.; Donovan, Dennis M.; Marlatt, G. Alan. (Eds). *Changing Addictive Behaviors: Bridging Clinical and Public Health Strategies*. New York: NY: Guilford Press.

Tucker, Jalie A.; Donovan, Dennis M.; and Marlatt, G. Alan. (Eds). (1999). *Changing Addictive Behaviors: Bridging Clinical and Public Health Strategies*. New York: NY: Guilford Press.

Valliant, George. (1983). *The Natural History of Alcoholism*. Cambridge, MA: Harvard University Press.

van Wormer, Katherine. (1987). "Group Work with Alcoholics in Recovery: A Phase Approach." *Social Work with Groups. 10*, (3), 81–97.

Volpicelli, Joseph and Szalavitz, Maia. (2000). *Recovery Options: The Complete Guide*. New York, NY: John Wiley & Sons.

Wallace, John. (1985). "Working with the Preferred Defense Structure of the Recovering Alcoholic," in Zimberg, Sheldon, Wallace, John, and Blume, Sheila. (Eds.) *Practical Approaches to Alcoholism Psychotherapy*. (Second Edition). New York, NY: Plenum Publishing.

Wegscheider, Sharon. (1981). *Another Chance: Hope and Health for the Alcoholic Family*. Palo Alto, CA; Science and Behavior Books.

Weil, Andrew, and Rosen, Winifred. (1983). *From Chocolate to Morphine: Understanding Mind-Active Drugs*. Revised: (1998). *From Chocolate to Morphine: Everything You Need to Know about Mind-Altering Drugs*. Boston, MA: Houghton Mifflin.

Wilber, Ken. (1998). *The Marriage of Sense and Soul: Integrating Science and Religion*. New York, NY: Broadway Books.

Woititz, Janet G. (1983). *Adult Children of Alcoholics*. Pompano Beach, FL: Health Communications.

Wolman, Richard N. (2001). *Thinking With Your Soul: Spiritual Intelligence and Why It Matters*. New York, NY: Harmony Books.

Zimberg, Sheldon. (1985). "Principles of Alcoholism Psychotherapy," in Zimberg, Sheldon, Wallace, John, and Blume, Sheila. (Eds). *Practical Approaches to Alcoholism Psychotherapy*. New York, NY: Plenum Publishing.

Zweben, Allen and Fleming, Michael. (1999). "Brief Interventions for Alcohol and Drug Problems." in Tucker, Jalie A.; Donovan, Dennis M.; Marlatt, G. Alan. (Eds). *Changing Addictive Behaviors: Bridging Clinical and Public Health Strategies*. New York: NY: Guilford Press.

# STUDY PACKAGE
# CONTINUING EDUCATION
# CREDIT INFORMATION

## ADDICTION, PROGRESSION,
## AND RECOVERY

Thank you for choosing PESI Healthcare as your continuing education provider. Our goal is to provide you with current, accurate and practical information from the most experienced and knowledgeable speakers and authors.

Listed below are the continuing education credit(s) currently available for this self-study package. **Please note, your state licensing board dictates whether self study is an acceptable form of continuing education. Please refer to your state rules and regulations.*

**Counselors:** PESI HealthCare, LLC is recognized by the National Board for Certified Counselors to offer continuing education for National Certified Counselors. Provider #: 5896. We adhere to NBCC Continuing Education Guidelines. These self-study materials qualify for 6 contact hours.

**Psychologists:** PESI is approved by the American Psychological Association to offer continuing education for psychologists. PESI maintains responsibility for the material. PESI is offering this self-study activity for 6.0 hours of continuing education credit.

**Social Workers:** PESI HealthCare, 1030, is approved as a provider for social work continuing education by the Association of Social Work Boards (ASWB), (540-829-6880) through the Approved Continuing Education (ACE) program. Licensed Social Workers should contact their individual state boards to determine self-study approval and to review continuing education requirements for licensure renewal. Social Workers will receive 6.0 continuing education clock hours for completing this self-study material.

**Addiction Counselors:** PESI HealthCare, LLC is a Provider approved by NAADAC Approved Education Provider Program. Provider #: 366. These self-study materials qualify for 7.0 contact hours.

**Nurses:** PESI HealthCare, LLC, Eau Claire is an approved provider of continuing nursing education by the Wisconsin Nurses Association Continuing Education Approval Program Committee, an accredited approver by the American Nurses Credentialing Center's Commission on Accreditation. This approval is accepted and/or recognized by all state nurses associations that adhere to the ANA criteria for accreditation. This learner directed educational activity qualifies for 7.2 contact hours. PESI Healthcare certification: CA #06538.

Procedures:  1. Read book.
2. Complete the post-test/evaluation form and mail it along with payment to the address on the form.

Your completed test/evaluation will be graded. If you receive a passing score (80% and above), you will be mailed a certificate of successful completion with earned continuing education credits. If you do not pass the post-test, you will be sent a letter indicating areas of deficiency, references to the appropriate sections of the manual for review and your post-test. The post-test must be resubmitted and receive a passing grade before credit can be awarded.

If you have any questions, please feel free to contact our customer service department at 1-800-843-7763.

**PESI HealthCare, LLC**
**200 SPRING ST. STE B, P.O. BOX 1000**
**EAU CLAIRE, WI 54702-1000**

**Product Number:** ZHS008695                     **CE Release Date:** 04/09/04

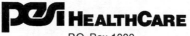
**HealthCare**

P.O. Box 1000
Eau Claire, WI 54702
(800) 843-7763

# Addiction, Progression, and Recovery

ZNT008695

This home study package includes CONTINUING EDUCATION FOR ONE PERSON: complete and return this original post/test evaluation form.

ADDITIONAL PERSONS interested in receiving credit may photocopy this form, complete and return with a payment of $25.00 per person CE fee. A certificate of successful completion will be mailed to you.

| For office use only |
| --- |
| Rcvd. _____ |
| Graded _____ |
| Cert. mld. _____ |

| C.E. Fee: **$25** | Credit card # _____ |
| --- | --- |
| | Exp. Date _____ |
| | Signature _____ |
| | V-Code* _____ (***MC/VISA/Discover:** last 3-digit # on signature panel on back of card.) (***American Express:** 4-digit # above account # on face of card.) |

**Mail to: PESI HealthCare, PO Box 1000, Eau Claire, WI 54702, or Fax to: PESI HealthCare (800) 675-5026 (fax all pages)**

Name (please print): _____ _____ _____
LAST            FIRST        M.I.

Address: _____

City: _____ State: _____ Zip: _____

Daytime Phone: _____

Signature: _____

• Date you completed the PESI HC Tape/Manual Independent Package: _____

• Actual time (# of hours) taken to complete this offering: _____ hours

## PROGRAM OBJECTIVES

How well did we do in achieving our objectives?

|  | Excellent |  |  |  | Poor |
|---|---|---|---|---|---|
| Identifying the original meaning of the word addiction and explaining why developing a passionate devotion to a healthy, positive addiction is often the only viable alternative for many people struggling with addictions. | 5 | 4 | 3 | 2 | 1 |
| Defining "compulsion" and explaining why compulsion, loss of control, and inability to abstain are among the most crucial elements of addiction. | 5 | 4 | 3 | 2 | 1 |
| Identifying many of the common signs, symptoms, and negative consequences typically associated with each stage of progression. | 5 | 4 | 3 | 2 | 1 |
| Describing five naturally-occurring stages of change on an Addiction Recovery Learning Curve. | 5 | 4 | 3 | 2 | 1 |
| Determining where clients presently stand on the five-stage Addiction Recovery Learning Curve. | 5 | 4 | 3 | 2 | 1 |

## POST-TEST QUESTIONS

1. The best generic definition of the word "addiction" would be:
   a. To develop physical dependence on a particular substance or activity and experience uncomfortable withdrawal symptoms when the substance use or activity is stopped.
   b. To develop increased tolerance for a particular substance or activity and the need to use more in order to achieve the desired effect.
   c. To experience harmful negative consequences as a direct result of habitually using a particular substance or activity.
   d. To habitually devote oneself or give oneself up to a particular behavior or activity.
   e. To develop a psychological dependence on a particular substance or activity marked by intense cravings and irresistible impulses to use the substance or activity.

2. Technically speaking, it could be said that there actually are no "alcoholics" or "addicts" because:

   a. These terms are nothing more than stigmatizing labels.

   b. There is no clear standard that can distinguish when problem use or abuse has progressed to the point where it can accurately be called alcoholism or addiction.

   c. These terms are not used in the official diagnostic terminology found in the Diagnostic and Statistical Manual of Mental Disorders (Fourth Edition—Text Revision) which is also known as the DSM-IV-TR.

   d. These terms are based on vague and exaggerated negative stereotypes.

   e. There is no universal agreement on the specific meaning of these words.

3. In the development of a harmful addiction, "loss of control" means that the user:

   a. consistently and compulsively uses more than intended to the point of intoxication every time they use.

   b. cannot reliably or safely predict the outcome once they have started to use.

   c. experiences unwanted negative consequences because of their use.

   d. experiences a serious deterioration of psychomotor coordination while using marked by either psychomotor retardation or agitation.

   e. is unable to safely drive a motor vehicle while using and will weave dangerously in and out of their lane or run off the road entirely.

4. The most effective teacher for many people suffering from serious harmful addiction—and for some people apparently the only teacher than can ever make a deep impression—is:

   a. Painful personal experience.

   b. Peer support and feedback.

   c. Intensive motivational therapy.

   d. Psychoeducational presentations.

   e. Psychoeducational discussion groups.

5. Which of the following statements about Driving While Intoxicated (DWI) is not true?

   a. It may be a genuine fluke in an otherwise normal, social, or occasional drinker.

   b. It is often an early warning sign that a harmful addiction might potentially emerge.

   c. It can be used to establish a diagnosis of alcohol abuse, all by itself, if it occurs more than once in a 12-month period.

   d. Some users may progress all the way into chronic, late stage alcoholism and still never experience it.

   e. It clearly establishes, all by itself, that the user is in the early stage of alcoholism at the very least.

6. Which of the following traits is not commonly found as a "predispositional characteristic" among people who develop serious problems with alcoholism, drug addiction, or other forms of harmful compulsive-addictive behavior:

   a. Over-sensitivity to unpleasant emotions and normal mood swings.

   b. Deficient motivation to control behavior and a desire for instant gratification.

   c. Inadequate techniques for controlling behavior and coping with problems.

   d. A pattern of automatic non-reflective yielding to impulses.

   e. Excitement seeking and low tolerance for boredom.

   f. Low frustration tolerance (LFT).

   g. An addictive or alcoholic personality structure.

   h. Diminished capacity to focus on the future consequences of present choices.

7. Which of the following statements best describes the "Abstinence Violation Effect" (AVE):

   a. It is a negative psychological reaction that occurs after an initial lapse into substance use—which involves guilt, shame, emotional distress, and a false addictive belief that further use is inevitable—often leading to an increased probability of full-blown relapse.

   b. It is the inevitable "loss of control" that almost automatically follows any lapse into substance use and thereby triggers a full-blown relapse.

   c. It is any specific sanction for continued use imposed by the legal system, an employer, or any other formal authority which has the legal right to require that a user abstain completely.

d. It is a healthy psychological defense that helps prevent an initial lapse into substance use because the user wants to avoid the guilt, shame, emotional distress, and increased probability of full-blown relapse that would follow.

e. It is the array of negative consequences caused by a full-blown relapse that is triggered by an initial lapse into substance use—and it may often involve many serious family, job, financial, legal, and health problems.

8. Which of the following is not a common symptom of chronic, late–stage harmful addiction?

a. Increasingly blatant and indiscriminate use in the form of benders, binges, and extended runs.

b. Drinking or using that may begin early and continue all day and night and prolonged periods of intoxication.

c. Increasingly severe and potentially life-threatening acute withdrawal symptoms.

d. Little or no recognition that any real problem exists related to using and virtually no desire to stop.

e. Severe and life-threatening medical and physical problems directly related to prolonged, heavy use.

9. The five stages of change on the Addiction Recovery Learning Curve are:

a. Continued Problem Use; Attempted Moderation; Attempted Abstinence; Attempted Spiritual Recovery; Sensible Spiritual Recovery.

b. Uncontrolled Use with Consequences; Attempted Common Sense Control; Attempted Analytical Abstinence; Attempted Spiritual Sobriety; Rational Spiritual Sobriety.

c. Uncontrolled Use with Consequences; Attempted Common Sense Control; Attempted Secular Sobriety; Attempted Spiritual Sobriety; Rational Spiritual Sobriety.

d. Uncontrolled Use with Consequences; Attempted Harm Reduction; Attempted Rational Recovery; Attempted Spiritual Recovery; Rational Spiritual Recovery.

e. Continued Consequences; Attempted Control; Attempted Abstinence; Attempted Spirituality; Rational Spirituality.

10. The Seven Simple Steps of Rational Spirituality are:
    a. Sense, Feel, Stop, Center, Think, Choose, Act
    b. Feel, Act, Sense, Stop, Center, Think, Choose
    c. Feel, Sense, Stop, Center, Think, Choose, Act
    d. Act, Feel, Sense, Stop, Center, Think, Choose
    e. Sense, Stop, Center, Think, Feel, Choose, Act

For additional forms and information on other PESI products, contact:
**Customer Service; PESI HEALTHCARE;**
**P.O. Box 1000; Eau Claire, WI 54702**
**(Toll Free, 7 a.m.-5 p.m. central time, 800-843-7763).**
**www.pesihealthcare.com**

**Thank you for your comments.**
**We strive for excellence and we value your opinion.**

# Professional Resources Available from PESI HealthCare

## Resources for Mental Health Professionals

*Addiction, Progression & Recovery,* by Dale Kesten, LCSW, LADC

*Assessing and Treating Trauma and PTSD,* by Linda Schupp, Ph.D

*Borderline Personality Disorder—Struggling, Understanding, Succeeding,* by Colleen E. Warner, Psy.D

*Case Management Handbook for Clinicians,* by Rand L. Kannenberg, MA

*Clinicians Update on the Treatment and Management of Anxiety Disorders,* by Deborah Antai-Otong, MS, RN, CNS, NP, CS, FAAN

*Collaborative Healing: A Shorter Therapy Approach for Survivors of Sexual Abuse,* by Mark Hirschfeld, LCSW-C, BCD & Jill B. Cody, MA

*Delirium—The Mistaken Confusion,* by Debra Cason-McNeeley, MSN, RNCS

*Depression and Other Mood Disorders,* by Deborah Antai-Otong, MS, RN, CNS, NP, CS, FAAN

*Effective Strategies for Helping Couples and Families,* by John S. Carpenter

*Grief: Normal, Complicated, Traumatic,* by Linda Schupp, Ph.D

*Psychiatric Emergencies,* by Deborah Antai-Otong, MS, RN, CNS, NP, CS, FAAN

*Sociotherapy for Sociopaths: Resocial Group,* by Rand L. Kannenberg, MA

## Resources for Nurses & Other Healthcare Professionals

*Heart and Lung Sounds Reference Library* (Audio CD), by Diane Wrigley, PA-C

*Infection Control and Emerging Infectious Diseases,* by William Barry Inman

*Legal and Ethical Standards for Nurses,* by Sheryl Feutz-Harter

*Managing Urinary Incontinence* (Audio CD), by Carol Ann White, RN, MS, ANPC, GNPC

*Mechanisms and Treatment of Disease: Pathophysiology—A Plain English Approach,* by Mikel A. Rothenberg, MD

*Oral Medication and Insulin Therapies: A Practical Guide for Reaching Diabetes Target Goals,* by Charlene Freeman

*Subclinical Signs of Impending Doom* (Audio CD), by Carol Whiteside, RN, PhD(c)

*Understanding X-Rays—A Plain English Approach,* by Mikel A. Rothenberg

**To order these or other PESI HealthCare products or to receive information about our national seminars, please call 800-843-7763**

www.pesihealthcare.com